P9-CJW-094

RUSSIA AND EURASIA

MILITARY REVIEW

ANNUAL

CONTRIBUTORS

Kathleen Addison is a Russian history specialist in Los Angeles.

David Beachley is a Russian affairs analyst with Science Applications International Corporation.

Sonia Ben Ouagrahm is an analyst with the Center for Non-Proliferation Studies at the Monterey Institute of International Studies.

Kenneth Currie is with the US Department of Defense.

Lester W. Grau, widely known for his numerous studies of the Soviet Army, is associated with the Foreign Military Studies Office, US Army Command and General Staff College, Fort Leavenworth, Kansas.

Randall Newnham is assistant professor in the Political Science Department of Penn State Berks-Lehigh Valley College.

Brian Taylor is assistant professor in the Political Science Department of the University of Oklahoma.

Sergei Zamascikov is an independent analyst.

Russia and Eurasia Military Review Annual

Edited by
Theodore W. Karasik

Volume 16
1992-1993

Academic International Press

With Volume 16
Russia and Eurasia Armed Forces Review Annual
is retitled
Russia and Eurasia Military Review Annual
in the interest of brevity.

RUSSIA AND EURASIA MILITARY REVIEW ANNUAL (REMRA)
Volume 16, 1992-1993

Copyright © 2004 by Academic International Press

All rights reserved. The reproduction or utilization of this work in
any form or by any electronic, mechanical, or other means, now known or
hereafter invented, including xerography, photocopying, and recording,
and in any information storage and retrieval system, by any individual,
institution or library, is forbidden under law without the written
permission of the publisher.

ISBN: 0-87569-252-4

Composition by Janice Frye and Ethel Chamberlain

Printed in the United States of America

By direct subscription with the publisher.

*A list of Academic International Press publications
is found at the end of this volume.*

ACADEMIC INTERNATIONAL PRESS
PO Box 1111 • Gulf Breeze FL • 32562-1111 • USA
www.ai-press.com

CONTENTS

CHARTS, TABLES, MAPS, FIGURES, INFORMATION

Preface

The present volume of Russian and Eurasia Military Review Annual (REMRA) contains information and analysis relating to the armed forces of the Soviet Union, Russia, the CIS, and other states. The purpose of this volume is to reflect military developments that occurred on the territory of the former Soviet Union since its disintegration at the end of 1991, and in the new Russian Federation, The Commonwealth of Independent States (CIS), and nonaffiliated independent states on territory of the old Soviet Union.

These developments clearly necessitate a change in REMRA's structure. Whereas REMRA will continue to carry important data relating to leadership and structure, as well as organization and other charts and tables, increasing attention will be devoted to understanding the processes unleashed by the collapse of the Soviet Union and their subsequent military consequences. Thus the present Volume 16 attempts to cast light on military aspects of the disappearance of the USSR during the two years immediately following, namely 1992 and 1993.

It is my hope to see REMRA become current as quickly as possible. To this end future volumes also will cover two-year periods. Volume 17 (1994-1995), Volume 18 (1996-1997), Volume 19 (1998-1999), and so on until current, whereupon annual coverage can resume.

Catching up confronts an editor with a host of problems. It is absurd to publish volumes that ignore present realities. It is equally unfortunate were REMRA to fail to provide a record of observers' views during the years in question. Thus several of the contributions below reflect later developments in tone and emphasis while seeking to present events from the viewpoints of participants. In this spirit I am including key Russian defense documents that illustrate Moscow's main concerns immediately following the Soviet implosion.

I want to thank Dr. David R. Jones, the former editor, whose guidance made this volume possible. My gratitude to the contributors to this volume is profound.

Again I dedicate this book to the Karasik, Greif, and Reya families, and especially to Sarah and Rachel, my daughters.

T.W.K.

ABBREVIATIONS

ABM	Anti-ballistic Missile Treaty	CGN	Nuclear Guided Missile Cruiser
ADA	Air Defense Artillery	CHG	Helicopter Carrier
Adm	Admiral	CIA	US Central Intelligence Agency
AGHS	Research Ship	CinC	Commander-in-Chief
AGI	Intelligence Collection Ship	CIRPES	Centre Interdisciplinaire de
AGOR	Survey Ship		Recherches sur la Paix et d'Études
ALCM	Air-launched Cruise Missile		Stratégiques
AGSS	Rescue Submarine	CIS	Commonwealth of Independent
AIFV	Armored Infantry Fighting Vehicle		States
Airmob	Airmobile	CL	Light Cruiser
AK	Kalashnikov Assault Rifle	CLQ	Command Cruiser
AMB	Airmobile Brigade	Co	Company
ANII	Artillery Scientific Research Institute	Col	Colonel
AO	Autonomous Oblast	Commo	Communications
APC	Armored Personnel Carrier	CPC	Patrol Craft
Arty	Artillery	CPD	Congress of People's Deputies
ASR	Submarine Rescue Vessel	CPSU	Communist Party of the Soviet
Asslt	Assault		Union
ASSR	Autonomous Soviet Socialist	CSBM	Confidence and Security Building
	Republic		Measures
ASW	Antisubmarine Warfare	CSCE	Conference on Security and
ATGM	Antitank Guided Missile		Cooperation in Europe
ATGW	Antitank Guided Weapon	CV	Aircraft Carrier
ATTU	Atlantic to the Urals (zone)	CVHG	Helicopter Carrier
AV	Aviation		
AWST	Aviation Week and Space	DDG	Guided Missile Destroyer
	Technology	DEWR	Defense & Economy World Report
		DM	Deutsche Mark
		DOSAAF	All-Union Voluntary Society for the
Batt	Battery		Support of Army, Aviation, and
Bde	Brigade		Fleet
BMD	Submarine Rescue Vessel		
BMP	Infantry Fighting Vehicle	EEC	European Economic Community
Bn	Battalion	ECM	Electronic Countermeasures
BNS	Baltic News Source	EW	Electronic Warfare
BPA	Bulgarian People's Army		
BTR	An Armored Personnel Carrier	FA	Frontal Aviation
		FAB	Frontal Aviation Battalion/Brigade
CDSP	Current Digest of the Soviet Press	FAC (9T)	Fast Torpedo Craft
CEP	Circle of Error Probable	FAC (G)	Guided Missile Craft
CFE	Conventional Forces in Europe	FAC (M)	Guided Missile Craft
CG	Guided Missile Cruiser	FAD	Frontal Aviation Division

FBIS	Foreign Broadcast Information Service	ITAC	Intelligence and Tactical Assessment Center, US Army
-SOV	Soviet Union	ITAR	Information Telegraph Agency of Russia
FEBA	Forward Edge of the Battle Area		
FF	Frigate		
FFG	Guided Missile Frigate	JIR	Jane's Intelligence Review
FFL	Light Frigate	JPRS	Joint Publications Research Service
FOFA	Follow-on Forces Attack	-UEA	Union Economic Affairs
FRG	Federal Republic of Germany	-UMA	Union Military Affairs
FSU	Former Soviet Union	-USA	United States of America
FUZhV	Fed. Upravlenie Zheleznodorozhnyk Voisk (Federal Dept. of Railroad Forces)	KAMAZ	Kamsky Avtomobilny Zavod
		KD	Kommersant Daily
FY	Fiscal year	KGB	Committee for State Security
		KP	Komsomolskaia pravda
GBTU	Main Armored Tank Directorate of MOD	KVS	Kommunist vooruzhennykh sil
		KZ	Krasnaia zvezda
GDL	Gas Dynamics Laboratory		
GDR	German Democratic Republic	LCAC	Air Cushion Landing Craft
Gds	Guards	LCM	Landing Craft, Mechanized
Gen	General	LMG	Light Machine Gun
GIRD	Group for the Investigation of Rocket Propulsion	LOC	Lanes of Communication
		LPD	Dock Landing Ship
GKChS	Gos. Komitet po Chrezvychainym Situatsiem (State Committee on Emergencies)	LSM	Amphibious/Medium Landing Ship
		LST	Tank Landing Ship
		LSU	Landing Ship, Utility
GKO	State Committee of Defense	Lt	Lieutenant
GLCM	Ground Launched Cruise Missile		
Gosplan	State Planning Committee of the Council of Ministers (USSR)	Maj	Major
		Mar SU	Marshal of the Soviet Union
GP	General Purpose	MBT	Main Battle Tank
GRAU	Main Rocket and Artillery Directorate of MOD	MCS	Minelayer
		MD	Military District
GSFG	General Strategic Force Generation	MFT	Military Forces in Transition (Sep 1991), U.S. Dept. of Defense
		MICV	Mechanized Infantry Combat Vehicle
HVAP	High Velocity Armor Piercing	MILBAL	Military Balance
HVAP(T)	High Velocity Armor Piercing (Tracer)	MILTECH	Military Technology, Bonn, 1977-
		MIRV	Multiple Independently Targetable Reentry Vehicle
ICBM	Intercontinental Ballistic Missile		
IISS	International Institute of Strategic Studies	MK	Moskovskie komsomolets
		MN	Moskovskie novosti
ICPSI	l'Institut Canadien Pour la Paix et la Sécurité Internationale	MOD	Ministry of Defense
		Mot	Motor, Motorized
IWEMO	Institute of World Economy and International Relations	MPA	Main Political Administration
		MR	Motor Rifle
Ind	Independent	MRB	Motor Rifle Brigade
INF	Intermediate-Range and Short-Range Missile	MRD	Motor Rifle Division
		MRL	Multiple Rocket Launcher
Inf	Infantry	MSC	Coastal Minesweeper

MSI	Inshore Minesweeper		Recon	Reconnaissance
MSO	Fleet Minesweeper		Regt	Regiment
MSU	Marshal of the Soviet Union		RFE/RL	Radio Free Europe/Radio Liberty
MVD	Ministry for Internal Affairs		RNII	Rocket Scientific Research Institute
NATO	North Atlantic Treaty Organization		RPC	River Patrol Craft
NCO	Non-Commissioned Officer		RPG	Rocket Propelled Grenade Launcher
NG	Nezavisimaia gazeta			
NIS	Newly Independent States		RSFSR	Russian Soviet Federated Socialist Republic
NKAO	Nagorno Karabakh Autonomous Okrug		RV	Reentry Vehicle
NKMV	People's Commissariat of Mortar Armament		SAFRA	Soviet Armed Forces Review Annual
NKOM	People's Commissariat for General Machine Building		SALT	Strategic Arms Limitation Talk
			SAM	Surface-to-Air Missile
NKPB	People's Commissariat of Ammunition		SAU	Surface-to-Air Missile Launcher
NPT	Non-Proliferation Treaty, Nuclear		SCI	Science, American Association for Advancement of Science
NSC	US National Security Council			
NSWP	Non-Soviet Warsaw Pact		SCLM	Sea Launched Cruise Missile
NYT	New York Times		SCUD	Surface-to-Surface Missile (SSM type)
NZ	Nezavisimaia gazeta			
			SDI	Strategic Defense Initiative, US
OMON	Special Purpose Police Unit		SGN	Nuclear Guided Missile Submarine
OMSDON	Operational Mission Police Rifle Division		sing.	singular
			SKB	Design Bureau Controlling Rocket Launcher Design and Development
OPNAZ	Operational Mission Police Unit			
			SLBM	Submarine Launched Ballistic Missile
Para	Parachute			
PC	Antisubmarine Corvette		SLCM	Sea-Launched Cruise Missile
PC	Patrol Corvette		SLOC	Sea Lanes of Communication
PCG	Guided Missile Corvette		SNF	Strategic Nuclear Force
PD	Parachute Division		Spetsnaz	Special Forces/Operations
PFA	People's Front of Azerbaijan		SPFA	Self-Propelled Field Artillery
PGR	Radar Picket Corvette		Sqdn	Squadron
PH	Hydrofoil Patrol Craft		SS	Attack Submarine
PHG	Hydrofoil Guided Missile Craft		SSA	Auxiliary Submarine
PHT	Hydrofoil Torpedo Craft		SSAN	Nuclear Research Submarine
Plat	Platoon		SSB	Ballistic Missile Submarine
POL	Petroleum, Oil, and Lubricants		SSBN	Nuclear Ballistic Missile Submarine
Postfactum	Russian information news and analytical service		SSG	Guided Missile Submarine
			SSGN	Nuclear Guided Missile Submarine
POW	Prisoner of War		SShA	United States of America
PRC	People's Republic of China		SSM	Surface-to-Surface Missile
PVO	Air Defense Aviation (Aviatsiia PVO)		SSN	Nuclear Attack Submarine
			SSQ	Communications Submarine
R	Ruble		SSQN	Nuclear Communications Submarine
REAFRA	Russia and Eurasia Armed Forces Review Annual		SST	Target Training Submarine

SSX	Attack/Tactical Submarine		u/i	Unidentified
START	Strategic Arms Reduction Talks		UN	United Nations
STAVKA	General Headquarters of the Supreme High Command		UNIDIR	United Nations Institute for Disarmment Research
STO	Council of Labor and Defense		US	United States
SVD	Dragunov Sniper Rifle		USSR	Union of Soviet Socialist Republics
SVE	Soviet Military Encyclopedia (Sovetskaia voennaia entsiklopediia)		VIZh	Journal of Military History (Voenno-istoricheskii zhurnal)
TASS	Soviet News Agency (Telegrafnoe Agenstvo Sovetskogo Soiuza)		VMF	Soviet Navy (Voennomorskoi flot)
TD	Tank Division			
TEL	Transporter-Erecter Launcher		VPK	Military Industrial Commission
Transp	Transport		VTA	Military Transport Aviation
TsK KPSS	Central Committee of the Communist Party of the Soviet Union		VV	Internal Troops
TVD	Theater of Military Operations		WGF	Western Group of Forces
			WP	Warsaw Pact
UEM	Ural Electrical Machine Building Plant		WT	Washington Times
			WTO	Warsaw Treaty Organization

I RUSSIA AND EURASIA MILITARY INDICATORS, 1992–1993

MILITARY AND SECURITY, 1992

CIS UNIFIED ARMED FORCES SUPREME COMMAND, NOVEMBER 1992

Commander-in-Chief of CIS Unified Armed Forces
Marshal of Aviation Yevgeny Ivanovich Shaposhnikov (b.1942)
(also Commander of Strategic Forces of CIS Unified Armed Forces)

Aide to the Commander-in-Chief of CIS Unified Armed Forces
Major General of Aviation Nikolai Sergeevich Stoliarov (b. 1947)
(also Chairman of the Committee for Work With Military Personnel)

First Deputy of the Commander-in-Chief of CIS Unified Armed Forces
Chief of the (Main) Staff CIS Unified Armed Forces Colonel General Viktor Nikolaevich
Samsonov (b. 1941)

Deputy to the Commander-in-Chief of CIS Unified Armed Forces
Chief of Civil Defense Colonel General Boris Yevgenevich Piankov (b. 1935)

RFE/RL Research Institute; Russia & Eurasia Facts & Figures Annual, 1993.

CIS STRATEGIC BOMBER LOCATIONS, 1992

Location	Location	Location
Uzin, Ukraine	Semipalatinsk	Kuibyshev GAZ*
Uzin, Ukraine	Semipalatinsk	Priluki, Ukraine
Uzin, Ukraine	Ukrainka	Zhukovskii
Mozdok	Ukrainka	Kazan MAP*

* Production facility

JIR, February 1992, 83.

CIS STRATEGIC LAND BASES, 1992

Belarus	Russia (continued)	Russia (continued)	Russia (continued)
Lida	Dombarovskii	Svobodny	Yuria
Mozyr	Drovianaia	Tatischevo	
	Irkutsk	Tatischevo	**Ukraine**
Kazakhstan	Kansk	Teykovo	Khmelnitskii
Derzhavinsk	Kartaly	Teykovo	Pervomaisk
Semipalatinsk	Kostromo	Ukrainka	Pervomaisk
Semipalatinsk	Kozelsk	Ukrainka	Priluki
Zhangiz-Tobe	Krasnoiarsk	Uzhur	Uzin
	Krasnoiarsk	Vypolzovo	Uzin
Russia	Mozdok	Yasnaia	Uzin
Aleisk	Nizhny-Tagil	Yoshkar-Ola	
Bershet	Novosibirsk	Yoshkar-Ola	
Bershet			

JIR, February 1992, 81.

FSU DRAFT FULFILLMENT BY REPUBLIC, 1990–1991

	Spring 1990 (percent)	Autumn 1990 (percent)	Overall 1990 (percent)	Spring 1991 (percent)
Armenia	7.5	37.5	22.5	16.5
Azerbaijan	100.0	58.0	84.0	100.0
Belarus	98.9	82.0	90.4	100.0
Estonia	40.2	31.6	35.9	30.3
Georgia	27.5	10.0	18.5	8.2
Kazakhstan	99.2	100.0	100.0	90.0+
Kyrgyzia	89.5	100.0	100.0	90.0+
Latvia	54.2	25.3	39.5	30.8
Lithuania	33.6	16.5	25.1	12.3
Moldova	100.0	92.0	96.0	81.5
RSFSR	98.6	92.2	95.4	100.0
Tajikistan	92.7	94.1	93.4	90.0+
Turkmenistan	90.2	100.0	96.1	90.0+
Ukraine	99.4	91.0	95.1	100.0
Uzbekistan	87.4	83.6	85.6	84.6

A detailed breakdown by republics for Autumn 1991 has not been published yet, but an official source declared that, as of early December 1991, the draft had been fulfilled. Union-wide, only by 22 percent.

JIR, February 1992, 73.

FSU MILITARY ETHNIC BREAKDOWN, 1985–1990

	Percentage of All Young Replacements Arriving						
	1985	1986	1987	1988	Spring 1989	Autumn 1989	1990
Russian speakers	45.3	44.9	43.7	42.1	41.3	42.1	66.5
Central Asians	31.4	32.3	33.6	33.2	30.0	44.2	10.7
Transcaucasians	13.4	14.3	14.4	15.8	23.0	5.8	6.5
Balts	1.4	1.2	1.1	1.1	1.1	0.001	—
From the Volga	3.8	3.4	2.9	3.3	1.5	3.4	14.1
Others	4.7	3.9	4.3	4.5	3.1	4.4	2.2

JIR, Feb 1992, 73.

CIS TROOP INCIDENTS IN TRANSCAUCASIA, 1991–1992

	Year	Total	Azerbaijan	Armenia	Georgia
Armed Attacks	1991	215	43	78	94
	1992	207	98	38	71
Number Killed	1991	24	8	8	8
	1992	30	11	6	13
Number of Weapons Stolen	1991	404*	218	131	49
	1992	4,076	3,939	73	64

* As reported.

Krasnaia zvezda, 25 June 1992.

CIS MILITARY HARDWARE ACCORDING TO CFE, 1992/FSU ARMS SALES, 1991

CIS MILITARY HARDWARE ACCORDING TO CFE, 1992

	Tanks	Tanks*	BBM's	BBM's*	Artillery Systems	Artillery Systems*	Combat Aircraft	Strike Helicopters	Naval Aircraft
Russia	6,400	1,425	11,480	995	6,415	1,310	3,450	890	300
Ukraine	4,080	950	5,050	700	4,040	800	1,090	330	100
Belarus	1,800	275	2,600	425	1,615	240	260	80	—
Moldova	210		210	130	250		50	50	—
Georgia	220		220	135	285		100	50	—
Armenia	220		220	135	285		100	50	—
Azerbaijan	220		220	135	285		100	50	—
Flanks:									
Russia	1,300	600	1,380	800	1,680		—	—	—
Ukraine	280	400	350		—		—	—	—

* For storage.

Nezavisimaia gazeta, 29 July 1992.

FSU ARMS SALES, 1991

Region	Total Volume of Deliveries (percent)
Africa	1
Asia	17
Europe	12
Latin America	1
Middle East	61
Near East	8

Weapons	Number Sold
Air Defense Systems	1
Armored Fighting Vehicles	658
Helicopter Gunships	1
Large-Caliber Artillery Systems	381
Missiles	1,783
Surface Ships	3
Tanks	553
Warplanes	40

Nezavisimaia gazeta, 29 September 1992. For more on FSU weapon systems and nuclear devices, see USSR Facts & Figures Annual/15, 17.

RUSSIAN MILITARY FORCES, 1992

Defense Budget: R411.30 bn

Strategic Nuclear Forces

Navy
Men	12,000
SSBN	55

Strategic Rocket Forces
Men	144,000
ICBM	1,400
MI-8	140

Strategic Aviation
Men	25,000
Bombers	581
TU-16	13
TU-22	60
IL-20	10
Tankers	75

Russian Armed Forces
Men	2,720,000
Reserves	3,000,000

Navy
Men	120,000
Conscripts	200,000
Submarines	250

Navy (continued)
Strategic Submarines	55
Tactical Submarines	183
Surface Combatants	192
Carriers	4
Cruisers	33
Destroyers	26
Frigates	129
Patrol and Coastal Combatants	305
Missile Craft	40
Torpedo Craft	29
Mine Warfare	218
Amphibious	80
Support	685
Merchant Fleet	2,800

Naval Aviation
Men	60,000
Bombers	235
SU-17	165
SU-24	100
SU-25	55

Naval Aviation (continued)
MIG-27	30
Fighters	35
Trainers	300
ASW	191
Tankers	18
Transport	58

Coastal Defense Forces
Men	12,000
Tanks	2,340
Electronic Reconnaissance	60
Artillery	204
SAM	250

Coastal Artillery and Rocket Troops
Men	4,500

Coastal Defense Troops
Men	13,000
Tanks	2,400
Artillery	992

General Purpose Forces

Ground Forces
Men	1,400,000
Tanks	29,800
Artillery	22,000
Mortars	2,000
SSM	900
Helicopters	3,200

Air Force
Men	300,000
Fighters	2,300
Electronic Reconnaissance	365
Trainers	1,500
Helicopters	320

Forces Abroad
Mongolia	3,000
Vietnam	500
Algeria	500
Angola	50
Cambodia	500
Congo	20
Cuba	4,300
India	500
Libya	1,000
Mali	20
Mozambique	25
Peru	50
Syria	500
Yemen	300

Russian Female Officers
Female Officers	657
Colonel	1
Lt. Col.	16
Majors	92
Captains	330
Lt. and Senior Lts.	218

JIR; MILBAL; Russia & Eurasia Facts & Figures Annual, 1993.

RUSSIAN MILITARY PRODUCTION SITES, 1992

Kazan	Tatarstan	Strategic bombers, helicopters, missiles, rocket engines, optical equipment, radio-communications equipment
Zelenodolsk	Tatarstan	Naval vessels
Glazov	Udmurtiia	Nuclear materials

RUSSIAN MILITARY PRODUCTION SITES, 1992 (continued)

Izhevsk	Udmurtiia	Armor vehicles
Izhevsk	Udmurtiia	Infantry weapons
Votkisk	Udmurtiia	Strategic missiles
Kemertau	Bashkiriia	Helicopters
Salavat	Bashkiriia	Optical equipment
Ufa	Bashkiriia	Communications equipment
Ufa	Bashkiriia	Engines

JIR; MILBAL; Russia & Eurasia Facts & Figures Annual, 1993.

RUSSIAN URANIUM PRODUCTION SITES, 1992

Aldan	Mining	Sliudianka	Mining
Karelia	Deposit (vanadium)	Vikhorevka	Mining
Krasnokamensk	Deposit	Vishnevogorsk	Mining
Lermontov	Mining and milling (molybdenum)		
Novogorny	Mining		

JIR; MILBAL; Russia & Eurasia Facts & Figures Annual, 1993.

RUSSIAN SECURITY ORGANS, 1992

Security Organs
500,000 employees

Federal Agency for Government Communications and Administration. In charge of security and codes for governmental communications and collection of signal intelligence.

Interior Ministry (MVD). Internal police and intelligence functions.

Military Intelligence (GRU). Responsible for military spying abroad and produces photographic intelligence. Subordinate to the Russian Ministry of Defense.

Ministry of Security. Contains former KGB components and is in charge of domestic and military counterintelligence, internal security and counterterrorism. Recently reacquired 240,000 border troops.

Presidential Committee for Leadership Protection. Protects Russian leadership. Contains the Alpha special forces.

Russian Intelligence Service. Former KGB first main directorate. Responsible for foreign spying and intelligence analyses.

JIR; MILBAL; WT; Russia & Eurasia Facts & Figures Annual, 1993.

RUSSIAN MILITARY LEADERS, NOVEMBER 1992

Russian Federation Ministry of Defense
Minister of Defense
Army General Pavel Sergeevich Grachev (b. 1948)

First Deputy Defense Ministers
Unknown
Colonel General Viktor Petrovich Dubinin (b. 1943 - d. 1992)
Andrei Afanasevich Kokoshin (b. 1945)

RUSSIAN MILITARY LEADERS, NOVEMBER 1992 (continued)

Deputy Defense Ministers
Colonel General Boris Vsevolodovich Gromov (b. 1943)
Colonel General Georgy Grigorevich Kondratev (b. 1944)
Colonel General Valery Ivanovich Mironov (b. 1943)
Colonel General Vladimir Mikhailovich Toporov (b. 1946)

Chief Military Inspector of the Armed Forces
Army General Konstantin Ivanovich Kobets (b. 1939)

Commanders-in-Chief
Commander-in-Chief of Strategic Rocket Forces
    Colonel General Igor Dmitrievich Sergeev (b. 1938)
Commander-in-Chief of Ground Foces
    Colonel General Vladimir Magomedovich Semenov (b. 1940)
Commander-in-Chief of Air Defense Forces
    Colonel General of Aviation Viktor Alekseevich Prudnikov (b.1939)
Commander-in-Chief of Air Forces
    Colonel General Aviation Petr Stepanovich Deinekin (b. 1937)
Commander-in-Chief of Naval Forces
    Admiral Feliks Nikolaevich Gromov (b. 1937)

Chiefs of Services
Chief of Rear Services
    Major General Vladimir Timofeevich Churanov (b. 1945)
Chief of Armaments
    Colonel General Viacheslav Petrovich Mironov (b. 1938)
Chief of Construction and Billeting
    Colonel General Nikolai Vasilevich Chekov (b. 1931)
Chief of Civil Defense
    Unknown
Chief of Main Directorate for Training and Distribution of Personnel
    Lieutenant General Yevgeny Vasilevich Vysotskii (b. 1947)

Commanders-in-Chief of Directions
Western Direction
    Army General Stanislav Ivanovich Postnikov (b. 1928)
Southern Direction
    Army General Nikolai Ivanovich Popov (b. 1930)
Far East Direction
    Colonel General Aleksandr Vasilevich Kovtunov (b.1933)

Commanders of Groups of Forces, Military Districts, and Fleets
Groups of Forces
Western Group of Forces
    Colonel General Matvei Prokofeevich Burlakov (b. 1935)
Northern Group of Forces
    Colonel General Leonid Illarionovich Kovalev (b. 1944)
Northwestern Group of Forces
    Colonel General Leonid Sergeevich Maiorov (b. 1941)
Transcaucasian Group of Forces
    Lieutenant General Fedor Mikhailovich Reut (b. 1946)

Military Districts
Far Eastern Military District
    Colonel General Viktor Stepanovich Chechevatov (b. 1945)

RUSSIAN MILITARY LEADERS, NOVEMBER 1992 (continued)

Military Districts (continued)
Leningrad Military District
   Colonel General Sergei Pavlovich Seleznev (b. 1944)
Moscow Military District
   Colonel General Leonty Vasilevich Kuznetsov (b. 1938)
North Caucasian Military District
   Colonel General Lev Sergeevich Shustko (b. 1935)
Siberian Military District
   Colonel General Viktor Andreevich Kopvlov (b. 1940)
Transbaikal Military District
   Colonel General Valery Stepanovich Tretiakov (b. 1941)
Ural Military District
   Colonel General Yury Pavlovich Grekov (b. 1943)
Volga Military District
   Colonel General Anatoly Ipatovich Sergeev (b. 1940)

Fleets
Baltic Fleet
   Admiral Vladimir Grigorevich Yegorov (b. 1938)
Black Sea Fleet
   Admiral Igor Vladimirovich Kasatonov (b. 1939)
Northern Fleet
   Admiral Oleg Aleksandrovich Yerofeev (b. 1940)
Pacific Fleet
   Admiral Gennady Aleksandrovich Khvatov (b. 1934)
Caspian Sea Flotilla
   Rear Admiral Boris Mikhailovich Zinin (b. 1941)

RFE/RL Research Institute; Russia & Eurasia Facts & Figures Annual, 1993.

RUSSIAN DEFENSE AND STATE SECURITY OFFICIALS, NOVEMBER 1992

Ministry of Security
Director-General: Colonel General Viktor
   Pavlovich Barannikov
Date of Birth: 1940
Date of Appointment: 17 January 1992

Foreign Intelligence Service
Director: General Yevgeny Maksimovich
   Primakov
Date of Birth: 29 October 1929
Date of Appointment: 26 December 1991

Ministry of Internal Affairs
Minister: Colonel General Viktor Fedorovich
   Erin
Date of Birth: unknown
Date of Appointment: 17 January 1992

Ministry of Defense
Minister: Army General Pavel Sergeevich
   Grachev
Date of Birth: 1 January 1948
Date of Appointment: 18 May 1992

**Supreme Soviet Defense and Security
   Committee**
Chairman: Major General Sergei Vadimovich
   Stepashin
Date of Birth: 1952
Date of Appointment: 28 February 1991

Border Guards
Commander: Lieutenant General Vladimir
   Ivanovich Shliakhtin
Date of Birth: 1940
Date of Appointment: 15 June 1992
Other Post: Deputy Minister of Security

RFE/RL Research Institute; Russia & Eurasia Facts & Figures Annual, 1993.

PERCENTAGE OF RUSSIAN DEFENSE INDUSTRY IN TOTAL PRODUCTION, 1992

	As Percentage of Total Output		As Percentage of Total Output
Diesel engines and		Sewing machines	100
diesel generators	88	Cameras	100
Computers	95	Video recorders	100
Rolled aluminum	94	Tape recorders	98
Rolled titanium	71	Refrigerators	98
Long-haul rail cars	33	Engine blocks	81
Gas and oil drilling		Vacuum cleaners	72
units	28	Washing machines	66
Television sets	100	Motorcycles	52

Ekonomika i zhizn, No. 18 (May 1992), 1.

FOREIGN INVESTMENT IN RUSSIAN DEFENSE INDUSTRIES, 1992

Name of Project	Enterprise	Credit Line
Automatic hosiery machines	Production Association Tulatochmash (Tula)	Hermes
Modern cranes	Imeni Kominternaplant (Novorossiisk)	Hermes
Blood transfusion systems	Tushino Engineering Plant	Hermes
Industrial and household sewing machines	Podolsk Concern	Hermes
Overlok sewing machines	Production Association Azovskii Optical & Mechanical Plant	Hermes
Enameling machines	Production Association Leningradskii Severny Plant	Hermes
Artificial leather, furniture, clothes	Production Association Progress (Kemerovo)	Italy
Minitractor engines	Production Tulskii Ammunition Works	Italy
Press-tools and molds	Serpukhov Radiotechnical Plant	Italy
Large washing machines	Production Association Poliot (Omsk)	Italy
Small washing machines	Votkinsk Plant Belgorod Radiotechnical Plant	Italy
Compact photo cameras	Production Association Krasnogorskii Plant	S. Korea
Compressors for refrigerators	Dvigatel Revoliutsii Plant (Nizhny Novgorod)	UK
AN-38 planes for local airlines	Tyumen Engine Manufacturing Association	Kuwait
Spinning units	Research and Production Association Elektromekhanika (Mias, Cheliabinsk Region)	Austria

Interfax, 15 October 1992, in FBIS-SOV, 21 October 1992, 25.

ARMENIAN MILITARY FORCES, 1992

Defense Budget: R250 mn

Armenian Military*		Armenian Military* (continued)		Russian Forces	
Men Within 15				Men	23,000
Years	Up to 300,000	Artillery	285	Tanks	600
Tanks	220	Aircraft	100	Artillery	350
Helicopters	270	Armored Vehicles	220	Helicopters	7
				SAM	80

ARMENIAN MILITARY FORCES, 1992 (continued)

* Equipment figures based on 15 May 1992 treaty on quotas per former republic.

JIR; MILBAL; Russia & Eurasia Facts & Figures Annual, 1993.

ARMENIAN MILITARY PRODUCTION SITE, 1992

Razdan   Radio electronic equipment

JIR; MILBAL; Russia & Eurasia Facts & Figures Annual, 1993.

ARMENIAN DEFENSE AND SECURITY OFFICIALS, 1992

State Administration for National Security
Chief: Valery Vagarshakovich Pogosian
Date of Birth: unknown
Date of Appointment: 2 February 1992

Ministry of Internal Affairs
Minister: Vano Smbatovich Siradegian
Date of Birth: 45 years old
Date of Appointment: 2 February 1992

Supreme Soviet Committee for Questions of Defense and Internal Affairs
Chairman: Gevork Bagdarian
Date of Birth: unknown
Date of Appointment: unknown

Ministry of Defense
Minister: Vazgen M. Manukian (acting)
Date of Birth: 1946
Date of Appointment: 20 October 1992
Other post: State Minister

RFE/RL Research Institute; Russia & Eurasia Facts & Figures Annual, 1993.

AZERI MILITARY FORCES, 1992

Defense Budget: R20 bn (est. 1993)

Azeri Forces		Azeri Paramilitary		Russian Forces	
Reserves in 15 yrs.	500,000	MVD Troop	20,000s	Men	62,000
Army	5,000	Karabakh People's		Tanks	1,250
Navy	1,000	Defense	12,000	Artillery	450
Tanks	297			Attack Helicopters	14
Helicopters	270			SU-24	30
Artillery	305			SU-25	30
Aircraft	100			MIG-25, SU-24	60
Armored Vehicles	396			SAM	135

JIR; MILBAL; Russia & Eurasia Facts & Figures Annual, 1993.

AZERI DEFENSE AND SECURITY OFFICIALS, 1992

Ministry of National Security
Minister: Fakhraddin Ayat ogly Takhmazov
Date of Birth: unknown
Date of Appointment: 16 May 1992

Ministry of Internal Affairs
Minister: Iskender Medzhid ogly Gamidov
Date of Birth: unknown
Date of Appointment: 16 May 1992

Ministry of Defense
Minister: Ragim Gaziev
Date of Birth: 49 years old
Date of Appointment: 18 March 1992

Committee for Defense of State Borders
Chairman: Iskander Imanverdi ogly Allakhverdiev
Date of Birth: 1947
Date of Appointment: 16 December 1991

AZERI DEFENSE AND SECURITY OFFICIALS, 1992 (continued)

Supreme Soviet Commission for State Security, Military Affairs, and Legal System
Chairman: Mamed Babash ogly Kuliev
Date of Birth: 1939
Date of Appointment: 5 February 1991

RFE/RL Research Institute; Russia & Eurasia Facts & Figures Annual, 1993.

BELARUSIAN MILITARY FORCES, 1992

Defense Budget: R17 bn

Strategic Nuclear Forces		Ground Forces (continued)		Air Force (continued)	
ICBM	54	Artillery	1,400	TU-26	40
Belarus Forces		SSM	60	SU-24	90
Men	90,000-125,000	MI-24	80	MIG-29	50
Reserves	350,000	MI-6	30	TU-16	13
		MI-8	90	TU-22	29
Air Defense		MI-24K	9	MIG-21	15
Men	10,000	MI-24P	6	MIG-25	30
MIG-23	65	MI-26	15	YAK-28	20
MIG-25	50	MI-2	27	MI-2	2
SAM	650	**Air Force**		MI-8	40
Ground Forces		Men	20,000	MI-24P	2
Men	95,000	TU-16	25		
Tanks	5,000	TU-22	65		

JIR; MILBAL; Russia & Eurasia Facts & Figures Annual, 1993.

BELARUSIAN MILITARY PRODUCTION SITES, 1992

Gomel	Radar systems
Minsk	Nuclear technology
Minsk	Optical equipment
Minsk	Radio communications equipment
Vitebsk	Radio communications equipment

JIR; MILBAL; Russia & Eurasia Facts & Figures Annual, 1993.

BELARUSIAN DEFENSE AND SECURITY OFFICIALS, NOVEMBER 1992

Committee for State Security
Chairman: Lt. General Eduard I. Shyrkouskii
Date of Birth: 1932
Date of Appointment: 30 October 1990

Ministry of Internal Affairs
Minister: Lieutenant General Vladimir
  Demianovich Yegorov
Date of Birth: 1939
Date of Appointment: 20 July 1990

Ministry of Defense
Minister: Colonel General Pavel Pavlovich
  Kozlovskii
Date of Birth: 9 March 1942
Date of Appointment: 22 April 1992

Border Troops
Commander: Major General Yevgeny
  Mikhailovich Bocharov
Date of Birth: 20 October 1948
Date of Appointment: 21 April 1992

BELARUSIAN DEFENSE AND SECURITY OFFICIALS, NOVEMBER 1992 (continued)

Supreme Soviet Commission for Questions of National Security, Defense, and the Struggle with Crime
Chairman: Major General Mechislav Ivanovich Grib
Date of Birth: 1938
Date of Appointment: 1990

RFE/RL Research Institute; Russia & Eurasia Facts & Figures Annual, 1993.

ESTONIAN MILITARY FORCES, 1992

Defense Budget: R135 million

Estonian Forces		Russian Forces		Russian Forces (continued)	
Men	2,000	Men	23,000	Artillery	20
		Tanks	250	SAM	250

JIR; MILBAL; Russia & Eurasia Facts & Figures Annual, 1993.

ESTONIAN MILITARY/URANIUM PRODUCTION SITE, 1992

Sillamae	Uranium, mining and milling

JIR; MILBAL; Russia& Eurasia Facts & Figures Annual, 1993.

ESTONIAN DEFENSE AND SECURITY OFFICIALS, 1992

Ministry of Internal Affairs
Minister: Lagle Parek
Date of Birth: 17 April 1941
Date of Appointment: 21 October 1992

Ministry of Defense
Minister: Hain Rebas
Date of Birth: 23 January 1943
Date of Appointment: 21 October 1992

Supreme Council Commission for Defense
Chairman: Rein Helme
Date of Birth: unknown
Date of Appointment: October 1992

Defense Union (Kaitseliit)
Commander: Kalle Eller
Date of Birth: unknown
Date of Appointment: unknown

Home Guard (Kodu Kaitse)
Commander: Andrus Wel
Date of Birth: 40 years old
Date of Appointment: 1992

RFE/RL Research Institute; Russia & Eurasia Facts & Figures Annual, 1993.

GEORGIAN MILITARY FORCES, 1992

Defense Budget: R6 bn

Georgian Forces

Army	Reserves	Paramilitary
20,000 men planned	500,000 men planned	3,000 with 13,000 planned

GEORGIAN MILITARY FORCES, 1992 (continued)

Georgian Military*		Russian Forces		Russian Forces (continued)	
Tanks	220	Army		Air Forces	
Helicopters	270	Men	20,000	MIG-23, MIG-29	80
Artillery	285	MI-8	40	SU-17	30
Aircraft	100	MI-26	25	SU-15, SU-27	40
Armored Vehicles	220	Tanks	1,500	SAM	175
		Artillery	370		
		Attack Helicopters	48		

* Equipment figures based on 15 May 1992 treaty on quotas per former republic.

JIR; MILBAL; Russia & Eurasia Facts & Figures Annual, 1993.

GEORGIAN DEFENSE AND SECURITY OFFICIALS, NOVEMBER 1992

Ministry of Defense
Minister: General Anatolii Kamkamidze
Date of Birth: 1938
Date of Appointment: 11 November 1992

Ministry of Internal Affairs
Minister: Major General Roman Levanovich
  Gventsadze
Date of Birth: unknown
Date of Appointment: 1992

Information and Intelligence Bureau
Director: Iraklii Batiashvili
Date of Birth: 30 years old
Date of Appointment: 3 May 1992

RFE/RL Research Institute; Russia & Eurasia Facts & Figures Annual, 1993.

GEORGIAN NATIONAL SECURITY AND DEFENSE COUNCIL, DECEMBER 1992

Chairman:	Eduard Shevardnadze	Members:	
Deputy Chairmen:	Tengiz Sigua	Irakli Batiashvili	Tedo Ninidze
	Jaba Ioseliani	Aleksandr Kavsadze	Aleksandr Chikvaidze
	Tengiz Kitovani	Anatoli Kamkamidze	Temur Khachishvili
		Kodar Natadze	

Sakartvelos respublika, 3 December 1992, in FBIS-SOV, 8 December 1992, 53.

KAZAKH MILITARY FORCES, 1992

Strategic Nuclear Forces		Kazakh National Guard	
ICBMs (SS-18)	104	Men	3,000-5,000
Bombers (TU-95H)	40		

Joint Russian-Kazakh Forces, 1992 (est.)

Army:		Air Force:		Air Force (cont.):	
Men	63,000	Men	30,000	MIG 25, SU-17,	
Battle Tanks	1,600	MIG-27, SU-24	140	SU-24	70
Artillery	1,500	MIG 23	100	MIG-25, MIG-31	60
SS-21	40			SAM	150
Attack Helicopters	25				

JIR; MILBAL; Russia & Eurasia Facts & Figures Annual, 1993.

KAZAKH MILITARY/URANIUM PRODUCTION SITES, 1992

Alma-Ata	Radio communication equipment	Uralsk	Machine guns
Petropavlovsk	Missile transport and launchers	Aksuyek-Kiyakti	Uranium mining
		Koktas	Uranium mining (copper)
Semipalatinsk	Nuclear weapons research	Ust-Kamenogorsk	Uranium mining and processing

JIR; MILBAL; Russia & Eurasia Facts & Figures Annual, 1993.

KAZAKH DEFENSE AND SECURITY OFFICIALS, NOVEMBER 1992

Committee for National Security
Chairman: Lieutenant General Bulat
    Abdrakhmanovich Baekenov
Date of Birth: 1942
Date of Appointment: 25 October 1991

Ministry of Internal Affairs
Minister: Vladimir Georgievich Shumov
Date of Birth: 1941
Date of Appointment: 17 April 1992

Ministry of Defense
Minister: Colonel General Sagadat
    Kozhakhmetovich Nurmagambetov
Date of Birth: May 25, 1924
Date of Appointment: 7 May 1992

National Guard
Commander: Major General Seilbek
    A. Altynbekov
Date of Birth: 48 years old
Date of Appointment: 19 March 1992

**Supreme Soviet Committee for National
    Security and Defense**
Chairman: Colonel Bulat Dzhanasaev
Date of Birth: 1952
Date of Appointment: 1 July 1992

Border Troops
Commander: Major General Bolat Zakiev
Date of Birth: 1950
Date of Appointment: 27 October 1992

RFE/RL Research Institute; Russia & Eurasia Facts & Figures Annual, 1993.

KYRGYZ MILITARY FORCES, 1992

Defense Budget: R730 mn

Kyrgyz National Guard
Formed 18 November 1991 with proposed
    5-7,000 active and 11,000 reserve.

Joint Russian-Kyrgyz Forces	
Active Personnel	12,000
Battle Tanks	200
Artillery	75
MIG-21, L-29, L-39	200
SAM	55

JIR; MILBAL; Russia & Eurasia Facts & Figures Annual, 1993.

KYRGYZ MILITARY/URANIUM PRODUCTION SITES, 1992

Ak-Tyuz-Bordunskii	Uranium mining (lead, thorium)
Bishkek	Munitions
Granitogorsk	Uranium mining and concentration (lead)
Kadzhi-Say	Uranium mining (lignite)
Kara-Balta	Uranium processing
Min-Kush	Uranium mining and milling (lignite)
Tyuya-Muyun	Uranium mining (vanadium)

JIR; MILBAL; Russia & Eurasia Facts & Figures Annual, 1993.

KYRGYZ DEFENSE AND SECURITY OFFICIALS, NOVEMBER 1992

State Committee for Defense Questions
Chairman: Major General Dzhanybek
  Asanbekovich Umetaliev
Date of Birth: 49 years old
Date of Appointment: 26 February 1992

Ministry of Internal Affairs
Minister: Colonel Abdybek Asankulovich
  Sutalinov
Date of Birth: unknown
Date of Appointment: 31 March 1992

State Committee for National Security
Chairman: Anarbek Kuramaevich Bakaev
Date of Birth: unknown
Date of Appointment: 26 February 1992

Supreme Soviet Committee on Military Affairs
Chairman: unknown

National Guard
Commander: Abdygul Abdrashidovich Chotbaev
Date of Birth: unknown
Date of Appointment: 28 February 1992

RFE/RL Research Institute; Russia & Eurasia Facts & Figures Annual, 1993.

LATVIAN MILITARY FORCES, 1992

Defense Budget: R257.4 million

Latvian Forces		Russian Forces		Russian Forces (cont.)	
Men	2,550	Men	40,000	Attack Helicopters	24
Latvian Home Guard		Tanks	200	MI-8	20
Men	12,000	Artillery	80	SAM	250

JIR; MILBAL; Russia & Eurasia Facts & Figures Annual, 1993.

LATVIAN DEFENSE AND SECURITY OFFICIALS, NOVEMBER 1992

Ministry of Internal Affairs
Minister: Ziedonis Cevers
Date of Birth: 29 January 1960
Date of Appointment: 20 November 1991

Ministry of Defense
Minister: Talavs Jundzis
Date of Birth: 1951
Date of Appointment: 19 November 1991

**Supreme Council Commission for Defense
and Internal Affairs**
Chairman: Peteris Simsons
Date of Birth: 1948
Date of Appointment: 1991

Security Service
Chairman: Colonel Juris Vectiraus
Date of Birth: 37 years old
Date of Appointment: 1992

Home Guard (Zemes sardze)
Chief: Girts Kristovskis
Date of Birth: unknown
Date of Appointment: 18 February 1992

RFE/RL Research Institute; Russia & Eurasia Facts & Figures Annual, 1993.

LITHUANIAN MILITARY FORCES, 1992

Defense Budget: Unknown

Lithuanian Military Forces		Russian Forces in Lithuania			
Men	7,000	Men	43,000	Artillery	260
National Guard	12,500	Tanks	1,000	SAM	125

JIR; MILBAL; Russia & Eurasia Facts & Figures Annual, 1993.

LITHUANIAN DEFENSE AND SECURITY OFFICIALS, NOVEMBER 1992

Ministry of National Defense
Minister: Audrius Butkevicius
Date of Birth: 24 September 1960
Date of Appointment: March 1990

Ministry of Internal Affairs
Minister: General Petras Valiukas
Date of Birth: 1948
Date of Appointment: 19 November 1991

Security Service
Director-General: Petras Plumpa
Date of Birth: 1939
Date of Appointment: 11 August 1992

Border Protection Service
Chief: Stanislovas Stancikas
Date of Birth: unknown
Date of Appointment: 1991

Supreme Council Commission for National Defense and Internal Affairs
Chairman: Saulius Peceliunas
Date of Birth: 19 January 1956
Date of Appointment: January 1992

RFE/RL Research Institute; Russia & Eurasia Facts & Figures Annual, 1993.

MOLDOVAN MILITARY FORCES, 1992

Defense Budget: R4.1 bn

Moldovan Armed Forces formed on 14 November 1991.

Moldovan Forces		Air Defense		Russian Forces (14th Army)	
Reserve in 15		SAM	80	Tanks	300
Years	300,000	**National Guard**		Artillery	330
Army		Men	4,000	Atttack Helicopters	40
Men	12,000			Scuds	24
Air Force		**Opposition Forces**			
MIG-29	30	Men (Dniester Army)	15,000		

JIR; MILBAL; Russia & Eurasia Facts & Figures Annual, 1993.

MOLDOVAN MILITARY PRODUCTION SITE, 1992

Kishinev   Electronic radio equipment

JIR; MILBAL; Russia & Eurasia Facts & Figures Annual, 1993.

MOLDOVAN DEFENSE AND SECURITY OFFICIALS, NOVEMBER 1992

Ministry of National Security
Minister: Major Vasile Calmoi
Date of Birth: unknown
Date of Appointment: 21 July 1992

Ministry of Internal Affairs
Minister: Major Constantin Antoci
Date of Birth: unknown
Date of Appointment: February 1992

Ministry of Defense
Minister: Lieutenant General Pavel Creanga
Date of Birth: unknown
Date of Appointment: 21 July 1992

Parliamentary Commission for Defense and Security Affairs
Chairman: Anatol Taran
Date of Birth: unknown
Date of Appointment: June 1992

RFE/RL Research Institute; Russia & Eurasia Facts & Figures Annual, 1993.

TAJIK MILITARY FORCES, 1992

Defense Budget: R1.5 bn

Tajik-Russian Forces

Air Defense		Army (continued)	
SAM	40	Tanks	680
Army		Artillery	360
Men	6,000	SS-21	4

JIR; MILBAL; Russia & Eurasia Facts & Figures Annual, 1993.

TAJIK URANIUM PROCESSING CENTERS, 1992

Chkalovsk	Uranium extraction, uranium, hexaflouride conversion
Taboshar	Uranium mining, uranium oxide extraction (vanadium)

JIR; MILBAL; Russia & Eurasia Facts & Figures Annual, 1993.

TAJIK DEFENSE AND SECURITY OFFICIALS, NOVEMBER 1992

Committee for National Security
Chairman: Alidjon A. Soliboev*
Date of Birth: unknown
Date of Appointment: 11 May 1992

Ministry of Internal Affairs
Minister: Guldastsho Imronshoev*
Date of Birth: Unknown
Date of Appointment: 5 November 1992

Ministry of Defense
Chairman: Major General Farrukh
    Rakhmanovich Niyazov
Date of Birth: 1935
Date of Appointment: 19 October 1992

* Replaced in December 1992.

RFE/RL Research Institute; Russia & Eurasia Facts & Figures Annual, 1993.

TURKMEN MILITARY FORCES, 1992

Defense Budget: Unknown

Turkmen-Russian Joint Forces

Men	34,000	SSM	24	MIG-23	85
Tanks	1,000	MIG-27, SU-17	60	MIG-25	30
Artillery	1,400	MIG-29	30	SAM	75

JIR; MILBAL; Russia & Eurasia Facts & Figures Annual, 1993.

TURKMEN DEFENSE AND SECURITY OFFICIALS, NOVEMBER 1992

Committee for National Security
Chairman: Major General Saparmurad Seidov
Date of Birth: 1942
Date of Appointment: 25 May 1992

Ministry of Internal Affairs
Minister: Colonel Serdar Charyyarov
Date of Birth: 1943
Date of Appointment: 17 September 1990

TURKMEN DEFENSE AND SECURITY OFFICIALS, NOVEMBER 1992 (continued)

Ministry of Defense Affairs
Minister: Lieutenant General Danatar Abdyevich Kopekov
Date of Birth: 1933
Date of Appointment: 27 January 1992

RFE/RL Research Institute; Russia & Eurasia Facts & Figures Annual, 1993.

UKRAINIAN MILITARY FORCES, 1992

Defense Budget: R116 bn

Strategic Nuclear Forces		Ukrainian Air Defense		Black Sea Fleet	
ICBM	176	Men	30,000	Bases	Sevastopol
TU-95H	21	SU-15	80		Odessa
TU-160	20	MIG-23	110		Poti
IL-78	20	MIG-25	80	Submarines	18
		SAM	2,400	Combatants	39
Ukrainian National Guard				Support Ships	240
Men	6,000	**Ukrainian Air Force**		TU-26	45
		Men	50,000	TU-16	25
Ukrainian Ground Forces		TU-16	30	SU-17	40
Men	150,000	TU-22	30	MIG-29	35
Tanks	8,000	TU-26	36	BE-12	23
Artillery	3,000	SU-24	282	MI-14	31
SSM	132	SU-25	30	KA-25	54
MI-24	240	MIG-23	80	KA-27	5
MI-6	60	MIG-29	220	AN-12	2
MI-8	280	SU-27	40	TU-22	6
MI-24K	8	TU-22	30	IL-20	1
MI-24P	5	MIG-25	15	MI-14	5
MI-26	20	SU-17	30	Tanks	600
MI-2	80	YAK-28	35	Artillery	200
		MIG-21	240		

JIR; MILBAL; Russia & Eurasia Facts & Figures Annual, 1993.

UKRAINIAN MILITARY/URANIUM PRODUCTION SITES, 1992

Location	Product	Location	Product
Chernovitsa	Optical equipment	Kiev	Transport aircraft
Dnepropetrovsk	Radar systems	Lugansk	Artillery and infantry
Dnepropetrovsk	Strategic missiles		weapons
Feodosiia	Naval ships	Lvov	Lasers
Izyum	Optical equipment	Nikolaev	Naval ships
Kharkov	Tanks	Pavlograd	Strategic missiles
Kharkov	Transport aircraft	Sevastopol	Naval ships
Kherson	Naval ships	Zaporozhe	Communications
Kiev	Artillery and infantry weapons		equipment
Kiev	Communications equipment	Zaporozhe	Engines
Kiev	Optical equipment	Zheltye Vody-Terny	Uranium mining and
Kiev	Radar systems		processing

JIR; MILBAL; Russia & Eurasia Facts & Figures Annual, 1993.

UKRAINIAN DEFENSE AND SECURITY OFFICIALS, NOVEMBER 1992

Security Service
Chairman: Colonel General Yevhen Kyrylovych
  Marchuk
Date of Birth: unknown
Date of Appointment: 6 November 1991

Ministry of Internal Affairs
Minister: Lieutenant General Andrii
  Volodymyrovych Yasylyshin
Date of Birth: 1933
Date of Appointment: 26 July 1990

Ministry of Defense
Minister: Colonel General Konstantin
  Petrovich Morozov
Date of Birth: 3 June 1944
Date of Appointment: 3 September 1991

National Guard
Commander: Major General Volodymyr
  Oleksiiovych Kukharets
Date of Birth: 1938
Date of Appointment: 22 October 1991

Border Troops
Commander: Colonel General Valery
  Aleksandrovich Gubenko
Date of Birth: 1939
Date of Appointment: 30 December 1991
Other Post: Chairman, State Committee
  for Defense of State Borders

RFE/RL Research Institute.

**Supreme Soviet Commission for Defense and
  State Security**
Chairman: V.P. Lemish
Date of Birth: unknown
Date of Appointment: 28 October 1992

State Committee for Defense of State Borders
Chairman: Colonel General Valery
  Aleksandrovich Gubenko
Date of Birth: 1939
Date of Appointment: 30 December 1991
Other post: Commander, Border Troops

Military Districts
Carpathian Military District
  Lieutenant General Vasily Timofeevich
    Sobkov (b. unknown)
Odessa Military District
  Lieutenant General Vitaly Grigorevich
    Radetskii (b. unknown)
Kiev Military District
  Lieutenant General Valentin Danilovich
    Boriskin (b.1942)

UKRAINIAN AIR FORCES, MARCH 1992

46th Smolensk Air Army

13th Heavy Bomber Division	Poltava
15th Heavy Bomber Division	Ozernoe
22nd Heavy Bomber Division	Bobruisk

(5 regiments, 125 bombers)

24th Vinnitsa Air Army

32nd Bomber Division	Starokonstantinov
56th Bomber Division	Cherlyianii
138th Fighter Division	Mirgorod

(8 regiments, 260 combat aircraft)

14th Lvov Air Army

4th Fighter Division	Ivano-Frankovsk
289th Bomber Division	Lutsk

(6 regiments, 215 combat aircraft)

JIR, March 1992, 131-136.

5th Odessa Air Army
(2 regiments, 90 combat aircraft)

17th Kiev Air Army

Kharkov Military Aviation School	Kharkov
Lugansk Military Aviation School	Bagerovo
Chernigov Military Aviation School	Chernigov

(240 combat-capable trainers,
525 jet trainers)

2nd Minsk Air Defense Army
(2 regiments, 80 interceptors)

8th Kiev Air Defense Army
(5 regiments, 195 interceptors)

UKRAINIAN GROUND FORCES, MARCH 1992

Carpathian Military District

24th Motor Rifle Division	Yavorov
26th Artillery Division	Kamenka-Bugskaia
110th District Training Center	Chernovtsii
66th Artillery Corps	
81st Artillery Division	Vinogradov

13th Combined Arms Army

17th Motor Rifle Division	Khmelnitskii
51st Motor Rifle Division	Vladimir-Volynskii
97th Motor Rifle Division	Slavuta
161st Motor Rifle Division	Iziaslav

38th Combined Arms Army

70th Motor Rifle Division	Ivano-Frankovsk
128th Motor Rifle Division	Nadvornaia

8th Tank Army

30th Tank Division	Novograd-Volynskii

Kiev Military District

169th District Training Center	Desna
254th Motor Rifle Division	Artemovsk

1st Combined Arms Army

25th Motor Rifle Division	Lubny
72nd Motor Rifle Division	Belaia Tserkov

6th Tank Army

17th Tank Division	Krivoi Rog
93rd Motor Rifle Division	Cherkasskoe

Odessa Military District

98th Air Assault Division	Bolgrad
28th Motor Rifle Division	Chernomorskoe
55th Artillery Division	Novaia Aleksandrovka
150th District Training Center	Nikolaev

14th Combined Arms Army
(forces in Ukraine only)

180th Motor Rifle Division	Belgorod

JIR, March 1992, 131-136.

UZBEK MILITARY FORCES, 1992

Defense Budget: Unknown

Uzbek-Russian Joint Forces		Uzbek-Russian Joint Forces (continued)	
Men	15,000	Attack Helicopters	24
Tanks	1,000	SU-17, SU-24, SU-25	165
Artillery	780	MIG-29, SU-15, SU-27	100
SSM	8	SAM	100

JIR; MILBAL; Russia & Eurasia Facts & Figures Annual, 1993.

UZBEK MILITARY/URANIUM PRODUCTION SITES, 1992

Location	Product	Location	Product
Chavlisay-Yangyabad	Uranium mining	Sumsar	Uranium mining
Chigirik	Uranium milling and processing	Tashkent	Radio communication equipment
Kyzyl-Dzhar	Uranium mining (gold)	Tashkent	Transport aircraft
Naugarzan	Uranium mining (flourite ores)	Uchkuduk	Uranium mining (gold)

JIR; MILBAL; Russia & Eurasia Facts & Figures Annual, 1993.

UZBEK DEFENSE AND SECURITY OFFICIALS, NOVEMBER 1992

Committte for State Security
Chairman: Gulam Aliev
Date of Birth: unknown
Date of Appointment: 12 June 1991

Ministry of Internal Affairs
Minister: Zakirzhon A. Almatov
Date of Birth: 1949
Date of Appointment: 16 September 1991

UZBEK DEFENSE AND SECURITY OFFICIALS, NOVEMBER 1992 (continued)

Ministry of Defense, National Guard Commander
Minister: Lieutenant General Rustam
Urmanovich Akhmedov
Date of Birth: 10 November 1943
Date of Appointment: 10 September 1991

Supreme Soviet Commission for Military Questions, State Security, and Soldiers' Social Security
Chairman: Vilor (Amanulla) Rakhmatullaevich
Niyazmatov
Date of Birth: 1937
Date of Appointment: 31 October 1990

RFE/RL Research Institute; Russia & Eurasia Facts & Figures Annual, 1993.

MILITARY AND SECURITY, 1993

CIS UNIFIED ARMED FORCES SUPREME COMMAND, SEPTEMBER 1993

First Deputy of the Commander-in-Chief of CIS Joint Armed Forces
Chief of the (Main) Staff CIS Joint Armed Forces
Colonel General Viktor Nikolaevich Samsonov (b. 1941)

Deputy of the Commander-in-Chief of CIS Joint Armed Forces
Colonel General Boris Yevgenevich Piankov (b. 1935)

RFE/RL Research Institute; Russia & Eurasia Facts & Figures Annual, 1993.

CIS NUCLEAR FORCES, 1993

The structure and composition of the CIS strategic forces. These comprise the Strategic Rocket Forces, naval strategic nuclear forces, and airborne strategic nuclear forces. The memorandum of understanding establishing initial figures in connection with the START Treaty between the USSR and the United States lays down that the grouping of intercontinental strategic missiles will comprise 1,398 missiles. Where are the missiles actually deployed and how many nuclear warheads do the carry? This is covered by the following table.

Missiles	Number of Missiles Deployed	Number of Warheads	Deployed at (Number of Missiles)
RS-10 (SS-11)	326	326	Bershet (60), Teykova (26), Krasnoiarsk (40), Drovianaia (50), Yasnaia (90), Svobodnii (60)
RS-12 (SS-13)	40	40	Yoshkar-Ola (40)
RS-16 (SS-17)	47	188	Vypolzovo (47)
RS-20 (SS-18)	308	3,080	Dombarovskii (64), Kartaly (46), Derzhavinsk (52), Aleisk (30), Zhangiz-Tobe (52), Uzhur (64)
RS-18 (SS-19)	300	1,800	Khmelnitskii (90), Kozelsk (60), Pervomaisk (40), Tatishchevo (110)
RS-12M (SS-25)	288	288	Lida (27), Mozyr (27), Teykovo (36), Yoshkar-Ola (18), Yuria (45), Nizhnii Tagil (45), Novosibirsk (27), Kansk (27), Irkutsk (36)

CIS NUCLEAR FORCES, 1993 (continued)

Missiles	Number of Missiles Deployed	Number of Warheads	Deployed at (Number of Missiles)
RS-22 (SS-24) rail-mobile	33	330	Kostroma (12), Bershet (9), Krasnoiarsk (12)
RS-22 (SS-24) silo-based	56	560	Pervomaisk (46), Tatishchevo (10)
Total	1,398	6,612	

More than 20 percent of the intercontinental strategic missiles deployed on the territory of the CIS countries are mobile, and 90 percent of their warheads are multiple warheads.

Sea-launched strategic nuclear forces. Northern Fleet: Nerpichia base (six Typhoon-class nuclear submarines with 120 RSM-52 missiles, each missile equipped with ten nuclear warheads. Izvestiia also discussed these boats in Nos. 50-52 in February 1992). Yagelnaia base (six Navaga-class nuclear submarines with 96 RSM-25 missiles, four Delta II nuclear submarines with 64 RSM-45s, and three Delta III, IV submarines with 48 RSM-50s). Olenia base (two Navaga IIIs, IV nuclear submarines with 32 RSM-50s, and seven Dolphin nuclear submarines with 112 RSM-54s). Ostrovnoi base (9 Delta I nuclear submarines with 108 RSM-40s).

Pacific Fleet: Rybachii base (three Navaga-class nuclear submarines with 48 RSM-25s, three Delta Is with 36 RSM-40s, and nine Delta III, IVs with 144 RSM-50s). Pavlovskoe base (three Navaga nuclear submarines with 48 RSM-25 missiles and six Delta I nuclear submarines with 72 RSM-40s).

The Russian Navy has 62 nuclear submarines with 940 strategic missiles.

Heavy strategic bombers are part of the Air Force's Long-Range Aviation. This means bombers with a range of more than 8,000 km and missile-carrying aircraft equipped with long-range nuclear air-launched cruise missiles (ALCMs).

At the time of the signing of the START Treaty the Soviet Union had 147 TU-95 and 15 TU-160 heavy bombers, of which 84 and 15 (respectively) carried long-range cruise missiles. These accounted for 735 and 120 nuclear warheads.

All heavy bombers were deployed on the territories of three former Union republics. At Mozdok and Engels in Russia, at Priluki, Uzin, and Ukrainka in Ukraine, and at Semipalatinsk in Kazakhstan. There are now 79 bombers on Russian territory (two TU-160s, 25 TU-95MSs, 45 TU-95K22s, and seven TU-95Ks), and 43 aircraft on Ukrainian territory, including 16 TU-160s. There are 40 TU-95MSs in Kazakhstan.

Long-Range Aviation also includes 34 tanker aircraft. These were all based at the Engels Airfield in Saratov Oblast. Just before the collapse of the USSR some were redeployed to Ukrainian territory. They are still there today.

The breakdown of the Commonwealth's strategic forces is as follows.*

Country	ICBMs A	ICBMs B	SLBMs A	SLBMs B	Heavy Bombers A	Heavy Bombers B	Total A	Total B
Belarus	81	81	—	—	—	—	81	81
Kazakhstan	98	980	—	—	40	240	138	1,220
Russia	912	3,970	788	2,652	79	271	1,779	6,893
Ukraine	176	1,240	—	—	43	372	219	1,612
Total	1,267	6,271	788	2,652	162	883	2,217	9,806

* A - Platforms, B - Warheads (zariady).

Izvestiia, 20 November 1993.

CIS DEFENSE STRUCTURE, MAY 1993

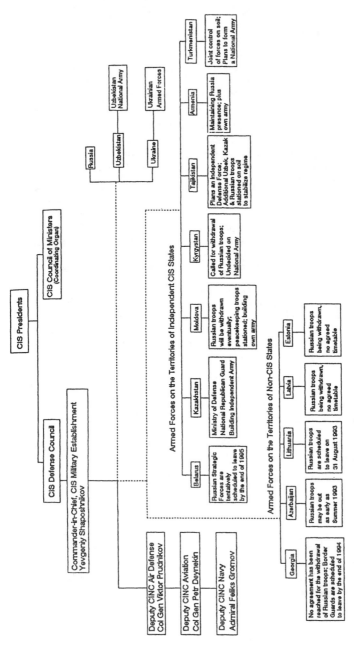

CIS Presidents

CIS Defense Council

CIS Council of Ministers (Coordinating Organ)

Commander-in-Chief, CIS Military Establishment Yevgeniy Shaposhnikov

Deputy CINC Air Defense Col Gen Viktor Prudnikov

Deputy CINC Aviation Col Gen Petr Deynekin

Deputy CINC Navy Admiral Feliks Gromov

Russia

Uzbekistan — Uzbekistan National Army

Ukraine — Ukrainian Armed Forces

Armed Forces on the Territories of Independent CIS States

Belarus — Russian Strategic Forces are tentatively scheduled to leave by the end of 1995

Kazakhstan — Ministry of Defense National Republican Guard Building Independent Army

Moldova — Russian troops will be withdrawn eventually; peacekeeping troops stationed; building own army

Kyrgystan — Called for withdrawal of Russian troops; Undecided on National Army

Tajikistan — Plans an independent Defense Force; Additional Uzbek, Kazak & Russian troops stationed on soil to stabilize regime

Armenia — Maintaining Russia presence; plus own army

Turkmenistan — Joint control of forces on soil; Plans to form a National Army

Armed Forces on the Territories of Non-CIS States

Georgia — No agreement has been reached for the withdrawal of Russian troops; Border Guards are scheduled to leave by the end of 1994

Azerbaijan — Russian troops may be out as early as Summer 1993

Lithuania — Russian troops are scheduled to leave on 31 August 1993

Latvia — Russian troops being withdrawn, no agreed timetable

Estonia — Russian troops being withdrawn, no agreed timetable

Russia & Eurasia Facts & Figures Annual, 1993

CIS MAJOR DEFENSE PLANTS, 1993

	Final Assembly Plants					Production Facilities				Total
	Missiles	Aircraft	Electronics	Shipyards	Land Arms	Nuclear	Chemical/ Biological	Major Components	Test Sites	
Russia	17	17	14	15	11	13	11	39	3	140
Ukraine	4	2	2	5	2	—	—	6	1	22
Kazakhstan	1	—	—	—	—	2	2	3	5	13
Belarus	—	—	—	—	—	—	—	3	—	3
Lithuania	—	—	—	—	—	—	—	2	—	2
Latvia	—	—	—	—	—	—	—	2	—	2
Estonia	—	—	—	—	—	2	—	2	—	4
Georgia	—	1	—	—	—	—	—	4	—	5
Armenia	—	—	—	—	—	—	—	2	—	2
Azerbaijan	—	—	—	—	—	—	—	1	—	1
Uzbekistan	—	1	—	—	—	—	—	1	2	4
Kyrgyzstan	—	—	—	—	—	—	—	1	1	2
Tajikistan	—	—	—	—	—	—	—	1	—	1
Moldova	—	—	—	—	—	—	—	2	—	2
Total	22	21	16	20	13	17	13	69	12	203

DEFENSE.

FSU AND RUSSIAN WEAPONS PRODUCTION, 1990–1992

Weapons Categories	1990 USSR	1991 USSR	1992 Russia
Tanks	1,300	1,000	675
Infantry Fighting Vehicles and Armored Personnel Carriers	3,600–3,900	2,100	1,100
Artillery	1,900	1,000	450
Bombers	35	30	20
Fighters/Fighter Bombers	575	350	150
Attack Helicopters	70	15	5
Submarines and Major SurfaceCombatants	20	13	8
Strategic Ballistic Missiles	190–205	145–165	45–75

AWST, 28 June 1993, 55.

RUSSIAN MILITARY LEADERS, SEPTEMBER 1993

Russian Federation Ministry of Defense

Minister of Defense
Army General Pavel Sergeevich Grachev (b. 1948)

First Deputy Defense Ministers
Chief of the General Staff of Armed Forces
    Colonel General Mikhail Petrovich Kolesnikov (b. 1939)

Deputy Defense Ministers
Colonel General Valery Ivanovich Mironov (b. 1943)
Colonel General Boris Vsevolodovich Gromov (b. 1943)
Colonel General Georgy Grigorevich Kondratev (b. 1944)
Colonel General Vladimir Mikhailovich Toporov (b. 1946)
Chief Military Inspector of Russian Federation
    Army General Konstantin Ivanovich Kobets (b. 1939)

Commander-in-Chief
Commander-in-Chief of Strategic Rocket Forces
    Colonel General Igor Dmitrievich Sergeev (b. 1938)
Commander-in-Chief of Ground Foces
    Colonel General Vladimir Magomedovich Semenov (b. 1940)
Commander-in-Chief of Air Defence Forces
    Colonel General of Aviation Viktor Alekseevich Prudnikov (b.1939)
Commander-in-Chief of Air Forces
    Colonel General of Aviation Petr Stepanovich Deinekin (b. 1937)
Commande-in-Chief of Naval Forces
    Admiral Feliks Nikolaevich Gromov (b. 1937)

Chiefs of Services
Chief of Rear Services
    Major General Vladimir Timofeevich Churanov (b. 1945)
Chief of Armaments
    Colonel General Viacheslav Petrovich Mironov (b. 1938)
Chief of Construction and Billeting
    Colonel General Nikolai Vasilevich Chekov (b. 1931)
Chief of Main Directorate for Training and Distribution of Personnel of Ministry of Defense
    Lieutenant General Yevgeny Vasilevich Vysotskii (b. 1947)

RFE/RL Research Institute; Russia & Eurasia Facts & Figures Annual, 1993.

RUSSIAN SECURITY COUNCIL OFFICIALS, OCTOBER 1993

Secretary	Oleg Lobov
Deputy Secretaries	Vladimir Rubanov
	Valery Manilov
Chief, Secretariat	Vladimir Markin
Administration for Information and Analysis	Vladislav Nasinovskii
Administration for Coordination and Interaction	Yury Nazarkin
Administration to Support Activity of Interdepartmental	
Commission to Fight Crime and Corruption	Andrei Makarov
Interdepartmental Foreign Policy Commission	(apparently vacant)
Interdepartmental Commission to Fight Crime and Corruption	Boris Yeltsin
Interdepartmental Commission for Ecological Security	Aleksei Yablokov
Interdepartmental Commission for Scientific-Technical	
Questions of Defense Industry	Mikhail Malei

Russia & Eurasia Facts & Figures Annual, 1993

RUSSIAN MILITARY FORCES, 1993

Defense Budget: R6 tr (projected 5 percent of GNP in 1994)

Strategic Nuclear Forces

Navy

Men	10,000
SSBN	52

Strategic Rocket Forces

Men	144,000
ICBM	1,204

Strategic Aviation

Men	19,000
Bombers	170
TU-16	13
TU-22	60
IL-20	10
Tankers	75

Strategic Defense

Men	21,000

Russian Armed Forces

Men	2,030,000

Air Defense

Men	230,000
Fighters	2,200
SAM	6,500

Army

Men	1,000,000
Tanks	25,500
Reconnaissance	7,000
Armored Ve- hicles	55,000
Artillery	42,000
Helicopters	3,500

Air Force

Men	170,000
Fighters	4,800
Bombers	300
Reconnaissance	100
Tankers	75
Helicopters	320

Naval Aviation

Men	60,000
Bombers	188
Aircraft	175
Helicopters	260
Tankers	6
Transport	420

Navy

Men	300,000
Conscripts	200,000
Submarines	219
Strategic Subma- rines	52
Tactical Subma- rines	153
Surface Combat- ants	170
Carriers	2
Cruisers	29
Destroyers	24
Frigates	114
Patrol and Coastal Combatants	163
Missile Craft	40

Navy (continued)

Torpedo Craft	27
Mine Warfare	210
Amphibious	75
Support	650
Merchant Fleet	2,700

Coastal Defense Forces

Men	12,000
Tanks	340
Armored Ve- hicles	2,000
Reconnaissance	60
Artillery	200
SAM	250

Coastal Artillery and Rocket
  Troops

Men	4,500
SSM	20

Chechen Forces

Men	65,000

Coastal Defense Troops

Men	13,000
Tanks	1,000
Armored Ve- hicles	1,400
Artillery	1820

Paramilitary and Opposition
  Forces

Border Troops	100,000

RUSSIAN MILITARY FORCES, 1993 (continued)

Paramilitary and Opposition Forces (continued)		Forces Abroad		Forces Abroad (continued)	
Armored Ve-		Vietnam	500	Mongolia	500
hicles	1,500	Algeria	500	Libya	1,000
Artillery	100	Angola	50	Mali	20
Aircraft	70	Cambodia	500	Mozambique	25
Naval Ships	300	Congo	20	Peru	50
		Cuba	2,000	Syria	500
		India	500	Yemen	300

JIR; MILTECH; RFE/RL Research Institute; Russia & Eurasia Facts & Figures Annual, 1993.

USSR AND RUSSIAN WEAPONS PRODUCTION, 1990–1992

Equipment	1990	1992	Percentage Decline
Attack Helicopters	70	5	-92.9
Artillery	1,900	450	-76.3
Nuclear Missiles	190	45	-76.3
Fighters/Bombers	575	150	-73.9
Personnel Carriers	3,600	1,100	-69.4
Submarines	20	8	-60.0
Tanks	1,300	675	-48.1
Bombers	35	20	-42.9

NYT, 3 December 1993.

RUSSIAN DEFENSE MATERIALS ADVANTAGES, 1990

Chemical/Allied Products
Aluminium oxide production processes
Lasant materials (lasers)
Polyurethane compounds
Self-propagating high-temperature synthesis
Synthetic rubber production processes
Turbulent reactor

Rubber and Miscellaneous Plastic Processes
Carbon adhesives
Carbon-carbon products
Componers
Rolivsans thermosetting cast resins

Fabricated Metal Products
Rotary-planetary mill machining
Small nuclear power reactors

Primary Metals Industries
Dynamic compacting synthesis
Elastomeric roll forming of sheet metal
Filament winding of thick section composites
  fabrication processes
Impulse processing methods
Plasma-mechanical metal processing

Primary Metals Industries (continued)
Vacuum processing of steel with synthetic
  slag and inert gases
Weldable aluminium-lithium alloys

Industrial/Commercial Machinery and Computer Equipment
Diesel engines
Fiber-optics modules for automatic control
  systems
Multiple-reflection optical systems
Waveguide holograms

Electronic and Other Electrical Equipment Components
Disk explosive magnetic generators
Explosive magnetohydrodynamic generators
High brightness negative ion sources
High power gas lasers
High power RF heaters for ionospheric
  modification
High power RF tubes
Laser instrumentation
Magnetic flux compression generators

RUSSIAN DEFENSE MATERIALS ADVANTAGES, 1990 (continued)

Electronic and Other Electrical Equipment Components (continued)
Microgravity-processed ultra-pure semiconductor single crystals
Pulsed power
Pulsed wave de-icing/anti-icing equipment
Spatial light modulators
Tacitrons
Vacuum microelectronics

Transportation Equipment
Dryogenic fuel aircraft engines
Fan-prop aircraft engines
Gas turbine helicopter engines
Wing with internal framework (lattice control surface or grid fin)

Measuring, Analyzing and Controlling Instruments: Photographic, Medical, Optical
Biochrome films
Diamond-coated surgical instruments

Measuring, Analyzing and Controlling Instruments: Photographic, Medical, Optical (continued)
Homosorption filter technology
Jet injection equipment for immunization
Lidar remote sensing
Microstructure laser devices
Performance enhancement electrical devices
Physiological measurement devices
Pseudorandom noise-coded waveform processing
Residual stress engineering measurement devices
Vaccine inhalator devices

Transportation Services
Space launch services
Commercial experimental payload services

Engineering, Accounting, Research, Management, and Related Services
Magnetohydrodynamic-accelerated simulation.

MILTECH, November 1993, 36.

RUSSIAN MILITARY-INDUSTRIAL COMPLEX EMPLOYMENT, 1992

Region	Military-Industrial Employment (th)	Percentage of Total Employment
Northwest	455.3	30.7
Urals	1,116.4	2J.7
(Udmurtia)	(167.7)	(55.3)
Volga-Vyatka	451.1	28.5
Volga	750.9	27.9
(Saratov Oblast)	(212.1)	(50.9)
Central	1,211.4	22.7
Western Siberia	472.5	22.7
(Novosibirsk Oblast)	(172.4)	(43.5)
Central Chernozem	247.2	22.6
Far East	178.3	17.8
Kaliningrad Oblast	18.9	15.0
Eastern Siberia	167.5	13.9
North Caucasus	255.1	13.7
North	92.2	9.4
Russian Federation	5,416.8	23.5

RFE/RL, January 1993.

RUSSIAN R&D PERSONNEL BY REGION, JANUARY 1992

	By Economic Region	By Republic, Territory, District
Total	100	
of which:		
Northern Region	1.2	100
including:		
Republic of Karelia		18.3
Republic of Komi		18.9
Arkhangelsk district		15.0
Vologda district		17.4
Murmansk district		30.5
North-Western Region	16.5	100
including:		
St. Petersburg	15.9	96.5
Leningrad district		1.6
Novgorod district		1.1
Pskov district		0.8
Central Region	42.4	100
including:		
Briansk district		0.8
Vladimir district		2.3
Ivanovo district		1.4
Kaluga district	1.3	3.1
Kostroma district		0.3
Moscow	29.0	68.4
Moscow district	5.4	12.8
Orel district		0.7
Riazan district		2.0
Smolensk district		0.8
Tver district		2.0
Tula district	1.4	3.2
Yaroslavl district		2.3
Volga-Viatka Region	4.3	100
including:		
Mari-El Republic		3.0
Mordovian SSR		2.5
Chuvash Republic		9.1
Kirov district		6.9
Nizhnii-Novgorod district	3.3	78.5
Centralno-Chernozemnii Region	3.2	100
including:		
Belgorod district		13.8
Voronezh district	1.8	54.4
Kursk district		12.1
Lipetsk district		9.1
Tambov district		10.6
Volga Region	7.9	100
including:		

RUSSIAN R&D PERSONNEL BY REGION, JANUARY 1992 (continued)

	By Economic Region	By Republic, Territory, District
Republic of Kalmykia-Halmg Tangch		0.5
Republic of Tatarstan	2.0	25.8
Astrakhan district		4.3
Volgograd district		11.8
Penza district		12.0
Samara district	1.6	20.3
Saratov district	1.5	19.0
Ulianovsk district		6.3
North-Caucasian Region	4.8	100
including:		
Republic of Adygeya		0.9
Republic of Daghestan		1.9
Kabardino-Balkarian Republic		3.8
Republic of Karachai-Cherkessia		0.4
North Ossetian SSR		2.9
Republic of Checheno-Ingushetia		4.1
Krasnodar Territory		20.6
Stavropol Territory		8.3
Rostov district	2.8	57.3
Ural Region	7.9	100
including:		
Republic of Bashkortostan	1.5	18.7
Udmurt Republic		6.4
Kurgan district		1.5
Orenburg district		2.9
Perm district	1.1	14.4
Sverdlovsk district	3.2	39.7
Cheliabinsk district	1.3	16.5
West-Siberian Region	6.9	100
including:		
Republic of Altai		0.1
Altai Territory		7.6
Kemerovo district		8.9
Novosibirsk district	3.0	43.6
Omsk district		14.0
Tomsk district		12.1
Tyumen district		13.8
East-Siberian Region	2.4	100
including:		
Republic of Buriatia		7.4
Republic of Tuva		1.1
Republic of Khakassia		0.5
Krasnoiarsk Territory	1.3	54.0
Irkutsk district		32.0
Chita district		5.0

RUSSIAN R&D PERSONNEL BY REGION, JANUARY 1992 (continued)

	By Economic Region	By Republic, Territory, District
Far East Region	2.1	100
including:		
Republic of Saha		
(Yakutia)		16.1
Primorsk Territory		43.6
Khabarovsk Territory		17.2
Amur district		6.8
Kamchatka district		3.3
Magadan district		5.9
Sakhalin district		7.0
Kaliningrad district	0.3	

SCI, 40-43.

RUSSIAN MILITARY AND SECURITY RESETTLEMENT ALLOCATIONS, 1993 (th sq m)

	Total	Plans of Ministries and Departments
Total residential building living space	5,386.7	3,434.23
Including Russian Ministry of Defense	3,700	2,700
Russian MVD	620	320
Including Internal Troops	220	40
Russian Ministry of Interior	545	102
Including Border Troops	345	50
Russian Foreign Intelligence Service (SVR)	7.3	—
Federal Agency for Government Communications and Information (FAPSI)	91.8	42.5
Main Administration for Protection of the Russian Federation (GUO)	1.1	—
Russian GKChS	35	7
FUZhV	112.2	95.3
Russian Ministry of Communications	11.4	8
Russian Special Construction	18.9	18.9
Dalspetsstroi FSU	28.2	28.2
Russian Ministry of Atomic Energy	15.5	15.5
FDSU	197	96
Russian Organization for Defense Sports and Techniques (ROSTO)	3.3	.72

Krasnaia zvezda, 26 June 1993.

RUSSIAN MILITARY AND SECURITY PENSIONERS' HOUSING ALLOCATION, 1993 (th sq m)

Locations	Total	Border Troops
Russian Federation—total	3,451.2	51.2
Republic of Bashkortostan	21.5	—

RUSSIAN MILITARY AND SECURITY PENSIONERS' HOUSING ALLOCATION, 1993
(th sq m) (continued)

Locations	Total	Border Troops
Republic of Buriatia	10.9	—
Republic of Dagestan	14.1	—
Karbardino-Balkar Republic	11.5	—
Karachayevo-Cherkess Republic	11.6	—
Republic of Karelia	30.4	.48
Republic of Komi	12.9	.24
Republic of Mari-El	25.2	—
Mordovan Soviet Socialist Republic	10.3	—
North Ossetian Soviet Socialist Republic	15.4	—
Republic of Tatarstan	47.1	—
Udmurt Republic	23.2	—
Ingush Republic	8.1	—
Chechen Republic	2	—
Chuvash Republic	12.6	—
Republic of Sakha (Yakutia)	4.4	—
Republic of Khakasia	7.1	—
Republic of Kalmykia—Khalmg Tangch	.4	—
Republic of Adygea	8.6	—
Republic of Gorno-Altai	3	—
Altai Krai	25.2	—
Krasnodar Krai	262.5	6.08
Krasnoiarsk Krai	25.1	—
Including Evenki Autonomous Okrug	.6	—
Maritime Krai	99.1	1.6
Stavropol Krai	118.1	1.12
Khabarovsk Krai	72.5	.96
Jewish Autonomous Oblast	5.3	—
Amur Oblast	103.9	.96
Arkhangelsk Oblast	14.1	.32
Including Nenetsk Autonomous Okrug	.5	—
Astrakhan Oblast	11.2	—
Belgorod Oblast	87.3	1.6
Briansk Oblast	45.4	—
Vladimir Oblast	77.8	1.28
Volgograd Oblast	92.8	—
Vologda Oblast	22.3	—
Voronezh Oblast	109.4	1.92
Ivanovo Oblast	29.1	—
Irkutsk Oblast	24.7	—
Including Ust-Orda Buriat Autonomous Okrug	.5	—
Kaliningrad Oblast	88.5	.8
Kaluga Oblast	51.4	1.6
Kamchatka Oblast	13.5	1.28
Kemerovo Oblast	17.1	—

RUSSIAN MILITARY AND SECURITY PENSIONERS' HOUSING ALLOCATION, 1993 (th sq m) (continued)

Locations	Total	Border Troops
Kirov Oblast	42.2	—
Kostromo Oblast	28.3	.6
Kurgan Oblast	16.5	—
Kursk Oblast	48.5	.6
City of St. Petersburg	32.3	2.4
Leningrad Oblast	72.5	.88
Lipetsk Oblast	30.2	.8
Magadan Oblast	2.7	—
Chukotsk Autonomous Okrug	.4	—
City of Moscow	25.2	3.2
Moscow Oblast	210.5	.8
Murmansk Oblast	32.9	—
Novgorod Oblast	45	1.28
Nizhegorod Oblast	61.6	1.92
Novosibirsk Oblast	36.9	—
Omsk Oblast	43.8	—
Orenburg Oblast	22.2	—
Orlov Oblast	37.7	.96
Penza Oblast	65.7	.6
Perm Oblast	34.5	—
Including Komi-Permiak Autonomous Okrug	3.4	—
Pskov Oblast	54.7	1.6
Rostov Oblast	97.2	1.76
Riazan Oblast	51.3	1.28
Samara Oblast	70.2	1.6
Saratov Oblast	139.5	.6
Sakhalin Oblast	13.5	.64
Sverdlovsk Oblast	29.7	—
Smolensk Oblast	49.8	.8
Tambov Oblast	55.5	.8
Tver Oblast	90.7	1.92
Tomsk Oblast	9.6	—
Tula Oblast	40.6	1.12
Tiumen Oblast	7.6	—
Including Khanty-Mansiisk Autonomous Oblast	.3	—
Ulianovsk Oblast	52.4	.8
Cheliabinsk Oblast	38.4	—
Chita Oblast	13.7	1.6
Yaroslavl Oblast	49	1.6

Krasnaia zvezda, 26 June 1993.

ARMENIAN MILITARY FORCES, 1993

Defense Budget: R250 mn (1991)

ARMENIAN MILITARY FORCES, 1993 (continued)

Russian Forces

Men	4,500	Tanks	200	Artillery	100

JIR; MILTECH; RFE/RL Research Institute; Russia & Eurasia Facts & Figures Annual, 1993.

ARMENIAN DEFENSE AND SECURITY OFFICIALS, JUNE 1993

State Administration for National Security
Chief: Eduard Grigori Simonyants
Date of Birth: Unknown
Date of Appointment: 16 Feb 1993

Ministry of Internal Affairs
Minister: Vano Smbatovich Siradegian
Date of Birth: Unknown (46 years old)
Date of Appointment: 2 Feb 1992

Supreme Council Committee for Questions of Defense and Internal Affairs
Chairman: Gevork Bagdasarian
Date of Birth: Unknown
Date of Appointment: Unknown

Ministry of Defense
Minister: Vazgen Mikaelovich Manukian
Date of Birth: 13 Feb 1946
Date of Appointment: 20 Oct 1992

DSOPSS.

ARMENIAN DEFENSE INDUSTRY INFORMATION, 1993

Armenian plants probably constituted less than two percent of the former Soviet defense-industrial base. Products from Armenian plants reportedly included instruments for Soviet submarines and ships, aircraft computer systems, other aviation electronics, telescope lenses, and other electronic equipment. Armenia has roughly three percent of the estimated former Soviet Union's military R&D facilities.

Armenia's strategic materials output includes gold, copper, aluminum, zinc, and molybdenum. The state is heavily dependent on imported fuel and ferrous metals.

DEFENSE, 23.

AZERI MILITARY FORCES, 1993

Defense Budget: R3 bn (est. 1993)

Azeri Military		Azeri Military (continued)		Azeri Paramilitary and Nagorno-Karabakh Forces	
Brigades: four motorized rifle, one tank, and two artillery		Helicopters	50		
		Artillery	285	MVD troops	20,000
Army	39,000	Aircraft	100	Karabakh People's	
Navy	2000	Armored vehicles	220	Defense	20,000
Tanks	220	Naval ships	13		

JIR; MILTECH; RFE/RL Research Institute; Russia & Eurasia Facts & Figures Annual, 1993.

AZERI DEFENSE AND SECURITY OFFICIALS, JUNE 1993

Ministry of National Security
Minister: Fakhraddin Ayat ogly Takhmazov
Date of Birth: Unknown
Date of Appointment: 16 May 1992

Ministry of Defense
Minister: Major General Dadash Garib ogly Rzaev
Date of Birth: Unknown (57 years old)
Date of Appointment: 21 Feb 1993

AZERI DEFENSE AND SECURITY OFFICIALS, JUNE 1993 (continued)

National Assembly Commission for State Security, Military Affairs, and the Legal System
Chairman: Mamed Babash ogly Kuliev
Date of Birth: 1939
Date of Appointment: 5 Feb 1991

DSOPSS.

Ministry of Internal Affairs
Minister: Major General Abdulla Museib ogly Allakhverdiev
Date of Birth: Unknown (52 years old)
Date of Appointment: 16 Apr 1993

Committee for Defense of State Borders
Chairman: Major General Iskander Imanverdi ogly Allakhverdiev
Date of Birth: 1947
Date of Appointment: 16 Dec 1991

AZERI DEFENSE INDUSTRY INFORMATION, 1993

Azerbaijan has less than one percent of the former Soviet defense industry and produces only minor components. Plants in the capital, Baku, produce computer components and display devices, printed circuit boards and other electronic subcomponents and associated electronic equipment. Less than one percent of the known former Soviet military R&D facilities are in Azerbaijan. The state's strategic materials production includes aluminum from a small plant in Sumgait, and oil from onshore complexes, principally at Baku and elsewhere on the Apsheron Peninsula, and from offshore fields in the southern Caspian Sea.

DEFENSE, 25.

BELARUSIAN MILITARY FORCES, 1993

Defense Budget: R692.4 bn (1994)

Strategic Nuclear Forces		Air Force		Air Defense	
ICBM	80	Men	14,000	Men	15,000
Belarus Armed Forces		Bombers	60	Fighters	75
Men	102,000	Fighters	130	SAM	650
Reserves	300,000	Reconnaissance	40	**Belarus Paramilitary**	
		Helicopters	300	Men	8,000
Ground Forces		Transport	40		
Men	50,000			**Russian Forces in Belarus**	
Tanks	3,300			Aircraft	270
Armored Vehicles	3,700				
Artillery	1,600				
SSM	60				

JIR; MILTECH; RFE/RL Research Institute; Russia & Eurasia Facts & Figures Annual, 1993.

BELARUSIAN DEFENSE AND SECURITY OFFICIALS, JUNE 1993

Committee for State Security
Chairman: Lieutenant General Eduard Ivanavich Shyrkouski
Date of Birth: 1932
Date of Appointment: 30 Oct 1990

Ministry of Defense
Minister: Colonel General Pavel Paulavich Kazlouski
Date of Birth: 9 Mar 1942
Date of Appointment: 22 Apr 1992

BELARUSIAN DEFENSE AND SECURITY OFFICIALS, JUN 1993 (continued)

Supreme Council Commission for Questions of National Security, Defense, and the Struggle Against Crime
Chairman: Major General Myachyslau Ivanavich Hryb
Date of Birth: 1938
Date of Appointment: 1990

Ministry of Internal Affairs
Minister: Lieutenant General Vladzimir Dzemyanavich Yahorau
Date of Birth: 1939
Date of Appointment: 20 Jul 1990

Border Troops
Commander: Major General Yevgeny Mikhailovich Bocharov
Date of Birth: 20 Oct 1948
Date of Appointment: 21 Apr 1992

DSOPSS.

BELARUSIAN DEFENSE INDUSTRY INFORMATION, 1993

Belarus has about five percent of the former Soviet defense-industrial base. Belarusian leaders have claimed that their defense industry contains 120 plants employing some 370,000 people. Belarus' major military contribution has been in vehicles and electronics. Minsk is the industrial center, providing military trucks and heavy-duty chassis for ballistic missile and air defense missile support equipment, including those for the Russian-produced SS-25 ICBM and at least one system Russia is currently trying to export—the SA-10 surface-to-air missile system. Minsk is also a center for the design and production of computers and computer-based command and control systems. A plant in Gomel has been the primary producer of radars for strategic ballistic missile defense.

Other Belarusian plants produce various components, such as avionics for military and civil aircraft. The Belarusian defense minister has claimed that the republic cannot produce everything that its armed forces need and that it would participate in cooperative ventures to produce equipment and weapons. Belarus has less than two percent of the identified former Soviet RDT&E facilities.

Belarus is largely dependent on other republics for most of its strategic materials. Foreign minister Petr Kravchenko said in a press interview that to achieve economic independence from Russia, Belarus would have to restructure its industry with advanced technology to make production more energy efficient and not so completely dependent on supplies of oil, gas, and iron ore. He cited in particular the need to transform the military and electrotechnical industry, the engineering industry, and the production of specialized instruments.

DEFENSE, 9.

ESTONIAN MILITARY FORCES, 1993

Defense Budget: 264.8 mn Kroons (1994)

Estonian Armed Forces		Russian Armed Forces	
Men (Army)	2,500	Men	7,000
Estonian Paramilitary		Tanks	40
Men	2,000	Armored vehicles	250
Naval ships for Maritime			
Border Guard and Coast Guard	8		

JIR; MILTECH; RFE/RL Research Institute; Russia & Eurasia Facts & Figures Annual, 1993.

ESTONIAN DEFENSE FORCES, 1993

Location	Unit	Location	Unit
Jagala	Kalev Infantry Battalion	Tallinn	Air Defense Battalion
Voru	Kuperjanov Infantry Battalion	Jagala	Communications Company
Johvi	Viru Infantry Battalion	Tallinn	Motor Transport Company
Tallinn	Independent Guards Battalion		

JIR, August 1993, 353.

MAJOR RUSSIAN BASES AND DEPLOYMENTS IN ESTONIA, 1993

Location	Unit	Location	Unit
Tallinn	56th Sverdlovsk A. Matrosov Motor Rifle Division, naval base	Parnu	Strategic air force base
Paldiski	Submarine base	Tartu	Strategic air force base

JIR, August 1993, 353.

ESTONIAN DEFENSE AND SECURITY OFFICIALS, JUNE 1993

Ministry of Internal Affairs
Minister: Lagle Parek
Date of Birth: 17 Apr 1941
Date of Appointment: 21 Oct 1992

State Assembly Commission for Defense
Chairman: Rein Helme
Date of Birth: 1954
Date of Appointment: Oct 1992

Defense Union (Kaitseliit)
Commander: Kalle Eller
Date of Birth: Unknown
Date of Appointment: Unknown

DSOPSS.

Ministry of Defense
Minister: Hain Rebas
Date of Birth: 23 Jan 1943
Date of Appointment: 21 Oct 1992

State Department for Defense and Border Protection
Director-General: Toomas Puura
Date of Birth: Unknown
Date of Appointment: Unknown

GEORGIAN MILITARY FORCES, 1993

Defense Budget: R6 bn (1992)

Georgian Armed Forces		Navy		Paramilitary and Opposition Forces	
Reserves		Men	100		
Men Planned	500,000	**Air Force**		National Guard	15,000
Army		Combat Aircraft	50	Abkhaz Forces	4,000
Men	20,000	**Russian Armed Forces**		South Ossetian Forces	2,000
Tanks	300	Army Men	20,000	Gamsakhurdian Forces	1,500
Armored vehicles	175	Aircraft	35		
Artillery	60				

JIR; MILTECH; RFE/RL Research Institute; Russia & Eurasia Facts & Figures Annual, 1993.

GEORGIAN DEFENSE AND SECURITY OFFICIALS, JUNE 1993

Ministry of Defense
Minister: Brigadier General Giorgi
    Karkarashvili
Date of Birth: Unknown (about 27 years old)
Date of Appointment: 6 May 1993

Information and Intelligence Bureau
Director: Iraklii Batiashvili
Date of Birth: Unknown (31 years old)
Date of Appointment: 3 May 1992

DSOPSS.

Ministry of Internal Affairs
Minister: Teimuraz Khachishivili
Date of Birth: Unknown
Date of Appointment: Nov 1992

**Parliamentary Commission for Defense and
    National Security**
Chairman: Nodar Natadze
Date of Birth: 1929
Date of Appointment: Nov 1992

ABKHAZIAN DEFENSE COUNCIL, APRIL 1993

Tamaz Nadareishvili—Chairman of the Council of Ministers of the Autonomous Republic of Abkhazia; chairman of Abkhazian Defense Council.

Geno Adamia—Major general, commander of the 23rd Mechanized Brigade of the Republic of Georgia Ministry of Defense 2nd Army Corps.

Guram Gabiskiria—Mayor of Sukhumi.

David Gulua—Colonel, minister of internal affairs of the Autonomous Republic of Abkhazia.

Yury Keshelava—Major general, head of the Information and Intelligence Service of the Autonomous Republic of Abkhazia.

Lorik Marshania—First deputy chairman of the Abkhazian Council of Ministers.

Ramaz Sichinava—First deputy chairman of the Council of Ministers of the Autonomous Republic of Abkhazia.

Zaur Uchadze—Major general, commander of the 24th Mechanized Brigade of the Republic of Georgia Ministry of Defense 2nd Army Corps.

Valery Kvaraia—Major general, commander of the Republic of Georgia Ministry of Defense 2nd Army Corps.

Sakartvelos respublika, 29 April 1993, in FBIS-SOV, 4 May 1993, 52.

GEORGIAN MILITARY AGE LIMITS BY RANK, 1993

Military Rank (except Navy)	Navy	Age Limit			
		Regular Personnel	Reserve		
			1st Category	2nd Category	3rd Category
1. Junior lieutenant, lieutenant, senior lieutenant, captain	junior lieutenant, lieutenant, senior lieutenant, captain-lieutenant	40	40	45	50
2. From major to colonel	captain 3rd rank, captain 2nd rank	50	50	55	55
3. Colonel	captain 1st rank	55	55	60	60
4. General	admiral	60	60	65	65

Sakartvelos respublika, 6 January 1993, in FBIS-SOV, 4 February 1993, 65.

GEORGIAN DEFENSE INDUSTRY INFORMATION, 1993

Georgia has less than one percent of the identified former Soviet defense industry. Its most significant military production facility—the Tbilisi aircraft plant—produces the SU-25 Frogfoot ground attack aircraft but is dependent on Russia for engines and some avionics and other components. Georgia
assembles no other major weapon systems. Electronics plants in Tbilisi, Akhmeta, Telavi, and Tsalka
produce microcircuits, sensors, and other microelectronics for military systems, including missiles,
produced in Commonwealth states. Georgia has less than two percent of the known former Soviet
military RDT&E facilities. There are two nuclear R&D institutes—in Tbilisi and Sukhumi—but no
nuclear production plants. Georgia produces about one-fifth of the former USSR's output of manganese ore—a key input in steel production—but no other significant strategic materials.

DEFENSE, 21.

KAZAKH MILITARY FORCES, 1993

Defense Budget: R69.3 bn (1993)

Strategic Nuclear Forces		Air Force		Russian Forces	
ICBMs	104	Fighters	140	Aircraft	80
Bombers	40	Reconnaissance	50	SAM	85
Army		Training Aircraft	95		
Men	44,000	**Republican Guard**			
Tanks	1,400	Men	2,500		
Artillery	2,000				
Attack Helicopters	50				

JIR; MILTECH; RFE/RL Research Institute; Russia & Eurasia Facts & Figures Annual, 1993.

KAZAKH DEFENSE AND SECURITY OFFICIALS, JUNE 1993

Committee for National Security
Chairman: Lieutenant General Bulat
   Abdrakhmanovich Baekenov
Date of Birth: 1942
Date of Appointment: 25 Oct 1991

Ministry of Defense
Minister: Colonel General Sagadat
   Kozhakhmetovich Nurmagambetov
Date of Birth: 25 May 1924
Date of Appointment: 7 May 1992

**Supreme Council Committee for National
   Security and Defense**
Chairman: Colonel Bulat Bakhizhanovich
   Dzhanasaev
Date of Birth: 1952
Date of Appointment: 1 Jul 1992

DSOPSS.

Ministry of Internal Affairs
Minister: Vladimir Georgievich Shumov
Date of Birth: 1941
Date of Appointment: 17 Apr 1992

National Guard
Commander: Major General Seilbek A.
   Altynbekov
Date of Birth: Unknown (49 years old)
Date of Appointment: 19 Mar 1992

Border Troops
Commander: Major General Bolat Zakiev
Date of Birth: 1950
Date of Appointment: 27 Oct 1992

KAZAKH DEFENSE INDUSTRY INFORMATION, 1993

Kazakhstan has about three percent of the identified former Soviet defense industry facilities, the largest military-industrial sector outside the Slavic republics. According to the Kazakh Minister of Industry, Kazakh defense industry comprised over fifty enterprises. A plant in Petropavlovsk produces the SS-21 SRBM. Other Petropavlovsk plants produce ballistic missile support equipment, torpedoes, and naval communications equipment. Another major torpedo producer is located in Alma-Ata. All of these plants rely on inputs of components from other states, primarily Russia. A plant in Ust-Kamenogorsk produces nuclear power reactor fuel and beryllium products, and a plant at Aqtau (Shevchenko) processes uranium ore. In addition, Kazakhstan has the only known plants outside Russia designed for production of chemical and biological warfare materials.

Kazakhstan's roughly one percent of the known former Soviet military RDT&E facilities are much more significant than the count indicates. Kazakh test ranges have played a vital role in the development and production of aerospace systems. The range at Vladimirovka is used for integration of aircraft with airborne weapons, the center at Saryshagan is used for development and flight-testing of strategic air defense missile and ballistic missile defense systems, and the center at Emba performs similar functions for tactical air defense missile systems. The facility at Tyuratam is used to launch spacecraft (including all manned missions) and to test liquid-propellant ICBMs. The Semipalatinsk Nuclear Weapons Proving Ground is one of two facilities in the former Soviet Union where nuclear weapons were tested. In 1991 Kazakhstan banned further nuclear testing and announced plans to convert the installation to civil uses.

Kazakh plants are key suppliers of such strategic materials as titanium, magnesium, tantalum, niobium, gold, silver, and alumina. Up to 1984, at least, the Soviets imported ore for the Ust-Kamenogorsk titanium-magnesium plant, apparently in part because of delays in developing the nearby Karaotkel ilmenite deposit. A plant in Pavlodar is one of the three largest producers of alumina in the newly independent states and is a major supplier to Russia's aluminum plants in Siberia.

DEFENSE, 13.

KYRGYZ MILITARY FORCES, 1993

Defense Budget: R800 mn (1992)

Air Force		Army	
Aircraft	200	Men	12,000
Russian Forces		Tanks	240
		Armored Vehicles	415
SAM	25	Artillery	240

JIR; MILTECH; RFE/RL Research Institute; Russia & Eurasia Facts & Figures Annual, 1993.

KYRGYZ DEFENSE AND SECURITY OFFICIALS, JUNE 1993

State Committee for Defense Questions
Chairman: Major General Dzhanybek
   Asanbekovich Umetaliev
Date of Birth: 26 May 1943
Date of Appointment: 26 Feb 1992

National Guard
Commander: Abdygul Abdrashidovich
   Chotbaev
Date of Birth: Unknown
Date of Appointment: 28 Feb 1992

State Committee for National Security
Chairman: Major General Anarbek Kuramae-
   vich Bakaev
Date of Birth: Unknown
Date of Appointment: 26 Feb 1992

Ministry of Internal Affairs
Minister: Major General Abdybek Asankulo-
   vich Sutalinov
Date of Birth: Unknown
Date of Appointment: 31 Mar 1992

KYRGYZ DEFENSE AND SECURITY OFFICIALS, JUNE 1993 (continued)

Supreme Council Committee on Military Affairs
Chairman: Unknown

DSOPSS.

KYRGYZ DEFENSE INDUSTRY INFORMATION, 1993

Kyrgyzstan has less than one percent of the former Soviet production plants. It manufactures torpedo components, small arms, and specialized vehicles on armored personnel carrier chassis but produces little else of defense significance. Most of the facilities are located in the capital, Bishkek. Less than one percent of the identified former Soviet RDT&E facilities are located in Kyrgyzstan. Among these is an underwater ordnance test area at Lake Issyk-Kul used for testing of torpedoes produced in Kazakhstan.

Kyrgyzstan produces few identified strategic materials. It processes uranium ore at a plant at Kara-Balty and is developing a gold mine and building a gold ore concentration plant near Kazarman.

DEFENSE, 19.

LATVIAN MILITARY FORCES, 1993

Defense Budget: 1,800 million Lats (1993)

Latvian Armed Forces		Navy		Russian Forces	
Men (157 women)	7,000	Men	300	Men	17,000
Officers	529	Naval Craft	5	Tanks	50
Only 116 have housing.		**Air Force**		Armored Vehicles	50
Reserves (Latvian Home		Aircraft	20	Artillery	50
Guard)	16,000			Combat Aircraft	120

JIR; MILTECH; RFE/RL Research Institute; Russia & Eurasia Facts & Figures Annual, 1993.

LATVIAN DEFENSE AND SECURITY OFFICIALS, JUNE 1993

Ministry of Internal Affairs
Minister: Ziedonis Cevers
Date of Birth: 29 Jan 1960
Date of Appointment: 20 Nov 1991

**Supreme Council Commission for Defense
and Internal Affairs**
Chairman: Peteris Simsons
Date of Birth: 1948
Date of Appointment: 1991

Home Guard (Zemes sardze)
Chief: Girts Kristovskis
Date of Birth: Unknown
Date of Appointment: 18 Feb 1992

Ministry of Defense
Minister: Talavs Jundzis
Date of Birth: 1951
Date of Appointment: 19 Nov 1991

Security Service
Chairman: Colonel Juris Vectiraus
Date of Birth: Unknown (38 years old)
Date of Appointment: 1992

DSOPSS.

MAJOR RUSSIAN BASES AND DEPLOYMENTS IN LATVIA, 1993

Riga	HQ, North Western Group of Forces; HQ 15th Air Army; naval base
Bolderaja	Submarine and ship repair yards
Daugavpils	Higher Air Force Engineer School
Jurmala	16th Motor Rifle Division
Liepaja	Naval base
Mucenieki	HQ, 27th Air Defense Corps

JIR, August 1993.

LITHUANIAN MILITARY FORCES, 1993

Defense Budget: 6 billion talonas (1993)

Lithuanian Military Forces		Navy		Paramilitary	
Men	9,800	Men	200	Border Guard	5,000
Army		Naval Ships	10	**Russian Forces**	
Men	4,300	**Air Force**		Men	2,000
Armored Vehicles	7	Men	250		
		Aircraft	6		

JIR; MILTECH; RFE/RL Research Institute; Russia & Eurasia Facts & Figures Annual, 1993.

MAJOR RUSSIAN BASES AND DEPLOYMENTS IN LITHUANIA, 1993

Vilnius	107th Motor Rifle Division
Kaunas	7th Guards Airborne Division
Klaipeda	3rd Guards Volnovkha-Evpatoriia Motor Rifle Division, naval base
Panevezys	16th Transport and Aviation Division
Rukla	Training center

JIR, August 1993.

LITHUANIAN DEFENSE AND SECURITY OFFICIALS, JUNE 1993

Ministry of National Defense
Minister: Audrius Butkevicius
Date of Birth: 24 Sep 1960
Date of Appointment: Mar 1990

Security Service
Director-General: Jurgis Jurgelis
Date of Birth: 9 Aug 1942
Date of Appointment: 30 Dec 1992

**Seimas Commission for National Defense
and Internal Affairs**
Chairman: Saulius Peceliunas
Date of Birth: 19 Jan 1956
Date of Appointment: Jan 1992

Ministry of Internal Affairs
Minister: Romasis Vaitekunas
Date of Birth: 1943
Date of Appointment: 10 Dec 1992

Border Protection Service
Chief: Stanislovas Stancikas
Date of Birth: Unknown
Date of Appointment: 1991

DSOPSS.

MOLDOVAN MILITARY FORCES, 1993

Defense Budget: R4.1 bn (1992)

Moldovan Armed Forces		Air Force		Russian Forces (14th Army)	
Men	9,400	Men	2,100	Tanks	100
Army		Aircraft	30	Artillery	120
Men	3,800	SAM	25	Attack Helicopters	10
Armored Vehicles	85	**Paramilitary and Opposition**		Scuds	12
Artillery	70	**Forces**			
		MVD Troops	2,500		
		Dniester Forces	10,000		

JIR; MILTECH; RFE/RL Research Institute; Russia & Eurasia Facts & Figures Annual, 1993.

MOLDOVAN DEFENSE AND SECURITY OFFICIALS, JUNE 1993

Ministry of National Security
Minister: Major Vasile Calmoi
Date of Birth: Unknown
Date of Appointment: 21 Jul 1992

Ministry of Defense
Minister: Division General Pavel Creanga
Date of Birth: 26 Oct 1933
Date of Appointment: 21 Jul 1992

Ministry of Internal Affairs
Minister: Major General Constantin Antoci
Date of Birth: Unknown
Date of Appointment: Feb 1992

Parliamentary Commission for Defense and Security Affairs
Chairman: Anatol Taran
Date of Birth: Unknown
Date of Appointment: Jun 1992

DSOPSS.

MOLDOVAN DEFENSE INDUSTRY INFORMATION, 1993

Moldova has less than one percent of the former Soviet Union's defense industry. It specializes in electronics, mostly subsystems and components used in military equipment produced elsewhere, primarily Russia. Plants in Chisinau produce military communications equipment and military computers. Moldova has less than one percent of the identified former Soviet military RDT&E facilities and no significant strategic mineral resources.

DEFENSE, 11.

TAJIK MILITARY FORCES, 1993

Defense Budget: R3.25 bn (1992)

Tajik Armed Forces		Russian Forces	
Men	2,500	Men	8,500
		Tanks	200
		Armored Vehicles	420
		Artillery	200
		SAM	10

JIR; MILTECH; Russia & Eurasia Facts & Figures Annual, 1993.

TAJIK DEFENSE AND SECURITY OFFICIALS, JUNE 1993

Committee for National Security
Chairman: Lieutenant Colonel Seidamir
  Zukhurov
Date of Birth: Unknown (42 years old)
Date of Appointment: Nov 1992

Ministry of Defense
Minister: Major General Aleksandr
  Vladimirovich Shishlyannikov

DSOPSS.

Ministry of Defense (continued)
Date of Birth: 3 Nov 1950
Date of Appointment: 21 Jan 1993

Ministry of Internal Affairs
Minister: Yakub Salimov
Date of Birth: Unknown
Date of Appointment: Nov 1992

TAJIK DEFENSE INDUSTRY INFORMATION, 1993

Tajikistan's defense industry constitutes less than one percent of the former Soviet Union's military-industrial base. A plant in Taboshar has produced solid-propellant rocket motors for strategic missiles. Tajikistan has no other identified defense industry facilities of significance and no identified military RDT&E facilities.

Tajikistan produces some strategic materials. The aluminum plant at Tursunzade is the third largest in the CIS and the world and is the industrial pillar of the Tajik economy. Sixty percent of the plant's output is exported to other former Soviet states, and it in turn relies on them for raw materials. Tajikistan mines gold ore and is expanding its own gold-processing capabilities. It operates one ore concentration plant at Taror and is building another concentration plant at Kansay and a gold refinery at Khudzhand (Leninabad). Tajikistan also operates a uranium ore concentration plant in Khudzhand.

DEFENSE, 17.

TURKMEN MILITARY FORCES, 1993

Defense Budget: R5 bn (1992)

Turkmen-Russian Joint Forces

Army		**Air Force**	
Army	28,000	Aircraft	80
Tanks	900	**Air Defense**	
Armored Vehicles	1,800	Aircraft	80
Artillery	900		

JIR; MILTECH; RFE/RL Research Institute; Russia & Eurasia Facts & Figures Annual, 1993.

TURKMEN DEFENSE AND SECURITY OFFICIALS, JUNE 1993

Committee for National Security
Chairman: Major General Saparmurad Seidov
Date of Birth: 1942
Date of Appointment: 25 May 1992

Ministry of Internal Affairs
Minister: Unknown

DSOPSS.

Ministry of Defense
Minister: Lieutenant General Danatar
  Abdyevich Kopekov
Date of Birth: 12 May 1933
Date of Appointment: 27 Jan 1992

UKRAINIAN MILITARY FORCES, 1993

Defense Budget: 544 bn karbovanets (1993)

Twenty motorized rifle and tank divisions, several airborne large units, three reinforced artillery divisions, and hundreds of special-forces units and large units.

Strategic Nuclear Forces

ICBM	166
Bombers	42
Tankers	20

Army

Men	217,000
Tanks	8,000
Armored Vehicles	6,000
Artillery	3,300
SSM	132
Helicopters	650

Air Force

Men	171,000
Bombers	115
Fighters	750
Reconnaissance	85
Transport	275
Helicopters	142
SAM	2,400

Navy

	3,000
Naval ships	3

Black Sea Fleet

Submarines	18
Combatants	39
Support Ships	240

Paramilitary Forces

National Guard	12,000
Border Guard	60,000

JIR; MILTECH; RFE/RL Research Institute; Russia & Eurasia Facts & Figures Annual, 1993.

UKRAINIAN DEFENSE AND SECURITY OFFICIALS, JUNE 1993

Security Service
Chairman: Colonel General Yevhen
    Kyrylovych Marchuk
Date of Birth: Unknown
Date of Appointment: 6 Nov 1991

Ministry of Defense
Minister: Colonel General Konstantin
    Petrovich Morozov
Date of Birth: 3 Jun 1944
Date of Appointment: 3 Sep 1991

Border Troops
Commander: Colonel General Valery
    Oleksandrovych Hubenko
Date of Birth: 1939
Date of Appointment: 30 Dec 1991
Other Post: Chairman of the State
    Committee for Defense of State Borders

State Committee for Defense of State Borders
Chairman: Colonel General Valery
    Oleksandrovich Hubenko

Date of Birth: 1939
Date of Appointment: 30 Dec 1991
Other Post: Commander of the Border Troops

Ministry of Internal Affairs
Minister: Lieutenant General Andrii
    Volodymyrovych Vasylyshyn
Date of Birth: 1933
Date of Appointment: 26 Jul 1990

National Guard
Commander: Lieutenant General Volodymyr
    Oleksiiovych Kukharets
Date of Birth: 1938
Date of Appointment: 22 Oct 1991

**Supreme Council Commission for Defense
and State Security**
Chairman: Valentyn Panteliovych Lemish
Date of Birth: Unknown
Date of Appointment: 28 Oct 1992

DSOPSS.

UKRAINIAN SECURITY COUNCIL, NOVEMBER 1993

Permanent Members of the Council

Kravchuk, Leonid Makarovych	President (Chairman of the Council)
Zvyahilskyy, Yukhym Leonidovych	Acting Prime Minister
Vasylyshyn, Andriy Volodymyrovych	Minister of Internal Affairs

UKRAINIAN SECURITY COUNCIL, NOVEMBER 1993 (continued)

Permanent Members of the Council (continued)

Zlenko, Anatoliy Maksymovych	Minister of Foreign Affairs
Marchuk, Yevhen Kyrylovych	Chairman, Security Service
Radetskyy, Vitaliy Hryhorovych	Minister of Defense
Shmarov, Valeriy Mykhaylovych	Vice Prime Minister

Members of the Council

Hubenko, Valeriy Oleksandrovych	Chairman, State Committee for Questions of Defense of Ukraine's State Border
Kostenko, Yuriy Ivanovych	Minister of Environmental Protection
Onopenko, Vasyl Vasylyovych	Minister of Justice
Paton, Borys Yevhenovych	President, Ukrainian Academy of Sciences
Pyatachenko, Hryhoriy Oleksandrovych	Minister of Finance
Spizhenko, Yuriy Prokopovych	Minister of Health

Uriadovii kurier, 4 December 1993, in FBIS-SOV, 7 December 1993, 41.

UKRAINIAN MILITARY SALARIES, 1993

Military Rank	Salary, Karbovantsi/Month	Military Rank	Salary, Karbovantsi/Month
Junior sergeant, petty officer 2nd class	1,500	Captain, captain lieutenant	6,500
Sergeant, petty officer 1st class	2,000	Major, captain 3rd rank	7,000
Senior sergeant, chief petty officer	2,500	Lieutenant colonel, captain 2nd rank	8,000
Ranking NCO, master chief petty officer	3,000	Colonel, captain 1st rank	9,000
Warrant officer	3,500	Major general, rear admiral	10,000
Senior warrant officer	4,000	Lieutenant general, vice admiral	11,000
Junior lieutenant	5,000	Colonel general, admiral	12,000
Lieutenant	5,500	General of the Army of Ukraine	14,000
Senior lieutenant	6,000		

Uriadovii kurier, 25 February 1993, in JPRS-UMA, 14 April 1993, 33.

UKRAINIANS AND RUSSIANS IN THE UKRAINIAN MINISTRY OF DEFENSE, AUGUST 1992

	Percent
Russians	57
Ukrainians	43

Molod Ukraiiny, 21 August 1992, in FBIS-SOV, 26 August 1992, 40.

UKRAINIAN DEFENSE INDUSTRY INFORMATION, 1993

Ukraine contains roughly fifteen percent of the former Soviet defense plants and military R&D facilities, some 700 plants with 500,000 employees directly employed in defense industry and perhaps another one million people contributing to defense output, according to Ukrainian estimates. It is the

UKRAINIAN DEFENSE INDUSTRY INFORMATION, 1993 (continued)

second-largest producer of military weapons and equipment after Russia. It is capable of assembling all major categories of military equipment—ships, missiles, transport aircraft, land arms, and radars— although not as diverse in types and models as those produced in Russia. Component and subsystem plants within Ukraine supply aircraft engines, avionics and other electronic systems, and missile parts for domestic use and for plants in Russia and other newly independent states. Ukrainian defense industry is not self-sufficient, despite its variety of defense output. It depends heavily on Russia for many components and subassemblies. Ukraine has up to fifteen percent of the known former Soviet military R&D facilities, including the sole pop-up test range for submarine-launched ballistic and cruise missiles.

Some Ukrainian facilities have unique capabilities, and others have been sole producers of key systems. Ukraine has the only shipyard in the former Soviet republics currently capable of building aircraft carriers. For missiles and space, Dnipropetrovsk Southern Machine-Building Plant has been the sole producer of the SS-18 ICBM and the SL-16 space launch vehicle, and a plant in Pavlohrad was the sole final assembly facility for the SS-24 ICBM.

Ukraine is also an important supplier of strategic materials for plants throughout the former Soviet Union. In 1991 it produced about half the union's iron ore, forty percent of its metallurgical coking coal, and one-third of its manganese ore and crude steel. Plants in Zaporizhzhya are important producers of aluminum, titanium, magnesium, and also specialty steels for military equipment. Ukraine depends heavily on Russian petroleum and natural gas for fuel and chemical industry inputs.

DEFENSE, 17.

UZBEK MILITARY FORCES, 1993

Defense Budget: Unknown

Uzbek Armed Forces		Army		Air Force	
Men	40,000	Men	38,000	Men	2,000
		Tanks	200	Fighters	100
Paramilitary		Armored vehicles	150	Transport	20
National Guard	700	Artillery	650	Russian Forces	
		SSM	5	Aircraft	32
		Helicopters	30	SAM	45

JIR; MILTECH; RFE/RL Research Institute; Russia & Eurasia Facts & Figures Annual, 1993.

UZBEK DEFENSE AND SECURITY OFFICIALS, JUNE 1993

Committee for State Security
Chairman: Gulam Aliev
Date of Birth: Unknown
Date of Appointment: 12 Jun 1991

Ministry of Defense
Minister: Lieutenant General
  Rustam Urmanovich Akhmedov
Date of Birth: 10 Nov 1943
Date of Appointment: 10 Sep 1991
Other Post: Commander of the Uzbek
  National Guard

**Supreme Council Commission for Military
  Questions, State Security, and Soldiers'
  Social Security**
Chairman: Vilor (Amanulla) Rakhmatulla-
  evich Niyazmatov
Date of Birth: 1937
Date of Appointment: 31 Oct 1990

Ministry of Internal Affairs
Minister: Lieutenant General Zakirzhon
  A. Almatov
Date of Birth: 1949
Date of Appointment: 16 Sep 1991

UZBEK DEFENSE AND SECURITY OFFICIALS, JUNE 1993 (continued)

National Guard
Commander: Lieutenant General Rustam
    Urmanovich Akhmedov
Date of Birth: 10 Nov 1943
Date of Appointment: 10 Sep 1991
Other Post: Minister of Defense

DSOPSS.

UZBEK DEFENSE INDUSTRY INFORMATION, 1993

Uzbekistan has less than one percent of the identified former Soviet defense industry. The state's major defense-industrial facility is the Tashkent Chkalov aircraft plant, which produces the IL-76 Candid transport and its Midas tanker and Mainstay AWACS variants, as well as components for air-to-surface missiles. The plant is now preparing for production of the IL-114, a new short-haul twin turboprop transport designed for civil and military uses. An associated aircraft components plant in Fergana manufactures assemblies for aircraft produced at Tashkent. The Fergana plant also modifies military transports for specialized missions. Tashkent-built aircraft are heavily reliant on engines and avionics supplied by plants in Russia. Tashkent electronics plants produce computers, integrated circuits, and other electronics components. Less than one percent of the known former Soviet RDT&E facilities were in Uzbekistan. Among these were the principal Soviet open-air biological warfare test range on Vozrozhdeniia Island in the Aral Sea and a chemical warfare test range on the Ustyurt Plateau.

Uzbekistan's strategic materials production includes gold and tungsten. The largest gold plant in the former Soviet Union is at a mining complex in Muruntau; other gold plants are at Altynkan and Samarkand. Tungsten ore is mined at Ingichka and processed at a concentrating plant nearby.

DEFENSE, 15.

II RUSSIAN AND EURASIAN MILITARY CHRONOLOGY, 1992-1993

CHRONOLOGY, 1992

JANUARY

- Turkmen Presidential Council member Alexander Bogdanov states that Turkmenistan intends to ask for partial control of the Caspian Sea Flotilla and the naval base at Krasnovodsk.
1 Russian Foreign Minister Andrei Kozyrev asserts that Russia is a natural partner of developed countries, especially the US.
2 Rumors circulate that Tajikistan is attempting to sell enriched uranium abroad.
2 Opposition forces from the Georgian Military Council oust Georgian President Zviad Gamsakhurdia The military council restores Tengiz Sigua to the post of prime minister and names Giorgi Karkarashvili as military commander. It also imposes a state of emergency and a curfew in Tbilisi.
2 Azeri President Ayaz Mutalibov declares presidential rule in the Nagorno-Karabakh capital of Stepanakert and the neighboring Shusha district "in order to coordinate measures to enforce the security of the population and restore constitutional order." At least thirty-six people have been killed in recent artillery attacks.
2 CIS commander-in-chief Yevgeny Shaposhnikov arrives in Minsk to discuss Belarusian defense plans and the future of the Belarusian Military District.
2-3 Moldovan Minister of National Security Anatol Plugaru and Moldovan Department for Military Affairs director General Nicolae Chirtoaca state that any former Soviet officers can join Moldovan troops as long as they profess loyalty to Moldova.
3 Dniester forces seize the MVD headquarters in Bendery.
3 Ukraine takes over control of all troops stationed on its territory with the exception of strategic nuclear forces. Servicemen begin taking an oath of allegiance to Ukraine.
5 Shaposhnikov discloses that only Russia, Kazakhstan, Armenia, Kyrgyzia, and Tajikistan are interested in maintaining unified command over the general purpose forces.
5 Shaposhnikov states that he has possession of one of three briefcases containing nuclear codes. One of the other cases is held by Russian President Boris Yeltsin; the third is in reserve.
5 Ukrainian defense minister Konstantin Morozov claims the Black Sea Fleet for Ukraine.
5 Russian Supreme Soviet Chairman Ruslan Khasbulatov states that Russia will not allow another republic to seize its fleets and armies.
6 Over 500,000 soldiers are sworn into the Ukrainian military.
6 Latvia and Russia sign an accord in which Latvia will provide food for Russian troops in exchange for petroleum products.

7 Gunmen fire on several thousand supporters of Gamsakhurdia in Tbilisi. Two people are wounded.

7 Estonia cuts off flour and cereals to CIS armed forces on its territory.

7 Estonian foreign minister Lennart Meri claims that short-range nuclear weapons still remain on Estonian territory.

7 Major General Nikolai Stoliarov, an aide to Shaposhnikov, states that the Black Sea Fleet may be transferred to Vladivostok to avoid seizure by Ukraine.

7-9 Lithuanian defense minister Audrius Butkevicius arrives in Germany to discuss European security, NATO, and German experience with Soviet troop withdrawal. On 8 January 1992 an agreement is signed which calls for Germany to train Lithuania's armed forces.

8 St. Petersburg Mayor Anatoly Sobchak accuses Ukraine of exploiting the idea of the CIS merely to acquire its own army. He claims that an Ukrainian army represents a "landmine under the future of all mankind."

8 Ukrainian President Leonid Kravchuk states that reliable telephone communications have been established between himself, Yeltsin, Belarusian Supreme Soviet Chairman Stanislav Shushkevich, and Kazakh President Nursultan Nazarbayev to prevent one side from launching a nuclear missile.

8 Twenty-five people are killed and seventy injured in two explosions when a ferry from Krasnovodsk in Turkmenistan docks in Baku.

8 Ukrainian President Leonid Kravchuk meets with US Congress Armed Services Committee chairman Les Aspin. Kravchuk reaffirms Ukraine's non-nuclear intentions and that his country does not plan to join NATO or other military blocs.

8 The Mejlis of the Nakhichevan Autonomous Republic of Azerbaijan vote to transfer to its jurisdiction all FSU army units and equipment on its territory.

9 Kravchuk criticizes CIS commander-in-chief Yevgeny Shaposhnikov as "backward(s)."

9 The Dniester Supreme Soviet places 20,000 former USSR troops within its jurisdiction under its authority and labels it the "Dniester Republican Guard."

9 An MVD battalion is robbed of weapons and its personnel beaten in route to Chisinau. The Dniester Republican Guard takes blame for the incident.

9 Georgian Military Council co-chairman Tengiz Kitovani asserts that the council would hand over power to a provisional government, which would rule until new elections are held.

9 Russia publishes its military oath.

9 Yeltsin warns Ukraine that "no one, not even Kravchuk, will take the Black Sea Fleet away from Russia," and insists that the fleet "was, is, and will be Russia's."

9 Russian first deputy premier Gennadii Burbulis declares that future Russian foreign policy will be conducted on principles of "patriotism" and "preservation of basic value of Russian diplomacy."

9 Chechen President Dzhakhar Dudaev meets with airmen in Groznyi and decides to create an air squadron.

10 Moldovan President Mircea Snegur meets with commanders of former USSR troops based in Moldova and asserts that he is willing to employ all officers and NCOs irrespective of nationality and to offer them and their families full social guarantees.

10 Ukraine cuts defense communications with the CIS command due to a dispute over Ukrainian views on nuclear weapons.

10 CIS officials notify Lithuania that planned military maneuvers on its territory have been canceled.

10 Ukraine begins to remove tactical nuclear weapons from its territory.

11 The Belarus Parliament votes to subordinate all former Soviet troops on its territory and to create a ministry of defense. The parliament also approves the text of Belarus' military oath which will be administered to those who entered the military as of November 1991. A Belarus national army of about 90,000 troops is envisioned.

11 Belarus defense affairs minister Petr Chaus announces that Belarus citizens serving outside of the country will be able to return home to serve. In addition, the Belarus defense minister states that a significant portion of the land occupied by military facilities (said to comprise more than ten percent of Belarus territory) would be returned to the people.

11 Russian and Ukrainian state delegations meet in Kiev and sign a communiqué that provides a framework on dividing former Soviet forces. The two sides set up a panel of experts to resolve defense disputes, and both agree to avoid taking "unilateral actions." They also agree that military units in Ukraine currently consist of both strategic and republican forces, and that a part of the Black Sea Fleet will be classified in the second category and will join the Ukrainian forces.

11 Yeltsin abolishes the Group of General Inspectors within the CIS Ministry of Defense. The move retires fifty-three marshals, an army general, and sixty-two lieutenants and colonels. Marshals Sergei Sokolov, Viktor Kulikov, Vasily Petrov, and Nikolai Ogarkov remain consultants and advisors.

13 Uzbek President Islam Karimov decrees that former USSR MVD troops in Uzbekistan will be placed under Uzbek control.

13 Azeri defense minister Tadzheddin Mekhtiev states that the four former republics that border on the Caspian Sea—Russia, Azerbaijan, Kazakhstan, and Turkmenistan—each had a right to claim a share of the Caspian Sea Flotilla. This force is made up of some eighty-five vessels, of which the four largest are frigates.

13 Belarus defense affairs minister Petr Chaus reveals that Minsk has diverted about 30 percent of funds intended for arms procurement to housing construction.

13 Kazakh President Nursultan Nazarbayev supports a unified CIS force and criticizes Ukraine for seeking to split the military.

13 Nazarbayev meets with Kazakh defense industry leaders to address their concerns over the economy.

13 The Lithuanian Supreme Council's presidium awards the "Jan 13" medal to Russian President Boris Yeltsin, fifty foreign politicians, diplomats, and journalists, and several hundred Lithuanians for their acts of bravery during the 1991 OMON attack on the Vilnius television tower.

13 Russian Deputy Prime Minister Yegor Gaidar rejects Russian Supreme Soviet Chairman Ruslan Khasbulatov's criticism and defends the decision of the government to sharply reduce military spending.

14 The Russian Constitutional Court unanimously annuls Yeltsin's decree merging the KGB and MVD.

14 Colonel Viktor Alksnis accuses FSU President Mikhail Gorbachev of having sanctioned KGB surveillance of leaders of all political parties, including Yeltsin.

14 Ukrainian defense minister Konstantin Morozov meets with Polish defense minister Jan Parys. During the meeting, Morozov stresses that Ukraine is developing a defensive military doctrine under which it would never start an armed conflict. He assures Poland that Ukraine has no territorial claims on its neighbors and will never use nuclear weapons.

14 Snegur cables Russian President Boris Yeltsin to complain about Russian mercenaries who support the Dniester Republican Guard.

14 Latvian deputy minister of Industry and Energy Ziedonis Blumbergs accuses the Northwestern Group of Forces of delaying its promise to supply Latvia with 100,000 tons of diesel fuel and 50,000 tons of gasoline. Only 100 tons of diesel fuel and 70 tons of gasoline have been delivered.

14 Latvian Prime Minister Ivars Godmanis warns that Riga will withhold food supplies to Russian troops unless petroleum is delivered from Russia. The prime minister also points out that Tyumen owes Latvia 600,000 tons of petroleum for 1990 and 1991 plus 300,000 tons of petroleum annually for Latvian work on Tyumen transportation infrastructure.

14 Nazarbayev and CIS commander-in-chief Yevgeny Shaposhnikov meet in Alma-Ata to discuss CIS forces. Both call for a unified army.

14 Estonian foreign minister Lennar Meri and Russian foreign minister Andrei Kozyrev meet to discuss the withdrawal of CIS/Russian troops from Estonia.

14 Shaposhnikov praises Nazarbayev for supporting a unified army.

15 Shaposhnikov visits Tajikistan and Turkmenistan to discuss the future of the CIS military.

15 Two airborne divisions in Lithuania issue an ultimatum to Russian President Yeltsin and CIS commander-in-chief Yevgeny Shaposhnikov to sign a withdrawal agreement with Lithuania granting social guarantees.

15 The Latvia Supreme Council requests aid from WHO and the Red Cross.

16 Former Azeri KGB chairman Ivan Gorelovskii is appointed Russian Foreign Intelligence Service deputy director.

16 Ukrainian chief of the General Staff Major General Georgy Zhivitsa claims that Kiev controls all former USSR military units on its territory and tactical nuclear weapons. The chief of staff also insists that "all ships on the territory of Ukraine belong to Ukraine."

16 Transcaucasus Military District commander Colonel General Valery Patrikeev asserts that the district should be under Russian control.

16 Deputy commander-in-chief of the CIS Armed Forces Colonel General Boris Piankov meets with Moldovan officials in Chisinau to discuss the status of the 14th Army.

17 Over five thousand officers meet in Moscow to discuss the future of the armed forces. The officers urge retention of a unified army and improved social guarantees for servicemen. One delegate demands the resignation of Shaposhnikov, causing him to storm out of the meeting.

17 Pro- and anti-Gamsakhurdia factions clash in Kutasis, Georgia.

17 Rutskoi blames Russian leaders for politicizing the armed forces.

18 Georgian Military Council troops attempt to occupy Abasha and Samtrdia.

18 Gamsakhurdia forces in Georgia attack two army bases in an attempt seize weapons.

18 Nazarbayev asserts that Kazakhstan is ready to sign the Non-Proliferation Treaty.

19 The Kazakh government announces that it will sell uranium only under the guidance and regulations of the International Atomic Energy Agency.

20 Latvians hold commemorative services for five men killed in Riga during the 1991 OMON assault on the Latvian Ministry of Internal Affairs.

20 Moldovan Minister of Internal Affairs Ion Costas appeals to the Helsinki Federation about the Dniester Republican Guard's violent attacks on Moldova.

20 Dniester Republican Guard forces seize forty-one military transport vehicles belonging to CIS military units stationed in Moldova.

20 Six are killed in clashes between students and law enforcement officials in Tashkent, Uzbekistan.

21 The Officers' Movement for the Revival of Russia emerges from the All-Union Officers' Assembly. The group's organizer is Major General Aleksandr Sterligov.

21 Commander of the Northwestern Group of Forces Colonel General Valery Mironov asserts that his forces are now under Russian jurisdiction.

21 Georgian Military Council troops occupy Abasha. Five are killed.

21 The Confederation of Mountain Peoples of the Caucasus meets in Makhachkala to discuss regional conflicts.

22 Thirty percent of Ukraine's tactical nuclear weapons are removed.

22 Georgian Military Council troops advance on Senaki.

22 The Latvian Supreme Council rules that Latvian customs officials are to inspect all CIS military transport vehicles before they depart Latvian territory.

22 CIS military affairs spokesman Lieutenant Colonel Leonid Ivashov states that Russia has agreed to finance 62.3 percent of the CIS military budget in 1992 while Ukraine will pay 17.3 percent and Kazakhstan 5.1 percent. The other members will make up the difference.

23 The Estonian Supreme Council orders all property belonging to the former Soviet Armed Forces be turned over to Estonia. The action is a

protest against removal of equipment that was supposed to be handed over to Estonia.

23 Gamsakhurdia supporters in Poti threaten to blow up parts of the town.

23 Kazakh deputy prime minister Yevgeny Ezhikov-Babakhanov announces that Kazakhstan will demand the right to monitor the Baikonur space center.

23 Shaposhnikov proposes assigning Ukraine only seven percent of the Black Sea Fleet.

24 The Russian Supreme Soviet approves a budget for the first quarter. The deficit is planned at 11.5 bn rubles (about 1 percent of GNP). The defense expenditure will be cut to about R50 bn, or 4.5 percent of the GNP.

24 A new Moscow government is formed.

24 Russian sources claim that 286,000 CIS servicemen and their families are homeless.

24 Gamsakhurdia supporters blow up three bridges near Khobi.

24 Abkhazia declares a state of emergency.

25 Nazarbayev announces that medium-range nuclear missiles are being removed from Kazakhstan and denies that the state plans to proliferate atomic materials throughout the Arab world.

25-26 The Ukrainian Union of Officers meets to discuss the country's security.

26 Mutalibov, speaking to journalists in Istanbul, reveals that Turkey is prepared to assist Azerbaijan in training officers for an Azeri national army.

26 Deputy chairman of the Belarus Parliamentary Security Committee Leonid Privalau states that the first load of tactical nuclear weapons has left Belarus for Russia.

26 Belarus foreign minister Petr Krauchenka claims that Belarus will be the first nuclear-free member of the CIS. He indicates that Belarus would be free of its long-range missiles by 1996 or 1997.

26 Thousands of Estonian Defense Forces parade through Tallinn in support of Savisaar.

27 The Estonian Supreme Council passes a military service law which states that mandatory service can last no more than eighteen months for all male citizens aged 18-28 and provides twenty-four months of alternative service. Those who served in the Soviet Army are exempt.

27 CIS Navy commander-in-chief Admiral Vladimir Chernavin arrives in Sevastopol and orders Black Sea Fleet personnel to swear an oath of loyalty to the CIS.

27 Media reports suggest that Omsk leaders want to export tanks and other military hardware.

27 The Turkmen Ministry of Defense is created.

27 Karimov abolishes the Tashkent OMON.

27-28 Georgian Military Council troops attack and capture Poti. Six people are killed and dozens wounded.

28 Kravchuk appoints new commanders to Ukraine's three military districts. General Valentin Boriskin is named commander of the Kiev MD (Military District), Lieutenant General Valery Stepanov for the Carpathian MD,

and Lieutenant General Vitaly Radetskii for the Odessa MD. By the same decree Viktor Chechevatov, Viktor Skokov, and Ivan Morozov are relieved of their duties.

28 The Uzbek Supreme Soviet adopts a resolution placing former USSR military units and schools on its territory under Uzbek jurisdiction.

28 Turkmen KGB chairman Danatar Kpekov is named head of the Turkmen Defense Ministry.

28 Yeltsin, Shaposhnikov, and CIS Navy commander-in-chief Vladimir Chernavin visit unexpectedly the port city of Novorossiisk to assure seamen that the Black Sea Fleet would not fall under Ukrainian control.

28 Head of the General Staff Academy, Colonel General Igor Rodionov, calls for his academy to become the training center for CIS officers. He argues that in the future it should be turned over to Russian supervision.

28 Forty people are killed when a civilian Azeri helicopter flying from Agdam to Shusha in Nagorno-Karabakh is shot down by a heat-seeking missile fired from Shushkent.

28 Petr Chaus is appointed to head the Belarus Ministry of Defense.

28 The Latvian Supreme Council orders local governments to monitor all Russian bases, installations, and buildings.

28 The Tajik Defense Committee rejects a claim by the Afghan resistance that the Tajik government is supplying weapons to the Afghan government.

28-29 Georgian Military Council troops capture Zugdidi. Three are wounded.

29 Yeltsin announces CIS and Russian arms cuts. He states that 600 strategic land and sea missiles have been taken off alert status as well as proposes eliminating 130 land based missile silos and halting production of heavy bombers and cruise missiles.

29 Belarus KGB chief Eduard Shirkovskii states that Western and Russian spies are infiltrating the state.

29 Yeltsin appears on nation-wide television to describe planned arms reductions in Russian and CIS military forces.

30 The CSCE admits Belarus, Ukraine, Azerbaijan, Kazakhstan, Kyrgyzstan, Turkmenistan, Tajikistan, Moldova and Uzbekistan into its membership.

31 Seven Moldovan policemen in Bendery are beaten by Russian Cossacks and Dniester Republican Guards.

31 Latvian defense minister Talavs Jundzis expects the Latvian Army to consist of 8,000 to 9,000 men. Fifty percent would serve as border guards. Jundzis hopes to arms the troops with weapons from the Northwestern Group of Forces.

31 A Russian delegation headed by Deputy Prime Minister Sergei Shakhrai holds talks in Vilnius on the withdrawal of Soviet troops from Lithuania.

31 The coordinating council of the All-Army Officers' Assembly meets and approves an appeal urging its representatives to take part in CIS meetings. Aleksandr Mochaikin is elected chairman.

31 A Russian delegation headed by Deputy Prime Minister Sergei Shakhrai holds talks in Vilnius on the withdrawal of Soviet troops from Lithuania.

FEBRUARY

1 Latvian Border Guards begin their duties. Minister of State Janis Dinevics is responsible for recruitment and supplies.

1 Yeltsin and US President George Bush sign a joint declaration of friendship, express the intention to reduce nuclear arsenals, to expand trade and economic cooperation, and to respect human rights.

2 The Ukrainian Supreme Soviet agrees to reduce military duty to eighteen months and naval service to two years.

2 Briva Latvija accuses the KGB of still operating in Latvia.

3 A Belarusian Supreme Soviet group of experts on military affairs determines that there are 160,000 troops on Belarusian soil. By 1994, the group argues, 80,000 will be in the Belarusian Army with a budget of R8 bn.

3 Estonia fails to reach agreement with Russia on troop withdrawals.

3 The Lvov oblast soviet passes a resolution calling for the Ukrainian Supreme Soviet to recognize the Ukrainian Insurgent Army of the 1930s to 1950s.

3 Major General Nikolai Stoliarov, while in Washington, states that tension in CIS armed forces is growing, particularly in Ukraine. He added that pressures to swear more than one military oath are splitting the armed forces.

4 Shaposhnikov states that he supports Yeltsin's arms control proposals. He also asserts that Russia and the United States are now allies.

4 Lieutenant General Vasily Vorobev states that Russia is the only CIS member to allocate funding for the first quarter of the 1992 CIS budget.

4 Estonian State and Border Defense Authority chief Toomas Puura asserts that his country is looking for cheap arms for its border guards. These arms may be supplied by departing CIS troops, Czechoslovakia, or the Chechen Republic.

5 Russian Deputy Prime Minister Sergei Shakhrai states that Russia will finance the withdrawal of Soviet Army troops from the Baltic states.

5 While meeting with German Economics Minister Juergen Moellemann, Nazarbayev asserts that Russian President Boris Yeltsin's disarmament proposal has "large gaps."

5 Poll data collected from the All-Army Officers' Assembly are published. Nearly 80 percent of all respondents state that the army must have the deciding vote on the army's future, while only 19 percent maintain that the army should wait for decisions by politicians. On the popularity of particular politicians, respondents have the most favorable feeling toward Nursultan Nazarbayev (65 percent), Aleksandr Rutskoi (36 percent), Viktor Alksnis (29 percent), and Boris Yeltsin (21 percent). The politicians arousing the greatest antipathy are Leonid Kravchuk (46 percent), Mikhail Gorbachev (45 percent), and Vladimir Zhirinovskii (33 percent). Some 70 percent of all respondents assert that they want a return to the USSR's borders.

5-7 Yeltsin meets with French President Francois Mitterrand to discuss disarmament issues and aid.

6-8 Chechens attack military and MVD bases in Chechenia. One is killed.

8 FSU defense minister Dmitry Yazov asserts in an interview from jail that the CIS Armed Forces could resemble the Warsaw Pact or NATO in structure.

10 Russian foreign minister Andrei Kozyrev warns of the threat of Islamic fundamentalism.

10 The Latvian foreign ministry sends a protest note to the Russian foreign ministry over the introduction of 500 FSU troops from Germany.

10 Ukrainian President Kravchuk believes that the biggest danger to the CIS is having a unified armed force.

10 Nazarbayev urges a unified CIS army.

11 CIS defense ministers meet in Minsk to discuss the army's future.

11 Moldovan Prime Minister Valeriu Muravschi announces that his country will not contribute to the CIS armed forces' budget.

11 A CIS nuclear-powered attack submarines collides with a US submarine near Kola Bay.

11 Moldovan Prime Minister Valeriu Muravschi asserts that Moldova will not make any financial contributions to CIS general-purpose forces. Instead, Moldova will only finance units of the ex-USSR armed forces that are stationed on Moldovan territory and accept Moldovan jurisdiction.

11 Turkmen President Saparmurad Niyazov's press service denies a report that Turkmenistan is training Azeri soldiers for service in Nagorno-Karabakh.

11 Five Iranians are detained by CIS Border Troops near the Turkmen town of Kersakhs. The Iranians are equipped with automatic weapons, grenades, and 60 mn Iranian rials.

12 Estonian customs officials intercept 15,000 pistols for delivery to Finland. The shipment originated from the Izhevsk Mechanics Factory in Russia's Udmurt republic.

12 Kebich warns that the CIS might fail if members do not resolve issues such as financing of the army and the structure of the armed forces.

12 Ukraine and Belarus refuse to sign military preparatory documents for the CIS summit in Minsk due to disagreement on the composition and redistribution of CIS forces among the commonwealth states.

12 Tajik opposition leaders hold a memorial meeting in Dushanbe to honor those killed during army and OMON attacks on demonstrators in February 1990. Nabiev offers a gesture of reconciliation by remaining the site Martyr's Square.

14 Kravchuk accuses CIS commander-in-chief Yevgeny Shaposhnikov of creating a joint stock company that is "surreptitiously" selling off the Black Sea Fleet. The attack comes during a CIS meeting in Minsk.

14 Six Russian aircrews fly SU-24 bombers from their airbase at Starokonstantinov in Ukraine to Belarus and then to Russia. The crews defect because they refused to take an oath of allegiance to Ukraine.

14 Georgian defense minister Lieutenant General Levan Sharashenidze asserts that Georgia "will definitely claim part of the Black Sea Fleet" and the naval base at Poti.

14 The CIS heads of state meet in Minsk and sign twenty documents on military and economic matters. One document seeks to regulate trade and economic cooperation and calls for the ruble to remain the sole monetary unit. Military accords are minor and few members sign all documents. Moldova fails to sign an agreement on strategic forces and Belarus does not sign an agreement on general purpose forces.

14 The All-Army Officers' Assembly calls on the CIS heads of state to suspend the withdrawal of troops from Germany, Poland, and the Baltics until "structures and mechanism" to provide social and legal protection are established.

15 Shaposhnikov is confirmed as commander-in-chief of the CIS Joint Armed Forces.

16 The Georgian observer delegation to the CIS summit in Minsk protests Russia's intent to sell the Black Sea Fleet.

16 Nazarbayev claims that Kazakhstan is a nuclear state since tests had occurred there since 1949. He also states that Kazakhstan will get rid of all nuclear weapons if the US, the former USSR, and the PRC do as well.

17 Yeltsin meets with US Secretary of State James Baker in Moscow to discuss nuclear disarmament.

17 Kravchuk protests to Russian President Boris Yeltsin over the "hijacking" of six long-range bombers from Ukraine to Russia.

17 The First Strategic Air Division, based at Uzin in Ukraine, renounces its subordination to Moscow and accepts Ukrainian jurisdiction.

18 Ukrainian defense minister Konstantin Morozov stresses that Ukraine's military will not be a threat to its neighbors.

18 The Latvian Supreme Council appoints Girts Kristovskis as chief of the Home Guard.

18 A group calling itself "Cossack Circle" is formed. Its members are officers and senior enlisted men of the former Soviet Armed Forces and those who support the military. The Riga branch reportedly has over 1,800 members. Branches are being formed in Liepaja and Daugavpils, where large numbers of troops are stationed.

18 Mutalibov dismisses Azeri defense minister Tadzhaddin Mekhtiev in response to pressure from the Azerbaijan Popular Front.

18 Shaposhnikov predicts that the former Soviet Armed Forces will split up into national armies.

18 Chechen President Dzhakhar Dudaev warns Russia that a "holy war" may erupt between the two entities.

19 Democratic Russia recommends Andrei Kokoshin for Russian defense minister.

19 Latvian defense ministry spokesman Auseklis Plavins claims that groups opposing independent Latvia have consolidated forces. These groups include Interfront, Council of War and Labor Veterans, and the Latvian Communist Party Operative Center.

19 More than twenty people are killed by heavy artillery fire in the Nagorno-Karabakh capital of Stepanakert.

19 Kravchuk attacks Russian President Boris Yeltsin for speaking for the CIS in nuclear arms reduction talks with the US.

20 Armenia, Azerbaijan, and Russia sign a communiqué agreeing on the need for an immediate cease-fire, for the restoration of communications and dispatch of humanitarian aid, and for continuing negotiations on a settlement of the Nagorno-Karabakh conflict.

21 Moldovan Minister of Defense Ion Kostash states that the Moldovan Army will be created on the basis of the 14th Army located on the right bank of the Dniester. Units located on the territory of the Dniester Republic will be given the status of an army on the territory of an independent state, and will be withdrawn to Russian territory in eighteen months to two years.

21 New fighting erupts near the towns of Agdam and Khodzhali.

21 Dienda reports that Latvia's new intelligence service is subordinate to the Latvian Ministry of Internal Affairs. The chief is Juris Kuzins. The department has four divisions with the following tasks: defense of Latvia's sovereignty; research on international relations; analysis of information; and administration of general affairs.

22 Latvia's National Independence Movement holds a protest demonstration in Riga. Thousands call for the departure of Russian troops.

22 Three CIS soldiers are killed in a clash with Azeris near Gyandzha while another twenty people are killed in an Azeri missile attack on Askeran.

22 Shaposhnikov calls for the return of 'age-old' Russian traditions, uniforms, and symbols in the armed forces.

22-23 NATO Secretary General Manfred Woerner meets with Ukrainian leaders, including President Leonid Kravchuk, Foreign Minister Anatolii Zlenko, and Minister of Defense Konstantin Morozov to discuss security issues.

23-25 A military construction unit rebels at Baikonur. Three soldiers are killed.

23 Russian security forces fight with batons to hold back several thousand pro-communist demonstrators who march in central Moscow to denounce Yeltsin's policies.

23 Rutskoi calls for the release of the August 1991 coup plotters.

24 Lithuanian attempts to remove Russian border guards from a customs post at the Klaipeda-Mukran ferry prove unsuccessful. Russian border guards also refuse to leave the post at Palanga, where the normal contingent of six to seven persons is supplemented by twenty-five armed soldiers.

25 Gamsakhurdia forces stage peaceful demonstrations in Tbilisi, Zugdidi, Senaki, Poti, and several towns in Abkhazia.

25 Chairman of the Abkhaz Supreme Soviet Vladislav Ardzinba proposes another state of emergency in Abkhazia following a series of bomb attacks on the main railway linking Abkhazia and Tbilisi.

25 Iranian Foreign Minister Ali Akbar Velayati and Mutalibov meet in Baku to discuss Iranian-led peace efforts over the Nagorno-Karabakh conflict.

25-27 The Lithuanian Parliament discusses the 1992 budget. Funding for the military is kept at the 1992 level with adjustments for inflation.

25 Yeltsin takes over supervision of the ministries of security, foreign affairs, and justice.

26 Russian Foreign Minister Andrei Kozyrev reveals that post-Soviet Russian interests include "a unified army, human rights, the protection of the Russian and the Russian-speaking population in other CIS states, and economic cooperation."

26 Ukraine, Tajikistan, Belarus, Moldova and Uzbekistan sign the Helsinki Final Act.

26 CIS chief of the General Staff, Colonel General Viktor Samsonov, visits Beijing for a six-day trip to discuss military cooperation and a reduction in military forces between Russia and the PRC.

27 A CIS air defense battalion unit withdraws from Mickunai, Lithuania. The unit is sent to Latvia. CIS troops still guard the base.

27 The Latvian Supreme Council adopts a budget of R6.6 bn for the first six months of 1992, including six percent for defense.

27 Myacheslau Hryb, chairman of the Belarusian Supreme Soviet Commission on Security, Defense, and the Fight Against Crime, asserts that Belarus will have a military of 90,000 men.

27 Kyrgyz MVD chairman Feliks Kulov is appointed Kyrgyz vice president.

27 Yeltsin decrees new duties to Vice President Aleksandr Rutskoi including supervision of the defense industry's conversion and arms sales.

28 Yeltsin visits the closed city Arzamas-16 to discuss the future of nuclear research.

28 Azeri President Ayaz Mutalibov announces that Baku has agreed to subordinate general purpose forces to both the Azeri president and to the CIS military command.

MARCH

• Fourteen warplanes are removed from Kyrgyzstan and flown to Russia.

• Moscow city officials arm themselves.

1 Commander of the ex-Soviet Caspian Sea Flotilla Rear Admiral Boris Zinin states that Azerbaijan will receive twenty-four combat and forty-nine "ancillary" ships from the Flotilla.

1 The town of Valga establishes a border to separate the Latvian side from the Estonian. The Latvian side is called Valka.

1-2 Dniester Republican Guards and Russian Cossacks seize Dubasary police headquarters. Two are killed and thirty-four policemen are taken prisoner.

2 Dniester Republican Guards and Russian Cossacks deploy forces on bridges across the Dniester River and on left bank roads in order to isolate the right bank.

2 Three hundred CIS airborne troops are sent to Nagorno-Karabakh to protect the 366th Motorized Infantry Regiment as it begins withdrawing from Stepanakert.

2 General Boris Gromov supervises the withdrawal of 300 CIS airborne troops from Nagorno-Karabakh.

3 The Georgian Military Council extends the state of emergency and curfew in Tbilisi because of nightly shootings.

3 Armenian protests block the CIS army troop withdrawal from Nagorno-Karabakh. One soldier is killed when Armenians open fire and troops refuse to surrender their weapons.

3 Moldovan peasants raid a CIS civil defense unit near Dubasary and seize weapons to fight the Dniester Republican Guards, and Russian Cossacks.

4 Fighting erupts between the Dniester Republican Guards, Russian Cossacks and Moldovan peasants in Cocieri. Nine are killed and twenty-nine wounded.

4 Yeltsin decrees that former Soviet troops in Germany, Poland, Mongolia, and Cuba will fall under Russia's jurisdiction.

5 The Russian Supreme Soviet adopts a Law on Security. The law sets up the legal foundations for the security of individuals, society, and the state from external and internal threats.

5 Shaposhnikov fires Air Force Major General Mikhail Bashkirov for pledging allegiance to Ukraine. Ukrainian Minister of Defense Konstantin Morozov promptly reinstates Bashkirov.

5 A cease-fire is announced between the Moldovan government and the Dniester region.

5 In a nation-wide speech Snegur charges that the Dniester Republic and the Russian media "are deliberately portraying the conflict as inter-ethnic…in an attempt to disguise the military-communist nature of the phantom "Dniester Republic" and to attract the support of the national patriotic forces of Russia."

5 The Latvian government decides that CIS personnel can exchange their apartments in Latvia for ones in Russia provided that the Latvian apartment goes to a Latvian returning to his homeland.

6-7 Commander of the CIS 14th Army Major General Yury Nekachev and his entire command staff are held prisoner in their headquarters in Tiraspol by Dniester Republic activists. The activists include the leaders of the Joint Council of Work Collectives and the Womens' Strike Committee. They demand that the 14th Army turn over its armament and vehicles to the Dniester Republic.

9 Zugdidi erupts in violence. Three policemen are killed in a bomb explosion and subsequent attack on police headquarters.

9 Dniester Republic armored vehicles fly the flag of the former Moldavian Soviet Socialist Republic and Dniester military posts display slogans such as "The Dniester Republic is a bulwark of internationalism."

9 Over 100 Iranians continue to be trained at the CIS naval base at Bolderaja.

10 Latvian Prime Minister Ivars Godmanis asserts that Latvia intends to take control of its borders and demands the departure of 2,000 CIS border guards.

10 Head of the Dniester Republic Military and Security Department Vladimir Ryliakov asserts that the republic stands for the preservation of "a single Army and a single economic space across the territory of the Soviet Union."

10 CIS 14th Army chief of staff Major General Viacheslav Sitnikov states that he is "under great social pressure" to come to the assistance of the

Dniester Republic. Local Russians have staged threatening demonstrations outside the 14th Army's barracks in Tiraspol.

10 The Financial Times reports that Ukrainian officers stationed in Azerbaijan are helping Azerbaijan establish its own army.

10 A joint meeting of the ruling Georgian Military Council and the Consultative Council decides to dissolve both bodies and create a temporary legislative and executive body known as the Georgian State Council which Eduard Shevardnadze heads. Dzhaba Ioseliani, one of the co-chairmen of the Military Council, serve as his deputy; acting prime minister Tengiz Sigua and Military Council co-chairman Tengiz Kitovani are also named members of the State Council.

11 The Estonian Supreme Council votes fifty-seven to one with one abstention to expel four former Soviet military representatives from the parliament. Soviet military troops in Estonia elected the four in March 1990.

11 A regiment of IL-78 refueling aircraft that is part of the strategic air division at Uzin is removed from the list of CIS strategic forces.

11 Rutskoi claims that tactical nuclear weapons are still located in Azerbaijan and Armenia.

12 Kravchuk announces that Ukraine will halt the withdrawal of tactical nuclear weapons from Ukraine to Russia because Kiev "...cannot guarantee that the withdrawn weapons will be destroyed, that they will be under the necessary control, or that they will not fall into the wrong hands."

13 Gamsakhurdia forces take hostage two senior Georgian defense officials and over forty national guardsmen in Zugdidi.

14 Chairman of the Union of Officers Stanislav Serekhov states that the US and NATO remain enemies.

14 CIS deputy commander-in-chief General Boris Piankov claims that all nuclear weapons have been removed from the Transcaucasus.

14-15 Dniester Republican Guards and Russian Cossacks attack Moldovan police units in three villages in Dubasary district in an attempt to eliminate the last remaining Moldovan police presence on the left bank of the Dniester. Russian forces also blow up two highway bridges over the Dniester River. Weapons depots are also targeted. Near Tiraspol, Dniester Republican Guards and Russian Cossacks carry away 1,100 Kalashnikov submachine guns along with 1.5 million cartridges, 1,300 grenade and mortar rounds, and 30 portable rocket launchers.

15 Iran negotiates a cease-fire between Armenia and Azerbaijan.

15 Belarusian Defense Minister Petr Chaus expresses his worry over the fate of Belarusian nuclear weapons transferred to Russian territory.

16 Yeltsin forms the Russian Ministry of Defense and names himself temporary defense minister.

16 First Deputy Prime Minister Gennadii Burbulis rules out a new coup.

16 Thirty people are killed or wounded during an attack on Fizuli.

16 Nazarbayev decrees the establishment of the Kazakh Republican Guard to protect the vital interests of the country and its citizens. It will be subordinate to the president.

17 Georgian State Council representatives and Gamsakhurdia supporters reach agreement to cease hostilities and release hostages.

17 UN special envoy Cyrus Vance meets with Acting Azeri President Yakub Mamedov and Prime Minister Hasan Hasanov in Baku to discuss a peaceful solution to the Nagorno-Karabakh conflict.

17 Shushkevich states that Belarus will continue to transfer tactical nuclear weapons to Russia.

17 Dniester Republican Guards and Russian Cossacks resume their offensive against the remaining Moldovan police posts in Dubasary.

17 Moldovan Prime Minister Valeriu Muravschi makes a televised speech in Russian announcing a unilateral cease-fire by the Moldovan police.

17 Kravchuk decrees that a "special regime" be formed on the Ukrainian-Moldovan border which bans the transit of armed groups and illegal entries into Ukraine.

18 Moldovan Prime Minister Valeriu Muravschi addresses an extraordinary session of the Moldovan Parliament. He asserts that "it was increasingly difficult to contain the Dniester Russian Guard and the Cossacks" in their offensive in eastern Moldova. The republic must either raise a military force or seek international support."

18 The Belarus Supreme Soviet votes to establish a national army.

18 Akaev tells a press conference in New Delhi that Kyrgyzstan plans to sell uranium under International Atomic Energy Agency supervision. He states that India could buy enriched uranium if it wished.

19 CIS defense ministers meet in Kiev. Thirty-four items are on the agenda.

19 Chief of the Russian delegation to Latvia Sergei Zotov claims that Russia wants to keep its radar station at Skrunda even after all troops are removed. Zotov states that there are 58,000 CIS troops in Latvia.

20 Yeltsin places former USSR border guards in the Baltic states under Russian jurisdiction.

20 The summit of the CIS heads of state opens in Kiev. Opinions differ over military, economic, and political issues. Seventeen documents are signed but key issues are not addressed. An agreement is reached on a CIS peacekeeping force but Armenia and Azerbaijan refuse to sign. Kravchuk and Yeltsin exchange harsh words over Russian domination of the CIS military and political structures. Finally, a statement is signed that the CIS wants to preserve Moldova's territorial integrity.

20 The CIS presidents confirm the appointments of CIS Armed Forces chief of the General Staff Colonel General Viktor Samsonov, CIS Strategic Armed Forces CinC Yury Maksimov, and CIS General Purpose Armed Forces CinC Vladimir Semyonov.

20 Shushkevich announces that the CIS General Staff refuses to accept Belarus' right to determine its defense policy.

20 Kravchuk insists on continuing the suspension of tactical nuclear weapons transfer to Russia.

20 Nazarbayev claims that Kazakhstan has the right to be a nuclear power despite the fact that it did so against its will.

21-22 The Confederation of Mountain Peoples of the Caucasus decides to establish an army.

24 The Azeri Parliament calls for the immediate creation of a 20,000 man national army.

25 The chairman of the Kyrgyz Supreme Soviet's Committee on Military Affairs states that Kyrgyzstan has no intention of establishing its own national army.

25 Karimov decrees the formation of the Uzbek Border Guards under the jurisdiction of the Uzbek National Security Service.

26 Yeltsin abolishes the position of state councillor for defense and dissolves the State Committee for Defense.

26 The chairman of the All-Russian Trade Union of Defense Industry Workers states that Russian defense industry exports are 3.8 times less in 1991 than in 1989.

26 Dniester President Igor Smirnov signs a decree ordering a partial mobilization of men up to the age of forty-five. Smirnov also signs a decree putting the Dniester Republic on Moscow time, which is one hour ahead of Chisinau.

26 A transformer station in Grigoriopol on the left bank of the Dniester is blown up. Power supplies to nearly all the Moldovan villages in the area are cut and half the farmland is deprived of irrigation water.

28 Gamsakhurdia forces occupy Abasha, Khobi, Senaki, and Tsalendzhik and dismisses the local authorities.

29 Snegur declares a state or emergency and orders Moldova's security forces to "liquidate and disarm the illegitimate armed formations" which are backing the Dniester "pseudo-state."

29 The Ukrainian Supreme Council warns that the Moldovan conflict could have dangerous consequences for the republic's neighbors.

30 Estonia creates a special police force to combat economic crime. It will consist of 100-140 officers and will be subordinate to the Estonian interior ministry.

30 Russia tells the CSCE that it is concerned about Russians in other areas of the CIS.

31 An attempted coup is launched against Chechen President General Dzharkhar Dudaev. Forces seize the broadcasting center, besiege Dudaev's official residence, and thousands of demonstrators gather in Grozny. Five are killed.

APRIL

1 Georgian forces engage supporters of ousted President Gamsakhurdia in Poti. Thirteen people are killed.

1 Special units of the Moldovan MVD attack Bendery leaving at least ten people dead.

1 Yeltsin places the 14th Army under Russian jurisdiction.

1 Russian Foreign Minister Andrei Kozyrev states that Russia "will be protecting the rights of Russians in other states of the (CIS)."

1 Shaposhnikov states that CIS troops always will be stationed in Kaliningrad Oblast.

2 The CIS high command promotes former commander of the Northern Fleet Admiral Felix Gromov to CIS Naval Forces first deputy commander-in-chief. He replaces Admiral Ivan Kapitanets who has retired.

3 Yeltsin appoints Colonel General Pavel Grachev and defense specialist Andrei Kokoshin as Russian first deputy defense ministers.

3 Yeltsin places himself as head of the Russian Security Council.

3 Yeltsin warns that Russia may take the Black Sea Fleet under its own jurisdiction.

4 In Alma-Ata, CIS foreign intelligence services agree that their republics will not spy on each other and will cooperate in intelligence activities. A coordinating organ, the Council of Heads of Intelligence Organs, is established. It is scheduled to meet four times a year.

7 US Secretary of State James Baker warns Kiev that American aid to Ukraine will be reduced if it does not resume tactical nuclear weapons transfers to Russia.

7 The Russian-led Crimean Republican Movement erects barricades in the streets leading to the Black Sea Fleet headquarters in Sevastopol.

7 Yeltsin asserts Russian jurisdiction over the Black Sea Fleet.

7 Shaposhnikov addresses the Russian Congress of Peoples Deputies. He supports a powerful Russian Army, criticizes the Russian Ministry of Foreign Affairs for not protecting Russian interests, and attacks Baltic leaders for trying to oust CIS troops.

7 CIS defense ministers sign ten out of eleven draft CIS military agreements. Ukraine and Azerbaijan do not initial documents concerning the creation of CIS common defense structures.

8 Rear Admiral Boris Kozhnin is appointed commander of the Ukrainian Navy.

8-9 The Ukrainian Parliament warns that Russia's moves against the Black Sea Fleet should be regarded "as an actual declaration of war against independent Ukraine."

9 Kravchuk suspends Ukrainian jurisdiction over the entire Black Sea Fleet.

9 Yeltsin suspends the decree calling for Russian jurisdiction over the Black Sea Fleet.

9 The Supreme Security Council of Moldova criticizes the Russian Congress of People's Deputies' resolution on the Dniester question as gross interference in the internal affairs of Moldova and a violation of the principles and norms of the UN Charter.

10-12 A cease-fire is declared. Observers arrive from Russia, Ukraine, Moldova, and Romania, and meet with the leaders of the Dniester Republic.

10-12 One thousand Azeri troops attack the village of Maraga in northern Nagorno-Karabakh and shell Stepanakert.

11 Dniester president Igor Smirnov issues a decree ordering all foreign armed formations to leave the territory of the left bank of the Dniester.

11 Belarus, Kazakhstan, Russia, and Ukraine fail to agree on how to implement START.

12 The Georgian State Council decrees the creation of a 20,000 man national army. Enlisted men will serve eighteen months.

13 The Estonian Supreme Council votes fifty-eight to five with fourteen abstentions to create a ministry of defense.

14 The Latvian Supreme Council debates over the continued presence of 120 former KGB members in the Latvian Ministry of Defense and the Latvian Ministry of Internal Affairs.

15 Azerbaijan and the CIS Main Naval Staff reach agreement on the division of the Caspian Sea Flotilla. The two sides agree that Azerbaijan and Russia would retain control of one quarter of the ships and facilities of the flotilla. The fate of the remaining 50 percent would be settled during negotiations with Kazakhstan and Turkmenistan.

16 Nazarbayev appoints Lieutenant General Anatoly Ryabtsev as head of the Kazakh National Guard. Ryabtsev, a Russian, is reportedly the commander of the 40th Army, currently based in Kazakhstan.

17 Krasnaia zvezda claims that Latvia is forming an eleven-ship navy manned by 1,000 sailors.

17 Ukrainian presidential advisor Nykola Mykhailchenko states that the transfer of tactical nuclear weapons from Ukraine to Russia has resumed.

17 The foreign ministers of Moldova, Russia, Ukraine, and Romania meet in Chisinau on the conflict in eastern Moldova. The ministers adopt recommendations on the disengagement of the forces in conflict, the disarming of irregular formations, and "maintaining the neutrality" and "defining the status" of Russia's 14th Army deployed in the area. The ministers also agree to set up three quadripartite bodies: a "group of military observers" to monitor the cease-fire, a "group of human rights rapporteurs," and a "mission of conciliation and mediation" to work out political solutions to the conflict.

18 Five Moldovan policemen are killed in two attacks in Bendery by Russian insurgents. Snegur warns that "the strategic aspirations of left-wing forces" in Russia [are] fanning the Dniester conflict [and] seeking to "drive a wedge between Moldova and Ukraine."

19 The Siberia Military District press center announces that servicemen can serve in areas of their choice.

20 Dniester President Igor Smirnov addresses the Russian 14th Army and calls for the creation of a 12,000-man Dniester National Army.

22 Lieutenant General Pavel Kozlovskii is appointed Belarusian defense minister. He was the first deputy commander and chief of staff of the Belarus Military District.

22 Ukraine again demands that it wants to be an equal party to Russia on START.

23 The CIS Military Committee for Personnel Work explores the reasons for 4,000 non-combat deaths over the last five years, one-fifth attributed to suicide.

23 Nazarbayev states that tensions between Russian and Ukraine over military issues is undermining CIS stability.

24 Head of the Russian Presidential Committee on Violence in Army Life Anatoly Alekseev claims that 300,000 Soviet soldiers have died since the end of WWII, many at the hands of their fellow servicemen.

25 Russian MVD troops withdrawal from South Ossetia. They had been in the region since December 1990.

25 Nazarbayev claims that each CIS member needs to build its own army but should maintain dual national and CIS control over these forces.

25 Latvia cuts off roads leading to the Baltic port of Liepaja where the CIS maintains a fleet of ships.

25 Karimov calls for each CIS state to build its own army but to maintain dual national and CIS control over these forces.

25 Niyazov claims that the CIS hardly exists and therefore fails to provide firm political control over the CIS Armed Forces. He also asserts that the Turkestan Military District ought to be disbanded, but suggests that the republic would be willing to negotiate with Russia over sharing the costs of funding the large troop contingent in Turkmenistan.

28 Latvia sends a diplomatic note to the US embassy in Riga describing a Libyan submarine undergoing repairs in Bolderaja.

28 CIS Naval Forces CinC Admiral Chernavin dismisses Black Sea Fleet officers who swear loyalty to Ukraine.

28 Kravchuk claims that all four CIS nuclear states and the US will sign START. Moreover, Kravchuk asserts that he wants security guarantees from the West against Russia.

28 Nazarbayev tells US President George Bush that Kazakhstan wants to sign a strategic alliance with the US.

28 Nine Russian government security guards are murdered in Kazan.

29 GRU chairman Colonel General Yevgeny Timokhin claims that his organization will be subordinated to the Russian government and not the CIS.

29 Latvian First Deputy Minister of Defense Dainis Turlajs accuses Russia of stalling on removing CIS troops from Latvian territory.

29 Israeli Minister of Defense Moshe Arens visits Latvia and meets with Latvian Foreign Minister Janis Jurkans and Latvian Minister of Defense Talavs Jundzis to discuss bilateral relations.

29 Landsbergis sends a telegram to Russian President Yeltsin demanding a halt in the transfer of new Russian troops to Lithuania. Troops are being flown to the military airports at Kazlu Ruda and Kedainiai, to which access by Lithuanian officials is barred.

30 Moldovan Minister of Defense Lieutenant General Ion Costas meets with the Swiss military attache in Moscow. The attache states that Switzerland "intends to establish links between the military institutions of the two countries with a view to strengthening Moldovan defense capabilities."

MAY

1 Unconfirmed reports suggest that Far Eastern Military District commander Colonel General Viktor Novozhilov is relieved of his command.

2 Nabiev orders the creation of a National Guard.

4 Russian Foreign Intelligence Agency chief Yury Kobaladze criticizes the West for attempts to force Russia to stop its intelligence activities abroad.

5 Russian State Secretary Gennadii Burbulis criticizes the US for pressuring Russia to halt a planned sale of booster rocket engines to India.

5 Thousands of Kumyks and Laks, many of them armed, confront each other in Karaman-Tyube, a locality a dozen kilometers north of Makhachkala.

5 Dniester Republican Guards blow up a highway bridge at Gura Bicului, east of Chisinau.

6 A train carrying the last shipment of tactical nuclear weapons from Ukraine arrives in Russia.

6 Azeri Minister of Defense Rahim Kaziev states that an agreement has been reached on the withdrawal of all CIS troops from Azerbaijan over a period of two years.

6 The former Belarusian Military District is liquidated.

7 Yeltsin decrees the creation of a separate Russian Army with himself as commander-in-chief.

7 Belarusian Minister of Defense Pavel Kozlovskii is promoted to colonel general and is assigned several deputies including former Belarusian Military District commander Colonel General Anatoly Kostenko and former Belarusian Minister of Defense Colonel General Petr Chaus.

7 Nazarbayev decrees that the Kazakh State Defense Committee is to be transformed into the Kazakh Ministry of Defense. Committee Chairman Sagadat Nurmagambetov is appointed Minister of Defense.

8 Tengiz Kitovani is appointed Georgian Minister of Defense. He replaces Lieutenant General Levan Sharashenidze.

8-9 Armenian forces launch an offensive and capture Shusha.

9 CIS Joint Armed Forces Command announces that Black Sea Fleet ships and submarines will no longer carry nuclear weapons.

10 Radio Erevan reports that forces of the Azeri Popular Front were engaged in military operations against Armenians in Nakhichevan.

11 Lithuanian Foreign Minister Algirdas Saudargas asks NATO to help force Russia to withdrawal CIS troops from the Baltics.

11 Latvia Foreign Minister Jaan Manitskii asks NATO to help force Russia to withdrawal CIS troops from the Baltics.

11 OMON is suspected in a bomb attack on a Latvian Home Guard armored vehicle and headquarters. No one is injured.

12 Nine people are killed as fighting continues along the Armenian-Azeri border, specifically in the Armenian town of Mardakert.

12 Fighting erupts in Kulyab. Six are killed.

13 Government and opposition forces agree on a plan to disarm persons possessing illegal firearms including the Tajik National Guard.

13 Georgian State Council chairman Eduard Shevardnadze and South Ossetian Parliament chairman Torez Kulumbegov meet and agree to a ceasefire.

13 CIS defense ministers meet in Tashkent and draft an appeal to the heads of state to preserve the joint armed forces during a transition to national armed forces.

13 The Ukrainian Ministry of Defense asks the Kiev patriarchate of the Ukrainian Autocephalous Church to prepare the first group of priests to serve the spiritual needs of the military.

14 An ammunitions dump explodes in Vladivostok. Sabotage is suspected.

15 The Azerbaijan Popular Front storms the parliament building in order to oust Mutalibov. One person is killed and several wounded. In addition the Front takes control of the Baku airport to prevent President Ayaz Mutalibov from leaving the country.

15 Ukraine takes control of long-range aviation formations and units deployed on its territory.

15 The summit of the CIS heads of state opens in Tashkent. Russia, Kazakhstan, Uzbekistan, Turkmenistan, Belarus, and Armenia are represented by their heads of state, the other five states by their premiers. Georgian State Council Presidium member Tengiz Sigua attends as an observer. Russia, Kazakhstan, Uzbekistan, Tajikistan, Kyrgyzstan, and Armenia sign a collective security agreement. Ukraine, Belarus, Azerbaijan, and Turkmenistan fail to sign due to disagreements. CIS states also agree on joint use of air space and the Baikonur and Plesetsk space launch facilities, the manning and financing of frontier troops, the formation of peacekeeping forces, and fulfilling the former USSR's obligations on chemical weapons.

16 Shooting erupts throughout Baku as the Azerbaijan Popular Front attacks Mutalibov supporters.

18 Armenian forces capture Lachin. Its fall signals the establishment of a land corridor from Armenia to Karabakh.

18 Nazarbayev arrives in the US for a five day state visit. While traveling to Washington the Kazakh president states that the CIS defense agreement signed in Tashkent on 15 May provides guarantees for Kazakh security and that his government will allow Russia to base its nuclear missiles in the country.

18 Army General Pavel Grachev is appointed Russian defense minister. He states that his primary task is the improvement of living conditions of Russian servicemen. More concretely, he asserts that the structure of the new Ministry of Defense will differ significantly from that of the old USSR ministry.

18-19 Some twenty-four people are killed and eighty-seven wounded during fighting in Dniester.

19 Russian Minister of Defense Pavel Grachev states that Russia will not withdraw its military forces from the Kurile Islands.

19 Nazarbayev meets with US President George Bush and promises to adhere to the START treaty.

19 Karimov claims that his country needs an army of 35,000 men.

19 Nakhichevan Foreign Minister Riza Abadov appeals to Turkey for arms to repel Armenian aggression.

19-20 Several units of Russia's 14th Army join the Dniester Republican Guards in military operations. Russian 14th Army commander Major General Yury Nekachev reportedly tells both Chisinau and Moscow that he has lost control over elements of his army.

20 Shaposhnikov warns against foreign intervention in the Nagorno-Karabakh dispute stating that it could lead to "a new world war."

20 The Russian Security Council meets for the first time. Rutskoi and the first deputy chairman of the parliament, Sergei Filatov, are appointed permanent members.

20 Snegur appeals to the populace for support against the Dniester forces. He claims that the integrity of the republic is "in mortal danger."

21 Russian Cossacks fly to the Russian 14th Army's airport in Tiraspol.

21 Commander of the Northwestern Group of Forces Colonel General Valery Mironov warns that a Dniester-type conflict could erupt in the Baltics.

22 Artillery fire continues between Armenia and Nakhichevan.

22 Russian defense minister Pavel Grachev asserts that he would not allow the honor and dignity of Russians to be insulted on the territory of any state.

22-23 Six soldiers of the Russian 14th Army are killed while attacking Moldovan positions.

23 Belarus, Kazakhstan, Russia, and Ukraine formally agree to the terms of the 1991 Strategic Arms Reduction Treaty (START).

23 Belarusian Defense Minister Petr Kozlovskii asserts that Belarus will reduce the military presence in the country. Sixty-two units will be disbanded before 1993 and up to 22,000 officers will retire in the next few years. The number of troops will be reduced by 40 percent, leaving 95,000 men.

24 Armenian officials meet with their counterparts from Azerbaijan and the US to discuss the conflict over Nagorno-Karabakh.

24 Estonian Border Defense Forces seize two military bases in Valga and near Tallinn.

24 A Gagauz detachment ambushes a Moldovan security detail which sought to stop a delivery of Alazan rockets to Gagauz militants. Two Moldovans are killed.

25 Armenia, Azerbaijan, Georgia, Moldova, Russia, and Ukraine announce to NATO how they will participate in the CFE treaty. Russia will keep 54 percent, Ukraine 27 percent, and Belarus 12 percent. Armenia, Azerbaijan, Georgia, and Moldova split the remaining seven percent.

25 Nazarbayev and Yeltsin sign a treaty on friendship, cooperation, and mutual aid in Moscow. The two countries agree to form a common military area with joint use of military installations and a common economic area. Both recognize the inviolability of each others borders.

26 CIS defense ministers meet in Moscow and agree on the composition of the CIS Strategic Forces. They will consist of the Strategic Rocket Forces, nuclear components from the Air Forces and the Navy, the ballistic-missile warning system and anti-missile defense systems, and space forces.

27 Yeltsin suggests that the Russian 14th Army will be removed from Moldova.

28 Russian 14th Army commander Major General Yury Nekachev opposes Russian President Boris Yeltsin's call to withdraw the army from Dniester. Nekachev expresses "doubt that the withdrawal would be easy to accomplish [because] more than half of the units' personnel consist of local inhabitants."

29 Dniester President Igor Smirnov asserts that he expects "soldiers and officers of the 14th Army to remain in the region and join the Dniester armed forces" in the event of the Russian 14th Army's withdrawal.

31 The Gagauz Republic Supreme Soviet appeals to Russia to include the Gagauz issue on the agenda for negotiations regarding the future of the Dniester region. The appeal states that "any attempt to ignore the will of the Gagauz people could lead to a large-scale conflict" and points out that there are now "three independent republics in place of the former Moldovan SSR."

JUNE

1 Akaev decrees that Kyrgyzstan assumes jurisdiction over military units stationed on its territory.

1 Russian defense minister Pavel Grachev accuses Moldova of inciting violence over the Dniester Republic. In addition, Grachev states that the withdrawal of Russian military units from the Caucasus, scheduled to begin that day, has been delayed at the request of the Armenian and Georgian governments.

1 Shaposhnikov announces his support of the 14th Army in Dniester because it is "under permanent attack by the Moldovans."

1 In a national address Snegur denounces "those who are trying to make Moldova into a base for continuing the imperial games of the former Union and its legal successor, Russia." While Moldova and other states "regarded the CIS as a means for discarding the former Soviet empire in a peaceful and civilized way, Moscow seeks to use the CIS as a new form of the USSR and to install pro-Moscow governments."

3 Estonia breaks off talks with Russia over the CIS military presence on Estonian territory.

3 Ossetian Popular Front (Ademon Nykhas) leader Alan Chochiev asserts that South Ossetia has a tactical nuclear warhead.

3 Yeltsin establishes a new commercial espionage agency attached to the office of the president.

4 Chechen President Dzhokhar Dudaev announces that the republic is determined to create a regular, national army numbering just over 7,000 men.

4 The Transcaucasus Military District press service denies that South Ossetia has a nuclear device.

4 The Moldovan defense ministry releases information documenting arms transfers from the Russian 14th Army to the Dniester Republican Guard.

5 Kravchuk names six generals, five of them Ukrainian, to top posts in the Ukrainian defense ministry. The new appointees are: Lieutenant General Ivan Bizhan, to first deputy defense minister; Lieutenant General Vasyl Sobkov, named chief of the Armed Forces Main Staff; Lieutenant General Anatoly Lopata, named deputy defense minister; Lieutenant General Ivan Oliinyk, named deputy defense minister for Armaments; Major General Oleksandr Ihnatenko, appointed deputy defense minister for Personnel and chief of the Personnel Directorate; and Lieutenant General

Mikhail Lopatin, named commander of Air Defense Forces. Lopatin is Belarusian.

5 Russian defense minister Pavel Grachev asserts that he would "answer any infringement upon the honor and dignity of the Russian population in any part of the CIS with the most resolute measures, right up to the dispatch of armed units."

6 Ukrainian defense minister Konstantin Morozov tells the Ukrainian Executive Committee of the Union of Officers that an order has been issued to remove from Ukraine over 6,000 officers who have failed to take the oath of loyalty to the republic.

8 Turkmenistan and Russia sign an agreement whereby Turkmenistan is to build its own armed forces on the basis of former Soviet units in the republic, but those forces would be controlled jointly by Russia and Turkmenistan. The protocol to the agreement calls for Moscow to retain control over certain air defense and air force units. Moscow will also provide some financing and technical supply during an unspecified transition period, while Turkmenistan will insure proper living conditions and supply for the military units.

8 The Russian foreign ministry and the Russian defense ministry protest the treatment of the military in the Baltics.

9 Twenty-eight people are killed in a rocket and shell attack on the South Ossetian capital of Tskhinvaki.

9 Twenty-one people are reported killed after two days of battles between supporters of Nabiev and a coalition of reformers and Muslim activists in Tajikistan.

10 Zheltoksan officials go on a hunger strike in Alma-Ata. They accuse the Kazakh authorities for repressing dissidents and giving up Kazakhstan's nuclear missiles.

10 Rahva Haal asserts that more Russian troops were being introduced into Latvia.

10 Yeltsin address the military high command. He calls for the creation of a Russian military big enough to protect a great nuclear power, supports the idea of strategic nuclear parity with the US, and hopes that Russia and Ukraine can work out their differences. Yeltsin also announces the appointment of Colonel General Viktor Dubynin as chief of staff of the Russian Army and first deputy defense minister. Dubynin's deputy will be Colonel General Mikhail Kolesnikov, while colonel generals Vladimir Toporov, Valery Mironov, and Georgy Kondratev are named deputy defense ministers.

11 Radio Lithuania reports that as of 1 January 1992, 34,852 officers and soldiers were stationed in the republic. At the present, there are about 180 military bases with about 68,000 hectares of land.

11 Georgian State Council Chairman Eduard Shevardnadze and Russian President Boris Yeltsin meet to discuss a settlement of the Ossetian conflict. A cease-fire is to start on 12 June 1992.

11 Kazakh soldiers mutiny in Arkhangelsk Oblast because they object to "having to serve in a foreign state."

12 Lieutenant General Leonid Kovalev is named commander of Russian forces in Poland. He had served as Odessa Military District chief of staff and had refused to take an oath of loyalty to Ukraine.

12 Azeri forces, including tanks and helicopter gunships, launch an attack on Armenian forces in Nagorno-Karabakh. Fifteen villages are recaptured but the fighting leaves hundreds dead.

12 Georgian guerrilla launch an artillery attack on Tskhinvaki killing thirteen people.

13 South Ossetian parliament chairman Oleg Teziev and Ossetian Popular Front leader Alan Chochiev are detained in North Ossetia for suspected involvement in an attack on a military depot.

13 A car bomb explodes outside the home of Georgian State Council Deputy Chairman and Mkhedrioni leader Dzhaba Ioseliani. Ioseliani is not hurt but seven other individuals are killed.

13 Nabiev attempts to create another Tajik National Guard.

13 CIS media reports that the Turkestan Military district will be disbanded by 30 June 1992. Kazakhstan, Kyrgyzstan, Turkmenistan, Tajikistan, and Uzbekistan fall within the district's supervision.

15 An ammunitions dump explodes in Kaliningrad Oblast killing one CIS naval officer.

15 Khasbulatov warns that Russia may try to neutralize Georgian units in South Ossetia.

15-18 Yeltsin arrives in the US. The Russian president and US President George Bush agree to make deep cuts in their countries' strategic nuclear weapons over the next decade, known as START II. The cuts will be in two stages: by the year 2000 each country would retain 3,800-4,250 nuclear warheads on strategic missiles, of which 1,000 could be on land-based missiles. The Russians would be allowed to keep roughly 600 warheads on so-called "heavy" missiles. These would be banned in the second stage, which would run until 2003. The total limit for this stage would be 3,000-3,500 missile warheads for each country. Finally, Yeltsin asks US President George Bush to "exert moral influence" on the IMF so it does not impose overly rigid conditions on Russia.

16-17 Fighting continues around Askeran district of Nagorno-Karabakh and Lachin.

16-18 The Coordinating Council of the CIS All-Army Officers Assembly meets in Moscow to discuss the need to protect the rights of servicemen.

17 Kravchuk endorses the US-Russian arms control accord but stresses that the agreement applies only to Russia.

17 Latvians commemorate the Red Army's invasion fifty-two years ago. Crowds call for the removal of Russian troops from Latvia.

18 Elite Kazakh troops clear the tent city in front of the Kazakh Supreme Soviet. No arrests are made.

18 Armenia and Azerbaijan reach a preliminary agreement at the CSCE-sponsored Karabakh peace talks in Rome to appeal for a cease-fire and to send international observers to the region.

18 The Dniester Republic begins to form its own army. The former deputy chief of staff of Russia's 14th Army, Colonel Stefan Kitsak, is promoted to major general, appointed defense minister, and formally instructed to form a Dniester army. Kitsak is an ethnic Romanian and a veteran of the Soviet invasions of Hungary, Czechoslovakia, and Afghanistan.

18 Two commanders are appointed to serve in the same position at the Sevastopol garrision where most of the Black Sea Fleet is moored. The Ukrainian defense ministry appoints Rear Admiral Boris Kozhin to oversee Ukrainian vessels while CIS Vice Admiral Vitally Larionov maintains his command over Russian ships.

18 Mkhedrioni deputy commander Tamaz Kurashvili is assassinated by a car bomb in Tbilisi.

19 Fighting continues in Bendery as Russian insurgents use armored vehicles to storm the last remaining police station.

20-21 Russian forces assist the Dniester Republican Guard and oust Moldovan forces from Bendery.

21 Shevardnadze blames Russia for the fighting in South Ossetia.

21 Kazakhstan is considering a draft defense budget of R19.1 bn for 1992 which is less than the R20.6 bn apportioned to Kazakhstan by the CIS military command. The budget allocates R825 mn for operations at the Baikonur space center and R974.8 mn for border troops.

21 Shaposhnikov states that Russian troops cannot be withdrawn from the Kurile Islands over the next years as claimed by Yeltsin.

22 Assistant commander of the Russian 14th Army Colonel Aleksandr Baranov states that "some" of the 5,000 Russian soldiers in the area participated in the fighting.

23 Ukrainian and Russian leaders hold a summit meeting in Dagomys. In military affairs, the accord restates Ukrainian and Russian adherence to CIS accords, consultations on implementing the START agreement and other international accords on limiting nuclear arms, and ratification of the CFE. Both countries attempt to defuse tensions surrounding control of the Black Sea Fleet by saying that both would get portions and contribute financial maintenance of the fleet.

24 In Georgia, Gamsakhurdia forces attack a CIS military base and seize arms, a tank, and occupy the Tbilisi TV tower. Four people are killed and twenty-six injured when the Georgian National Guard retakes the tower.

24 Shevardnadze, Yeltsin, and the leadership of North and South Ossetia meet in Sochi to sign a cease-fire agreement and the deployment of peace-keeping troops.

24 Abkhazian militants attack the Abkhaz Ministry of Internal Affairs and beat up Minister Givi Lominadze and two deputies.

25 Nabiev empowers the Ministry of Internal Affairs, National Security Committee, and the State Defense Committee to form military detachments to confiscate illegal weapons from armed groups.

25 An assembly of officers based in Tajikistan issues a statement that criticizes the decision by the republic's parliament to take control of military

units in Tajikistan. They argue that all military property and equipment in the republic should belong to Russia.

25 Russian defense minister Pavel Grachev tells ex-USSR military commanders in the Baltic states that they have the right to shoot if attacked.

27 Members of the Islamic opposition kill 34 people and wound 200 during an attack on a kolkhoz in Vakhsh district of Kurgan-Tyube Oblast.

28 Major General Aleksandr Lebed replaces Major General Yury Nekachev as head of the Russian 14th Army. Lebed immediately labels Moldova's actions as "genocide."

29 Colonel General Boris Gromov, the former commander of the Soviet 40th Army in Afghanistan and former USSR first deputy MVD chairman under Boris Pugo, is named a Russian deputy defense minister.

30 Armed gunmen fire on the Nurek hydroelectric station and damage the transformer.

JULY

1 Black Sea Fleet commander Igor Kasatonov states that Ukraine wants 90 percent of the disputed fleet while Russia is prepared to give Kiev only 22 percent of it.

1 Two are killed during a gun battle on the Tajik-Afghan border during the transfer of two grenade launchers, eleven pistols, nineteen grenades and two radio transmitters into Tajikistan.

1 Commander of the Russian 14th Army Major General Aleksandr Lebed claims Bendery as "an inalienable part of the Dniester Republic" and "the Dniester Republic itself a small part of Russia."

2 The Tallinn City Council votes to restrict the movements of Russian troops and equipment within city limits.

2 The Council of Russian Foreign Policy holds its first meeting. The council, which consists of various deputies, journalists, scientists and businessmen, seeks to protect the rights of Russians living in neighboring states. During the meeting Russian Foreign Minister Andrei Kozyrev, as well as top Americanist Georgy Arbatov, and former Yeltsin adviser Sergei Shakhrai, warn of a growing anti-government alliance.

2 Ukrainian Deputy Foreign Minister Boris Tarassuk announces that Ukraine's parliament had ratified the CFE treaty. Tarassuk also said that Ukraine would continue to maintain the second largest army in Europe, even after putting into effect the CFE-mandated reductions.

2 Security forces prevent a Birlik and Erk demonstration.

2-3 CIS defense ministers meet in Moscow. The meeting fails to remove tensions between Ukraine and Russia over administrative control of nuclear weapons on Ukrainian territories. However, agreements on anti-missile defense and control over space projects, air defense, and on a council of collective security are signed.

3 Yeltsin and Moldovan President Mircea Snegur meet in Moscow. The two presidents agree in principle to a cease-fire, creation of a demarcation corridor between the forces, the introduction of "neutral" peacekeeping forces, the granting of a "political status" to the left bank of the Dniester

by the Moldovan Parliament and, ultimately, bilateral negotiations on withdrawing Russia's 14th Army from Moldova.

4 Georgian, Russian, and North and South Ossetian negotiators meet in Vladikavkaz and agree to withdraw all armed forces from South Ossetia and to create a peacekeeping force of 500 troops.

4 Landsbergis and National Defense Minister Audrius Butkevicius participate in ceremonies in Klaipeda formally inaugurating the activities of the Lithuanian Coastal Defense.

4 Commander of the Russian 14th Army Major General Aleksandr Lebed asserts that he "can no longer regard Moldova's President as a legitimate president" as he has "created a fascist state."

6 The CIS heads of state meets in Moscow. They agree in principle to create peacekeeping forces consisting of 2,000 to 10,000 soldiers with their first assignment to enforce and monitor a cease-fire in Moldova. Ukraine's demands on administrative control over nuclear forces fails to be solved. The participants agree to restructure the CIS Border Forces by dismissing CIS Border Forces CinC Ilya Kalinichenko and establishing a CIS Council of Commanders of Border Forces. In a personnel move Colonel General Boris Piankov is confirmed as CIS deputy commander.

6 Shaposhnikov announces that the main functions of the CIS commander is centralized control over strategic nuclear arms, coordination of military doctrines and military reforms of CIS member states, and the settling of armed conflicts both in side the CIS and on its periphery. The CIS command will have 300 military and 100 civilian employees and will be subordinate to the CIS heads of state. The CIS command will also manage meetings of the CIS Council of Defense Ministers. The council will have a committee for coordinating nuclear strategy and a secretariat.

6 Three hundred Gamsakhurdia supporters blow up two rail bridges and attack Mkhedrioni headquarters in Tsalendzhika where Dzhaba Ioseliani met with his units. Six people are killed.

7 Russian Ground Forces commander-in-chief Colonel General Vladimir Semenov arrives in Moldova to arrange a cease-fire. Moldovan First Deputy Minister of Defense Pavel Creanga, Dniester Republican Guard commander Stefan Kitsak, and Semenov sign the agreement. The agreement provides for an immediate and unconditional cease-fire; the redeployment of all armored vehicles, artillery, rocket launchers, and mine and grenade throwers to designated locations behind the front lines; the withdrawal of snipers and the recall of covert operations units to their barracks; the wide dissemination of these orders through the mass media; and the creation of joint groups of monitors from Moldova's Ministry of Defense, the Dniester National Guard, Russia's 14th Army, and Russia's Ministry of Defense. The cease-fire is not part of the multilateral peacemaking operation initiated by the CIS.

8 CIS Black Sea Fleet commander Admiral Igor Kasatonov accuses Ukraine of violating the Dagomys agreement by resubordinating a marine regiment from the fleet to the Odessa Military District.

8 High-ranking representatives of Russia's ministries of defense and security, reacting to recent statements by Foreign Minister Andrei Kozyrev and others, deny that they are planning a coup.

8 The Russian Supreme Soviet ratifies the CFE Treaty.

8 The Russian Supreme Soviet authorizes the use of Russian troops in Moldova.

8 One person is killed, two wounded, and eighteen captured during a gun battle on the Tajik-Afghan border. Chief of the Central Asian Border District Boris Gribanov asserts that the violators are all residents of Kurgan-Tyube Oblast and had undergone military training in Afghanistan.

8 Kazakhstan signs the 1975 Helsinki Final Act.

8 Kyrgyzstan signs the 1975 Helsinki Final Act.

9 Georgian Deputy Prime Minister Aleksandr Kavsadze is kidnapped after his car is blown up.

9 The Russian, Moldovan and Dniester military observers find that Dniester forces have not complied with the cease-fire agreement.

9 Snegur calls for CSCE peacekeeping mechanisms in Moldova.

9 The Russian government announces that sixteen regions in the country will be closed to foreigners. Foreigners will not be permitted to travel without special permission from the Ministry of Security to the Kamchatka peninsula, the city of Komsomolsk on Amur, the island of Russkii in Primorie, several districts in Moscow and St. Petersburg. The regions of Orenburg, Nizhegorod, Arkhangelsk, Murmansk, Ekaterinburg, Cheliabinsk, Kaliningrad, Volgograd, Astrakhan, Krasnoiarsk, Mordovia and some other districts are also restricted.

9 Yeltsin issues a presidential decree entrusting the secretary of the Russian Security Council, Yury Skokov, with special powers to implement the council's decisions and presidential decrees on security issues.

9 In Kurgan-Tyube Oblast, the main highway passes from the control of rival fighting groups to that of the republican OMON and residents of the Kurgan Tyube and Kulyab oblasts turn in over 120 firearms to interior ministry authorities.

10 Armenia, Azerbaijan, Belarus, Georgia, Kazakhstan, Russia and Ukraine sign the CFE agreement.

10 Director of the CIS Naval Press Service Captain Valery Novikov warns that CIS naval personnel are very upset over delays in receiving their pay. R1.5 bn had yet to be distributed.

11 CIS Black Sea Fleet commander Igor Kasatonov and Ukrainian Naval commander-in-chief Boris Kozhin meet in Sevastopol to sign an agreement that neither side will take unilateral actions.

11 A Black Sea Fleet naval infantry unit seizes the military commandant's office of the Sevastopol garrison and forcibly remove the Ukrainian commander.

11-12 Fighting intensifies between Armenia and Azerbaijan. Armenian forces kill thirty Azeris in the Mardakert region of Nagorno-Karabakh.

13 A delegation from the French defense ministry General Staff holds a meeting in Vilnius with Landsbergis, Foreign Minister Algirdas Saudargas, and National Defense Minister Audrius Butkevicius to discuss the creation of closer ties between the military of the two states. A group of Lithuanian officers will study at the French War Academy.

14 Estonian and Russian military forces exchange gunfire when a Russian vehicle fails to stop at an inspection post.

14 Russian and US arms-control experts release a statement indicating that the two sides will continue to work together toward creating a joint global system of defense against ballistic missiles.

14 The Turkmen Cabinet of Ministers begins formation of the republic's armed forces. The cabinet also moves to create a national guard, with an initial strength of 1,000.

14 Five hundred Russian and 350 Georgian troops move into South Ossetia as peacekeepers.

15 A Russian parliamentary investigation of the Russian Ministry of Security results in a purge of 2,000 employees.

15 Yeltsin signs a decree drafting thousands of officers from the army and the ministries of the interior and security to work in tax investigation bodies.

16 CIS foreign and defense ministers meet in Tashkent to discuss deploying peace-keeping forces within the CIS.

16 Kazakh state advisor Tulegen Zhukeev and defense minister General Sagadat Nurmagambetov meet with a delegation from the US defense department in Alma-Ata. Nurmagambetov emphasizes that all strategic nuclear weapons on Kazakh territory will be dismantled on schedule.

16 A NATO delegation visits Kyrgyzstan.

16 Lithuanian Deputy Prime Minister Zigmas Vaisvila sends a telegram to Lieutenant General Fedor Melnichuk, first deputy commander of the Northwest Group of Forces, asking that Russian military exercises in Lithuania planned for the second half of July 1992 be canceled since they are in violation of Lithuania's sovereignty.

16 Moldovan defense minister Major General Ion Costas and national security minister Anatol Plugaru are released from the posts.

16 Niyazov issues a decree approving alternative service on important construction sites for military conscripts who have valid reasons for refusing military service.

17 Uzbekistan, Afghanistan, and Pakistan hold their first trilateral trade meeting in Islamabad. The meeting focuses on agreements for transport links between the three states, including measures to repair roads destroyed in the Afghan war.

18 Tajik Supreme Soviet acting head Akbarsho Iskanderov visits Afghanistan in an attempt to seek Afghan help in stopping the flow of weapons into Tajikistan.

20 Over 1,000 national guards in Tashkent swear allegiance to Uzbekistan. Duties will include preventing terrorist actions, freeing kidnapped prisoners, guarding important economic installations, and dealing with natural disasters.

20 Belarus and Russia sign a military cooperation agreement which covers both conventional and nuclear weapons.

20 Ukrainian National Security Service chief Yevhen Marchuk and Russian Minister of Security Viktor Barannikov sign documents on cooperation of their international and regional activities.

21 Estonia proposes that Russia withdrawal its border guards to the frontier set in the 1920 Tartu Peace Treaty.

21 Deputy chairman of the Kyrgyz State Committee on National Security Valery Verchagin reveals that the committee has begun to develop the main principles of Kyrgyz national security. While Kyrgyz priorities focus mainly on relations with major regional powers such as China, Turkey, Iran, and Pakistan, the committee also takes into account the interests of the US and Russia. The committee, which was formally the republican KGB, concerns itself with preventing terrorism, investigating corruption, and the narcotics trade.

21 Yeltsin criticizes the Russian military of corruption and abuse of office.

21 Russian Minister of Defense Pavel Grachev states that Russian troops will be trained as peacekeeping troops over the next several years for possible deployment both with UN peacekeeping forces and with proposed CIS peacekeeping units.

21 A frigate from the Black Sea Fleet with a rebellious crew bolts from a training exercise at its home port of Donuzlav, raises the Ukrainian flag, and sets sail without permission for Odessa.

22 The Russian defense ministry Press Center announces that the Volga-Ural Military District, joined in September 1989, again is split into separate administrative units.

22 Kurgan-Tyube Oblast officials demand that Nabiev declare a state of emergency in the oblast and request that a CIS peacekeeping force be sent to the region to stop fighting motivated by political, religious and inter-clan disputes.

23 Ukraine and Russia agree to the creation of a parliamentary commission to supervise observance of the Dagomys agreement and another on cooperation between the Russian and Ukrainian commanders of the Black Sea Fleet.

24 The Russian government decrees that Russian defense firms will be issued licenses by the Ministry for Economic Relations for the export of arms components to other countries, including those in the CIS.

24 Turkmenistan and Russia sign a protocol on border troops.

26 Except in the Black Sea Fleet and the Caspian Sea Flotilla, CIS naval ships begin to fly the Russian naval flag.

27 Belarusian First Deputy Prime Minister Mikhail Miasnikovich states that Belarus intends to sell surplus arms abroad.

27 CIS Naval commander-in-chief Admiral Vladimir Chernavin becomes Russian Naval commander-in-chief and a member of the Russian Ministry of Defense Collegium. Chernavin asserts that the Baltic Fleet would remain in the Baltic, and that the fleet command hoped to secure bases in Tallinn, Estonia, and in Liepaja, Latvia, as well as several other places.

27 The Russian General Staff submits to the Supreme Soviet a document calling for a freeze in proposed troop reductions on the Kurile Islands.

27 Russian Security Council secretary Yury Skokov rejects coup attempt rumors.

27 A cease-fire is announced after a meeting in Khorog between leaders of Tajikistan's political parties, the armed bands that have been fighting in the country's southern regions, members of the clergy, and leaders of all the country's regions.

28 Shushkevich states that Russian troops numbering about 30,000 will remain in Belarus for seven years.

28 The flagship of the Ukrainian Navy, the 6,000-ton *Slavutich,* is launched at Nikolaev.

29 Azerbaijan and Russia sign a two-year cooperation agreement on guarding Azerbaijan's southern borders with Iran and Turkey.

29 The Lithuanian government confirms the existence of a Russian government decree dated 9 July 1992 which authorizes the sale to Lithuania of small arms and ammunition for $52.4 mn to be paid in rubles or in exchange for food and consumer goods.

29 Russian, Moldovan, and Dniester units take up peacekeeping positions throughout Moldova.

30 First Deputy Chief of the Russian General Staff Colonel General Mikhail Kolesnikov warns that the breakup of the USSR has rallied the NATO alliance and encouraged it to build closer ties with former Warsaw Pact members and with several former Soviet republics. Kolesnikov asserts that growing instability could lead to direct intervention by Western powers in the former USSR under the pretext of establishing international control over nuclear weapons.

30 Russian Minister of Defense Pavel Grachev orders that Russian officers are entitled to shoot to kill in cases of arbitrary actions against themselves or army installations.

30 Russia and the US sign an agreement in which Washington will provide up to $25 mn for the destruction of Russian chemical weapons.

31 Russian TV reports that Ukraine is willing to offer nineteen high-performance TU-160 Blackjack bombers for sale at an estimated price of $13 mn each.

AUGUST

- Russian General Aleksandr Vladimirov claims that President Boris Yeltsin has lost control over the military.
- Two Ukrainian soldiers are killed while serving as UN peacekeepers in Bosnia.
- Shooting erupt between Uzbek border guards and Afghans.
2 Azerbaijan plans to send eighty soldiers to Turkey for military training.
2 Thirty Russian soldiers attack Estonian guards at the Narva River border crossing.

2 Officers celebrating Russian Airborne Forces Day cause disturbances in a number of Russian and Ukrainian cities, including Moscow, Tyumen, and Kiev.

2 Tajik Democratic Party chairman Shodmon Yusupov claims that CIS troops stationed in Tajikistan have interfered in the country's civil war.

3 Latvian Supreme Council deputy chairman Andrejs Krastins requests that Russia withdraw its intelligence network from the country.

3 Yeltsin and Ukrainian President Leonid Kravchuk meet in Mukhalatka and agree on the main points of a prospective treaty on friendship, cooperation and partnership between their two states. The two leaders also agree to place the disputed Black Sea Fleet under joint control for a three-year interim period.

4 The Estonian Supreme Council shortens the term of compulsory military served from 18 to 12 months due to economic burdens faced by the state.

4 Kazakhstan's Supreme Soviet Committee for National Security and Defense deputy chairman Sergei Subbotin expresses doubt as to how far the agreement reached by Yeltsin and Kravchuk to remove the Black Sea Fleet from the jurisdiction of the CIS command corresponds to the general position of the CIS countries.

4 Russian foreign minister Andrei Kozyrev denounces his critics and rejects the so-called Eurasian line in foreign policy.

5 Georgian Border Forces commander Colonel Otar Gumberidze states that Georgia expects to complete the creation of its border forces by May 1994.

5 Russia and Azerbaijan agree to transfer 30 percent of the Caspian Sea Flotilla to Azerbaijan.

5 Employees of Tajikistan's National Security Committee declare their intent to stage a sit-down strike if Nabiev does not withdraw a decree removing Committee chairman Alizhon Solibaev.

6 The presidium of the Belarusian Parliament claims that the Yalta agreement between Russia and Ukraine on the Black Sea Fleet violates CIS agreements.

6 The Uzbek Law on Defense is released. The law rejects military action as a means of settling disputes and rejects any territorial claims on any other states. It describes Uzbekistan as "aspiring to neutrality," which corresponds with the decision to join the non-aligned movement. Uzbekistan will not produce, acquire, or station nuclear weapons on its territory. The law states that the Uzbek Armed Forces will be built according to the principle of reasonable sufficiency and that in case of martial law the president will serve as commander-in-chief.

7 Rutskoi addresses the Council of Atamans and suggests that the Cossacks form their own military units on contract.

8 Chairman of the Russian Supreme Soviet Committee of International Affairs, Yevgeny Ambartsumov, calls for the development of a Russian foreign policy doctrine similar to the US Monroe Doctrine.

9 Rumors circulate again about Tajikistan selling enriched uranium. Apparently Tajik businessmen are planning to sell enriched uranium abroad to

representatives of various states, including Saudi Arabia, Iraq, Iran, Turkey, and Pakistan.

10 Yeltsin signs a law which closes all regions of the country involved in developing, producing, storing or utilizing weapons of mass destruction, processing radioactive materials, and accommodating military or other facilities.

11 Eleven security officials including Georgian interior minister Roman Gventsadze are kidnapped in Zugdidi.

11 Niyazov decrees that all former Soviet Border Forces are now under Turkmenistan's jurisdiction. Major General Akmurad Kabulov is named commander of the Turkmen Border Forces.

12 CIS high command representative Colonel Vasily Volkov announces that a protocol on procedures for using CIS peacekeeping forces is signed. Azerbaijan, Belarus, Ukraine, and Turkmenistan reportedly did not sign the protocol.

12 Moldovan and Russian delegates begin to discuss the status of Russia's troops in Moldova. These cover the 14th Army and the 300th Paratroop Regiment in Chisinau.

13 Nagorno-Karabakh declares a state of emergency and orders the mobilization of men aged 18-45.

13 CIS Lieutenant General Valery Manilov states that the CIS high command has rejected the introduction of peacekeeping forces in Armenia and Azerbaijan.

13 Georgian National Guard units begin searching for kidnapped officials.

14 Nineteen people are killed when the Georgian National Guard engages in battles with Abkhaz MVD troops in Sukhumi.

14 Russian 14th Army commander Major General Aleksandr Lebed addresses the Council of Atamans of Russian Cossack Hosts and calls for "the revival of the Russian great-power state."

14 All kidnapped Georgian officials except three are released.

15 Russian defense minister Pavel Grachev sends a telegram to the Georgian and Abkhaz leadership calling on them to guarantee the safety of Russian troops stationed in Abkhazia.

15 Ukrainian Deputy Defense Minister for Armaments Lieutenant General Ivan Oleinyk states that 2,450 tanks, 2,220 armored combat vehicles, and large caliber artillery pieces are scheduled to be destroyed at factories in Zhitomir, Kiev, Lvov, Nikolaev, and Kharkov according to the CFE treaty.

16 Black Sea Fleet ships begin to evacuate 1,700 Russians from Sukhumi.

16 A Russian paratroop regiment is sent from Gyandzha in Azerbaijan to Sukhumi to protect Russian military facilities and help evacuate Russian vacationers and the families of Russian troops.

17 Shevardnadze announces that Georgia had reasserted its authority over Abkhazia.

17 In Osh, the chairman of the Kyrgyz Supreme Soviet's State Defense Committee, Major General Janybek Umetaliev, and Uzbek defense minister Lieutenant General Rustam Akhmedov sign a protocol on cooperation in military affairs.

17 Dniester National Guard elements volunteer to fight in Serbia against Bosnia.
18 The CIS Armed Forces Committee of the Chiefs of Staff meets in Moscow. Chiefs of staff and deputy defense ministers from member states except Moldova participated.
18 Georgian National Guard troops under defense minister Tengiz Kitovani storm the Abkhazian parliament building.
18 Nazarbayev decrees the formation of Kazakh Border Troops. Kazakhstan also assumes jurisdiction over the former Dzerzhinskii Higher School for Border Troops in Alma-Ata which, along with Kazakhstan's border troops, will be subordinate to the republic's National Security Committee (former KGB) rather than to the military.
19 Abkhaz parliament chairman Vladislav Ardzinba retreats to Gudauta with 1,500 Abkhaz National Guard.
19 Abkhaz parliament chairman Vladislav Ardzinba and Georgian state council member Ivlian Khaindrava agree on a withdrawal plan.
20 Russian chief of the General Staff General Viktor Dubinin states that Kazakh and Russian officials reached agreement on keeping Russian nuclear weapons in Kazakhstan for seven more years. Dubinin states that this allows the Russian military to continue using the Emba and Sary-Shagan test sites.
20 Russian foreign minister Andrei Kozyrev defends Moscow's policy towards the Yugoslav conflict and rejects nationalists who argue that Russia support Serbia due to the "infamous Slavic factor."
20 Chief of the Russian General Staff General Viktor Dubinin states that Russian and Kazakh officials have reached agreement on keeping Russian strategic nuclear weapons in Kazakhstan for seven more years.
20-21 Georgian troops withdraw from Sukhumi.
22 Yeltsin makes Russian military appointments: Colonel General Vladimir Semenov, CinC of Ground Forces; Colonel General Igor Sergeev, CinC of Strategic Forces; Admiral Feliks Gromov, CinC of Naval Forces; Colonel General Viktor Prudnikov, CinC of Air Defense Forces. Semenov and Prudnikov are already serving in similar roles in the CIS military command.
22-23 Thirty-five people are killed and over 100 wounded in two Azeri air raids on Stepanakert.
23 The Georgian State Council orders preparations for mobilization to counter insurgencies from the Confederation of Mountain Peoples.
24 An anti-tank missile is fired into the apartment of Georgian Defense Minister Tengiz Kitovani.
24 The Russian Security Council states that Russia will take steps to end the Abkhaz conflict.
24-25 Forty Georgian troops and five Abkhaz are killed near Sukhumi and Gagra. Two more are killed during an exchange of prisoners.
25 Russian defense minister Pavel Grachev meets with PRC defense minister Qin Jiwei in Moscow to discuss force reductions in East Asia and the Pacific.

26 Three are killed when Abkhazians attack the Sukhumi railway station.

26 Moldovan defense minister Major General Pavel Creanga and Russian defense minister Pavel Grachev sign an agreement to withdraw the 300th Paratroop Regiment from Chisinau.

27 Three are killed when a hydrofoil comes under attack from an unmarked helicopter in Georgian territorial waters.

27 The Russian Prosecutor General's office initiates criminal proceedings against the Confederation of Mountain Peoples for "terrorist acts."

27 Yeltsin issues a decree transforming the Transcaucasus Military District into the Group of Russian Troops in Transcaucasia with headquarters in Tbilisi.

27 Five members of the Democratic Party of Tajikistan are gunned down in their offices and three members of Lali Badakhshan are killed in their homes.

29 An assassination attempt is made on Elchibey. A Kamaz truck driver attempted to ram Elcheibey's police escort.

29 Abkhaz parliament chairman Vladislav Ardzinba and Georgian defense minister Tengiz Kitovani sign a cease-fire agreement in Sochi. The agreement fails to take hold.

30 Dozens are killed in fighting between Abkhazian and Georgian forces near Gagra. Simultaneously, an "unidentified" warship shells Georgian troops from the Black Sea.

30 Georgian groups launch an attack on Gudauta, the headquarters of Abkhaz parliament chairman Vladislav Ardzinba.

31 CIS military observers from Russia, Kazakhstan, and Kyrgyzstan travel to southern Tajikistan to assess the civil war within the country.

31 The CIS Joint Armed Forces Chief Command is formally established.

31 US President George Bush announces that the US and Russia had initialed an agreement to ensure that highly enriched uranium from dismantled nuclear weapons would be used only for peaceful purposes.

31 A group of opposition demonstrators raid the Tajik presidential palace and hold government employees and members of the president's staff hostage.

SEPTEMBER

2 A mass rally and military parade is held in Tiraspol on the second anniversary of the "Dniester Soviet Socialist Republic."

3 CIS Council of Defense Ministers meets in Moscow. Russia and Ukraine continue to argue over administrative control of nuclear weapons. Ukraine insists that the strategic forces on its territory should be under the jurisdiction and control of the Ukrainian Ministry of Defense.

3 Yeltsin, Shevardnadze, Abkhaz parliament leader Vladislav Ardzinba, and representatives of the peoples of the North Caucasus sign a cease-fire agreement in Moscow. A tripartite commission is formed to implement the agreement.

3 The presidents of Uzbekistan, Kazakhstan, Kyrgyzstan, and Russia issue a warning to the government and political groups of Tajikistan labeling the civil war in that country a danger to the CIS, and announcing that

Russia and the Central Asian states intend to intervene. The statement mentions dangers such as the large-scale smuggling of arms from Tajikistan's southern neighbors.

3   The Tajik Supreme Soviet's presidium and its Cabinet of Ministers issues a statement declaring no confidence in Nabiev and removes him from power.

3   Tajik Minister of Internal Affairs Mamadaez Navzhuvanov resigns.

4   Kulyab Oblast Soviet deputy chairman Sasiddin Sangov is found dead.

5   Russian Foreign Intelligence Service leader Yevgeny Primakov declares that "Russia has no interest in leaving its borders open so that they can be crossed by gangs carrying weapons and drugs" in Central Asia.

5   Several hundred people are killed in Kurgan-Tyube.

5-6   Fifteen people are killed in Gudauta and Gagra as Georgian troops withdraw from Abkhazia.

7   Four Georgian soldiers are killed and twenty-nine wounded in three separate clashes in Abkhazia and a major railway line was destroyed by an explosion near Ochamchire.

8   Shevardnadze accuses Abkhazia of violating the cease-fire agreement and asserts that Abkhazia has no control over its armed forces.

8   Latvian Supreme Council deputy Mihails Stepicevs accuses Russia of trying to drive a wedge between the Baltic states by holding separate talks with each one over troop withdrawals.

8   The Dniester Republic Supreme Soviet approves the establishment of the Dniester Air Force.

8   Ukrainian parliament chairman Ivan Plyushch leads a delegation to Washington to meet with US Secretary of Defense Dick Cheney, National Security Adviser Brent Scowcroft, and other US officials.

8   Karimov appeals to UN Secretary General Butros-Ghali that unrest in Tajikistan could lead to more tension throughout the region.

9   Another assassination attempt is made on Elchibey.

9   The tripartite commission formed to implement the 3 September cease-fire meets in Sukhumi to sign a new cease-fire agreement but fails to reach agreement on disbanding the Abkhaz National Guard.

10   The fifth round of CSCE-sponsored Karabakh preparatory peace talks end in Rome without reaching an agreement.

10   CIS troops from Russia, Kazakhstan, Kyrgyzstan, and Uzbekistan take up positions on the Tajik-Afghan border.

11   US state department officials assert that Russia has refused arms inspectors access to military facilities under the CFE Treaty.

11   Seven people are killed in a shoot-out between guards on the Tajik-Afghan border and a group of Tajiks returning from Afghanistan.

12-13   Dozens of Azeris and Armenians are killed in heavy fighting in the Armenian-controlled Lachin corridor that links Nagorno-Karabakh with Armenia.

12-16   Georgian and Abkhazian troops engage in battle near Gagra. Many are killed and dozens injured.

14 Army General Konstantin Kobets is named chief military inspector of the Russian Armed Forces.

16 Ukrainian parliamentarians indicate that Ukraine may retreat on pledges to transfer ballistic missiles to Russia.

17 The Russian defense ministry warns that Russian forces reserve the right to fight back if attacked.

17 Kulyab Oblast authorities appeal to Central Asian leaders and Russia to send CIS troops to stop the fighting in Tajikistan.

17 Ukrainian Minister of Defense Konstantin Morozov states that Kiev intends to build two operational commands based on the three existing military districts in Ukraine. He also asserts that a new service, the Air Defense Troops, would be formed by combining the Air Force and Air Defense Forces.

18 Azerbaijan launches an offensive against Armenian units in Nagorno-Karabakh and advance to within ten kilometers of Stepanakert.

18 The Georgian defense ministry demands a part of the former Soviet Air Force and Navy.

18-20 Fighting rages in rural areas of Kurgan-Tyube Oblast and Dushanbe. A thousand people seize seven buses in the capital to join the fighting in Kurgan-Tyube. Two columns of trucks are sent to Kulyab Oblast with food because there is a danger of starvation.

19 In Sochi the defense ministers of Armenia, Azerbaijan, Georgia, and Russia sign an agreement on a cease-fire in Nagorno-Karabakh. Observers from Armenia, Azerbaijan, Georgia, Ukraine, Belarus, and Kazakhstan will monitor the cease-fire.

19 A bus carrying Georgian troops is blown up near Gagra. Six are killed.

20 Georgian defense minister Tengiz Kitovani meets with Russian defense minister Pavel Grachev in Sochi to review the work of the tripartite commission.

22 The Russian Navy receives new appointments. Admiral Valentin Selivanov, formerly commander of the Leningrad naval base, is appointed chief of the main staff. Vice admirals Georgy Gurinov and Vasily Eremin are appointed deputy commanders. Vice Admiral Aleksandr Gorbunov is appointed deputy commander for combat readiness.

23 Georgian, Russian, and South Ossetian negotiators sign a new cease-fire agreement.

23 Nazarbayev visits France for a three day visit. He signs the CSCE Charter.

25 Shaposhnikov confirms that CIS nuclear missiles still target the US.

25 The Russian government claims to have halted the sale of three Kilo-class diesel submarines to Iran due to US pressure.

27 Armed groups from Kulyab seize four tanks, an armored transporter, and an armored car from Russian forces stationed in Kurgan-Tyube, and capture five members of the Russian unit.

27 Kurgan-Tyube City Council chairman Nurali Kurbanov claims that hundreds of people, including the city's chief law enforcement official, are

killed in an attack on the city by Tajik forces loyal to deposed President Nabiev.

28 Landsbergis addresses the UN General Assembly. The speech focuses on the need for the Russian military to leave the Baltic states.

28 Ten Russian soldiers oust unarmed Lithuanian soldiers from a building in Kaunas. The Russians later leave the building, but three unarmed officers remained on the second floor. The first floor is controlled by Lithuanian troops.

28 Russian defense budget figures are released. Expenditures total between R1.55 and 1.65 trillion in July 1992 prices compared to R632 bn in 1992. The increase is due to personnel and housing construction costs. Procurement spending is set at R170 bn.

29 Shaposhnikov warns European countries against interfering in talks between CIS states over nuclear weapons control.

29 Latvian Minister of State Janis Dinevics and Deputy Minister of Interior Martins Virsis protest against Russia using Latvian territory for "submarine trade" to Iran and Libya.

30 In Krasnaia zvezda Shaposhnikov calls for Russian supervision over CIS nuclear weapons. In addition, the CIS CinC asserts that the US wants to create a "unipolar world" and calls for CIS to play a role between the North and the South.

30 Reports indicate that leaders of the opposing sides in Tajik civil war say they only control 20 percent of their forces.

OCTOBER

• Azerbaijan deploys tanks and armored cars along its border with Iran.

1 Black Sea Fleet commander-in-chief Admiral Igor Kasatonov is reassigned as Russian Navy first deputy commander-in-chief.

1 Abkhazia announces that the withdrawal of fighters from the Confederation of Mountain Peoples of the North Caucuses has been halted because of continued Georgian attacks.

1 Kravchuk rejects CIS Marshal Yevgeny Shaposhnikov's call for increased Russian control over nuclear weapons.

2 Dniester Republic president Igor Smirnov appoints Colonel Stanislav Khazheev as Minister of Defense. In addition, further decrees raise the age limit for officers serving with the Dniester forces from fifty to sixty years of age. Smirnov discloses that Dniester forces are currently comprised of 35,000 men.

2 3,000-4,000 Abkhaz national guardsmen and volunteers from the North Caucusus capture the town of Gagra after heavy fighting. One hundred people are killed.

3 The Georgian State Council votes to seize all former Soviet military equipment on Georgian territory.

3 Shevardnadze's helicopter is fired upon as he travels to Sochi for talks with Russian military officials.

4 Russian defense minister Pavel Grachev warns Georgia that attempts to take control of Russian military equipment would be repelled by force.

5   Two Russian naval vessels arrive in the Persian Gulf to participate in the international peacekeeping duties.

6   President Lennart Meri calls for a "rapid, orderly and complete" withdrawal of foreign military forces from Estonian territory.

6   The Latvian Ministry of Defense criticizes the Association for the Defense of Veterans Rights and claims that it "cannot be assessed as anything other than interference by the Russian Army in Latvia's internal affairs."

6   Yeltsin announces that the government has increased MVD personnel by 50,000 men and proposes using the Army to combat crime.

6-7   The CIS defense ministers meet in Bishkek.

7   Ukraine deploys National Guard units in the Crimea.

7   Georgia accuses Russia of sending T-72 and T-80 tanks to Abkhazia.

8   Landsbergis states that the withdrawal of Russian troops from Lithuania has proceeded in an orderly manner. He places importance on the removal of the 107th Division from Vilnius. He asserts, however, that some Russian military leaders spoke of instructions from Moscow to postpone the handing over of installations.

8-9   A CIS summit is held in Bishkek where a join session of the heads of state and heads of government occurs. On the issue of nuclear weapons control, Belarus and Kazakhstan agree to hand over their launch codes to Russia and to dismantle their weapons within three years. Ukraine refuses to go along with this idea. Moreover, a CIS draft treaty on defense and collective security is signed except by Moldova and Ukraine. It calls for members to defend each other from external threats. Finally, in a personnel move, General Yury Maksimov is removed from his position as CIS CinC for Strategic Rocket Forces. No replacement is named.

8-9   Twenty percent of the population in Sukhumi flees as Abkhazian forces prepare to engage Georgian militia.

11   Abkhazian troops open fire on a Georgian helicopter killing two Georgian civilians.

12   Azerbaijan and Russia sign an agreement on mutual security and friendship.

12   Russian border troops seize *Solo,* a Greenpeace ship, near Novaia Zemlia.

13   Shushkevich states that Belarus will eliminate all its nuclear weapons in two and a half years. Kebich dismisses two lieutenant generals for "abuse of power" and "failure to manage military property." Three deputy defense ministers reportedly are also severely reprimanded and several top posts are eliminated.

13   The Russian Navy rejects Georgian charges that it has violated its territorial waters.

13   Uzbekistan offers to send military troops to Tajikistan.

14   A closed session of the Kyrgyz Parliament votes against sending peacekeeping forces to Tajikistan because it is "an internal matter."

14   Kravchuk meets with Indian defense minister Sharad Pawar in Kiev to discuss military-political issues.

15 Georgian foreign minister Aleksandre Chikvaidze and Russian foreign minister Andrei Kozyrev meet in Moscow but fail to produce an acceptable formula for resolving the Abkhazian conflict.

15 Russian defense minister Pavel Grachev announces that nuclear missiles outside of Russia have been taken off alert status.

15 Russian negotiating positions delay efforts to move forward on START II.

16 The CIS high command expresses concern over the disintegration of the former Soviet air defense system in Central Asia and the Caucasus. Radar stations continue to close as military specialists flee ethnic fighting.

16 Data concerning the 1983 attack on Korean Airlines Flight 007 is released. The files show that the Soviets withheld information.

16 Georgian parliament speaker-elect Eduard Shevardnadze warns that failure to secure a settlement on the Abkhazian conflict will lead Georgia to use military force to recover lost territory.

17 Shaposhnikov asserts that a Russian unilateral withdrawal from the Kurile Islands is "meaningless," and that it would be necessary to strengthen border guards in the area if the islands are demilitarized.

17 Yeltsin and director of Russian foreign intelligence Yevgeny Primakov meet with US CIA director Robert Gates in Moscow.

19 A Russian troop train carrying troops, six tanks and eleven missile systems is detained in Riga because it arrived in Latvia from Estonia without an entry permit and failed to halt for inspection at Lugazi border post.

19 Yeltsin signs a decree prolonging the Russian moratorium on nuclear weapons tests until 1 July 1993.

19 Acting Tajik President Akbarsho Iskandarov sets up a security council consisting of the leadership of Tajikistan's legislature and the Cabinet of Ministers, and appoints film-maker and opposition leader Davlat Khudonazarov his chief presidential advisor.

20 Officials in Leninabad Oblast appeal for Russian troops to help save the country.

21 Abkhaz parliament chairman Vladislav Ardzinba and Russian foreign minister Andrei Kozyrev meet in Moscow in attempt to resolve the Abkhazian-Georgian conflict. Ardzinba accuses Georgia of wishing to create "a new unitary state structure" that would entail the abolition of any autonomy for Abkhazia.

21 Atyrau Oblast chairman Sagat Tugelbaev orders the closure of nuclear missile test sites within the oblast's territory.

21 The Russian Ministry of Defense announces a suspension of troop withdrawals from the Baltic states.

21 The commander of the Russian motorized division stationed in Tajikistan authorizes his men to shoot without warning if their personal safety is threatened.

21-22 The Belarusian Supreme Soviet ratifies the CFE Treaty. Belarus defense minister Pavel Kozlovskii states that the CFE agreement permits Belarus to retain 1,800 tanks, 2,000 armored vehicles, and 130 combat aircraft. He claims that over the next forty months Belarusian forces would not exceed 100,000 soldiers.

22 Belarus Deputy Minister of Defense Aleksandr Tushinskiy and US Under Secretary of Defense Frank Wisner sign a series of nuclear agreements in Washington. The agreements include an umbrella agreement providing the legal framework for US assistance and two implementing agreements. One calls for up to $5 million in US aid to equip and train Belarus personnel to deal with any emergency that might arise during the removal of nuclear weapons. The second is designed to help Belarus establish export control systems to prevent the spread of atomic or chemical weapons.

22 Russian scientist Vil Mirzaianov is arrested for disclosing secret information on Russia's chemical weapon's program.

23 Russian Navy CinC Admiral Feliks Gromov states that the Baltic Fleet will be transferred to Baltiisk in Kaliningrad Oblast.

24 Some 200 armed supporters of the Azerbaijan Popular Front occupy the MVD and TV center in Nakhichevan in an attempted coup.

24 The Russian foreign ministry issues a statement on the Tajik civil war. The statement says "A real threat of a further escalation of the conflict and of expansion of the civil war persists. This is fraught with disastrous consequences for the territorial integrity of Tajikistan and the security of the entire Central Asian region. The destiny of Russian citizens and the Russian-speaking population in that country is a matter of particular concern for the leadership of the Russian Federation."

24 Kulyab Oblast forces enter Dushanbe and seize the presidential palace. Leader of Kulyab Oblast forces and former speaker of the Tajik Supreme Soviet Safarali Kenzhaev accuses the anti-current coalition of democratic, nationalist, and Islamic groups of seeking to force the rise of a Muslim state.

24-25 Fighting continues in Dushanbe with hundreds of people killed.

25 Officers from the Third Klaipeda Division of the Russian coast guard state that they have no intention of leaving Lithuania because conditions at their new bases are unsatisfactory.

25 Ukrainian defense minister Konstantin Morozov describes the recent appointment of Vice Admiral Petr Svyatashov as chief of staff of the Black Sea Fleet as a "one-sided action" breaching previous agreements.

26 Black Sea Fleet ships and sailors are blockaded in Poti. Abkhazians fear the ships will be used by Georgia.

26 The Tajik government regains control of Dushanbe. Russian armored forces escort Kulyab forces out of Dushanbe.

27 Kyrgyz Vice President Feliks Kulov states that Tajik Acting President Akbarsho Iskandarov had asked him to resume his peace mission and that Pamiris from Gorno-Badakhshan were seizing motor vehicles and taking hostages.

27 Russian Supreme Soviet guards, under the command of Ruslan Khasbulatov, surround the editorial offices of Izvestiia.

27 In a speech given at the Russian foreign ministry Yeltsin criticizes the organization for its "improvisations, inconsistencies and contradictions."

27 The Russian security ministry Collegium warns of the danger of "anticonstitutional structures which endanger the rebirth of the Russian state."

28 Caspian Flotilla chief of staff Captain Yury Startsev states that only one warship and twenty ships would remain at the flotilla's former headquarters in Baku.

28 Kazakhstan endorses the UN resolution endorsing the Chemical Weapons Convention.

28 A Russian SU-25 and a Georgian aircraft fire air-to-air missiles at each other but neither aircraft is hit.

28 The last former Soviet combat troops leave Poland eighteen days ahead of schedule.

28 Kulyab Oblast Soviet executive committee chairman Dzhumakhon Rizoev is assassinated.

28 Ukrainian defense minister Konstantin Morozov states that Ukraine wants to dispose of its nuclear weapons but had not received enough foreign assistance to remove them.

29 Yeltsin orders a halt to the withdrawal of Russian troops from the Baltic states because Moscow cannot provide housing.

29 The Russian government calls for a one-to-two-year moratorium on discussing the return of the Kurile Islands to Japan.

29 Yeltsin names Colonel General Leonid Maiorov as Russian Federation Commissioner for Questions of Temporary Housing and Withdrawal of Forces and Fleets from the Baltic States. Russian Security Council official Yury Skokov is assigned to coordinate negotiations with the Baltic states.

29-31 Kravchuk visits the PRC. While in Beijing Kravchuk denies that Ukraine intends to sell the 67,500-ton aircraft carrier *Varyag* to China.

30 Latvian Supreme Council chairman Anatolijs Gorbunovs asserts that Russian President Boris Yeltsin's directive on halting troop withdrawal indicates that Russia intends to defend its people in Latvia with the help of the army.

30 Yeltsin states that implementing presidential rule would violate the constitution but the Russian people could change his mind.

31 Yeltsin visits Astrakhan, the new home of the Russian Caspian Sea Flotilla.

31 Tajik TV reports 18,500 people killed in southern Tajikistan since May 1992.

NOVEMBER

1 Sukhumi is shelled.

1 The commander of Russian border troops in Tajikistan, General Vitaly Gritsan, asserts that a group of Uzbeks from southern Tajikistan had kidnapped Kadriddin Aslonov, the recently-appointed chairman of the Kurgan-Tyube Oblast Soviet Executive Committee.

2 Russian defense authorities hand over to Estonia all military properties located in the town of Viljandi.

2 Georgian President Eduard Shevardnadze criticizes Georgian Army units who seized Russian arms stored at a depot in the town of Akhaltsikh.

2 Yeltsin declares a state of emergency in North Ossetia and Ingushetia.

2 Russian forces attack Georgian forces deployed in Abkhazia.

2 Ukrainian chief of staff Georgii Zhivitsa claims that several thousand conscripts have deserted since the beginning of this year.

3 Belarusian defense minister Pavel Kozlovskii states that while the Belarusian conscript army would remain multi-national, the proportion of ethnic Belarusians is gradually increasing within the officer corps. He asserts that by the middle of next year it is expected that approximately one-half of all the officers will be Belarusian.

3 Abkhazian forces battle Georgian troops in the suburbs of Sukhumi.

3 Russian 14th Army commander Major General Aleksandr Lebed addresses the Joint Council of Work Collectives. He denounces as "servile" the "Dniester" leadership's recent proposals to Chisinau concerning the delimitation of powers and charges that the Dniester leadership is becoming bureaucratized while allowing the republican guard to "die a slow death."

3 An extraordinary session of the presidium of the South Ossetian Supreme Soviet condemns the actions of Ingush extremists and warns that if Ingush armed formations are not immediately withdrawn from North Ossetian territory "the people of South Ossetia would…take the necessary measures to repel the aggressors."

3 The South Ossetian Supreme Soviet condemns the Ingush and warn that it will retaliate if attacked.

3 Russia and Cuba sign an agreement to allow Moscow to continue operating an electronic intelligence facility in Cuba.

3 Tajik General Mukhriddin Ashurov, commander of the Russian motorized division stationed in Tajikistan, claims that his troops have assumed responsibility for maintaining the curfew in Dushanbe in addition to guarding key buildings and manning roadblocks on all approaches to the city.

4 Shaposhnikov warns that the military withdrawal from the Baltic states should not be pushed because it could have explosive consequences for both Russia and the Baltics.

4 The leaders of Kazakhstan, Kyrgyzstan, Uzbekistan, and Tajikistan meet in Alma-Ata to discuss how to end the fighting in Tajikistan. The participants issue a five-point statement, calling for the Russian motorized division stationed in Tajikistan to continue its peacekeeping role until a CIS peacekeeping force can be formed, and for the creation of a governing council in Tajikistan that would include representatives of all factions and parties.

4 Yeltsin and North Ossetian Supreme Soviet chairman Akhsarbek Galazov discuss the violence between Ossetians and Ingush.

4 The Russian Supreme Soviet ratifies the START Treaty.

5 CIS military officials fail to agree on a document establishing the composition of the CIS strategic forces.

5 North Ossetian officials report that a cease-fire in the region was being observed and that hostages were being exchanged. The officials also report that 115 people had been killed and 272 wounded in the battles with the Ingush.

5 Afghan veteran Ruslan Aushev is named chief Russian administrator in Ingushetia.

5 Japanese sources report that all tactical nuclear weapons have been removed from the former Soviet Pacific Fleet.

5 Ukrainian First Deputy Prime Minister Ihor Yukhnovskii suggests that Kiev ought to sell or auction off to the highest bidder nuclear warheads that remain in the country.

6 Belarusian officials state that all food, tobacco, and alcoholic beverages may be purchased only with coupons.

6 The Georgian Parliament elects President Eduard Shevardnadze as head of state and assumes his duties as commander-in-chief.

6 Lithuania buys two anti-submarine frigates from Russia.

6 Russian General Viktor Filatov visits Herzegovina and Belgrade and denounces Russian foreign minister Andrei Kozyrev for not supporting Serbia.

7 Two Russian soldiers are killed by snipers in North Ossetia.

8 Russia and Turkey agree to an arms sale worth $75 mn.

9 Abkhazian parliament chairman Vladislav Ardzinba accuses the Transcaucasus Military District of supplying arms to Georgian forces.

9 Moldovan Colonel Nicolae Chirtoaca requests NATO intervention in Moldova.

10 Georgian interim prime minister Tengiz Sigua nominates General Nodar Gudzhabidze as commander of the general headquarters and Lieutenant Colonel Kamkamidze to serve as commander-in-chief of the Georgian Armed Forces.

10 Russian troops enter Ingushetia.

11 Georgian tugs and fishing vessels blockade the port of Poti.

11 Lithuanian prime minister Aleksandras Abisala asserts that he fears the West would not do anything to stop Russia if it moved militarily against the Baltic states.

11 Russian troops pull back from territory claimed by Chechenia.

12 CIS Armed Forces CinC Boris Piankov states that the enduring potential for hostilities breaking out in the CIS, particularly in Central Asia and the Caucasus, makes the creation of CIS peacekeeping forces a necessity.

12 Shaposhnikov calls for a Russian-Ukrainian summit to discuss the disposition of nuclear weapons still deployed in Ukraine.

12 Chechen military forces are placed on high alert after Russian troops suspend their withdrawal.

12 Russian foreign minister Andrei Kozyrev and French foreign minister Roland Dumas sign an agreement under which France will help Russia dismantle part of its nuclear weapons.

12 Tajik foreign minister Khudoberdy Kholiknazarov meets with Russian defense minister Pavel Grachev and argues that a state of emergency should be declared in Tajikistan and enforced by a Russian military division.

13 A government commission investigating the deaths of 450 Azeri civilians in Khodzhali in February 1992 reveal that troops of the Russian 366th Regiment participated in the murders.

13 According to a Russian source, Azeri interior minister Iskander Gamidov claims that Azerbaijan has a total of six nuclear weapons, and that "if the Armenians do not come to their senses" he would authorize a nuclear strike against Erevan.

13 Russian deputy prime minister Sergei Shakhrai is appointed a full member of the Russian Security Council.

14 Russian defense minister Pavel Grachev denies that the army is involved in plans to establish a state of emergency or to disband parliament.

15-16 Russian and Chechen forces negotiate and then agree to a new withdrawal attempt.

16 Russian defense minister Pavel Grachev orders all weapons not in combat units be handed over to central facilities.

17 Rutskoi, in a speech delivered in Omsk, claims that the Crimean peninsula and other territories that were part of Russia should be returned. He also calls for an end to radical reform.

17 Ukrainian defense minister Konstantin Morozov states that Kiev had no intention of selling its nuclear warheads and that it would eliminate the weapons jointly with Russia.

18 Shaposhnikov states that he favors a NATO-style arrangement for the CIS in which each of the members would provide a specified number of troops to join the unified forces to carry out assignments of common interest.

18 While visiting South Korea, Yeltsin hands over the black box containing tapes with recorded reports from the Korean Air Lines Flight 007 shot down in September 1983.

19 The Estonian foreign ministry protests the presence of Russian warships in Estonian territorial waters. Apparently, a Russian submarine and a destroyer were in the vicinity of Ruhnu Island in the Gulf of Riga.

19 Lithuania freezes Russian Army funds.

19 Yeltsin addresses the Korean National Assembly and proposes halting nuclear submarine production in two or three years.

19 Deputy prime minister Sergei Shakhrai orders Russian forces in the North Ossetia-Ingush conflict zone to be in a state of heightened combat readiness.

20 More than 500 Russian troops are removed from Cuba.

20 The Tajik Parliament votes to introduce CIS peacekeeping forces into the country.

21 CIS Council of Defense Ministers' secretary Lieutenant General Leonid Ivashov warns that the armed forces of the FSU have been divided among the successor states in an "irrational" manner.

21 Commander of the Ukrainian Navy Rear Admiral Boris Kozhin states that Ukraine's naval doctrine will require an occasional naval presence outside the Black Sea.

22 Russian chief of the General Staff Viktor Dubinin dies after a lengthy battle with cancer.

22 Kravchuk informs US senators Sam Nunn and Richard Lugar that the START treaty has been submitted to the Ukrainian Parliament and he expects it to be ratified by January 1993.

23 Yeltsin meets with the Russian Ministry of Defense Collegium and the commanding officers of military districts, fleets, and other major units. Rutskoi and Khasbulatov also attend. Yeltsin emphasizes the military's role in ensuring state security and stability.

23 Forty-nine Ingush hostages are handed over to Russian MVD Troops and militia.

23 US senators Sam Nunn and Richard Lugar announce that Ukraine will receive financial compensation for dismantling its nuclear warheads.

24 The Kuldiga regional council decides to stop supplying electricity to the Skrunda ballistic missile early warning station.

24 ABC television network reports that the former Soviet Navy dumped more than 11,000 containers of solid radioactive waste and barrels filled with 43 mn gallons of liquid radioactive waste at a total of twelve ocean sites over the years.

26 Five youths murder GRU Colonel Vladimir Zenin.

27 The Georgian Parliament appoints General Anatolii Kamkamidze as Minister of Defense.

29 Dniester security minister Vadim Shevtsov confirms that he is really Vladimir Antyufeev, a former high official in the Latvian KGB and supervisor of OMON in Riga.

30 In Termez the defense ministers of Kazakhstan, Kyrgyzstan, Uzbekistan, and Russia in a meeting with CIS Armed Forces commander Yevgeny Shaposhnikov and chairman of Tajikistan's Supreme Soviet Imomali Rakhmonov decide to establish a CIS peacekeeping force for Tajikistan.

30 Lithuanian defense minister Audrius Butkevicius visits the PRC to discuss bilateral relations.

30 South Korea announces Yeltsin failed to give all the tapes from KAL 007's black box.

DECEMBER

1 The Russian Supreme Soviet extends the state of emergency in North Ossetia and Ingushetia until 30 January 1993.

1 The Russian military begins to contract servicemen for two-to-three-year periods.

1 GRU first deputy chairman Colonel General Yury Gusev dies in an auto crash.

2 The last Russian Border Guard detachments leaves Ventspils.

2 Russian Unity member Mikhail Astafev criticizes the US-Russian arms pact of June 1992 for allowing US access to any Russian installation.

3 Russia, Kazakhstan, Kyrgystan, and Tajikistan and the PRC agree to pull most of their troops back 100 kilometers on each side of the 7,500-km border between China and the four CIS states.

3 Latvia bars the transit of 105 Russian tanks until the government approves their movement.

3 Authorities begin to disarm illegal formations in North Ossetia and Ingushetia.

5 Russian defense minister Pavel Grachev addresses the Congress of People's Deputies. He calls for "a moratorium on the Army's involvement in politics for the sake of stabilization and Russia's revival."

7 Shevardnadze warns that all political means for resolving the Abkhaz crisis have been exhausted and that a military solution may be necessary.

7 Fighting erupts between pro-communist forces and the Islamic-Democratic forces near Dushanbe.

7 Over 80,000 refugees from the Tajik civil war gather near the Afghan border.

8 Uzbek Ministry of Internal Affairs officials travel to Kyrgyzstan to arrest Birlik supporters.

10 Russian defense minister Pavel Grachev addresses the Congress of People's Deputies and promises that the military will stay out of politics.

10 The Congress approves a resolution subordinating security forces around the Parliament to a new parliamentary security department.

11 At the Seventh Russian Congress of People's Deputies Shaposhnikov calls for "strong coordinating bodies" between Kazakhstan, Uzbekistan, Kyrgyzstan, Tajikistan, and Armenia. He states that Turkmenistan and Belarus favor closer integration into a NATO-type security system.

11 Acting Lithuanian president Algirdas Brazauskas visits Latvia and calls for financial aid to accelerate the withdrawal of Russian troops from the Baltic states.

11 Ukrainian foreign minister Anatolii Zlenko asserts that the republic intends to ratify START and join the Non-Proliferation Treaty.

13 US Secretary of State Lawrence Eagleburger meets with Russian foreign minister Andrei Kozyrev in Stockholm to discuss obstacles that have been delaying the conclusion of START II.

13 Fighting continues in Dushanbe as government and opposition military commanders meet.

14 In Georgia a Russian military helicopter carrying dozens of passengers including women and children is shot down. There are no survivors.

14 Moldova and Romania sign a bilateral military agreement in which Bucharest will train the Moldovan Army.

14 Russian Minister of Security Viktor Barannikov delivers a hardline speech to the Congress. He claims that his agency is struggling against the "subversive activities of western secret services and [their] efforts to transform Russia into a raw materials' appendage of the developed countries." Barannikov also accuses the West of trying to gain control of Russia's nuclear arsenal.

14 Russian Prosecutor General Valentin Stepankov signs indictments in the case of the August 1991 coup attempt. Simultaneously, four of the eleven accused are freed on bail. They are former speaker of the USSR Parliament

Anatoly Lukianov, Army General Valentin Varennikov, and two KGB generals, Viacheslav Generalov and Yury Plekhnov.

14 In an unconventional move made without warning, Russian foreign minister Andrei Kozyrev simulates what a hard shift to the right would mean for Russian foreign policy during a speech to the council of CSCE foreign ministers in Stockholm.

14 Ukraine and Russia disagree over who owns ship repair facilities in the Black Sea Fleet.

15 Belarus and Poland sign a cooperation statement between their military establishments.

15 Yeltsin and German Chancellor Helmut Kohl meet in Moscow and agree that Russian forces will depart Germany by mid-1994. Germany will offer Russia DM500 mn to help speed the process.

15 Fighting between small opposition groups and units loyal to the new government continues around Dushanbe.

15 Over a dozen Russians are taken hostage in Dushanbe.

15 Ukraine announces that it needs more time to study START.

15 Russia flies twenty SU-17 jet fighters to the PRC.

16 The Belarusian Parliament votes by an overwhelming margin not to join the CIS collective security treaty signed in Tashkent.

16 Georgian officials deny that Georgia is responsible for shooting down a Russian helicopter killing dozens because the missile came from Abkhazian-controlled territory.

17 The Russian Parliament passes a resolution calling for Russia to use its UN Security Council veto to prevent military intervention in the former Yugoslavia.

17 Russian Security Council official Yury Skokov is appointed chairman of the council's Foreign Policy Commission.

17 US Secretary of State Lawrence Eagleburger warns Ukraine that continued delay in ratifying START and the Lisbon Protocol would harm US-Ukrainian relations.

19 Estonian General Staff deputy commander Colonel Raul Luks reports that the Estonian Armed Forces have started their first exercises with 1,000 personnel. He states that the scenario is to counter aggression from neighboring states "where a totalitarian regime has gained power."

20 Yeltsin calls US president George Bush to discuss the possibility of signing START II.

21 Shaposhnikov meets with representatives from the CIS. He complains that the CIS collective security treaty and agreements on peacekeeping forces have failed to work. Moreover, he states that a recent inspection of the Strategic Rocket Forces revealed security violations.

21 Kazakh defense minister Colonel General Sagadat Nurmagambetov announces that Kazakhstan's military doctrine will be purely defensive.

21 The Russian Parliament debates the costs to Russia of UN sanction against the former Yugoslavia, Iraq, and Libya. While the Committee on International Affairs and External Economic Relations has estimated the

cost to Russia of sanctions at $15 bn, a representative of the Ministry of External Economic Relations implies that the estimate is inflated.

21 Yeltsin and US president George Bush discuss obstacles to signing START II.

21 While in Moscow Tajik prime minister Abdumalik Abdullodzhonov reveals that due to the civil war in Tajikistan, 10,000 to 20,000 have died in Tajikistan, that there are 70,000 Tajik refugees in Afghanistan, and 120,000 Tajik families are homeless.

26 Russian foreign minister Andrei Kozyrev states that "there [is] no alternative to the peace process" in Bosnia, and that UN military action would "lead nowhere."

26 The bodies of three Russian servicemen are found near the town of Kofarnihon, a stronghold of the Tajik opposition.

28 Shaposhnikov calls for the CIS to set up a defensive military alliance but expresses concern about the combat readiness of the forces.

28 The 107th Motorized Rifle Division of the Russian Army completes its withdrawal from its base in Vilnius.

28 Democratic Russia announces its support for Yeltsin in the April 1993 referendum on the new Russian constitution.

28 Both U.S. Secretary of State Lawrence Eagleburger and Russian foreign minister Andrei Kozyrev express satisfaction with their talks in Geneva to finalize START II. The treaty would cut each country's nuclear arsenal to roughly 3,500 warheads by 2003.

29 Abkhazian forces attack Sukhumi.

29 Ukraine announces that it will need at least $1.5 bn to remove nuclear weapons on its territory.

30 The Russian defense ministry declares that its troops outside Russia will take "the most decisive measures, including armed actions, to defend their honor, dignity, and life" if "unlawful actions" against them and their families continue.

CHRONOLOGY, 1993

JANUARY

3 In a Moscow ceremony Russian president Boris Yeltsin and US president George Bush sign the START II strategic nuclear arms reduction treaty.

4 In an appeal to UN Secretary-General Boutros Boutros-Ghali, Georgian Parliament chairman Eduard Shevardnadze calls for the immediate dispatch of UN peacekeeping forces to Abkhazia.

6 Tajikistan's National Security Committee announces that the government is in control of most of the country. Anti-government resistance remains strong only in the Garm, Dzhirgatal, and Komsomolabad districts east of Dushanbe, and the government has not determined how to rout the opposition from these areas.

7 Chairman of Tajikistan's Supreme Soviet Imomali Rakhmonov imposes a state of emergency and curfew on Dushanbe and nearby districts.

10 A delegation that includes senior officers of the Russian Foreign Intelligence Service and KGB veterans arrives in the United States to discuss the new role of intelligence in the post-Cold War period. The delegation, headed by General Vadim Kirpichenko, meets with American congressmen and representatives of the US intelligence community to examine prevention and/or countering of illegal proliferation of nuclear weapons and other advanced weapons systems and technologies, narcotics trafficking, terrorism, and organized crime.

11 According to data provided by the Northwestern Group of Forces, on 1 January some 27,000 Russian troops occupied about 70,000 hectares of land in Latvia. These forces have 29 tanks, 73 armored vehicles, 12 antiaircraft artillery, 36 howitzers, over 2,500 automobiles, over 60 airplanes (of which 11 are transport), 11 helicopters, 12 submarines, and about 130 ships (of which 29 are warships).

13 Foreign minister Andrei Kozyrev signs the United Nations Convention of Chemical Weapons on behalf of Russia in Paris.

13 Coup rumors sweep Tbilisi.

14 Lt. Gen. Aleksandr Lebed, commander of Russia's 14th Army in Moldova, warns allegedly corrupt Dniester republic leaders that he is "sick and tired of guarding the sleep and safety of crooks."

15 Vasilii Lipitskii, chairman of the Civic Union's Executive Committee, states that his party would like to know whether the Russian government had agreed to the plan for air strikes against Iraq. If so, this meant that a "very narrow circle of individuals had taken on the colossal responsibility for events which may have long term consequences." If Russia was not consulted, he argued that "this means that Russia is no longer considered a great power and member of the UN Security Council."

15 Russian president Boris Yeltsin states that Russia was ready to guarantee Ukraine's security.

15 The former chief of the Control Administration of the Russian President's Office, Yury Boldyrev, submits to Yeltsin a report recommending that several generals of the Western Group of Forces (WGF) be stripped of rank for corruption and embezzlement.

15 The chairman of the Ukrainian Republican Party, Mykhailo Horyn, asserts that, having given up all its short-range nuclear arms, Ukraine should not eliminate the rest of its nuclear arsenal unless other nuclear powers do so.

18 In Chisinau Moldovan defense minister Pavel Creanga and Ukrainian first deputy defense minister Ivan Bizhan initial an agreement that provides for the creation of a common air defense system, exchanges of military information of joint interest, and exchanges of military specialists.

20 Lt. Gen. Aleksandr Lebed, commander of Russia's 14th Army in Moldova, warns that hostilities may resume "at any moment" in the city of Bendery on the right bank of the Dniester and calls for a referendum to determine whether the city should belong to Moldova or to the left-bank Dniester Republic.

21 The CIS Nuclear Policy Committee fails to solve the ongoing argument over ownership and control of the former Soviet strategic nuclear weapons stationed in Belarus, Ukraine, and Kazakhstan. Russia insists that these weapons can only belong to one country—itself.

25 CIS CinC Marshal Yevgeny Shaposhnikov reiterates his claim that Russia should be the sole owner of former Soviet strategic nuclear weapons.

28 During a visit to India, Yeltsin signs several agreements on arms sales and production.

30 Russian defense minister General Pavel Grachev and General John Shalikashvili, CinC of NATO forces in Europe, state that their armed forces could collaborate in preventing local conflicts and in combating the spread of nuclear weapons.

FEBRUARY

1 Nazarbaev visits NATO headquarters in Brussels.

1 Coup rumors sweep Moscow.

1 In a speech devoted to the fiftieth anniversary of the Battle of Stalingrad Yeltsin pays tribute to the heroism and perseverance of the Red Army and the Soviet people during the decisive World War II battle. Yeltsin uses the occasion to stress the difficulties faced by the Soviet people in 1943 with those faced by Russians today, and calls for a similar application of determination and courage to overcome them.

3 Polish defense minister Janusz Onyszkiewicz and his Ukrainian counterpart, Konstantin Morozov, sign a defense cooperation agreement in Kiev. The agreement covers disarmament, training, and information exchanges.

4 The Belarus Parliament ratifies a number of key arms control agreements. The 360-member Parliament passes the START-1 treaty and Lisbon Protocol by a 218 to 1 vote, with 60 members abstaining, despite an earlier call by the 130-member Belarus faction for a delay in ratification. The Parliament also ratifies the Nuclear Nonproliferation Treaty, an agreement with Russia on the status of the nuclear weapons in Belarus, and an agreement coordinating Russian and Belarusian military activities.

4 Russian defense minister Pavel Grachev arrives in Dushanbe to discuss the status of the Russian 201st Motorized Division which has been stationed in Tajikistan throughout the civil war. Grachev also discusses Russian assistance to Tajikistan in creating a national army.

4 Law enforcement representatives claim that the Tajik civil war in 1992 took around 20,000 lives.

5 Several members of the anti-government opposition are arrested in Tajikistan on suspicion of attempting an armed coup and causing the civil war of 1992. Among those arrested is former dissident Mirbobo Mirrakhimov, who headed Tajikistan's State Radio and TV under the coalition government.

5 Russian defense minister Pavel Grachev suggests that a civilian could be named to head the Ministry of Defense sometime after 1995, "when the situation in the army stabilizes." He states that the General Staff would

then manage the uniformed military while the defense ministry would concern itself with military-political issues and weapons policy. Grachev also reports that 2,218 generals now serve in the Russian army and that the proportion of generals had fallen from one for every 530 soldiers and 169 officers in 1987 to one for every 1,262 soldiers and 312 officers today.

9 Lt. Gen. Aleksandr Lebed, commander of Russia's 14th Army in Moldova, condemns the "parade of sovereignties" of the former Soviet republics as a "darkening of the mind" and predicts that sovereignty will lead to wars; "therefore it is necessary to eradicate it."

9 The Azerbaijan Popular Front claims that the seizure by Armenian forces of part of Nagorno-Karabakh's Mardakert district was the direct result of "provocative action" by leading officials, including defense minister Rahim Gaziev, and was intended to bring about a coup.

12 Moldovan president Mircea Snegur claims that supporters of Moldovan-Romanian unification may be planning a coup to overthrow the legal authorities and to provoke civil war.

14 The Azeri Ministry of Defense claims that Russian troops stationed in Armenia, armed with heavy artillery and tanks, participated in an Armenian offensive in the north of Nagorno-Karabakh.

16 Akaev tells leaders of the country's democratic parties and movements that government and legislature should not waste time in fighting each other, as they are in Russia, but should cooperate to find ways out of Kyrgyzstan's economic crisis.

16 The command of the Russian Strategic Rocket Forces charges that Ukrainian authorities have failed properly to maintain strategic nuclear weapons still based in Ukraine and has suggested that this neglect could lead to a catastrophe rivaling Chernobyl.

16 Lt. Gen. Ivan Oliinyk is dismissed from his post as Ukrainian deputy defense minister for Armaments. The dismissal reportedly came for abuse of office. Meanwhile, Ukrainian president Leonid Kravchuk appoints Lt. Gen. Vladimir Antonets as commander-in-chief of Ukraine's recently united Air Force.

18 Tajikistan's recently appointed defense minister Aleksandr Shishlyannikov states that the Russian 201st Division remains the guarantor of stability in Tajikistan. He claims that the republic is currently forming Ground Forces and an Air Force, with Air Defense Forces to follow.

19 A gas pipeline is attacked in Georgia which cuts off all natural gas delivers to Armenia. The attack is the third one within a month.

19 A Ukrainian-Moldovan agreement on military cooperation is signed by the defense ministers, Generals Konstantin Morozov and Pavel Creanga, in Chisinau. According to the communique the agreement provides for the creation of a common air defense system of the two countries; exchanges of intelligence; joint maneuvers, drills, and tactical studies; cooperation in the training of military personnel; mutual support in repairing and servicing military equipment; and sharing experience in the creation of national armies.

21 Azeri president Abulfaz Elchibey appoints Afghan veteran Major General Dadash Rzaev as defense minister. Rzaev is the fifth Minister of Defense since the post was created.

21 Shevardnadze flies to the Abkhaz coastal town of Sukhumi following an overnight air raid by Russian warplanes in which one person was killed and eight injured.

23 Hard-line communists, ultra-nationalists, and disgruntled military officers turn the first Russian "Defenders of the Fatherland Day," into a noisy anti-government demonstration with between 20,000 and 40,000 participants including five of the leading plotters from the 1991 attempted coup.

23 Minister of Defense Pavel Grachev asserts that Moscow no longer considers either NATO, Japan, or South Korea to be its enemies. He suggests instead that the most likely source of conflict for Russia is the South, and states that Russia is moving particularly to build up its forces in the North Caucasus Military District.

23 Shevardnadze accuses the Russian military leadership of seeking an armed conflict with Georgia, and states that if Russian troops are not withdrawn from Abkhazia and Adzharia, Georgia may be constrained to announce a general mobilization "to defend the country."

24 Belarus military spending in 1993 reportedly will be R56.5 billion or 6.3 percent of the total budget.

27 Defense ministry representatives from the CIS states which have signed the Collective Security Agreement meet in Moscow to discuss concrete plans for promoting closer military integration. Armenia, Kazakhstan, Kyrgyzstan, Tajikistan, and Uzbekistan take part in the meeting. The secretary of the CIS Defense Ministers' Council, Lt. Gen. Leonid Ivashov, said that all seven documents on the agenda were approved. Although details of the agreements are not provided, the participants reportedly decide to create a working commission charged with drawing up proposals for implementing the Collective Security Agreement, including the establishment of a single air defense system.

28 Maj. Gen. Ruslan Aushev, a 38-year-old medal-winning veteran of the war in Afghanistan, is elected the first president of Ingushetia. Of the 142,223 voters who participated in the election 99.99 percent are said to have voted for Aushev, who was the sole candidate. The turnout was 92.66 percent.

MARCH

3 The Russian Security Council meets under the chairmanship of President Boris Yeltsin to discuss the basic principles of the country's new foreign policy concept prepared not by the foreign ministry but by the Foreign Policy Commission of the Security Council chaired by the council's secretary, Yury Skokov. Following the convening of the Russian Security Council, Yeltsin meets with commanders of Russia's military districts, fleets, and service branches.

3 Russian and Ukrainian security chiefs sign a package of protocols aimed at promoting joint efforts in the battle against drug trading and terrorism.

3 Shevardnadze returns to the Abkhaz capital of Sukhumi to assess the capability of the Georgian troops in the region. Shevardnadze denies rumors that Georgia is preparing to abandon Sukhumi to the Abkhaz forces, affirming that additional Georgian troops were being deployed to counter a possible Abkhaz assault.

3 Russian and Ukrainian security chiefs sign a package of protocols aimed at promoting joint efforts in the battle against drug trading and terrorism.

3-4 Coup rumors sweep Moscow.

4 Belarus defense minister Pavel Kozlovskii puts forward a proposal to forbid servicemen from taking part in political activities even in their free time and when they are off-base.

5 Russian defense minister Pavel Grachev bans all exercises, as well as movements of troops and military equipment, in the Moscow region during the forthcoming Congress of People's Deputies.

6 Russian defense minister Pavel Grachev states that he intends to keep the armed forces out of politics.

6 Tajikistan's Minister of Internal Affairs, Yakubzhon Salimov, states that government troops finally captured the Ramit Gorge east of Dushanbe from opposition forces.

10 Yeltsin's press spokesman Viacheslav Kostikov warns that the Congress had brought the country to "a very dangerous situation."

10 Deputy chairman of Tajikistan's Council of Ministers, Munavarsho Nazriev, states that groups of the armed Tajik opposition tried to escape mopping-up operations by government troops by fleeing into Kyrgyzstan, but were stopped by Tajik and Kyrgyz government forces.

11 Several Western newspapers assert that Boris Yeltsin had privately asked several Western leaders whether they would support him if he takes "emergency measures" to preserve his rule in a bitter power struggle with the parliament. These "measures" could include the introduction of direct presidential rule and the disbanding of the Congress of People's Deputies.

15 Russian foreign minister Kozyrev stops in Vilnius during his trip from Kaliningrad to Helsinki for the meeting of the Council of the Baltic Sea States. He notes that the situation of the Russian-speaking population in Lithuania is better than in Latvia and Estonia, but that agreements on Russian troop withdrawal and guarantees for servicemen and retired soldiers still have to be signed.

16 Abkhaz troops launch a major offensive against Georgian forces located in the Sukhumi area.

20 A US attack submarine collides with a Russian ballistic-missile submarine in the Barents Sea.

21 The Russian ministers of defense, security, and the interior emphasize their "neutrality" on Yeltsin's decrees on a special regime.

24 Deputy prime minister Sergei Shakhrai states that if hardliners oust the president "they will have to use force or other means" to remove Boris Yeltsin from the Kremlin.

25 Col. Gen. Anatoly Lopata is named chief of the Main Staff and a first deputy defense minister of the Ukrainian Armed Forces.

25 NATO experts state that they have evidence that the authority of defense minister Pavel Grachev is diminishing in the Russian Armed Forces because he is perceived as being too close to Yeltsin. The same sources claim that Vice President Aleksandr Rutskoi is currently lobbying for support in the military.

25 In his address to the nation on the eve of the Ninth Congress, Yeltsin accuses the leadership of Parliament of secretly plotting to oust him.

25 The collegium of the Russian defense ministry issues an appeal on urging servicemen once again to avoid becoming involved in politics.

29-30 Sangak Safarov, head of the pro-communist Tajik People's Front, and Faisuli Saidov, one of his military commanders, are killed in the southern town of Kurgan-Tyube. The circumstances of their deaths are unclear. Tajik interior ministry officials claim that the two men were shot during a violent quarrel, while the Tajik Parliament presidium issues a statement that the two men were killed by hired assassins.

APRIL

2 Nazarbaev issues a decree on the creation of naval forces in Kazakstan.

4-5 President Bill Clinton and Yeltsin meet in Vancouver, Canada, to discuss security and economic issues.

6 Armenian forces launch a new offensive in Nagorno-Karabakh.

9 The Belarus Supreme Soviet overrides the objections of Shushkevich and votes to strengthen ties with Moscow by joining the CIS collective security agreement.

10-11 The influential Union of Ukrainian Officers adopts a resolution that calls for: maintenance of Ukraine's status as a nuclear power; suspension of the Yalta agreement that regulates Russian and Ukrainian activities with respect to the Black Sea Fleet; and the discharge of all officers not taking an oath of allegiance to Ukraine or who are in some fashion obstructing the construction of a Ukrainian national army.

13 German defense minister Volker Ruehe and his Russian counterpart, Pavel Grachev, sign a cooperation agreement between the two defense ministries following talks in Moscow. The agreement calls for exchanges of both information and personnel. Members of the Russian Armed Forces will train in Germany and members of the Bundeswehr are to visit Russia.

15 In Azerbaijan, interior minister Iskander Gamidov resigns. He was criticized for his affiliation with the pan-Turkish National Labor Party (Gray Wolves) and for using physical violence against political moderates. His successor is Major General Abdullah Allahverdiev.

16 An Armenian defense ministry spokesman charges that Turkey is sending arms and troops to Azerbaijan via Nakhichevan, and hinted that Armenia might shoot down Turkish transport planes that crossed its air space.

28 Yeltsin releases Vice President Aleksandr Rutskoi as head of the Interdepartmental Commission of the Security Council for Struggle Against Crime and Corruption.

MAY

1 A Labor Day demonstration turns violent when security forces attempt to prevent some 2,000 demonstrators from marching on Red Square and then from moving the rally to the Vorobevie Hills. The Russian interior ministry claims that 12 demonstrators and 27 police were hospitalized. One person, an OMAN officer, later dies.

3 An SU-24 fighter plane from the Tajik Air Force is shot down by a Stinger missile fired from Afghanistan.

4 By a vote of 82-0-1, the Estonian Parliament appoints a retired United States officer, 61-year-old Estonian-American Colonel Alexander Einselm, as commander-in-chief of the Estonian defense forces.

4-5 An explosion at the Inguri Hydro Electric Station in western Georgia, which supplies up to 40 percent of Georgia's electricity, causes widespread power blackouts in Tbilisi and elsewhere in Georgia.

4-5 Secretary of State Warren Christopher visits Moscow to meet with Yeltsin. They discuss the crisis in Bosnia-Herzegovina. Yeltsin urges the Bosnian Serb Parliament to accept the Vance-Owen peace plan.

5 Russia renews its call for a comprehensive nuclear test ban.

5 US senators Sam Nunn and Richard Lugar meet with Russian parliamentarians to discuss the START-2 ratification process. Senator Nunn observes that the START-2 ratification process is being slowed by the ongoing political struggles in Russia.

5 Ukranian president Kravchuk states that he favors an informal security alliance between Ukraine, Slovakia, and "other states of the region."

6 Loti Kobalia, leader of the armed supporters of ousted Georgian president Zviad Gamsakhurdia, meets with Abkhaz acting defense minister Sultan Soslanaliev to discuss ways of ending the war in Abkhazia.

6 Prime Minister-designate Panakh Guseinov states that Azerbaijan accepts the terms of the US-Russian-Turkish peace plan for Nagorno-Karabakh.

7 Russian defense minister Pavel Grachev claims that the Russian military might eventually be reduced to an all-volunteer force of about one million troops.

10 US Ambassador at Large Strobe Talbott meets with Ukrainian president Leonid Kravchuk, foreign minister Anatoly Zlenko, and the Minister of Defense Konstantin Morozov. Talbott was originally scheduled to meet only with lower-ranking officials, reportedly in response to President Clinton's refusal to meet Ukrainian prime minister Leonid Kuchma earlier this year. US-Ukrainian relations have been strained over Ukraine's failure to ratify START-1 and sign the Nuclear Nonproliferation Treaty. Following his meeting with Kravchuk, Talbott states he understands Ukraine's concerns over scrapping the nuclear weapons on its territory without security guarantees or adequate funds for their dismantling and states that the promised $175 million for dismantling the weapons is a starting point, not the final offer.

11 Yeltsin fires secretary of the Security Council Yury Skokov and deputy prime minister Georgy Khizha.

11 Russian defense minister Pavel Grachev and his Turkish counterpart, Nevzat Ayaz, sign an agreement providing for cooperation in military training and arms production.

12 The ministers of Internal Affairs from Russia, Armenia, Georgia, Kazakhstan, Kyrgyzstan, Tajikistan, Turkmenistan, Uzbekistan, Ukraine, and the non-CIS republics of Latvia and Estonia meet in Erevan. The meeting focuses on the problems of organized crime, arms trade, drugs, and other illicit activities.

12 Ukraine accuses Romania of abusing UN sanctions against rump Yugoslavia to hold up Ukrainian trade. Foreign minister Anatoly Zlenko claims that since early April about 160 Ukrainian barges, mostly carrying commodities for the metallurgical industry in Hungary and Austria, have been detained for lengthy searches of up to three or four weeks in the Romanian port of Galati.

13 At a meeting of the defense ministers of the CIS states Russia opposes two draft agreements presented by the CIS command that would have increased integration and formed joint CIS forces. While nine of the CIS states sent delegations to the meeting, Ukraine did not. Russia specifically objects to plans for the creation of standing CIS forces during peacetime. Finally, Russia claims that under the terms of the May 1992 Lisbon Protocol that it is the sole inheritor of the USSR's nuclear weapons.

14 At their summit in Moscow, Russian president Yeltsin and Shevardnadze call for a cease-fire in Abkhazia and the withdrawal from the combat zone of heavy military equipment and artillery.

15 Russian president Boris Yeltsin and Moldovan president Mircea Snegur meet in connection with the CIS summit. The two note with satisfaction that the Dniester cease-fire is holding and "highly appreciated the activity of the Russian-Moldovan-Dniester peacekeeping forces."

17 A state of emergency is declared in the Khasavyurt district of Dagestan. A dispute over land led to an armed clash between local Dargins and Kumyks, in which one person was killed.

18 Kyrgyzstan's prime minister Tursunbek Chyngyshev claims that Uzbekistan's president Islam Karimov has promised to drop measures taken by Uzbekistan against Kyrgyzstan in retaliation for the latter's introduction of its own currency.

18 Russian defense minister Pavel Grachev visits Lithuania. In his talks with President Algirdas Brazauskas he states that, although Russia had no wish to delay the withdrawal of Russian troops past the 31 August deadline, the shortage of railroad cars might make this necessary.

19 The Ruthenian (Rusyn) Association of Subcarpathia sets up a "provisional government" in Ukraine's Transcarpathian Oblast. The body intends to ask the UN and foreign governments for recognition that Transcarpathia, which belonged to Hungary until 1920 and to Czechoslovakia until 1945, be recognized as an independent republic or, through a referendum, be reunited with Slovakia.

19 In the course of a stormy debate in the Azerbaijan National Assembly, parliament deputy speaker Tamerlan Karaev condemns as "a betrayal of the people's interests" the agreement signed on 14 May on the Armenia-Nakhichevan border by Nakhichevan Parliament chairman Geidar Aliev and Armenian first deputy chairman Ara Sarkisyan.

19 By a vote of 52 to 9 with 1 abstention, the Estonian Parliament passes a law on local elections. Non-citizens and citizens of other countries are allowed to vote if they have resided in the election area for the past five years, but cannot run as candidates.

20 The Nagorno-Karabakh Republic rejects a US-Russian-Turkish proposal for settlement of the Karabakh conflict because Turkey was violating UN Resolution 822 on Karabakh by preventing the delivery of humanitarian aid to Armenia.

26 Armenia and Azerbaijan formally approve the US-Russian-Turkish sponsored peace plan for Nagorno-Karabakh. However, the Nagorno-Karabakh Defense Committee rejects the plan on the grounds that it did not provide guarantees for the safety of the population of Nagorno-Karabakh or stipulate an end to the Azeri economic blockade.

27 Ukrainian defense minister Konstantin Morozov warns that ships from the Black Sea Fleet raising the Russian flag might be expelled from Ukrainian territorial waters and their crews deprived of any chance of receiving Ukrainian citizenship.

28 Shushkevich clarifies the republic's position on the CIS collective security pact. He states that the use of Belarusian troops beyond the country's borders is only permissible through a decision by the republic's Supreme Soviet. Furthermore, Belarus has the right to discontinue its participation in the collective security system from the moment all Russian military and strategic forces have been withdrawn from its territory within the parameters of its international agreements and obligations.

29 Afghan and Tajik rebels attack a Russian border post. Three border guards are killed, and four others injured.

30 Yeltsin issues a decree prolonging the state of emergency in parts of North Ossetia and Ingushetia.

30 Over 200 ships of the Black Sea Fleet have raised the Russian naval ensign.

JUNE

2 Ten accords related to the pullout of Russian troops from Latvia are signed in Moscow. Agreement is not reached, however, on the completion date of the troop withdrawals or on the future of Russian strategic facilities in Latvia.

2 A detachment of fighters from the Dniester Russian forces in eastern Moldova arrive in Abkhazia.

3 Armored vehicles and military patrols are deployed in Baku.

3 The long-awaited debate in the Ukrainian Parliament on ratification of START-1 and adherence to the Nuclear Nonproliferation Treaty (NPT)

begins. Foreign minister Anatoly Zlenko makes a strong plea to lawmakers to move forward with the confirmation of Ukraine's non-nuclear status by ratifying both treaties. Zlenko's report is sharply criticized by deputies representing all shades of political opinion, including the Democratic chairman of the parliamentary foreign affairs commission, Dmytro Pavlychko, all of whom explicitly or implicitly accuse the foreign minister of yielding to external pressure instead of defending Ukraine's interests.

4 Renegade detachments of troops led by Surat Guseinov, who was dismissed from the post of commander of Azerbaijan's forces in Nagorno-Karabakh in February 1993, attack an Azeri army base in Gyandzha. About sixty people are killed.

4-5 Separatists take control of Lenkoran in southeast Azerbaijan close to the Iranian border and distribute leaflets in Evlakh and Mingechaur calling for a campaign of civil disobedience.

5-6 The US and Russian defense ministers meet in the German town of Garmisch and discuss means of increasing cooperation in defense matters. Aspin states that the US Navy is changing its submarine operations so as to reduce the chance that US and Russian submarines will collide.

6 While in Sukhumi, Shevardnadze raises the possibility that Georgian troops may take offensive measures to end the conflict with Abkhazia.

7 Extensive rioting, looting, and arson at the Baikonur space center occurs in Kazakhstan. This is at least the third such incident, and the most serious since February 1992, when three Kazakh soldiers were killed during a mutiny.

8 Estonian prime minister Mart Laar tells parliament that his government does not expect to attain its goal of having the approximately 7,000 Russian troops out of the country by 1 August.

8 Addressing a meeting of Azerbaijan's National Assembly, Elchibey rules out the use of force to end the uprising in Gyandzha and states that negotiations have begun with military commander Surat Guseinov.

9 A Russian delegation led by foreign minister Andrei Kozyrev takes steps to mitigate the conflict in Abkhazia through a series of meetings with Georgian and Abkhaz leaders in Tbilisi and Gudauta.

10 Yeltsin uses a speech to top-ranking army and navy officers to defend his political program and to praise what he described as progress in restoring control over the armed forces and raising morale in the officer corps. Yeltsin states that Russia should adopt basing practices similar to those used by the US in order to maintain a Russian military presence in Moldova, in the Caucasus states of Georgia and Armenia, and in Central Asia. He again links the withdrawal of Russian troops from Estonia to the rights of Russians living there and housing for the departing military.

11 Yeltsin names the commander-in-chief of the CIS Joint Armed Forces, Marshal Yevgeny Shaposhnikov, to the post of secretary of the Russian Security Council.

14 The Nagorno-Karabakh Supreme Soviet Presidium votes 6-5 to accept the CSCE peace plan.

16 Rebels loyal to Surat Guseinov ignore an appeal by President Abulfaz Elchibey to surrender and continue their eastward advance and take the towns of Akhsu and Geokchai.

16 An armed group under the control of former Deputy Minister of Defense Alikram Gumbatov takes control of Lenkoran close to the Azerbaijan-Iranian border and calls on Elchibey to resign.

17 Russian and Ukrainian presidents Boris Yeltsin and Leonid Kravchuk, prime ministers Viktor Chernomyrdin and Leonid Kuchma, and defense ministers Pavel Grachev and Konstantin Morozov meet outside Moscow. One of the principal topics of discussion is the Black Sea Fleet. Yeltsin states Russia's willingness to provide security guarantees to Ukraine if it ratifies the START-1 and NPT treaties. The two sides agree to split the Black Sea Fleet.

17 Rebels loyal to Surat Guseinov take the town of Shemakha, 77 miles west of Baku, encountering no resistance.

17 Elchibey dismisses the ministers of national security and internal affairs, reportedly at the insistence of National Independence Party chairman Etibar Mamedov.

18 Elchibey flees Baku by private plane for his home town of Ordubad in Nakhichevan.

18 In a TV address, Geidar Aliev assumes the powers of president.

18 The Russian foreign ministry accuses Estonia of "aggressive nationalism" and warns that "the line of confrontation taken by Tallinn" may have serious consequences, not only for Estonia but also for the Baltic region.

19 Approximately 2,500 refugees, mostly Abkhaz and ethnic Russians, are evacuated from Tkvarcheli.

20 Russian troops are placed on alert in North Ossetia and Ingushetia due to growing tensions.

21 Prime minister Adolfas Slezevicius visits the United States and asks US national security advisor Anthony Lake to send observers to monitor the withdrawal of Russian troops from Lithuania.

22 Troops loyal to rebel Colonel Surat Guseinov stroll Baku.

23 The foreign minister of Belarus, Pyotr Krauchenka, asserts that other countries should provide funds in addition to the $74 million proposed by the United States for the elimination of its nuclear weapons.

23 The Clinton administration warns Russia against the planned sale of rocket-fuel ingredients to Libya.

23 Russian deputy foreign minister Vitaly Churkin unveils a seven-point declaration outlining considerations that should be taken into account in talks on Bosnia. The most important aspects are that Russia rejects the "legalization" of land taken by force or by ethnic cleansing in Bosnia, and Russia demands that the external border of Bosnia-Herzegovina be preserved.

23 Russian foreign minister Andrei Kozyrev calls for a further extension of the moratorium on nuclear testing being observed by Russia, France, the UK, and the US.

23 An assembly of Black Sea Fleet officers denounces the Moscow agreement signed by President Yeltsin and President Kravchuk that would split the fleet.

24 Russian prime minister Viktor Chernomyrdin cancels a planned visit to Washington over US accusations that Russian plans to sell sophisticated missile technology to India violates international export regulations.

24 Russian president Yeltsin accuses Estonia of unfriendly actions toward his country and charges that "there is ethnic cleansing similar to apartheid going on in Estonia."

24 A NATO Political Committee delegation holds talks with Lithuanian president Algirdas Brazauskas. Brazauskas speaks about the country's political and economic situation and asks for NATO's support in helping Lithuania become a member of the EC.

26 The chairman of Georgia's Parliament, Eduard Shevardnadze, meets with Kravchuk. One of the issues discussed in their 45-minute meeting was possible Ukrainian mediation in settling the Abkhaz conflict.

28 Rebel leader Surat Guseinov holds talks with Aliev in Baku, after which Guseinov announces that his revolt is over and pledges loyalty to Aliev.

30 A session of Azerbaijan's National Assembly votes 38 to 1 to appoint Surat Guseinov prime minister with responsibility for the ministries of defense, security, and the interior.

JULY

1-4 Abkhaz forces launch a major offensive.

2 The chairman of the Russian Committee on State Security and Defense, Sergei Stepashin, notes that any expansion of NATO to include Poland, Hungary, and the Czech Republic would be tantamount to creating a "cordon sanitaire" around Russia.

2 The Ukrainian Parliament votes 226 to 15 in favor of an amendment to a document on Ukraine's foreign policy objectives that asserts that the nuclear weapons on Ukrainian territory are Ukraine's property.

3 Azeri security forces attack several thousand supporters of ousted President Abulfaz Elchibey in Baku.

3 Proteges of acting president Aliev are appointed ministers of security and the interior.

4 Shevardnadze narrowly misses being hit by shrapnel from an Abkhaz shell as he travels by car to the town of Shroma to talk with Georgian soldiers.

5 Russian defense minister Pavel Grachev and chairman of Kyrgyzstan's State Committee on Defense Dzhanibek Umetaliev sign two agreements on military cooperation. One agreement provides for either country to lease land for military installations on the territory of the other, the rent to be paid in equipment and training. Both sides also undertook to maintain supply systems for military units and to place orders for equipment with local industries. The agreements also covered social and legal protection and provision of housing for military staff stationed on each other's territory.

6   Shevardnadze declares martial law effective throughout Abkhazia.

7   Georgian prime minister Tengiz Sigua asserts that Georgia would recall its ambassador from Moscow if Russia did not stop supplying the Abkhaz separatists with arms, equipment, and ammunition.

7   Polish defense minister Janusz Onyszkiewicz and his Russian counterpart Gen. Pavel Grachev sign an agreement on military cooperation. The agreement provides for technical cooperation and the exchange of specialists and information.

9   The UN Security Council unanimously approves sending fifty military observers to Georgia as soon as a cease-fire holds.

9   The commander of Russia's 201st Motorized Rifle Division in Tajikistan, Major General Mukhriddin Ashurov, is replaced by Colonel Viktor Timofeev, who was previously a division commander in Russia's Kaliningrad Oblast.

10   Ukrainian foreign minister Anatoly Zlenko sets out his blueprint for Ukrainian security policy, stressing the importance of creating a collective security zone stretching from the Baltic to the Black Sea. He argues that existing groups, such as the Visegrad group, need to be "widened and deepened." While Zlenko did not mention Russia directly, he rejects Russia's claim to a special role in peacekeeping and regional security in the former USSR. Zlenko notes that the new North Atlantic Cooperation Council is an important development but he is also critical of NATO for not moving quickly enough to reform itself to deal with the post-Cold War environment.

10-11   Russian president Boris Yeltsin and German chancellor Helmut Kohl held a two-day summit at Lake Baikal to discuss bilateral relations, Russian troop withdrawals, and integration of Russia into Europe.

12   Russian deputy foreign minister Boris Pastukhov states that Russian-mediated peace talks in Moscow failed to produce a cease-fire agreement and have been suspended indefinitely.

13   Russian deputy prime minister Sergei Shakhrai, while in Sochi, proposes using a trilateral peacekeeping force to settle the Abkhaz conflict in a manner similar to that employed in South Ossetia, where Russian, Georgian, and North Ossetian troops were deployed.

13   About 200 Tajik rebels and their Afghan supporters capture a Russian border post in Tajikistan and destroy a nearby village. The attack kills some 28 Russian soldiers, 6 Tajik interior ministry troops, between 100 and 200 civilians, and an undisclosed number of rebel fighters.

14   Russian Border Guards, supported by troops of Russia's 201st Motorized Rifle Division and Tajik interior ministry forces, take back a Tajik post near the Afghan border attacked the previous day.

15   Russia's Parliament approves an urgent order to the Russian government to take "all necessary measures to protect and ensure the safety" of Russian Border Guards in Tajikistan.

15   The Azerbaijan National Assembly hears an interim report on the findings of its commission to investigate the circumstances of the attack by government troops on the headquarters of Surat Guseinov's private army in Gyandzha on 4 June.

16 Assassination rumors against Aliev sweep through Baku.

16 Musavat Party chairman and former National Assembly speaker Isa Gambarov and two former security ministers are arrested.

16-17 A high-level Russian military delegation, led by Minister of Defense Pavel Grachev, is in Tajikistan to coordinate a response to intensified attacks by Afghan-backed Tajik rebels.

17 Police break into the headquarters of the Azerbaijan Popular Front, beat and detain a number of Front officials, and rip out telephones and fax machines.

19 Tajik and Russian warplanes bomb a strategic rebel stronghold east of Dushanbe.

20 Imomali Rakhmonov, Tajikistan's head of state, stresses the importance of reopening the strategic Dushanbe-Khorog road, currently blocked by rebels.

20 Leader of the independent Mkhedrioni armed formation and Parliament deputy Dzhaba Ioseliani blames Russia for the escalation of the conflict in Abkhazia. He warns that if Sukhumi falls to the Abkhaz separatists his units will create a "second Afghanistan" for Russia by starting a guerrilla war.

20 A UN technical team led by American George Sherry begins work in Tbilisi to prepare for the arrival of fifty UN military observers.

21 Russian special envoy Boris Pastukhov and Shevardnadze approve a draft agreement for a cease-fire in Abkhazia.

21 Marius Yuzbashian, Armenian KGB chief for ten years until October 1988, is shot three times while walking his dog in a Erevan park.

22 Shushkevich completes the process of acceding to the Nuclear Nonproliferation Treaty during a visit to Washington. Shushkevich and US defense secretary Les Aspin also sign three agreements providing for $59 million in US assistance for removal of nuclear weapons from Belarus and cleansing of former weapons sites.

22 Armenian troops engage Azeri forces in Agdam.

22 Kyrgystan's top defense official, Major General Dzhanibek Umetaliev, chairman of the State Committee on Defense, is removed. Umetaliev is replaced by his own first deputy, Myrzakan Subanov.

22 Defense minister Pavel Grachev accuses Ukraine of moving to take over control of the nuclear weapons on its territory. Grachev states that the Ukrainian defense ministry on 3 July issued an order concerning the status of nuclear weapons installations which provided for canceling all Russian directives concerning them, and transferring the installations and the special units guarding them to the 43rd Missile Army, administratively controlled by Ukraine.

22 Marshal Yevgeny Shaposhnikov transfers his set of launch authorization codes to Russian defense minister Grachev shortly after resigning from his position as commander of the CIS Joint Armed Forces. This confirms the fact that Russia has de facto taken full control of launch authority from the CIS command, and puts an end to any CIS nuclear force.

22 More clashes occur along the Tajik-Afghan border, with Russian troops firing on rebel positions on Afghan territory. Unconfirmed reports also

state that there has been more fighting in the mountains east of Dushanbe, where Tajik interior ministry forces are trying to destroy rebel strongholds.

23 Karabakh forces backed by tanks take the strategic town of Agdam after street fighting in which up to 500 Azeri soldiers are killed. Karabakh forces advance to within one kilometer of Fizuli.

23 Ukrainian defense minister Konstantin Morozov suggests that Ukraine may try to join the Nuclear Non-proliferation Treaty with the special status of a "transition country" with nuclear weapons.

24 Foreign minister Andrei Kozyrev, addressing a consultative meeting of ASEAN foreign ministers in Singapore, proposes the creation of a "regional security community" in the Asian-Pacific region whose mechanisms would include centers for preventing conflicts and for overseeing arms trading in the region, and a Russian-ASEAN committee to coordinate Russia's broader dealings with Southeast Asia nations.

24 Aliev calls on the UN to "restrain" Armenian aggression, arguing that "any references by the Armenian side to the fact that the armed forces fighting in Nagorno-Karabakh are not subordinate to the Republic of Armenia are without foundation."

24-26 The Russian military continues its artillery bombardment across the Tajik-Afghan border.

26 The Abkhaz Parliament debates and approves a plan to end the conflict with Georgia.

26 Yeltsin announces at a meeting of the Security Council that Minister of Security Viktor Barannikov has been reprimanded for his ministry's lack of preparedness for events on the Afghanistan-Tajikistan border.

27 Yeltsin dismisses Minister of Security Viktor Barannikov for "violation of ethical norms and serious failures in the leadership of his ministry, including the Border Troops."

27 In Sochi, Georgian Parliament speaker Vakhtang Goguadze, Deputy Chairman of the Abkhaz Supreme Soviet Sokrat Dzhindzholia, and Russian foreign minister Andrei Kozyrev sign a cease-fire agreement.

27 Following a three-hour meeting between visiting foreign minister Konstantin Morozov and Secretary of Defense Les Aspin, Pentagon officials announce that Ukraine has begun dismantling some of its ten-warhead SS-19 long-range nuclear missiles.

28 Yeltsin names Nikolai Golushko acting Minister of Security. He worked for the KGB for over 25 years and was appointed chairman of the Ukrainian KGB in 1987. In 1992 he joined the Russian Ministry of Security as one of Barannikov's deputies.

28 Kazakh president Nursultan Nazarbaev and Uzbek president Islam Karimov issue a joint appeal in Almaty to the other CIS heads of state to hold an emergency summit. The two presidents complain that "regional separatism, the isolationism of individual states and their desire to get out of the crisis on their own or at the expense of the economic interests of neighboring states" are taking the place of economic integration.

30 Gamsakhurdia supporters seize the town of Senaki in Western Georgia but withdraw after Jaba Ioseliani, head of the paramilitary Mkhedrioni group, said he would eject them by force.

30 Kravchuk states that Ukraine's 46 SS-24 strategic nuclear missiles are not covered by START-1 and that the question of destroying the SS-24s must be dealt with in a separate treaty between Ukraine, Russia, and the US.

31 In accordance with the Latvian-Russian agreement on allowing prisoners to serve out sentences in their homeland, Sergei Parfenov, the former deputy chief of the OMON forces in Riga, is turned over to Russia.

AUGUST

1 The Russian government issues a threat to launch a preemptive strike on the Tajik-Afghan border if Tajik opposition forces and their Afghan supporters continue to concentrate along the Afghan side of the border.

1 A first contingent of Russian troops who are part of a tripartite cease-fire monit-oring group arrive in Abkhazia.

1 Viktor Polyanichko, the head of the interim administration in the areas of North Ossetia and Ingushetia which are under emergency rule, is ambushed and killed.

3 Russia's First Deputy Minister of Foreign Affairs Anatoly Adamishin, on a trip through Central Asia to discuss the situation in Tajikistan, meets Niyazov and is told that Turkmenistan will not participate in any joint military actions in Tajikistan.

5 The Washington Post reports that the Clinton administration is close to adopting a policy calling for the US to intercede diplomatically in regional and ethnic disputes in the former Soviet Union. The document is known as Directive 13.

5 Vice President Aleksandr Rutskoi, speaking to military veterans on the fiftieth anniversary of the Battle of Kursk, asserts that he believes the former USSR will be resurrected and will "again become a superpower which can guarantee peace on earth."

7 The heads of state of Kazakhstan, Kyrgyzstan, and Tajikistan meet with Boris Yeltsin to seek a solution to the conflict on the Tajik-Afghan border. In a declaration issued at the end of the meeting, the summit participants commit themselves to increasing the numbers of their troops guarding the border, promising additional military, economic, and humanitarian aid to Tajikistan, and threaten retaliatory measures if outside attacks on the border continue. A separate declaration on the inviolability of borders that commits the signatories to prevent activities by individuals or groups on their territory seeking to alter borders is also signed.

8 CIA official Fred Woodruff is shot and killed while riding in a car with Eldar Guguladze, Shevardnadze's security chief, near the village of Natakhtari outside Tbilisi.

9 Deputy Defense Minister Konstantin Kobets claims that the Ministry of Finance owes the Ministry of Defense more than R1.5 trillion and that, as a result of the funding shortfall, more than 60 percent of all servicemen were not paid in July and many received no pay in June.

10 Yevgeny Shaposhnikov, former USSR Minister of Defense and subsequently CinC of the CIS Joint Armed Forces, offers to resign from his current post as chief of the Russian Security Council.

10-15 Afghanistan's foreign minister Amin Asalla visits Dushanbe for talks with the government of Tajikistan on ending the fighting on the Tajik-Afghan border and on repatriation of the thousands of Tajik refugees who fled to Afghanistan after Tajikistan's present government took power in December 1992. They issue a communique in which the Afghan side promises to try to stop attacks on Tajikistan from its territory, and the Tajik side undertakes not to allow attacks against Afghanistan except in self-defense.

10 The head of the directorate for arms control and disarmament of the Ukrainian Ministry of Foreign Affairs, Kostyantyn Hryshchenko, denounces Russia's assumption of control over all former Soviet nuclear weapons.

11 Russian president Boris Yeltsin promises Kuchma during their meeting that Russia would pay Ukraine for nuclear weapons transferred to Russia.

16 Ukrainian Minister of Defense Konstantin Morozov and his German counterpart, Volker Ruehe, sign an agreement on military cooperation that provides for official and working visits between delegations of the armed forces of the two countries.

16 The Azeri Parliament condemns what were termed "separatist actions" by Alikram Gumbatov, head of the self-proclaimed Talysh-Mugan Republic located on Azerbaijan's southeastern border with Iran. Gumbatov is accused of links with the Islamic Hezbollah group and with "Mafia clans" said to be financing him. He was further said to have 3,000 armed supporters plus 80 armored vehicles.

16 The State Defense Committee of Kyrgyzstan announces that 122 young men from Kyrgyzstan would be sent for officer training to military schools in Russia, while another 40 would be sent to Uzbekistan. Several dozen cadets from Kyrgyzstan are currently studying in Turkey.

16 Lithuanian prime minister Adolfas Slezevicius is received by Valdis Birkavs in Riga. They discuss Baltic security and Russian troop withdrawal as well as Lithuania's plan to construct a petroleum terminal near the Latvian border. The two also examine ways to improve cooperation in resolving economic, energy, and border problems.

18-19 Armenian forces take the town of Dzhebrail, south of Nagorno-Karabakh and fourteen kilometers from the Azeri-Iranian frontier. An estimated 60,000 refugees from Fizuli and Dzhebrail are displaced by the fighting.

21 Sergei Sarkisyab, head of the Nagorno-Karabakh self-defense forces, is appointed Armenian defense minister.

22 The Russian foreign ministry breaks off troop withdrawal talks with Lithuania. A statement asserts that the Russian troops eventually will leave in accordance with the norms of international law, but within a timetable suitable for Russia, about which Lithuania would be informed.

23 Russian foreign minister Andrei Kozyrev warns Poland, the Czech Republic, and Slovakia against joining NATO and reasserts Russian strategic interests in the Baltic region. He asserts that attempts by Poland to gain

NATO membership would merely strengthen "reactionary forces" in Russia.

23-24 The CIS Council of Defense Ministers meets. Participants agree, first, to transform the supreme command of the CIS Joint Armed Forces into a permanent headquarters for coordinating military cooperation, to be subordinated to the CIS Council of Defense Ministers. The decision abolishes the post of CIS commander-in-chief, formerly held by Yevgeny Shaposhnikov, and names CIS Main Staff chief Viktor Samsonov as temporary head of the new headquarters. The representatives of the six signatory states to the CIS Collective Security Treaty sign a document to promote military cooperation in eleven areas, including setting up a common air defense system and drafting a long-term concept on developing the CIS Joint Armed Forces. In addition, they approve a Russian proposal that would apparently set up a Collective Security Council to include the heads of CIS states, their defense and foreign ministers, as well as a secretary general.

24 Lt. Gen. Aleksandr Lebed claims to have been authorized to discharge some political functions by his superiors in Moscow. "I have taken on, and strive to rigorously fulfill, the roles of peacekeeper, diplomat, and neutral party."

24 Tens of thousands of Azeri civilians continue to flee towards Iran to escape the ongoing fighting in the region of Dzhebrail in southern Azerbaijan.

24 A meeting of the CIS Council of Foreign Ministers in Moscow reaches agreement on eight documents, including joint initiatives on fighting terrorism, drugs, pollution, and the spread of weapons of mass destruction to be presented to the 48th UN General Assembly.

25 Yeltsin states that Russia has no objection to Polish NATO membership.

26 Telephone negotiations between Azerbaijan deputy Parliament chairman Afiaddinn Dzhalilov and Nagorno-Karabakh foreign ministry representatives fail to lead to the hoped-for talks on a cease-fire.

27 Armed units subordinate to the Azerbaijan Popular Front occupy Nakhichevan airport and prevent the unloading of voting papers for the 29 August referendum.

30 Nazarbaev tells a congress of the Global Anti-Nuclear Alliance in Almaty of Kazakstan's concerns about the effects of nuclear testing at China's Lop Nor test site.

31 Russian troops officially complete their departure from Lithuania.

31 Reflecting ongoing efforts by Russian political leaders to win support within the armed forces, Yeltsin spends a full day visiting troops and observing exercises in the Moscow Military District.

SEPTEMBER

1 The head of the Nagorno-Karabakh government, Robert Kocharyan, claims that Iranian troops "had been visually observed" crossing the Azeri-Iranian border.

1 Russian defense minister Pavel Grachev and high-ranking Georgian officials agree on the continued stationing of Russian troops in Georgia.

2   Turkmenistan and Russia sign a bilateral agreement on military coopera-
    tion.
3   Ukrainian and Russian leaders meet in Massandra and sign treaties on
    security issues. The Russian side evidently surprises the Ukrainian delega-
    tion by the toughness of its position on the debt issue and by proposing
    that Ukraine settle this problem without delay by selling its share of the
    Black Sea Fleet and leasing Sevastopol to Russia. When President Krav-
    chuk and other members of the Ukrainian delegation finally arrive back
    in Kiev, they deny that any deals concerning the sale of Ukraine's share
    of the Black Sea Fleet or Ukraine's surrender of its nuclear warheads to
    Russia had been made.
3   Yeltsin announces that he and Ukrainian president Leonid Kravchuk had
    agreed at a summit meeting in the city of Massandra on the Crimean
    peninsula that Ukraine would turn over its share of the Black Sea Fleet
    in exchange for "more or less" the cancellation of Ukrainian debts to
    Russia. Yeltsin also announces that agreement was reached on the return
    of nuclear warheads from Ukraine to Russia for dismantling.
6   Russian Border Guards patrolling the Armenian-Turkish frontier twice
    come under fire from Turkish territory.
9   Russian foreign minister Andrei Kozyrev meets with Tajik leaders in Du-
    shanbe and claims that more Russian troops will be sent to the country.
9   Armenia declares that it has evidence that Azerbaijan is receiving military
    equipment from Ukraine.
9   President Yeltsin's Kremlin guard, or Main Protection Directorate, takes
    over the official dacha of Valery Zorkin, chairman of Russia's Constitu-
    tional Court.
10 Ukrainian defense minister Konstantin Morozov informs Kravchuk that
    he will disclaim all responsibility for Ukraine's southern defenses if the
    Massandra agreement to sell Ukraine's half of the Black Sea Fleet is im-
    plemented.
12 Addressing a meeting in Kutaisi, Shevardnadze warns that supporters of
    ousted president Zviad Gamsakhurdia have one month to lay down their
    arms or be liquidated.
13 Lt. Gen. Aleksandr Lebed wins 88 percent of the votes in a four-way race
    for a seat in the Dniester Republic Supreme Soviet.
15 Russia's ambassador to Poland, Yury Kashlev, asserts that Russia's stance
    on possible Polish membership in NATO has been "oversimplified and
    misunderstood."
15 An Aeroflot TU-134, with about fifty passengers and crew on board, is
    hijacked during a scheduled flight from Baku to Perm. The hijackers—
    reportedly four in number—are said to be members or supporters of the
    pro-Iranian Hezbollah. After a refueling stop in Kiev, the plane lands at
    an airport near Oslo. All passengers are released unharmed, and the hi-
    jackers give themselves up.
15-16 Fighting erupts on two different fronts in Georgia. Forces loyal to ousted
    president Zviad Gamsakhurdia are fighting in western Georgia for the

control of the main rail line. Abkhaz forces break the seven-week cease-fire.

16 About 140 members of the Volunteer Home Guard Service in Kaunas flee to the forests with their weapons because they are prompted by fears that the Lithuanian government is planning to dissolve the service.

17 Prime Minister Viktor Chernomyrdin reiterates his position that the Kuriles will not be ceded to Japan.

18 Yeltsin appoints Oleg Lobov, whose job as first deputy prime minister went to Yegor Gaidar, as the new secretary of the Security Council.

20 Abkhaz forces surround Sukhumi.

21 Abkhaz forces shoot down a Georgian aircraft. Dozens are killed.

21 The Supreme Soviet votes to impeach Yeltsin and swears in Aleksandr Rutskoi as acting president. Rutskoi appoints Viktor Barannikov, Andrei Dunaev, and Vladislav Achalov as ministers for security, interior, and defense, respectively.

22 The Ministry of Security signals its support to Yeltsin by announcing that it had received special directives from the Office of the President and that they would be "fulfilled unconditionally."

22 Minister of Defense Pavel Grachev assures Yeltsin of the loyalty of the armed forces.

22 A second Georgian civilian aircraft bursts into flames on landing at Sukhumi after being hit by a heat-seeking missile; some 20 of the 81 passengers and crew manage to escape.

27 Russian Supreme Soviet first vice chairman Yury Voronin tells the Congress of People's Deputies that a detachment from the Dniester Republic had arrived in Moscow and joined the defenders of the Russian parliament building.

27 President Bill Clinton meets for an hour with Baltic presidents Lennart Meri (Estonia), Guntis Ulmanis (Latvia), and Algirdas Brazauskas (Lithuania). Clinton expresses US support for the early, unconditional, and rapid withdrawal of Russian troops from Estonia and Latvia. While Meri demands that Russian president Boris Yeltsin speed the withdrawal, Ulmanis raises concern about Russia's hopes to retain some military installations in Latvia. Brazauskas states that he was worried about the military build-up in Kaliningrad and supported its demilitarization. The three presidents also gave Clinton a letter stating that the termination of Radio Free Europe Baltic-language broadcasts is "premature and unsettling for the Baltic countries."

27 Abkhaz forces capture Sukhumi.

28 A bomb explodes outside the US embassy in Tallinn.

28 Russian first deputy defense minister Andrei Kokoshin states that the leadership of the armed forces is united in its willingness to implement instructions from the Russian president and government. More specifically, Kokoshin said that the Ministry of Defense Collegium, which includes all deputy and first deputy defense ministers, supported Grachev.

28 Clashes continue to break out in Moscow.

28 Troops surround the Russian parliament building.
29 The Russian government gives an ultimatum to the legislature to leave the Russian Parliament building by 4 October.
29 Clashes continue to break out in Moscow.
29 Latvian president Guntis Ulmanis tells the UN General Assembly that although the UN and CSCE have passed resolutions calling for the speedy withdrawal of Russian troops from his country, talks on their removal are making little progress.
29-30 Forces loyal to ousted Georgian president Zviad Gamsakhurdia withdraw from the coastal town of Ochamchira, paving the way for its capture by Abkhaz troops.
30 Lt. Jonas Maksvytis, who led the Volunteer Home Guard Service in Kaunas in an insurrection, voluntarily surrenders to the Lithuanian police.

OCTOBER

1 The press service of the Belarusian Ministry of Defense announces that the withdrawal of Russian troops from the country should be completed in 1996 instead of 1998, when all nuclear weapons should be removed under the Lisbon Protocol.
2 Aliev claims that security officials have foiled a plot to assassinate him by a Turkish citizen and Azerbaijan Popular Front members with links to the extreme right wing Grey Wolves organization.
2 Russian president Boris Yeltsin issues a decree which awards medals to 200 servicemen in Russia's 14th Army.
3 Violence sweeps Moscow as pro- and anti-government forces clash. Rioters break through police lines surrounding the Parliament building. Pro-Rutskoi and Khasbulatov forces attack the Moscow mayor's office. Armed with grenades, the rebels attempt to seize the Ostankino broadcast center, shutting down the first Russian TV channel. Ostankino's Radio Maiak also goes off the air, but the Russian second TV channel continues to broadcast. A number of people are killed and wounded in the attack at Ostankino. Work at the ITAR-TASS office is briefly disrupted when protesters blockade it.
3 First Deputy Prime Minister Yegor Gaidar calls on citizens of Russia to support the president and government. Speaking on Russian TV he states, "Honestly, tonight we need your support. We cannot place responsibility for saving democracy just on the police and internal ministry troops. We call those who are ready to support Russian democracy to assemble at the Moscow's mayor's office to protect our future, our children's future and to prevent making our country a huge concentration camp for decades."
3 Yeltsin issues a decree stipulating that Prime Minister Chernomyrdin is to assume presidential powers if Yeltsin could not carry out his duties. In addition, Yeltsin declares a state of emergency for Moscow.
4 The Taman Guards Division, airborne troops from Tuva, and the Dzherzhinsky Division attack the Russian Parliament building with automatic weapons and tanks, setting the White House ablaze. Dozens are killed.

4 The top leaders of the opposition, Ruslan Khasbulatov, Aleksandr Rutskoi, and General Albert Makashov, surrender after government forces
storm the Russian Parliament. They are taken to the Ministry of Security's
Lefortovo Prison. Prior to their surrender, Khasbulatov and Rutskoi asked
Western ambassadors to guarantee their safety, the Belgian embassy playing a mediating role.

4 The United States, Britain, Germany and the European Community express support for Yeltsin's use of force against the Russian Parliament.

4 The Russian government suspends the activities of a number of extreme
nationalist and communist opposition groups. Among the suspended
groups are the National Salvation Front, the Russian Communist Party,
the Communist Youth Organization (Komsomol) and the Officers' Union.

4 Georgian troops retake the western town of Khoni.

4 Ukraine's Minister of Defense Konstantin Morozov resigns because of
political conflicts within Parliament.

5 The Russian Parliament continues to burn.

5 Moscow and the city authorities report that some 5,000 militiamen are on
duty under the state of emergency. Sniper fire continues and shooting is
reported from districts in the vicinity of Parliament. Early in the morning
of 5 October the headquarters of the ITAR-TASS news agency comes
under fire. One person is reported killed and several are injured. Outside
Moscow the country is reported calm, though anti-Yeltsin demonstrations
are reported in St. Petersburg and some other cities.

5 According to the Main Medical Directorate of Moscow the total casualties from 9 a.m. on 3 October to 6 a.m. on 5 October numbered some 526
people. Of this number some 421 were hospitalized. Fifty-nine people are
reported to have died during this period. Other reports suggest that sixty
people were killed in the attack on the Ostankino TV studio.

5 According to the Washington Post Russian military leaders were split over
whether or not to support Boris Yeltsin during a crucial meeting of the
Ministry of Defense Collegium on the eve of the 4 October crackdown in
Moscow.

5 The Russian government criticizes the storage of nuclear warheads at the
Pervomaisk ICBM site. The number of warheads at the site is 6-8 times
higher than the limit, and both temperature and radiation levels have increased as a result.

5 Over 300 armed Tajik oppositionists cross the border from Afghanistan
but are stopped by Russian and Tajik forces.

6 The commander of Russian forces in Germany, Col. Gen. Matvei Burlakov, states that the army's participation in the assault on the Parliament
building was a limited action and should not be construed as a sign of
unconditional loyalty to Yeltsin's program of reform.

6 The Russian government formally requests that the limits on flank de-
ployments of weapons covered by the CFE treaty be revised upwards.

7 Five members of the Volunteer Home Guard Service in Kaunas are arrested for stealing twenty Kalashnikov automatic rifles to sell on the black
market.

7 Komsomolskaia pravda reports that highly placed supporters of Boris
  Yeltsin in the presidential apparatus are accusing Russian defense minister
  Pavel Grachev of, at the least, incompetence in his management of the 4
  October assault on the White House. The Yeltsin aides are reported to
  have said that Grachev dragged his feet on involving army troops in the
  operation, and that it was in fact Deputy Defense Minister Konstantin
  Kobets who finally took command of the situation.

7 Yeltsin awards interior minister Viktor Erin with the country's highest order—the title of Hero of the Russian Federation. The title is also awarded
  to eight soldiers, four posthumously, for suppressing the rebellion on 3-
  4 October. The heads of the ministries of defense and security, Nikolai
  Golushko and Pavel Grachev, respectively, are awarded, together with
  Deputy Defense Minister Konstantin Kobets, the Order of Personal Courage.

8 Col. Gen. Vitaly Hryhorovych Radetskii is approved as Ukraine's new
  defense minister by Parliament.

8 The new Russian Procurator General, Aleksei Kazannik, formally arrests
  and charges Ruslan Khasbulatov, Aleksandr Rutskoi, Viktor Barannikov,
  Andrei Dunaev, and Vladislav Achalov with "organizing mass disorders"
  under Article 79 of the Russian criminal code.

8 Russian foreign minister Andrei Kozyrev states that Russia strives to create effective peacekeeping forces as a means of dealing with regional conflicts in the former Soviet Union as well as in other parts of the world.

8 In the New York Times an article claims that the Soviet Union developed
  a command and control system option to allow nuclear weapons to be
  fired automatically under special circumstances. The system could be
  enabled by the Russian military or political leadership if it appeared that
  the leadership would not survive a nuclear strike. Normally the system is
  designed to maintain strict centralized control.

8 Armenian president Levon Ter-Petrossian, acting Azeri president Geidar
  Aliev and Georgian Parliament chairman Eduard Shevardnadze hold two
  hours of frank discussions with Russian president Boris Yeltsin in Moscow. Agreement is reached on the need to coordinate efforts in conflict
  mediation with the help of international organizations, and on the deployment of Russian troops to restore rail links from the Black Sea to Tbilisi
  and to Armenia.

8 Addressing the UN General Assembly, Moldovan foreign minister Nicolae Tiu solicits support for the withdrawal of Russian troops, which are
  meant "to keep Moldova in Russia's sphere of influence" and "to separate the Transdniester from Moldova."

9 The heads of the Russian and Georgian general staffs sign a treaty on the
  legal status of the Russian troops currently stationed in Georgia together
  with eight protocols including one on the joint use of all port facilities and
  airfields.

9 The state of emergency and curfew that were declared in Moscow on 3
  October are extended for eight more days.

9 Kravchuk appoints Vice Admiral Volodymyr Bezkorovainy as Ukraine's new navy commander. He replaces Borys Kozhyn. Previously, Bezkorovainy commanded the nuclear submarine force of Russia's Northern Fleet.

11 Brazauskas states he hopes to improve contacts with NATO.

11 Ulmanis asserts that Latvia would like to join NATO.

11-13 Yeltsin departs Moscow for a three-day trip to Japan. On 12 October he officially offers condolences for "the inhuman treatment of Japanese prisoners of war" interned in the USSR in 1945 and subsequently. Yeltsin, who arrived in Tokyo the previous evening, spent the morning meeting with the Japanese emperor and empress. Later he confers with Prime Minister Morihiro Hosokawa and his top economic advisors. Yeltsin and his Japanese hosts announce the signing of a number of agreements, including a joint declaration on Japanese-Russian relations. The two sides pledge in the declaration to resolve the Kurile Islands territorial dispute on the basis of respect for "law and justice." Japanese prime minister Morihiro Hosokawa tells reporters that Yeltsin agreed to honor a 1956 joint declaration in which the USSR announced its readiness to negotiate the return of the two smallest of the four disputed Kurile Islands, with the future of the other two to be left to subsequent negotiations.

12 Addressing the UN General Assembly, the acting head of the Azeri delegation, Yashar Aliev, stated that the complete and unconditional withdrawal of Armenian forces from all occupied territory in Azerbaijan is an essential precondition for convening the CSCE Minsk conference on a settlement of the conflict.

12 Ukraine's foreign minister, Anatoly Zlenko, states that granting special status for Russian peacekeeping operations is unacceptable.

13 General Albert Makashov, a longtime opponent of Boris Yeltsin and a leader of the military forces supporting the Russian Parliament, is charged with "organizing mass unrest."

13 Turkmen Minister of Defense Danatar Kopekov issues a statement denying Russian press reports that Afghan air force planes bombed Turkmen territory.

14 Ukrainian air crews evacuate 7,000 Georgian refugees from Abkhazia.

14 Speaking to a meeting of Afghan War veterans, defense minister Pavel Grachev states that Boris Yeltsin should remain president until at least 1996.

14 Lt. Gen. Aleksandr Lebed, commander of Russia's 14th Army in Moldova, resigns his recently won mandate as a deputy to the Dniester Republic Supreme Soviet.

15 Russian foreign minister Andrei Kozyrev allegedly sends a letter to Secretary of State Warren Christopher indicating that Russia might veto new UN sanctions against Libya for protecting two suspects in the downing of the Lockerbie flight in 1988.

17 Senior Japanese government officials protest resumed dumping by the Russian Navy of radioactive waste in the Sea of Japan.

17 Yeltsin military aide General Dmitry Volkogonov states that security and defense ministry leaders had indeed been slow in throwing their support behind Boris Yeltsin during the 3-4 October disturbances in Moscow.

17 Gamsakhurdia's forces capture the strategic rail junction of Samtredia.

18 Shevardnadze reports that the Georgian Army "has practically disintegrated."

18 Nazarbaev visits China to discuss political, and economic cooperation. The two sides agree to set up a group of experts to discuss nuclear testing sites in their respective countries.

18 Lithuanian defense minister Audrius Butkevicius resigns.

19 Gamsakhurdia's forces close in on Kutaisi.

19-20 Ukraine's Parliament meets in closed session to debate security issues. The Parliament approves a military doctrine which makes nuclear disarmament conditional on Western security guarantees. Kravchuk accuses the West of not helping Ukraine in its efforts to disarm. After the closed debate over Ukrainian military doctrine confusion emerges between Ukrainian officials on their obligations under START-1 and the Lisbon Protocol. Kravchuk, in reaffirming his commitment to see the START-1 treaty ratified, suggests that after its ratification all SS-19 ICBMs in Ukraine would be scrapped. Dmytro Pavlychko, chairman of the parliamentary committee on foreign relations, again asserts that only 36 percent of the delivery vehicles on Ukrainian territory would be dismantled.

20 Two nuclear warheads leak radiation while sitting in a railroad car on the Russian-Ukrainian border. The leak has been ongoing since 5 October. Ukraine has sought guarantees and compensation from Russia for the warheads and their materials.

20 Under strong pressure from Japan, South Korea, and the US, Russian authorities decide to cancel a second planned dumping of liquid nuclear waste into the Sea of Japan.

20 During his visit to France, Russian foreign minister Andrei Kozyrev and French foreign minister Alain Juppe sign an accord providing for some $70 mn in assistance to Russia for nuclear weapons dismantling.

20 The Czech government announces that it will give two million koruny ($66,000) worth of surplus military equipment to Lithuania.

20-25 Georgian forces launch a major counteroffensive against Gamsakhurdia's forces and eject them from Poti, Khoni, and Lanchkhuta. The rail junction of Samtredia is also recaptured. Russian forces are rumored to be assisting the Georgian military.

22 Kravchuk calls for the creation of a new Central European security zone reflecting the new political realities of the post-Soviet era.

22 Deputy Chairman of the Democratic Party of Tajikistan Oynikhon Bobonazarova is arrested and accused of treason and membership in an armed organization that aims to overthrow the government.

22-23 Secretary of State Warren Christopher holds meetings with Russian officials in Moscow. Christopher states that Russia enthusiastically supports the US proposal to restrict NATO expansion to a plan of gradual growth.

Yeltsin calls the plan "brilliant" and "terrific" following meetings at his dacha with Christopher.

23 Armenian forces attack the towns of Kubatli, Zangelan, and Goradiz in southeastern Azerbaijan.

24 Nazarbaev meets with Secretary of State Warren Christopher in Amalty. Nazarbaev promises that Kazakhstan will ratify the Nuclear Non-proliferation Treaty by the end of this year. Christopher and Nazarbaev also reportedly eliminate all remaining problems connected with a draft "umbrella agreement" that will govern the payment of US denuclearization aid to Kazakhstan.

25 Secretary of State Warren Christopher and Ukrainian foreign minister Anatoly Zlenko sign an umbrella agreement that will clear the way for the US to dispense up to $175 million in aid to "denuclearize" Ukraine. Christopher also meets with Kravchuk, who promises to submit the START-1 treaty, the Lisbon Protocol, and the Nuclear Non-proliferation Treaty to parliament for ratification. Christopher also offers Ukraine an economic aid package worth $155 mn to help jump-start its economic reforms. He signs an agreement that will provide $27 mn to improve safety conditions at the Chernobyl power plant and four other nuclear power stations.

26 Ukraine's foreign ministry asks for a review of the CFE treaty. A ministry statement criticizes the treaty as being based on an outdated confrontation between two blocs. As a result, Ukraine is being forced to move tanks and other armored vehicles away from the Black Sea region and closer to the central European states.

26 Secretary of State Warren Christopher meets with Shushkevich and Prime Minister Vyacheslav Kebich in Minsk. Christopher presents the US "partnership for peace" initiative which would s'low Belarus to collaborate with NATO countries in military planning and exercises, and would give Belarus the right to consult with NATO nations in case it is threatened.

26 Secretary of State Warren Christopher, upon arriving in Riga, states that the US wants an early and complete pullout of Russian troops from Latvia.

26 Aleksandr Troshin is appointed deputy secretary of the Security Council. Troshin is a "technocrat" who received his education at the Moscow Aviation Institute's engineering and economics department, after which he worked in Gosplan. Most recently he served as first deputy minister of economics.

27 The three Baltic foreign ministers—Trivimi Velliste of Estonia, Georgs Andrejevs of Latvia, and Povilas Gylys of Lithuania—are said to back a new NATO partnership program to allow all former Warsaw Pact states and former Soviet republics, as well as four neutral European countries— Austria, Switzerland, Finland, and Sweden—to participate in a broad range of the alliance's activities.

27 According to the Estonian Ministry for the Environment, the environmental damage caused by the presence of Soviet and Russian troops over

more than fifty years amounts to 15,279,547,000 kroons (about $1.2 bn). Military airfields are the worst source of pollution (9 bn kroons), followed by military warehouses (2.5 bn kroons), weapons and other testing grounds (2.16 bn kroons), missile bases (about 328 mn kroons). Specific sums are not given on damage caused by radar stations, fuel tanks, ports, and other sites.

27 At a press conference in Riga following a meeting with the three Baltic foreign ministers, Secretary of State Warren Christopher states that the US welcomes the departure of Russian troops from Lithuania.

28 US defense secretary Les Aspin and Belarusian Minister of Defense Pavel Kozlovskii sign a memorandum in Washington providing for regular high-level US-Belarus military meetings and setting up a defense working group.

28 Ukraine and Slovakia sign a bilateral military agreement.

28-29 Forces loyal to ousted Georgian president Zviad Gamsakhurdia launch a counterattack and retake the town of Khobi. Georgian forces retake the town again the following day.

29 Iran, Turkey, and Azerbaijan call on the UN Security Council to convene a session to discuss renewed fighting in southern Azerbaijan.

29 Russian media reports that Russian defense minister Pavel Grachev will be dismissed for his actions during the October 1993 uprising.

31 Former KGB general Oleg Kalugin is detained by police in London in connection with the murder of Bulgarian dissident Georgy Markov in 1978.

NOVEMBER

• Fighting renews in the Khatlon and Gorno-Badakhshan regions.

2 Azeri president Geidar Aliev establishes a defense council to counter "the extreme deterioration of the military and political situation." He also appoints Colonel Nadzhameddin Sadykhov commander-in-chief of the Armed Forces.

2 Georgian government forces fight their way into the town of Khobi after subjecting it to heavy artillery bombardment

2 The Russian Security Council approves Russia's new military doctrine. The document is not released.

2 In Moscow talks are held between Yeltsin, foreign minister Andrei Kozyrev, and French prime minister Edouard Balladur. Kozyrev highlights the special relationship between France and Russia and states that the French side cannot imagine European security and political integration without Russia.

2 In an interview with the Hamburg weekly, Stern, Yeltsin states that Russia is prepared to do its part in realizing the "partnership for peace" concept for delaying the expansion of NATO to Eastern Europe as elaborated by NATO in October 1993.

3 Russian foreign minister Andrei Kozyrev claims that Russia is radically revising and reconsidering its interests in Eastern Europe. He states that Russia wishes to see Eastern Europe act as a bridge between Russia and Western Europe. Kozyrev reiterates Moscow's opposition to the expansion of NATO eastwards.

4 Ukraine states that the new Russian doctrine on the use of nuclear weapons is causing security concerns in Ukraine. According to the Russian defense minister, Pavel Grachev, Russia will not use nuclear arms against a country which has no nuclear weapons of its own and has signed the NPT agreement. Ukraine possesses numerous nuclear warheads and has not signed the NPT agreement.

4 A first wave of some 200 Russian marines from the Black Sea Fleet land in Poti to guard railway lines and roads in western Georgia against attack from troops loyal to ousted president Zviad Gamsakhurdia.

4 Testifying before the Senate Foreign Relations Committee, Secretary of State Warren Christopher states that a preliminary US government assessment of Russia's recently announced military doctrine determines that it did not undermine the "crucial principle" of respect for the sovereignty and territorial integrity of other former Soviet republics.

5-6 Russian foreign minister Andrei Kozyrev meets with his Ukrainian counterpart, Anatoly Zlenko, in Odessa. The two discuss implementing agreements reached during the Massandra summit regarding nuclear weapons and the division and sale of the Black Sea Fleet. The sale of Russian gas and oil to Ukraine is also on the agenda.

7 Brazauskas meets with Kazakh president Nursultan Nazarbaev in Almaty to discuss improving bilateral relations. Nazarbaev expressed interest in using the Lithuanian port of Klaipeda for trading purposes.

8 A second wave of 750 Russian marines and 40 armored vehicles land in Poti. The mission is described as humanitarian.

8-11 Russian defense minister Pavel Grachev visits China. The two sides sign a five-year military cooperation accord.

8 Foreign minister Andrei Kozyrev clarifies Russia's position on the question of tightening UN Security Council sanctions against Libya. Kozyrev states, "We will even use the veto if we have to in order to block this resolution, not because we are protecting terrorists, but because this resolution must take into consideration Russia's economic interests."

8 Western sources report that Azerbaijan has enlisted a force of Afghan mujahidin to bolster its army.

8-9 Lithuanian president Brazauskas meets with Chinese president Jiang Zemin and Chinese prime minister Li Peng in Beijing. The talks primarily focus on economic questions, especially Chinese trade to Europe through the Lithuanian port of Klaipeda.

9 A conference of leaders of the security services of Russia, Kazakhstan, Kyrgyzstan, Uzbekistan, and Tajikistan agree to coordinate protection of Tajikistan's border with Afghanistan and in normalizing the situation within Tajikistan.

11 The Ukrainian Parliament delays the START-1 debate.

11 The Ukrainian Parliament adopts a law banning paramilitary organizations. The law is aimed at the radical nationalist Ukrainian National Self-Defense Organization (UNSO), which has sent fighters to Abkhazia and Moldova and has staged a number of demonstrations in Ukraine in recent months.

12 Yeltsin criticizes Minister of Defense Pavel Grachev for hesitancy in calling Russian Army troops into action against pro-parliament forces on the night of 3-4 October 1993.

15 A North Korean diplomat is expelled from Russia for trying to recruit Russian missile specialists.

16 Russian foreign minister Andrei Kozyrev meets with Uzbek president Islam Karimov to develop a "strategic partnership" with Russia.

16 Russia's new military doctrine is publicly released. The doctrine includes among the external threats to Russia the suppression of the rights and legitimate interests of Russian citizens living abroad (presumably in the former Soviet republics), efforts by outside powers to interfere in the internal affairs of Russia, and attacks on Russian military installations located on the territory of foreign states. The doctrine includes in its list of items considered to be potential military threats to Russia a clause including "the widening of military blocs and alliances damaging the security interests of the Russian Federation." A more serious level of threat, that called "direct military threats to Russia," includes any attempts to interfere with support systems for strategic weapons, a clear reference to Ukraine.

16 Russia and Bulgaria sign an agreement on military cooperation.

17 Yeltsin and Russian defense minister Pavel Grachev observe military exercises in the Tula region.

17 Russia continues to ask for CFE changes.

17 Party of Russian Unity and Concord chairman Sergei Shakhrai claims that he fears the possibility of a military take-over in Russia.

18 Russian foreign minister Andrei Kozyrev ends a two-day visit to Dushanbe and exchanges documents that ratify the treaty of friendship and co-operation between Russia and Tajikistan.

18 Russian prime minister Viktor Chernomyrdin flies to Vilnius to sign nine bilateral agreements and a protocol. The most important document is a most favored nation trade treaty that halved Russian duties on goods imported from Lithuania. Other agreements are on social guarantees for ex-servicemen, pensions, cooperation between interior ministries, air and motor transport communication, and Russian military transit from Germany.

18 The Ukrainian Parliament ratifies START-1 by a surprisingly wide margin (254 to 9, out of 440 members). The Lisbon Protocol is ratified as well, with the reservation that Article Five, which commits Ukraine to join the non-proliferation treaty as a non-nuclear state, does not apply.

19-20 The chief military commanders of Estonia (Major General Aleksander Einseln), Latvia (Colonel Dainis Turlais), and Lithuania (Major General Jonas Andriskevicius) meet in Tallinn and decide to create a joint 650-man Baltic battalion in 1994 that will be trained for UN peace-keeping operations. English will be the primary language of communication.

20 Armenia and Azerbaijan blame each other for an incident during which the convoy of Yeltsin's special envoy to Nagorno-Karabakh, Vladimir Kazimirov, came under fire from Armenian territory at a border crossing between the two countries.

20 Russian foreign minister Andrei Kozyrev warns that Ukraine's resolution on START-1 leaves an "alarming impression" and that Ukraine is leaving open the possibility of not eliminating its weapons.

23 Shushkevich criticizes Russian attempts to pressure Ukraine into becoming a non-nuclear state.

23 The Estonian government issues a decree establishing the procedure for granting residence permits to retired foreign military personnel and their families. Anyone who retired from the military before 20 August 1991 and was born before 1 January 1930, has a spouse or minor child who is an Estonian citizen or legal permanent resident, or the Estonian government deems his presence in Estonia to be necessary, can apply for a residence permit.

23 Russia hints that it will apply economic pressure on Ukraine if it fails to adjust its views on START-1.

25 Director of Russian Foreign Intelligence Service Yevgeny Primakov states that the incorporation into NATO of Poland, Hungary, and the Czech and Slovak republics would not accord with Russian national interests.

27 A bomb explodes near the motorcade of Mkhedrioni leader Dzhaba Ioseliani. No one is injured.

27 Deputy defense minister Boris Gromov expresses his concern over Kazakhstan's policy on nuclear weapons.

28 Rail traffic resumes between Termez in Uzbekistan and Kurgan-Tyube after members of the Tajik opposition blow up bridges and segments of track along a stretch of 84 km, thereby cutting off supplies to a large part of southern Tajikistan.

29 President Bill Clinton and Kravchuk discuss the recent Ukrainian Parliament ratification of START-1 during a 30-minute telephone conversation. Clinton expresses his concern over the conditions attached to ratification, while Kravchuk reiterates his intent to resubmit the treaty to the new Ukrainian Parliament, scheduled to be elected in March 1994.

30 One of the defendants in the August coup trial, former KGB chairman Vladimir Kriuchkov, states that Gorbachev was not isolated in Crimea in August 1991.

DECEMBER

1 Georgia and Abkhazia sign an eight-point memorandum of understanding to end the conflict between them.

1 Participants in the CSCE foreign ministers' annual conference in Rome fail to reach agreement on the wording of a statement on Nagorno-Karabakh after Armenia objects to a reference to Azerbaijan's territorial integrity, and Azerbaijan similarly protested a proposed Armenian reference to the right to self-determination.

1 Kazakh Minister of Science Galym Abilsiitov states that his country wants Russia to assume responsibility for the Baikonur space center and the town of Leninsk under a lease agreement.

1 Addressing a conference on Black Sea cooperation in Kiev, Kravchuk states, "We do not view nuclear weapons as weapons but as material wealth and we demand compensation for them." He also puts forward a number of proposals regarding security in the Black Sea basin. They include detailing naval training activities; adopting a declaration on the inviolability of naval borders; elaboration of memoranda on the inadmissibility of members utilizing their naval forces against other Black Sea Region Assembly members, or allowing the use of their territory for aggression against other members.

2 Major General Vitaly Yakovlev, deputy chief of staff of the Russian defense ministry's Main Directorate for Nuclear Weapons, warns that it might be unsafe, and even impossible, to dismantle nuclear warheads from Ukraine if they have exceeded their six-year service life.

2 The chief of the Administration of Military Tribunals, Colonel General Anatoly Muranov, claims that over 13,000 servicemen were arrested in 1993 for crimes such as corruption, desertion, and illegal sale of weapons and equipment.

2 Lithuanian president Algirdas Brazauskas holds talks with Latvian president Guntis Ulmanis in the west Latvian town of Nica. They discuss forming a five-plus-three political and economic alliance between the five Nordic Council countries and the three Baltic states.

2-7 Estonian Armed Forces commander Major General Aleksander Einseln, economic minister Toomas Sildmae, and other officials and businessmen, visit Jordan, Kuwait, and Turkey to discuss economic, political, and security issues.

3 Secretary of State Warren Christopher discusses nuclear arms with Ukrainian foreign minister Anatoly Zlenko in Brussels after the meeting of the North Atlantic Cooperation Council and emphasizes economic incentives, saying that the "totality of US-Ukrainian relations can be realized only if Ukraine meets its obligations." Christopher warns that economic aid from Washington would flow freely only if Kiev moves on the nuclear disarmament issue and economic reform.

6 Tajik first deputy Supreme Soviet chairman Abdulmajid Dostiev states that Tajikistan's leadership has not and does not intend to negotiate with the armed Tajik opposition.

6 The Azeri National Assembly passes a law on censorship providing for the closure for one month of publications that print material deemed to contain military secrets or to insult state figures.

7 Russian foreign minister Andrei Kozyrev asserts that Sevastopol has always been a Russian naval base and would remain so.

8-9 Yeltsin travels to Brussels for official visits to Belgium, NATO, and the European Union. During the second day of Yeltsin's two-day visit to Brussels Russia and the European Union sign an agreement on economic cooperation. The Russian president also meets with NATO secretary general Manfred Woerner for further discussions on NATO expansion.

9 Alikram Gumbatov, who seized power in the Caspian border town of Lenkoran in late June and proclaimed an autonomous Talysh-Mugan Republic, is apprehended by Azeri law enforcement officials.

9 The Supreme Court of the Dniester Republic in Tiraspol pronounces sentences on the six supporters of the Moldovan Popular Front accused of murder and diversion in the armed conflict between Moldova and the Dniester Republic in summer 1992. Ilie Ilascu was sentenced to be shot, and the rest to long terms in jail.

13 Swedish defense minister Anders Bjoerck warns that his country would not remain neutral if any of the Baltic states were attacked. His comments come in response to the election success of Russian nationalist Vladimir Zhirinovskii.

13 Estonian prime minister Mart Laar notes that the Russian election results should prompt the European Union to integrate the Baltic states more quickly and NATO to provide security guarantees.

13 Vice President Albert Gore visits Kazakhstan. While there the Kazakh Supreme Soviet votes 283 to 1 to accede to the Nuclear Non-proliferation Treaty. Gore and Nazarbaev also sign an umbrella agreement governing the payment of US denuclearization aid. Some $70 million will be provided to dismantle SS-18 silos, while an additional $14 million will be spent on nuclear weapons safety and emergency response equipment.

15 Yeltsin accuses Ukraine of cheating and deception in its dealings over nuclear weapons.

15 The head of Russia's border troops, Colonel General Andrei Nikolaev, states after a brief visit to Tajikistan that CIS forces on the Tajik-Afghan border may need strengthening because of the danger of massive attacks in the spring by Tajikistan oppositionists based in northern Afghanistan.

15 In Tallinn, Estonian, Latvian, and Lithuanian presidents Lennart Meri, Guntis Ulmanis, and Algirdas Brazauskas issue three joint statements. One calls on democrats to "consolidate the democratic gains of the past few years on the European continent and democratic values in Europe." Calling NATO "the main long-term guarantor of our security," the presidents express the hope that the "partnership for peace" program to be discussed at the NATO summit in Brussels on 10-11 January 1994 would not be an "empty bottle" but have an adequate content. Another statement calls on the Nordic Council countries to support the Baltic initiative to have regular joint meetings of Nordic and Baltic foreign ministers.

16 Chechen rebel army units surround the presidential palace in Grozny. They later retreat after talks between representatives of the units and President Dudayev.

17 Yeltsin signs a decree on the creation of the Presidential Security Service headed by Maj. Gen. Aleksandr Korzhakov. The new entity will be independent of the Main Administration for Government Protection.

17 Yeltsin signs a decree which calls for all the Federal Immigration Service to take over control of immigration at the borders from the Border Guards service, and to register all non-Russians entering Russia, including asylum-seekers.

20-21 Deputy Foreign Minister of Ukraine Boris Tarasyuk confirms reports that some twenty SS-24s will be taken off alert by the end of 1993. Ukrainian parliamentarians react angrily to the deactivation announcement.

21 While about thirty Russian pensioners and war veterans protest, a crane in Narva removes the last public statue of Lenin in the Baltic states, Western agencies report.

21 Relations between Russian troops stationed in the east Georgian town of Telavi and members of Dzhaba Ioseliani's Mkhedrioni paramilitary deteriorate into a "permanent bloodfeud" which claims fatalities on both sides.

21 Yeltsin signs a decree disbanding the Ministry of Security and replacing it with the Federal Counterintelligence Service. Former chief of the Ministry of Security, Nikolai Golushko, is appointed director of new service. His former first deputy, Sergei Stepashin, retains the same position in the newly created entity. The new service will be directly responsible to Yeltsin.

22 The Belarusian Ministry of Defense states that 27 of its 81 strategic SS-25 missiles have been withdrawn to Russia. These were withdrawn from the Postavi Division in the northern part of the republic. The remaining 54 missiles are based with two other divisions and must be withdrawn by the end of 1996 in accordance with bilateral agreements between Russia and Belarus.

22 The CIS defense ministers meet in Ashgabat. They decide to formally transform the CIS Joint Military Command into the CIS Joint Staff Committee. Russia agrees to pay half the costs for its upkeep.

22 Yeltsin gives a press conference on the results of the Russian elections and other issues. Yeltsin calls the dissolving of the Ministry of Security a good move because it was "last bulwark of the former Soviet totalitarian system," and insisted that it was to be "disbanded, not reorganized."

22 Ukrainian defense minister Vitaly Radetskii tells the CIS defense ministers in Ashgabat that Ukraine is now prepared to contribute to the work of the Council of Defense Ministers, and plans to have permanent representatives at the headquarters of the CIS joint forces. The Ukrainian defense ministry later denies these comments.

22 Ukrainian authorities arrest six people involved in a plot to smuggle sixty sealed glass ampules, together with 100 kilograms of mercury and weapons from Ukraine.

23 Russia and Turkmenistan sign several agreements. First, Russian president
    Boris Yeltsin and Niyazov sign an accord on dual citizenship. It is the first
    such agreement between two Soviet successor states. A second agreement
    signed formalizes the status of Russian troops in Turkmenistan. The
    agreement calls for Russia to assist Turkmenistan in building its own mili-
    tary with Ashgabat providing full funding for Russian officers in the Cen-
    tral Asian state.

23 A joint meeting of CIS foreign and defense ministers in Ashgabat agrees
    to extend the CIS peacekeeping mandate in Tajikistan for another year.

23-24 Four gunmen burst into a school in Rostov on Don and take a number of
    school children hostage. After given ransom and a helicopter they fled,
    with intermediate stops, to Dagestan, where they abandon the helicopter
    and attempt to escape by foot. The men are later captured and the hos-
    tages released.

24 The fourteenth summit meeting of CIS member states in Ashgabat results
    in a number of agreements. CIS leaders agree to start implementing an
    accord on economic union despite the fact that some parliaments still
    have not ratified the document. In addition, they agree to a resolution on
    the organizational-financial aspects of the Commonwealth economic
    court; an agreement on state social aid to families of servicemen killed in
    Afghanistan; an agreement on pensions and state insurance for the staff
    of interior ministries; a resolution on an interstate radio-navigation sys-
    tem; and an agreement on interstate transportation of dangerous and haz-
    ardous cargo. Among the agreements not signed are a Russian draft
    accord on rights of national minorities. The final summit declaration in-
    directly rebuffs the policies promoted by Russian nationalist Vladimir
    Zhirinovskii. In personnel matters, the Ashgabat summit elects Boris
    Yeltsin chairman of the CIS for a period of six months. In addition, Rus-
    sian diplomat Gennady Shabannikov is appointed general secretary of the
    CIS Collective Security Council, also for a period of six months. Finally,
    the summit set up a new body, the Council of Commonwealth Foreign
    Ministers.

24 A confrontation takes place at Tbilisi airport between Georgian defense
    minister Giorgi Karkarashvili and Georgian security minister Igor Geor-
    gadze as the Georgian delegation returns from the CIS summit in Ashga-
    bat. Georgadze reportedly accuses Karkarashvili of having lost the war in
    Abkhazia and disrupting the signing of the CIS military agreement in
    Ashgabat, threatens to arrest him, whereupon the two men come to blows.

25 A memorandum of understanding signed by Viktor Chernomyrdin and
    Kazakh prime minister Sergei Tereschchenko calls for Russia to lease the
    Baikonur launch facility, the Semipalatinsk nuclear testing range, and the
    Sary Shagan air defense missile test site. The leases will run for 99 years.

27 The head of the dissolved Ministry of Security, Nikolai Golushko, states
    that he and his people are concerned about the abolishment of the min-
    istry. Speaking at a press conference in Moscow, Golushko claims that
    such a move was "abrupt" in light of the October 1993 uprising.

28 Karabakh Armenian forces are forced to retreat from mountain positions sur-
    rounding Agdam, east of Nagorno-Karabakh, following fierce fighting that
    resulted in heavy casualties on both sides. The fierce battle is attributed to
    the presence of Afghan mujahidin and Azeri orders to shoot deserters flee-
    ing the front line. Fighting is also continuing in Mardakert district.
28 The Belarusian Parliament allocates R692.4 billion for the republic's mili-
    tary budget for 1994.
28 The Baltimore Sun reports that Russian scientist Vil Mirzaianov will stand
    trial on charges of divulging state secrets. Mirzaianov was charged in
    October 1992 after he told Moscow News and The Baltimore Sun of
    evidence of continuing Russian chemical weapons research and produc-
    tion.
29 Russian defense minister Pavel Grachev announces that the Russian mili-
    tary would be reduced to a force size of 2.1 million by the end of 1994
    and that no further reductions would be made. Grachev notes that the
    military's participation in the October crisis prevented civil war and the
    disintegration of the country.
29 Reiterating Russia's already clear opposition to the rapid incorporation of
    former Warsaw Pact states into NATO, Russian foreign minister Andrei
    Kozyrev states that such a move would play into the hands of Vladimir
    Zhirinovskii.
29 Coup rumors sweep Tbilisi.
30 Yeltsin signs a decree on the creation of the Chief Command of the Rus-
    sian Federation Border Guards. The new service will be subordinated
    directly to the Russian president and headed by the present commander-
    in-chief of the Border Guards, Andrei Nikolaev.
31 Gamsakhurdia is found dead.

FORMATION OF THE CIS MILITARY

Sergei Zamascikov

BACKGROUND

The rapid turn of events that followed the failed August 1991 coup led to the dissolution of the Soviet Union and led some of the resulting republics to form an alliance in the Commenwealth of Independent States (CIS). While the Soviet Union was disintegrating, the West focused its attention on the striving of the republics for political and economic independence, downplaying its concern over the military ramifications of the Soviet breakup. From the West's point of view the weakening and fragmentation of grand Soviet military power was a positive. And the formation of the Joint CIS Strategic and Conventional Forces at the CIS meeting in Minsk on 14 February 1992 was looked at as a sign that the military assets of the former Soviet Union (FSU) were under control.

At the same meeting the CIS member states also sent a very clear signal that the military assets of the once formidable Soviet military machine would be split among the armies of the independent member states.[1] Since this meeting Russia, Ukraine, Belarus, Armenia, Georgia, Azerbaijan, Moldova, Kazakhstan, Uzbekistan, Lithuania, Latvia, and Estonia have formed their own armed forces. Most of the Soviet republics also have begun forming national-guard-type units. In addition, unofficial or semi-official paramilitary units either were formed or under formation in most of the FSU republics and even in some territories. The deterioration of the economic stiuation in the former Soviet Union is causing political instability and exacerbating ethnic tensions which, in turn, may create pressure for all FSU republics to have their own armed forces.

Beyond this movement to develop independent military formations, the fate of what was once the Soviet military remains unsettled. While Marshal Yevgeny Shaposhnikov, the commander-in-chief of the CIS armed forces, is now formally subordinated to the ruling Council, the men under his command cannot answer "what is the purpose of their existence, what are their missions, who is their enemy and to which country they owe allegiance...."[2]

The command of the border guard troops is in the process of being transferred from the center to local authorities, as has already happened in Ukraine, Armenia, Georgia, Azerbaijan, and the Baltic states. The transfer is not happening painlessly. According to one commander, only Russia so far has been paying its share of the troops' upkeep and the budget has been financed only at 55 percent.[3] As for the future of the Russian Army, its missions are the subject of hot debate. The Army will clearly inherit the bulk of what is left of the USSR/CIS military. The future of Russian defense policies will largely be determined by the state of Russia's economy and by the policies of its neighbors. Most Russian officials plan to keep the armed forces at between 1.2 and 1.5 million men.[4] What this military instability means for the West is that it may be dealing now with a far more serious problem than it did when it faced the stronger, but somewhat restrained and tamed, late Soviet Union. The West must closely watch military developments in the FSU republics. This chapter examines the origins, the current environment, and the prospects for the armed forces in each of the FSU republics.[5]

The rapidly changing situation in the CIS, with new laws being passed on an almost daily basis, the ongoing reorganization of the armed forces, the conflicts between local political leadership and military commanders, and armed conflict in many places, makes any study of this subject outdated even before it is finished.

RUSSIA
Russia Before August 1991

Following Boris Yeltsin's election to the chairmanship of the Russian Federation parliament and Russia's declaration of sovereignty in June 1990, the issue of whether Russia should have its own armed forces emerged as a major controversy. Early on Yeltsin introduced the position of the defense minister.[6] Initially, according to Yeltsin's own statement, this ministry was to have 20 military experts on its staff. The ministry's functions were to include monitoring troop readiness, conscription, and military exercises of the Soviet forces deployed in the Russian Soviet Federated Socialist Republic (RSFSR), and constructing military installations and bases on Russia's territory.[7] This ministerial position was designed to assert Russia's control over some key military issues and to challenge the Soviet Union's monopoly on military and security policy.

In January 1991 the Russian government established the RSFSR State Committee on Defense and Security, with Col. Gen. Konstantin Kobets as its head. This move was criticized by Lieutenant General Tarasov, a military professional, as an effort to "disorganize, weaken, and ultimately abolish" the USSR Armed Forces.[8] Colonel General Kobets' appointment as head resulted from a major compromise between Yeltsin, Gorbachev, and the Soviet High Command. According to Kobets the Soviet military leadership agreed to let Yeltsin supervise the "ministry of defense" under the condition that they appoint their own man to head the ministry. The deal that Gorbachev and the military were able to force on Yeltsin in exchange for giving him this ministry seemed clearly to favor the central government. The new RSFSR Committee was to be responsible for the conscription, pre-induction training, military housing, and conversion of defense industries, that is, for all issues the central government found difficult to handle. The Soviet military leadership intended to offer a similar deal to any other republic wanting to establish its own "defense minister." This effort sought to ensure that the Soviet General Staff and government retained the leading role in military and security policy, while meeting nationalist calls for an increased role in these areas.

After August 1991

Since the August 1991 coup Russia has changed drastically. General Kobets and his subordinates placed themselves behind Yeltsin and defended the "White

House" during the confrontation. Ironically, it was Kobets' connections at the USSR Ministry of Defense that proved crucial in keeping open the lines of communication and avoiding mass bloodshed.[9]

After the coup the RSFSR Ministry of Defense was reorganized. Until March of 1992, when the independent Russian Ministry of Defense was formally created, General Kobets served as Minister of Defense.[10] On April 3, 1992, Colonel General Pavel Grachev, the former First Deputy Minister of Defense of the CIS, was appointed First Deputy Minister of Defense of Russia. His primary responsibilities, unlike Kobets, were to work with the CIS command to coordinate the transfer of assets and personnel to Russia.

In the first few months following the creation of the Russian Armed Forces Grachev made several imprtant moves and issued statements that allowed some educated guesses about the direction it intended to follow. Grachev proceeded to place officers like himself (mostly Afghan war veterans) in key Ministry of Defense positions. Today, among his six deputies, four are so-called "afghantsy." Afghan war veterans also head significant directorates in the Ministry of Defense and the Russian General Staff. Although President Yeltsin stated that he intends the Russian Ministry of Defense to become a "military-civilian institution," Grachev's first deputy, Dr. Andrei Kokoshin, is a prime candiate.

The "young turks" entrusted with forming the new Russian military face a formidable task.[11] The morale of the officers and enlisted personnel is at an all-time low. The bulk of combat-ready forces of the FSU are either stationed in Germany or about to become an integral part of armies of other independent states. And, most important, severe budget constraints make it impossible to modernize the old Soviet weaponry and equipment that Russia inherited.[12]

The Russian military leadership's first steps are, in fact, logical: to develop a new military doctrine and to begin the reform in the armed forces based on the new doctrine. The draft of the new military doctrine, discusssed and approved, was presented to Yeltsin on September 1, 1992.

The New Russian Military Doctrine

The new draft of Russian military doctrine, published in May 1992, replaces the USSR Ministry of Defense doctrine of November 1990.[13] The Russian military leadership severely criticized the Soviet doctrine, primarily because it was overly "defensive" and because it lacked a defined program for modernizing the armed forces. The new doctrine lays out Russian views on the nature and requirements of future war. While it is labled "draft" in a nod to the legislators, it clearly represents the position of the Russian military leadership.

While speaking at the conference discussing the new military doctrine Col. Gen. Rodionov stated, "It is time to give up such notions as 'defensive doctrine,' 'defensive strategy,' and 'defensive armed forces.'" His views were supported by Grachev.[14] The doctrine departs from the Gorbachev/Yazov line of "defensive" thinking. Under the 1990 doctrine defense was considered a useful form of military action and a preemptive strike was excluded as an option. The 1992 doctrine posits that the Russian Armed Forces will conduct defense and offense and should be ready to seize strategic initiatives to destroy the opponent. The troops, the new military doctine states, will be trained to conduct "all forms of military action."

Another important difference between the two doctrines is that the main wartime objective of 1990 version was to "repel aggression," while the main objective of the 1992 version is to "repel aggression and defeat the opponent."[15] The most controversial part of the new Russian military doctrine deals with the definition of future threats to Russia's security, which include striving for regional dominance by some states or a coalition of states, "the introduction of foreign troops in contiguous states and the buildup of forces near the Russian borders," and "violation of the rights of Russian citizens and of persons ethnically and culturally identified with Russia." The latter may be interpreted as a potential source of conflict in the FSU states with sizable Russian minorities.

The new tougher Russian military leadership's views contrast sharply with the political line of the country's Ministry of Foreign Affairs, which still stresses the "new political thinking" of broad cooperation with the West. In fact, the military's analysis of Russia's strategic interests expressed in the new doctrine manifestly contradicts the assessment of the liberal civilian analysts and politicians. These new military adherents of "Realpolitik" evidently have support at the highest level of the Ministry of Defense.

In the ongoing conflict between the Ministry of Defense and the foreign ministry the most important criticism leveled by the military against the current Russian foreign policy concerns the assessment of Russia's strategic interest vis-a-vis the West. While the Ministry of Foreign Affairs and many civilian politicians argue that Russia and the United States should cooperate in the military field, many high-ranking officials of the Russian Ministry of Defense still see the West, and the United States in particular, as a threat. Col. Gen. Rodionov, chief of the General Staff Academy, stated in his address at the May 1992 Ministry of Defense-sponsored conference that "Russia's interests in every important region (the Baltics, Eastern Europe, Middle, Near and Far East) to a certain degree are in opposition to the interests of other states, and, first of all, US interests."[16] And in his public address Col. Gen. Kolesnikov, first deputy chief of Russia's Armed Forces General Staff, said "the revival of Russia as a new strong regional power is not in the interests of the US and NATO." According to Kolesnikov, the United States is trying to help the disintegration of the CIS. He also thinks that the West may interfere militarily in the affairs of the FSU under the pretense of maintaining stability and control over the FSU's nuclear weapons.[17] It is not clear how much influence the Ministry of Defense may have on Yeltsin's policies. Voices like these coming from the high-ranking members of the military establishment clearly have an audience.

Force Structure

According to the Ministry of Defense plan restructuring the USSR Armed Forces into the new Russian military will involve three stages and take six to eight years to complete. The total number of troops located in Russia today is approximately 2.0 million, with another 500,000 to 600,000 serving in units and formations under Russia's jurisdiction elsewhere.[18] By the year 2000 the number of personnel in the Russian Armed Forces will be reduced to 1.5 million.[19] The Ministry of Defense decided not to follow the recommendations of some of the more radical reformers, such as General Aleksandr Vladimirov and Andrei Kokoshin, who wanted to build the new armed forces from scratch. The first organizational moves by the new Russian defense authorities point to a reform based on the existing CIS framework. Through 1995 the current structure in terms of services, branches, and command and control system will be retained.

Some of the key features include the following.

• A new element will be introduced during the 1992-1995 period: mobile rapid deployment forces. This will be a new operational-strategic formation with elements of airborne troops, naval infantry, light Ground Forces formations, units of military tranport aviation, and helicopters, as well as support and reinforcement.

• Strategic Nuclear Forces groupings. Specific composition "will be determined by the strategic offensive arms agreements that have been secured."[20]

• New conventional groupings of troops will be created on Russian territory by 1995, "effectively from scratch."[21] According to the existing plans which, of course, are subject to revision, the so-called "new operational groupings" will consist of forces of constant readiness, rapid-reaction forces, and strategic reserves. There was discussion about forming three to five such groupings.

• Ground Forces structure during 1992-1995 will transition from an army/division basis to a corps/brigade basis. As a result, by 1995 the number of corps will be increased by half and the number of divisions reduced by two-thirds, but the number of brigades will have risen by almost a factor of six.

Russia has a adequate base for creating strong armed forces. Most of the strategic nuclear forces are located on its territory, including 1,035 ICBMs, 70 heavy bombers, 62 SLBM with 940 warheads, command and control centers, and antimissile and space defense installations. Conventional forces include the military assets and units of seven former Soviet military districts. Russia also claims under its jurisdiction units of the Western (Germany) and Northwestern groups of forces, the Transcaucasian Military District, and the 14th Army (located in Moldova).[22] This gives it approximately seventy divisions. Also stationed in Russia are one Air Defense district and five PVO armies, several air armies (with more than 2,000 aircraft), a number of Spetsnaz units, the operational bases of four fleets, and the central command headquarters of all the CIS armed forces service branches.

Russia's National Guard

On 19 August 1991, the first day of the abortive coup, Yeltsin declared the need to form a national guard. This declaration obviously reflected the Russian president's desire to have his own security force to protect the country's fragile democracy against new coup attempts. Yeltsin's declaration was enthusiastically suported by Russia's Vice President Aleksandr Rutskoi. Subsequently Rutskoi, an Air Force major general, became a key person in the ongoing process forming Russia's National Guard.[23]

According to Rutskoi, the Guard's organizing committee includes representatives from the Russian parliament's legislative and security committees, the government's executive branch, the KGB, the police, and some other institutions.

Members of Rutskoi's staff—Aleksandr Sterligov, Gennadii Yankovich and Pavel Aleksandrovskii—play key roles in the committee's work. In the end, the committee's composition of KGB, military, and some former Party apparatchiks may raise some suspicion among the democratic opposition about the Guard's reliability.

Unlike the national guard in some other FSU republics, the Russian Guard will not be formed from existing MVD units. Instead, personnel will be selected among more than 10,000 volunteers. The core of the Guard will be formed from Afghan veterans who defended the "White House" during the August 1991 coup. The rest, particularly the officers, will be chosen from volunteers from the MVD and Spetsnaz units.[24]

The first and, probably for the time being, only Guard unit will be a brigade of nine battalions numbering between 3,000 and 5,000 men. The brigade will have basic infantry weapons and equipment but will be reinforced with air defense, anti-tank units, and perhaps armored personnel carriers and tanks as well.

Besides protecting the president and the government, the Guard will fight natural disasters and mount anti-drug and counter-terrorist operations. In an emergency situation it can serve as a back-up to the existing anti-riot control units of Russia's Ministry of Internal Affairs.

The creation of Russia's Guard remains very controversial. Its critics usually point to the fact that the Guard does not have any unique missions and duplicates existing military and law enforcement structures. According to opponents, this is a luxury that Russia cannot afford. Others suggest the Guard take over some functions of existing MVD units and be subordinated to the Russian Ministry of Internal Affairs.[25] It appears that the views of those in support of the Guard will prevail, particularly because of Rutskoi's strong support.

Military Formations of Russia's Autonomous Regions

Since the Russian republic itself is a federation, some of its so-called "autonomous" republics and regions may create their own military or paramilitary forces.

Chechen Republic. Although the Chechen republic is formally under Russia's jurisdiction, it has proclaimed its independence under the leadership of the newly elected president, former Air Force Major General Dzhokhar Dudaev, and has created military formations.

The so-called Muslim Chechen Army was set up during the confrontation between Dudaev's government and Yeltsin when the latter declared martial law in the Chechen Republic and sent the MVD troops to maintain order. Dudaev, in turn, declared a mobilization call-up of all able-bodied males in November 1991. According to some reports, the Muslim Chechen Army then numbered 62,000 men.[26] The real number of Dudaev's army is around 4,000-5,000 men.

The Chechen Army consists of three branches: the republican guard, the territorial defense reserve drawn from civilians, and the special forces. The special forces, which are modeled after the Soviet armed forces' assault units, seem to have the better trained armed units. Most of its personnel were recruited from among veterans of the Soviet Airborne Troops, naval infantry, special forces of the MVD, and the Border Guards. Many are Afghan war veterans. The Muslim Chechen Army leadership has indicated that their weapons and equipment have been purchased through all available channels without consideration of cost.[27] This obviously means they were stolen from the CIS military and MVD units or obtained through organized crime networks, where the Chechen presence is quite widespread.

Tatarstan. While the Chechen republic remains the only Russian administrative unit with its own armed forces, the Republic of Tatarstan, Russia's largest autonomous unit, has also begun taking steps toward forming its own army. At its first congress the Tatar youth organization Azatlyk passed a resolution calling for the creation of the "Armed Forces of the Republic of Tatarstan" on a strictly volunteer basis.[28] Given the strong separatists tendencies in this republic of five million with a large percentage of Muslims, these calls should be taken seriously.

Dagestan. Dagestan has 1.8 million people and more than thirty nationalities. With martial traditions dating back many centuries, it should come as no surprise that many military formations are based on nationalities. The largest armies belong to the Chechens, Avars, Laks, Kumyks, Lezgins, and Azeris. The largest among these formations is Avar People's Front, named after Shamil, who was a prominent leader of the anti-Russian resistance in the 19th century. During the conflicts the Avars have had with the Kumyks, the former were able to call up about 30,000 armed supporters. The Kumyks, according to some estimates, have about 15,000 to 20,000 armed fighters including special "mobile groups" with 2,000 to 3,000 men. They apparently consist of Afghan war veterans and those who served in the special forces.[29]

Prospects For The Future

Now that Russia finally has decided to field its own armed forces, their size, shape, and missions will be determined by two factors: the state of its economy, and relations with its neighbors, particularly Ukraine. Since both factors are unlikely to improve in the immediate future, the military and the right wing will strive to preserve the existing Soviet military structures under Russian control.

The new structures of the Russian Armed Forces are still in the formative stage. Although a year has passed since they were formed, there is still no military doctrine. The draft of the military doctrine submitted by the Ministry of Defense proposes to keep the existing force structure until 1995.[30] This suggests a rather conservative approach to a military reform.

Regardless of the planned defense cuts, Russia will continue to play a major role as the regional and global nuclear superpower. With its forces stationed in the various ethnic "hot spots" of the FSU, the Russian Army may find itself involved in various conflicts on behalf of Russian or Slavic populations. This role of regional peacekeeper could become particularly dangerous if power in Russia falls into the hands of a conservative and chauvinistic regime.

UKRAINE
Before August 1991

In declaring its sovereignty on 16 July 1990 Ukraine proclaimed the right to establish its own armed forces and to establish the terms of military service by its citizens. Dmytro Pavlychko, the head of the Ukranian Parliament Commission on Foreign Affairs and a leading member of the radical Narodna Rada parliamentary faction, Rukh, said that "the creation of national armies, including the Ukrainian army, is a normal, legitimate process in attaining the republic's genuine sovereignty."[31] The promotion of an independent Ukrainian national army has been particularly strong in western Ukraine, where memories of the long underground resistance to the Red Army by both the Ukrainian Insurgent Army (UPA) and the Organization of Ukrainian Naionalists (OUN) are still fresh. The Special Committee to Resurrect the Armed Forces of the Ukraine has been established in Lvov.

Many Ukrainians believe that the independent Ukrainian People's Republic was defeated by the Bolsheviks in 1919 because it did not have its own armed forces. Ukraine was always a battlefield for invading armies and has hardly ever experienced real independence and security. It is not surprising that Yurii Shcherbak, the leader of the Ukrainian Green Party, says that Ukraine should not repeat the mistake Kuwait made of not possessing sufficient armed forces after it was occupied by Iraq.[32]

An array of pro-independence political parties, organizations, and parliamentary deputies have readily supported the goal of creating a national army. On 3-4 February 1991 a conference was held in Kiev devoted to Ukrainian foreign and domestic security. The unprecedented event brought together representative of Rukh, the Association of Democratic Soviets and Democratic Blocs of Ukraine, the Committee to Resurrect the Armed Forces in Ukraine, and even a few representatives from the General Staff and the Kiev Air Defense Academy.[33] Speaking at the conference the head of Rukh's military collegium, Vitalii Chychyl, an 18-year veteran of the Strategic Rocket Forces who resigned for political reasons, described his main task as "consolidating all the healthy forces among Ukrainian officers, serving in Ukraine and beyond its borders, around the question of a Ukrainian National Army. We call...upon Communist...as well as democratic officers to make wise decisions, so that we may resolve the very important issue of creating our national military."[34] The conference agreed unanimously that Ukraine needs a national army. The conference worked out a concept for the creation, in stages, of armed forces in the republic.

Stage I, from February until summer 1991, is to be legislative. Laws were to be adopted on military concription, state security, and the transfer of all military industrial enterprises on the republic's territory to the jurisdiction of the Ukrainian government. The republic's budget for the next year was to stipulate a special article of expenditures for forming the republican army on a professional basis. Simultaneously, allocations to the all-union military budget were to be drastically cut.

Stage II is to begin with the formation of a national guard corps. Later, an air force, a navy, and organs of state security would be formed. Inasmuch as Ukraine has been declared a nuclear free zone in accordance with the Declaration of Sovereignty, all nuclear weapons located on its territory are to be transferred or sold to Russia.[35] Participants of the conference could hardly have imagined that most of their decisions, which seemed so radical at the time would become reality in the space of only six months.

After August 1991

The aborted August coup in Moscow had a catalytic effect on the formation of the Ukrainian Armed Forces. After proclaiming its complete independence from the Soviet Union on 24 August 1991 the Ukrainian parliament voted to place all existing military formations on the republic's territory under its jurisdiction. On 3 September 1991 the republic appointed its first minister of defense, Maj. Gen. Konstantin Morozov. Morozov, who had served as the air army commander in Ukraine, was given the monumental task of drawing up plans for the republic's armed forces and national guard.

Unlike his counterparts in some other newly independent states, Morozov was chosen primarily for his professional qualities rather than for his political loyalty alone. He chose to remain, at least until the end of October 1991, on the payroll of the USSR Ministry of Defense and was able to maintain good professional contacts with the new USSR minister of defense, Marshal Shaposhnikov, and the then chief of the General Staff Army General Lobov.

The first step of the new minister of defense and his staff was to present a broad package of legislative proposals to the republic's parliament. On 22-23 October 1991 the Ukrainian Supreme Soviet approved on first reading a package of laws "On the Defense of Ukraine," "On the Armed Forces of Ukraine," "On the Republican Guard," "On the State Border of Ukraine," "On the Border Troops of Ukraine," and "On the Social and Legal Protection of Military Troops Performing Service on the Territory of Ukraine." The other two decrees created the Ukrainian Defense Council and outlined a Ukrainian concept for defense and national security.[36] The Ukrainian legislature devoted much more attention to its armed forces than did its Russian counterpart. Before it went on vacation in the summer of 1992, the Ukrainian parliament adopted about eighty acts in the military and security field.

These new laws are more democratic than the ones the Russian legislature passed. Ukrainian servicemen are allowed to form their own organizations, sue their commanders, and leave the country just like any other citizen of Ukraine.[37] In response to the military's increasing grievances the Ukrainian parliament was the first of the CIS countries to pass the "Act on Social and Legal Defense of Servicemen and Their Families" in December 1991.[38] This act provided for many essential privileges both during service and after retirement. Taking such a position helped to gain the loyalty of most of the military on its territory.

The republic's legislature also ruled that in 1992 the technical and organizational foundations of the armed forces were to be established, and the entire process was to be completed by 1994-1995.[39] The military reform plan, which was developed based on this legislation, consisted of three stages. Stage one (1992-

1993) was to establish mechanisms of command and control. Stage two (1993-1994) was to develop a unified plan for using the country's armed forces. Stage three (1995) was to develop the plans for mobilizing and training the armed forces reserve and for completing the personnel reduction to 400,000 men from the present 657,000.[40]

Ukraine's Military Doctrine

At present Ukraine lacks an official military doctrine. According to press reports, the new doctrine will have a defensive character based on the principle of "defense sufficiency." Ukraine, according to these accounts, is planning to be a non-allied nation pursuing a policy of neutrality. One of the drafts of the military doctrine states that if an enemy engaged Ukraine in a local military conflict, the Ukrainian Army will rely primarily on its air force and missile troops and use "precision-guided weapons."[41]

Major opposition parties also advanced their own proposals, which are rather radical and often anti-Russian. The influential Ukrainian Republican Party considers that the major threat to Ukraine will come from the East and wants the bulk of the armed forces to be stationed along the border with Russia. It also wants the Ukrainian Army to be 500,000 strong and not 200,000 to 220,000 as in the Ministry of Defense proposal.

The Ukrainian National Assembly takes an even more radical approach. It thinks that because of its geopolitical situation Ukraine cannot remain neutral. It is calling for creating an anti-Russian defense treaty with the Baltic, Caucasus, and Central Asian states. It is quite obvious, even from this brief review, that Ukraine's military doctrine will continue to be subject to heated internal debate. It is in the West's strategic interest to follow these debates very closely.

Force Structure

One of the issues that caused considerable debate both inside and outside the republic had to do with the size and composition of Ukraine's Armed Forces. After parliament passed the laws on defense, most parties agreed to scale down their numbers considerably.[42] During his visit to Germany in January 1992 Ukrainian President Leonid Kravchuk said that conventional troop strength in his country will be reduced to about 220,000. This figure seems to respond to Helmut Kohl's statement of 28 January 1992 that it makes no sense to give humanitarian and financial assistance to FSU republics that want to create armed forces large enough to alter the existing balance of forces in Europe.[43] In 1994 the realistic number for the Ukrainian Armed Forces will be closer to 200,000.

Ukrainian media accounts and personal interviews with the republic's government officials suggest that the structure of Ukraine's armed forces will have this look.

• The Ukrainian Ground Forces (the number to be determined by the factors described above) will be formed from the assets of the Soviet Ground Forces units stationed on the republic's territory. Russian and other non-Ukrainian officers will be offered the opportunity either to leave or pledge allegiance to the

Ukrainian government, and Ukrainian officers serving outside Ukraine are invited to come back and join.

• All conventional forces based on Ukrainian territory, including the Navy and the Air Force, are subordinated to the Ukrainian Ministry of Defense.

• All strategic forces, while temporarily stationed in Ukraine, are to remain under CIS control, with unspecified Ukrainian participation.

• Ukraine is to create a national guard on the basis of MVD units.

• Ukranian Border Guard Troops will be a conscript force based on drafting only citizens of Ukraine, with the officer and noncommissioned officer corps hired on a contract basis.[44]

• Ukraine will form its own railroad and civil defense troops.[45]

Clearly, it appears that Ukranian Armed Forces will have ground troops, air force, and navy and will be divided into three operational-level commands based on the existing headquarters of the former Soviet Transcarpathian, Odessa, and Kiev military districts. The ground troops will consist of several army corps, 7-8 divisions, 6-7 motorized infantry and tank brigades, and 2-3 army aviation brigades.

The Ukrainian Air Force will have three ground and one naval group and will be subordinated to the three operational commands and to the Navy. Fighter aviation will be charged with the air defense mission. All CIS air defense installations, including missile, radar, space, and other units of the Eighth PVO Strany Army based in Ukraine, will become part of the Ukranian Air Force and will be renamed "Forces of Aerospace Defense." The naval forces will be formed from those ships and units of the Black Sea Fleet claimed by Ukraine and will be divided into brigades and include naval aviation and coastal defense units.[46] Ukraine will have one military academy and three higher military schools. Six hundred officers will work in the Ministry of Defense Headquarters.[47]

Ukraine has enough of former Soviet assets to form formidable armed forces. It inherited 6,204 tanks, 6,394 armored personnel carriers, more than 3,000 artillery systems, and 1,431 aircraft. Even with the cuts mandated by the CFE agreement it has the capability to have one of the largest and best equipped armed forces in the region. Unlike the other states of the FSU, Ukraine also has an abundance of native officers and noncommisioned officers.

On 6 December 1991 the Ukrainian parliament adopted an oath of loyalty which pledges the soldiers' service to Ukraine, to its constitution and laws, and to its liberty and independence. The Ukrainian government, urged by the republic's ministry of defense, insisted that all servicemen stationed within its borders take this oath. Those who refused were given a chance either to retire or leave.

Despite strong resistance from Moscow, most officers and enlisted men appear to be willing to swear allegiance to Ukraine. In the first two months 352,000 servicemen of approximately 657,000 stationed there took the oath.[48] The major reasons for this rapid change of allegiances was the collapse of the Soviet Union and that those who take the oath to Ukraine were promised housing, better pay, and scarce food coupons.[49]

Predictably, the issue of the military oath was surrounded by controversy. Admiral Kasatonov, the former CIS commander of the Black Sea Fleet, forbade his subordinates to take the oath. This order was disobeyed by some of them. The most dramatic example of the confrontation was the defection to Russia of six Ukraine-based bombers with their crews flying their regimental colors.[50]

While political tensions betwen Russia and Ukraine remain high, the CIS/ Russian professional military are changing their attitude toward their Ukrainian colleagues. Moving away from the bitter confrontational stance of the initial period of the Russian-Ukrainian military debate, some conservative Russian military writers began to voice cautious praise of Ukraine's military policies. This praise particularly applied to Ukraine's well-formulated position on military affairs as well as to its policy to preserve as much of the existing Ukraine-based Soviet military infrastructure as possible inside the newly-formed Ukrainian Armed Forces. By supporting Ukrainian policies the Russian military conservatives attempted to put some pressure on their own reform-minded leadership.[51]

Ukraine's National Guard

The Ukraine National Guard was officially established on 4 November 1991 by the Ukrainian parliament.[52] Major General V. Kukharets, coming appropriately from the MVD troops, became the new defense chief. Accordingly, as in most of the other republics, Ukraine's national guard was heir to the forces and hardware of the USSR's MVD units. By decree all MVD units, including their bases, training centers, and equipment, have been transferred to the Ukrainian government.

The first National Guard units numbered 6,000 troops drawn from MVD units stationed in Ukraine. According to Kukharets, by April 1992 plans were in place to increase the Guard to 30,000 men. All recruits must have more than a high school education, must be at least 165 centimeters tall, and must be in good physical health.[53] To meet National Guard personnel requirements Ukraine initially planned to retain the old conscription principle. Unlike army recruits, those called to serve in the National Guard drew 300-400 rubles a month at September 1992 prices and were offered an opportunity to sign a contract and become professional soldiers.

The Ukrainian Law on the National Guard assigns to it functions generally similar to those assigned to MVD troops of the former USSR, including:

• Defense of the republic's territorial integrity.

• Assistance during emergencies and catastrophes.

• Protection of the foreign consulates and embassies.

• Guarding and transporting prisoners.[54]

Ukraine's Position on Nuclear Weapons

Ukraine has more nuclear weapons stationed on its territory than France and England combined. Most of these weapons are termed modern "heavies," the

SS-19 and SS-25. It has thirty strategic bombers. After Ukraine declared independence the future of nuclear weapons on its territory became the center of attention. While the Ukrainian government has declared many times that the republic has no intention of maintaining nuclear weapons of its own and wants to become a nuclear-free zone, some opposition members have raised objections to transferring Ukraine-based nuclear weapons to Russia.[55]

After the referendum of 1 December 1991 on independence and the election of the republic's president Ukraine's position on nuclear weapons has become somewhat clearer. The republic appears to be serious about becoming a nuclear-free zone. However, it wants some control over all nuclear weapons as long as they remain on its territory. As Ukrainian president Leonid Kravchuk put it at a meeting with the foreign observers, "We will stand for the liquidation of nuclear weapons, tactical and strategic, and this should be done in a process of negotiation with all countries. Ukraine only wants control over the weapons on its territory, but it doesn't want a button."[56] Kravchuk appears to want a collegial decision-making body in which Ukraine would have a seat, along with the other republics that have nuclear arms on their territories.

It is less clear exactly how Ukraine is planning to become nuclear-free. Ukrainian officials have said that the weapons deployed on their territory should not be moved to Russia, but rather destroyed under the supervision of the UN or another international agency. While no formal decision has been made yet, independent Ukraine is unlikely to press for this particular type of denuclearization. Of course, a great deal will depend on Ukraine's future relations with Russia.[57]

Ukraine's ambivalence on this point is demonstrated by how President Kravchuk dealt with tactical nuclear weapons stationed on Ukrainian soil. Speaking at a press conference at the end of his visit to Germany in February 1992, Kravchuk said that all tactical nuclear weapons would be removed from Ukrainian soil by the summer of 1992, and all strategic nuclear missiles would be dismantled by the end of 1994.[58] Then, on 12 March, in an abrupt reversal of previous agreements, Kravchuk said that he had stopped the transfer of tactical nuclear weapons from his republic to Russia for dismantling. According to Kravchuk, the reason for this decision was "the chaos and uncertainty" in Russia and the fact that there were no guarantees that, once moved, these weapons "will not fall into evil hands."[59] After considerable pressure from the West, Ukraine finally agreed to transfer all tactical nuclear weapons to Russia. The transfer was completed by mid-April 1992.

On 23 May 1992 Ukraine, along with Belarus and Kazakhstan, which also have strategic weapons on their territories, joined the United States and Russia in signing the START Treaty. Nonetheless, the process of Ukraine's full and final denuclearization will likely encounter many other obstacles.

The Black Sea Fleet Dispute

The question of who is to control the Black Sea Fleet, or rather, how this is to be divided between Ukraine and Russia, is one of the most contentious issues in both countries. Several solutions have been offered by the various parties to this debate:

• Ukraine wants to keep all Black Fleet assets, save the "strategic" ones that carry nuclear weapons. This includes part of the submarine force, some of the major combatants, and part of the naval air force.

• The Russian General Staff wants to give Ukraine only a relatively small part of surface combatants and coastal defense forces. The rest is considered part of the "strategic force" by the General Staff.

• Some moderates in Russia, including members of the movement "Military for Democracy," want this issue to be resolved based on international law, the size of Ukraine's share of the naval systems proportional to its contribution to the former USSR military budget. According to Capt. 2nd Rank G.M. Melkov, the Ukrainian share of the military budget was between 10 percent and 16 percent of the total.[60]

The Ukrainian position may not be very far from the one advocated by the Russian moderates. The official newspaper of Ukraine's defense ministry, for example, advanced this justification of the claims to the Black Sea Fleet.

> According to all international laws, if the state collapses, its property, including the Navy, is divided relative to the share of each republic, which means that Ukraine should have 18 percent of all property. Thus, the entire Navy must be divided among all former republics of the USSR. Ukraine can claim more ships than there are now in the Black Sea Fleet. And the Navy should be divided in proportion not to numbers, but to types and tonnage of the ships.[61]

The battle over the fleet ended in a temporary truce at the Yeltsin-Kravchuk meeting in Crimea on 3 August 1992. A treaty was signed that subordinates the fleet directly to the Ukrainian and Russian presidents until 1995. They are to be jointly responsible for the appointment of its commander. The conscripts, 50 percent Ukrainian and another 50 percent from Russia, will pledge allegiance to their respective governments.

Such dual subordination will decrease the fleet's combat readiness. One cannot assume that neither Yeltsin nor Kravchuk attach great importance to the Black Sea Fleet's strategic missions. Also, such a bilateral Russian-Ukrainian decision on the fate of what is supposed to be the CIS property is likely to draw protests from other Commonwealth members.[62]

The continuing quarrel between Russia and Ukraine has more than the future of the fleet at stake. Any definitions and principles agreed upon in ongoing negotiaions likely will carry over to other strategic assets stationed on Ukrainian soil as well. Whatever the ultimate Ukrainian share proves to be, much of it may be sold or scrapped. According to Viktor Antonov, the Ukrainian minister in charge of defense industries conversion, his country has no intention of sending its ships into the Mediterranean. Antonov suggested that the fleet in Ukrainian hands would be used for defensive purposes only. He argued that "just because we say no one has the right to decide what is in our territory does not mean that we intend to keep it all."[63]

Prospects For The Future

Ukraine is probably the only CIS member that has a concept for developing its armed forces. Despite rhetoric suggesting the contrary, the ongoing disputes with Russia over Crimea and the Black Sea Fleet are apparently going to be resolved peacefully. In the next five years Ukraine will emerge as a major European power with a modern armed forces of over 200,000 men, as well as a large blue-water navy. It will have a major defense industry and nuclear capabilities.[64] A peaceful resolution of its conflicts with Russia does not necessarily mean good neighborly relations. In fact, it is very likely that political tensions between these two "super neighbors" will continue. If such tensions become serious enough, a future Ukrainian government may choose to reconsider its commitment to nuclear non-proliferation treaties. At the same time, the possibility of armed conflict with Russia remains very low.

BELARUS
Before August 1991

After declaring its state sovereignty on 27 July 1990 Belarus proclaimed its right to establish its own armed forces and determine the terms of military service by its citizens. Compared to its southern neighbor, Ukraine, Belarus was relatively slow in addressing the issue of its own independent armed forces. The first efforts to put the matter onto an organizational footing came from the Belarusian Social Democratic Society in March 1991. The Social Democrats were the first to call for development of a national security system for Belarus and for creation of republican military formations.[65]

After August 1991

On 20 August 1991 a leading member of the Belarusian Social Democratic Society, Lt. Col. Mikhail Statkevich, announced the establishment of the Belarusian Association of Servicemen (BZV), a group that sought to go beyond the confines of the Social Democratic Society and appeal to all military personnel wishing to devote themselves to fulfilling Belarus' defense requirements. The Belarusian declaration of independence in August 1991 led Statkevich and others to conclude that the formation of a Belarusian national army and national guard should be an immediate, rather than a long-term, goal. In that connection the BZV saw itself as an ally of the democratic forces in the parliament and in society at large.[66]

By the fall of 1991 Belarus' leadership had placed under its jurisdiction civil defense units, staffs, military commissariats, and border and railroad units deployed on its territory. The parliament's National Security and Defense Commission prepared documents defining the functions of the new Security Council and the Ministry of Defense, and defined concepts of reform and organizational development of its own armed forces.[67] Conservatives strongly opposed the government's decision to establish its own military in Belarus. When the package of military reform proposals was presented to the Belarusian Supreme Soviet on 16-17 September

1991 it fell victim to the strong resistance of conservative groups who drew their support from the staunch pro-Moscow stance of the Belarusian Military District commander, Col. Gen. Kostenko.[68]

On November 15, 1991 Belarus' parliament finally approved legislation establishing the Ministry of Defense Affairs. Nevertheless, no one was chosen to fill the ministerial post. Although the Supreme Soviet Commission on National Security, Defense, and the Fight against Crime called for action on creation of a national guard on 25 October 1991, the decision on that matter was postponed once again.[69]

It was not until 11 December 1991, after the birth of the CIS, that Col. Gen. Petr Chaus was appointed to the post of defense minister. Chaus, a Belarusian, was chief of staff of the Baltic Military District before becoming deputy head of USSR Civil Defense in the summer of 1991. On 11 January 1992 the republic's parliament voted to rename the defense affairs ministry the Ministry of Defense and to introduce the oath of allegiance to Belarus.[70] Parliament did not go so far as to subordinate the conventional forces on the Belarusian territory to its own jurisdiction. They were put under control of the Council of Ministers of Belarus, which is led by the conservative former Communist Party official Vyacheslav Kebich.

Force Structure and Military Doctrine

After announcing on 14 February 1992 its intention eventually to follow Ukraine in creating its own armed forces, Belarus nonetheless seemed eager to avoid provoking the kind of sharp conflicts as those between Kiev and Moscow. There is no controversial issue such as the Black Sea Fleet to resolve and, thus far, there has not been much interest on Belarus' part in publicly laying claim to the former Soviet equipped forces. The removal of tactical nuclear arms, which was completed on 28 April 1991, and the planned elimination of Belarus' long-range nuclear systems, ultimately will lead to a reduction in the number of troops within the republic that are subordinate to joint CIS control. The overall task is to form a force of 80,000 from the estimated total of 160,000 troops of the former Soviet Armed Forces stationed in the Belarusian Military District.[71]

There has been little discussion about the future shape and missions of Belarusian armed forces. Probably the most credible assessment so far came from Col. Leonid Privalov, the deputy chairman of Belarus' parliament Commission on Security, Defense and the Fight Against Crime. He said that the republic's future army should be based on the existing forces, facilities, and equipment of the former Belorussian Military District. In his view the national army would be limited to 4-5 divisions manned at full strength. In the transitional period, which according to Belarusian leadership is to last two to three years, the republic would be unable to train, equip, or supply its army independently and must rely on the old centralized supply system now controlled by the CIS General Staff.

This position was later supported by the new Belarusian Minister of Defense, General Kozlovskii. In May 1992 he said that sixty-two large units were to be disbanded by the end of the year. "In the next few years," according to Kozlov-skii, "up to 22,000 officers will have to retire." The number of troops will be reduced by 40 percent, leaving 95,000 men serving in the ground, air, or air defense forces. Pointing out that the offensive potential of Belarus is considered to be the greatest in Europe, Kozlovskii said that his short-term goal is to develop a defense doctrine and destroy the vestiges of the old offensive doctrine.[72]

Belarus has certainly inherited more military equipment than its armed forces can possibly use. There are two tank armies and one combined-arms army sta-tioned on its territory. Even under the CFE limits Belarus is allowed to keep 1,800 tanks, 2,600 armored personnel carriers, and 1,615 artillery systems. It also has 260 modern aircraft and 80 helicopters. Since the country's leadership seems to be committed to having relatively small armed forces and a defensive doctrine, it is likely to either sell or simply discard the surplus military hardware. None-theless, thanks to the rich "inheritance" that Belarus received from the FSU armed forces, it is likely to have one of the most modern and best equipped armies in Europe.

Prospects For The Future

By 1995 Belarus plans to have its own 80,000-90,000-strong armed forces. Since the republic has no ethnic trouble spots, it will likely continue to maintain good relations with its neighbors, which include Russia, Ukraine, Poland, and Lith-uania. There is no reason to believe that Belarus will create obstacles to with-drawal of the only nuclear weapons it has on its territory, the mobile SS-25 missiles.

BALTIC STATES

During their independence in the interwar years all three Baltic states maintained their own armed forces. After the 1940 annexation by the Soviet Union these forces were disbanded and most of the officers were killed by Stalin. It is note-worthy that these armies offered no resistance to the Red Army during the an-nexation. The Baltic states have a history of being nonviolent, peaceful nations.

All three republics also contributed their own national units to the Red Army after the 1917 revolution and during World War II. The best-known of these units was the Red Latvian Riflemen Corps, which became one of the crack units the Bolsheviks used against the opposition, Even so, representatives of the indig-enous nationalities in these units did not exceed 30 or 40 percent.[73]

By the spring of 1991 all Baltic states passed legislation allowing for the estab-lishment of their own military and police forces. This process started well before the formal break from the USSR, although all three republics proceeded cautiously to avoid provoking retaliation by the central government. The Baltic states also developed joint policies for talks with the USSR government on mili-tary questions, each republic independently preparing detailed drafts.[74] These policies deem the presence of the USSR troops on the territories of the repub-lics to be a "politically and economically destabilizing factor" and request their withdrawal in "short term." The "General Principles of Baltic Republics' Security," jointly developed by Latvia, Lithuania, and Estonia, also provides for creation of national defense formations.[75]

The first reaction of the Soviet military to these demands was predictably negative. Maj. Gen. A. Litvinov, the special liaison of the Soviet Ministry of Defense with "State Organs of Power and Administrations of the USSR in the Union Republics," acknowledged that the ministry was prepared to discuss "all questions" with the republics' leadership, but said that many of their demands were "an empty phrase."[76] Even after Russia and the rest of the world formally recognized the independence of the Balts, the status of the Soviet Armed Forces and their withdrawal timetable remained unclear. For example, after a 27 February 1992 meeting with German parliamentarians General Mironov, commander of CIS troops in the Baltics, said that withdrawal of the 120,000 troops under his command would take about five years. He noted that some troops preferred to stay and that housing problems must be solved before more troops could depart.[77]

LATVIA

This republic was among the first in 1990 to pass a law on alternative service that allowed conscientious objectors to work in various low-skill, menial labor positions for three years instead of serving the usual two years in the Soviet Armed Forces. Since this alternative to military sevice is performed in Latvia, it has been selected by a growing number of young men. In the spring of 1990 only 49.8 percent of those subject to conscription chose to serve in the USSR military forces. In Riga there were some 550 young men performing alternative service, which included working as bus and streetcar drivers, firemen, and auxiliary policemen. The total number of those who chose the alternative service was 2,500 as of August 1990.[78]

On 25 September 1990 the Latvian parliament amended the Law on Alternative Service to give those who object to service in the USSR military a wider choice of occupations, including jobs at the Ministry of Internal Affairs as border guards and in customs, in maintaining public order, and in agriculture, all in Latvia.[79] The amended law also allowed soldiers from Latvia who deserted from the Soviet Armed Forces to perform alternative service in the republic. These developments predictably caused strong criticism from the Soviet military, which claimed that many conscripts use alternative service as a loophole to evade the draft. The Soviet woes about conscription in the republic were exacerbated by the Latvian authorities, who refused to cooperate with the military commissariats and even stopped supporting them financially.[80]

In January 1991 the first volunteer detachments were organized in Riga to guard the building housing the government and communications offices against an expected Moscow-organized coup. On 26 January the Council of Ministers of Latvia decided to establish a defense department, which was to assume the guarding of strategically important sites.[81] On 3 April 1991 the People's Front of Latvia decided to stop coordinating and financing these volunteer detachments.

The principal reason cited was that the given tasks "were not handled effectively by the new department."[82]

At the same time the People's Front urged the Council of Ministers to continue to work more energetically on establishing a Latvian national army or guard. Unlike many other republics of the former Soviet Union, the Latvian government could not simply take over existing MVD troop units and build a national guard on their basis. Although the MVD was formally subordinated to the Latvian government, a part of the militia initially refused to accept authority of the newly appointed minister loyal to the Latvian government. Until the coup attempt in August 1991 two parallel judicial systems existed. Some militia precincts had sworn loyalty to the Latvian government, others declared that were there a conflict between Latvian and Soviet law they would enforce the latter.

The most notorious case was the MVD Spetsnaz unit, the OMON, which refused to be subordinated to the Latvian authorities and even attempted to take over the ministry building in February 1991. The OMON was eventually removed from the authority of the Latvian MVD by Moscow and placed under the Vilnius Internal Troops division HQ while based in Riga. After the coup attempt the unit was transferred to Russia.

The existing militia in Latvia is only one-third Latvian. The other two-thirds are of mixed ancestry. This raised a question about whether a militia which is predominantly non-Latvian should be the only existing armed unit subordinated to the republic. To correct this situation the Latvian parliament passed a law transforming the militia into what is commonly known in the West as a "police force" and subordinated it to the municipal authorities.[83]

Because of this complicated political situation the process of forming a Latvian military started much later than in the neighboring states of Lithuania or Estonia. It was not until late November 1991 that the parliament appointed Talavs Jundzis as minister of defense. The parliament also passed laws on the armed forces and created a Latvian military consisting of four major components.

• Border guard troops, to consist of 5,000 men and include ground detachments and naval units.

• Ground forces of about 5,000 men, which include four battalions of a rapid deployment force (composed of four light infantry battalions, a reconnaissance battalion, a communications company, and an engineering company) to be used in emergencies and to fight organized crime and civil disturbances.

• An air force.

• Territorial defense forces (opolchenie) recruited on a volunteer basis from the local population "loyal to the Latvian state. These units, similar to the ones established in Lithuania, will largely consist of reservists, and a small professional core numbering 300-400 men.[84]

The Latvian military presently is armed with light infantry weapons and has no artillery. There are plans to buy some military equipment and ammunition from the withdrawn Russian troops.

The budget of the Latvian Ministry of Defense is projected to be somewhere between from three and five percent of the republic's total budget.[85] According to the Latvian defense ministry leadership, the officer corps initially will consist primarily of former Soviet Army officers, particularly those with the senior ranks.[86] The intent is that eventually these officers will be replaced by a local cadre trained in the republic as well as in Western military schools. Today, young officers who receive ROTC training in college and want to join the army are required to complete a six-month retraining course. Latvia later plans to open its own military academy in Malpils.

LITHUANIA

Discussions of a Lithuanian national army began immediately after the republic declared its independence from the Soviet Union in March 1990. In the spring of 1990 the Lithuanian Defense Department was created and it began to form volunteer detachments charged with traditional police duties. The struggle for control of the republic's Ministry of Internal Affairs, which was formally subordinated to Moscow, was one of the major reasons for creating this department. From the very beginning the functions of the Defense Department, as identified by its director, General A. Butkevicus, included guarding important government buildings, civil defense, fire fighting, customs control, rescue and national emergency mission. It was to form a voluntary "national guard service;" and "if the government so decides" create a national army.[87]

In September 1990 the Lithuanian government established its own intelligence service to provide information about the situation in the republic and abroad. Also in September 1990 a border force was formed and charged with controlling the flow of goods and commodities across the republic's border. This force of approximately 2,200 men began operations in October 1990.

In 1991 the Defense Department began to call its first volunteers for the Territorial Defense Forces. In 1991 the Defense Department also started to conscript young men primarily for border guard and national guard duties, The total number of personnel serving with these forces is estimated between 10,000 and 15,000.[88] The Territorial Defense Forces' units are organized as companies, detachments, and "druzhiny" (regiments). The druzhina commanders are appointed by the head of the Defense Department, the other commanders by the chief of staff.

The volunteers in the Lithuanian ArmedForces are to perform their duties on a part-time basis. They sign a contract to attend training sessions four times a week. Once a year they are called up for a 20-day training camp, where they may be used for other missions as well, "depending on the circumstances."[89] The professional cadre, officers, and noncommissioned officers, are trained in Kaunas, where the officers' school is located, and in Vilnius, where the training units for noncommissioned officers are located. The training courses for the officers and noncommissioned officers last six and three months, respectively.[90]

Presently, Lithuania has the following military forces.

• Territorial Defense Forces of voluntary service organized territorially in 66 companies, plus a 500-man professional staff.

• Rapid deployment forces of 5,000 men recruited on contract to combat organized crime, terrorism and possible other emergencies, in coordination with the neighboring countries.

• Forces of civil defense—1,000-1,500 men.

• Border guards—5,000 men.[91]

The border guards and civil defense forces have a combination of conscript and professional staff, while the Territorial Defense Forces and rapid deployment units are all volunteers.[92] Besides the Defense Department units there are other independent paramilitary armed formations in Lithuania. Some of these are the offspring of organizations that existed in Lithuania before World War II. One of these militarized organizations, Siauliu Saiunga, was resurrected in 1988. It has its own uniforms and regulations. After the events of January 1991 this organization publicly swore allegiance to the Lithuanian government. Its structure includes companies and quick-reaction detachments, the so-called "Green Armbands." According to one report they have 1,500 Simonov semi-automatic rifles and about a thousand artillery tubes of World War II vintage in their arsenal.[93] The Lithuanian parliament also passed a Law on Alternative Service Obligation. Citizens of the Lithuanian Republic who are age 19 to 27 are eligible for alternative (labor) service.[94]

ESTONIA

In April 1990 the Estonian parliament passed a law declaring the Soviet conscription law illegal within Estonia. The legislation also established an alternative civilian service for those unwilling to serve in the Soviet Army. Not surprisingly, most of those drafted subsequent to this date preferred to perform civilian service working in hospitals or police forces.

In December 1990 the government of Estonia reached a compromise with the Soviet military authorities allowing all Estonians citizens to serve inside the republic.[95] In March 1991 the Estonian parliament passed the Law on Defense, which set forth concepts for creating national formations of the republic's defense force. Like Lithuania's law, this Estonian law established a border guard service and custom control to monitor the movement of goods and people across its frontiers. The core of Estonian armed forces was formed around two militarized national formations, "Kodukaitse" and "Kaitseliit," which were first used for guarding the parliament and other government buildings in Tallinn. The overall strength of these detachments is estimated at 3,000-4,000 men.[96]

Estonia first announced the formation of its own defense forces in June 1991.[97] The declared mission of the defense forces is to protect Estonia's independence and territorial integrity and ensure the security and the rights of citizens. On November 11, 1991 Ants Laaneots, acting director of the Estonian Defense Forces, formally announced the beginning of the first conscription into

Estonian armed forces.[98] First reports from the draft boards were not very encouraging. Young men from Estonia appear only slightly more willing to serve in a local defense force than in the Soviet military. According to the published conscription figures, Estonian defense officials have been unable to fulfill their quota of conscripts in the first two phases of the current call-up. The first phase began in November 1991 and brought 207 men, about 30 percent less than needed. The second phase began on December 2 and produced 205 men, again less than the officials wanted. Most of those who did not appear were ethnic Estonians.[99]

The structure of the Estonian armed forces being formed is similar to that of Latvia and Lithuania.

- Border guards.

- Forces of territorial defense.

- Forces of civil defense.

- Rapid deployment force.

The total number is planned to be between 5,000 and 6,000 men.

Similar to the other Baltic states, Estonian legislation also established an alternative civilian service for those unwilling to serve in the regular army.

Prospects for the Future

The presence of the large contingent of Russian troops remains the most destabilizing factor in the Baltics. These troops are unlikely to leave the Baltics before the pullout from Germany is completed. In the meantime all three Baltic states are creating their own militaries rapidly.

MOLDOVA
Before August 1991

In September 1990 Moldova suspended the obligation of its citizens to serve in the Soviet Armed Forces and created its own Department of Military Affairs with its own armed units.[100] The first national guard battalion, Tigris-Tigrina, was formed in November 1990. It consists of volunteers, many of whom are "veterans" of the armed clashes with the separatists in the Gagauz region of the republic in October 1990. On 23 November 1990 Tigris-Tigrina officially was blessed by a Kishinev priest and a republic-wide fundraising effort began for the national guard.

In December 1990 the Moldovan parliament passed The Law on the National Guard, and the Department of Military Affairs began forming a second battalion. But in January 1991 the Law on the National Guard and the suspension of the USSR Law on Universal Military Service Obligation were revoked as part of a political compromise with Moscow whereby several pro-independence laws were revoked in response to Gorbachev's request. On 12 April 1991 the republic's legislature reinstated the suspension, this time with the added option for conscripts to serve in the newly established Moldovan Corps of Carabinieri. The total strength of this corps is projected to be 10,000. The government plans to recruit veterans of the airborne, border guard, internal troops and Afghan war veterans.[101] In 1991, 3,000 men were drafted into Moldova's Corps of Carabinieri.

Since spring 1991 the military draft has been conducted in Moldova only in accordance with the republic's law.[102] Since that time, according to Col. Chirtoaca, head of Moldova's Department of Military Affairs, the USSR conscription law "has no legal force in Moldova," and refusal to serve shall not be punishable. All draftees were given the option to serve on the territory of the republic "without augmenting the Soviet troop levels here." In 1991, 3,000 men were drafted into Moldova's Corps of Carabinieri. Service outside the republic is permitted only on the basis of individual application along with written parental approval. The Moldovan government also instructed the Department of Military Affairs and the local administration to provide "socially useful employment" for runaway conscripts.[103]

After August 1991

On 30 December 1991 Moldovan President Mircha Snegur issued a decree subordinating all structures and troops of the former USSR civil defense units in his republic to Moldova's Civil Defense Service.[104] This was the first step toward "privatizing" FSU military equipment. Following the February 1992 talks with the CIS deputy minister of defense, Boris Piankov, Moldovan Minister of Defense Ion Kostas stated that his country's armed forces are to be created based on the 14th Army units located on the right bank of the Dniester River. Units located on the territory of "Dniester Republic" will be withdrawn to Russia in eighteen months to two years.[105]

According to the plan submitted to Moldova's parliament its armed forces will consist of four major groupings and number 20,000 men. Each is to have one mechanized brigade and helicopter squadron. Each military grouping is to be subordinated to its own territorial command—a grouping that is similar in concept to the Soviet military districts. Moldova also plans to have air defense forces (one PVO brigade) and an air force with about 100 airplanes and helicopters.[106]

There are two regions in Moldova that have their own paramilitary forces. These regions, Trans-Dniester and Gagauzia, declared their independence from Moldova and are not recognized by the Moldovan government.

Trans-Dniester

"Workers teams" in this largely Russian-speaking region were created in the fall of 1990 soon after the region declared itself the "Independent Republic of Trans-Dniester." Although the official strength of these teams was never announced, the conservative Council of Workers Collectives that directs them indicates that they have several thousand armed members. During the bloody clashes with Moldovan police in Gagauzia in the fall of 1990 Trans-Dniester security engaged the opposition in the town of Dubasary, leaving three people killed and fourteen wounded.[107]

Since these first confrontations the situation in Moldova grew even more complicated. Starting in the late fall of 1991 the armed clashes between Moldovan military formations and Trans-Dniester republic units began rapidly to escalate to widespread armed confrontation involving at times thousands of armed men on each side. The casualties among the population are now numbered in the hundreds. The situation in Trans-Dniester could grow into Karabakh-like conflict.[108]

The armed forces of the Trans-Dniester republic include 1,500 "guard units" that include the former militia force armed with automatic weapons, 70 armored vehicles, 16 old T-34 tanks, and multiple rocket launchers. A 600-man "Dniester" battalion, poorly armed territorial defense detachments, and volunteer Cossack detachments came from southern regions of Russia to help the rebels. The total strength of Trans-Dniester armed forces is about 15,000 men.[109] In June 1992 the Trans-Dniester republic began to form a regular army, according to its commander Gen. Stefan Kigak. It will have a core of volunteers but will be staffed mainly with conscripts. Weapons and equipment are being purchased, not confiscated, from the 14th Army.[110]

Most of the Moldova's government forces fighting in Trans-Dniester consist of OMON units that function as specially trained volunteer police forces. They are often joined by non-governmental volunteer detachments of various sizes who are not subordinated to Kishinev.

Gagauzia Region

There are no reliable reports about "self-defense detachments" in this region of Moldova. According to various media accounts, they were formed largely independently from each other after martial law was introduced in the region at the end of October 1990. The only organization in Gagauzia that openly declared it will continue the armed struggle for independence is the Party of National Revival "Arkalyk." Its leader, Ivan Burgudzhi, has been arrested and charged with illegal weapons possession and with instigating a violent overthrow of the existing political system. The Gagauz-elected government declared its commitment to a peaceful resolution of the existing conflict with Moldova. However, the clashes with the Kishinev government continue. The Gagauz self-defense detachments were dispatched on 3 February 1992 to guard the territory's borders. They were armed with machine guns and mortars and prepared for combat.[111]

PROSPECTS FOR THE FUTURE

The situation in Moldova remains very tense and the possibility of new interethnic clashes resulting in a full-fledged civil war remains high. This state of affairs is complicated by the presence of the units of the Russia's 14th Army in the middle of the conflict. Each party, the Moldova government and the Trans-Dniester administration, wants the 14th Army on its side. The military is desperately trying to remain neutral. After visiting the region, Aleksandr Rutskoi, Russia's vice president, wanted the 14th Army to serve as a guarantor of a peace separating the fighting parties. However, the lamentable experience of using CIS forces in Nagorno-Karabakh is likely to result in the withdrawal of the army to Russia.

Moldova is likely to remain an explosive region of the CIS. Kishinev is forming its own regular armed forces, staffed with ethnic Moldovans. The separatist Trans-Dniester is likely to continue its armed resistance. The planned withdrawal of the Russian 14th will make the situation even more complicated. The Trans-Dniester forces are unlikely to prevail in full-fledged military conflict with the central government, but they are certainly able to mount a long-standing and bloody guerrilla resistance. This situation has the potential to spread into neighboring states, Russians being sympathetic to their separatist ethnic kin and Romania openly supporting the central government.[112]

CAUCASUS
Azerbaijan

In late 1989 the first armed detachments of the Peoples Front of Azerbaijan (PFA) were formed. On 12 January 1990 the Committee for National Defense was established in Baku. After Soviet troops established martial law in Baku on 20 January 1990, all military structures were dissolved and the leaders, including the chairman of the PFA, Etibar Mamedov, were arrested.

Some Azeri armed guerrilla detachments have been fighting in Nagorno-Karabakh and in the Nakhichevan region since 1990. The first intense fighting was reported between Azeri and Armenian forces at the border with the Nakhichevan region, near the villages of Sadarak, Germechatakh, and Shada, as early as January-February 1990. In January 1990 the PFA began drafting young unmarried men into its armed detachments and training them for guerrilla operations in Nagorno-Karabakh.[113]

After the withdrawal of Soviet troops in December 1991 Azerbaijan started to create its own "National Defense Army." In January 1992 Azeri ex-president Mutalibov said, "We are forming units that can fight like an army and when we attack something we should be able to hold it, to eliminate the Armenian terrorists and not to give it away."[114] Mutalibov complained that he was unable to buy weapons from Russia or other countries to arm these units adequately. According to him, in January 1991 Azerbaijan had a 2,000-3,000-strong volunteer force fighting the Armenian militia in Nagorno-Karabakh. After the Tashkent agreement in the spring of 1992 that gave Azerbaijan a large share of the weapons and military equipment of the 4th Army and the Caspian Flotilla, its newly formed military began to arm itself frantically and in an unorganized manner.

The withdrawal in December 1991 of the estimated 5,000 Soviet troops deployed in Nagorno-Karabakh brought a new escalation of a warfare that already had cost more than 2,000 lives. Between November 1991 and summer 1992 Azerbaijani forces have been in constant retreat, culminating in the loss of Nagorno-Karabakh, and also of the Azeri town of Lachin. These victories have given Armenia a corridor into the disputed territory to allow supply of Karabakh.

At least one military expert attributes these defeats to the poor training of Azerbaijani troops. There are also several reports blaming the failures in Nagorno-Karabakh on the lack of coordination and unsatisfactory performance of the Azerbaijani Ministry of Defense. There was virtually no communication between units and the high command. There was never full mobilization, and would-be volunteers were frustrated by bureaucracy in Baku.[115]

The embarrassing military defeats Azerbaijan suffered at the hands of Armenians prevented the conservative parliament from reinstating President Mutalibov in May 1992. The new government, which came to power in May 1992, changed the military leadership and managed to improve its performance substantially. As a result, during the July-August offensive the Azeri side was able to recapture most of the territory the Armenians had taken during their spring offensive. Severe fighting in Karabakh continues, with neither side having an upper hand.[116]

The new Azeri administration made an effort to establish centralized control over the republic's military formations. They now fall under the command of the minister of internal affairs and include the national army, the police, and OMON. Some non-official military such as the Grey Wolves became part of OMON.[117]

Nagorno-Karabakh

This territory has been involved in fierce ethnic fighting for more than three years. Reliable information about the numbers and state of its armed forces is obscure and most of the reporting from this region is biased. The most reliable estimates are:

• NKR forces of self-defense, which include the entire male population from the age of eighteen to sixty, approximately 40,000- 50,000.[118]

• Volunteer detachments from Armenia, 20,000-30,000.

• Mercenary units, 1,500-2,000.[119]

Armenia

The first military-type formations began to appear in early 1988. By summer 1990 the armed forces were divided between two hostile groups, the Armenian National Army (ANA) and the Armenian National Movement (ANM).

Until September 1990, ANA was the largest military group in Armenia. Its commander, Rasmik Vasilian, maintained that his units would be subordinated only to a freely elected republican parliament. When ANM was elected to a majority position in August 1990, ANA refused to surrender to the ANM militia, its archrival. On 30 August 1990 a deputy of the parliament, Viktor Aivazian, was killed while negotiating with ANA. This assasination forced parliament to declare ANA and other military groups not subordinated to the government to be illegal. The ANA leader Vasilian and his staff surrendered and ANA was disarmed and integrated into ANM. Some of the ANA armed detachments operating at the border with Azerbaijan and in Nagorno-Karabakh remain active. According to some reports, after the official disbandment of ANA one of these groups attacked villages in a Kazakh region of Azerbaijan and fought with Soviet Army units. July 1992 estimates put ANA strength at only 600 to 750 men.[120] Besides ANA, Armenia has other underground armed formations. The largest of these formations is the Erkrapai with an estimated strength of 1,000, and the David Sasunskii Battalion with an estimated strength of 150. There are about thirty other known unofficial military detachments with as many as 20-150 men each.

From 1990 through early 1992 various armed groups were established in Armenia, most of which claimed to protect the republic's frontiers or to fight for independence of Nagorno-Karabakh.Various estimates put the total strength of the armed detachments in Armenia at anywhere from 2,000 up to 140,000. They are armed with personal weapons including AK-47, and artillery including dispersement guns such as Alazan-type, helicopters, non-guided missiles, grenade launchers, and 165 flame-throwers. Most of the weapons were probably stolen from the police and Soviet Army units. More than 800 weapons and over 130,000 rounds of ammunition were stolen from military stocks in the Transcaucasian republics in 1990.[121]

During 1991 and 1992 attacks on Soviet and CIS army units stationed in the Caucasus grew even more widespread. Armenian military formations and guerrilla groups are capturing large numbers of modern arms including BM-21 MRL systems. The Armenian government never officially endorsed any of these groups and at least until 1992 publicly maintained that the republic does not have its own army.

The first official Armenian armed national formation, an Armenian OMON regiment, was created in early 1991. Armenia began drafting conscript-age youth into this national formation and recruiting volunteers from those serving in the Soviet Armed Forces. The unit, which is supposed to be more than 1,000 strong, is divided into battalions and has "all the necessary armaments and equipment." Later, five independent companies were formed to serve at the Azeri-Armenian border. The recruits were paid 300 to 350 rubles a year in 1991 prices. These so-called self-defense detachments are part of the Ministry of Defense and can be considered an integral element of the Armenian military. For example, Armenian Minister of Defense Vasgen Sarkisian declared in his televised address on 7 May 1992 that "Armenia has its own army which is located at our border with Azerbaijan. Today, every second man is ready to fight for our republic and sacrifice his life."[122]

The Armenian border defense system is quite efficient and has a well-defined structure subordinated to the Armenian Ministry of Defense. Locally self-defense detachments are subordinated to the border-commandant zone, or pograngkomendatura. Each administrative district has such a structure and is commanded by Soviet Army veterans of Armenian decent. The commandant is in charge of all military and paramilitary units in the area including the state security detachments, militia, and territorial defense forces.

After the draft was introduced in the spring of 1991 Armenia was able to bring the number of its forces, officially called the Armenian Self-defense Forces, to approximately 80,000. They comprise 30,000 members of the police force and 50,000 men in the national military forces. Since Armenia is scheduled to receive a substantial portion of the arsenal of the 7th Guards Army stationed there, it may have a well-equipped and well-trained military that all states in the region must reckon with. It has shown that it can conduct successful future military operations in Nagorno-Karabakh, where it took over key Azerbaijani strongholds.

Georgia

On 29 December 1990 the Georgian parliament passed the law On Creation of the Internal Troops-National Guard of the Georgian Republic. President Zviad Gamsakhurdia indicated that the National Guard would number 13,000 men.[123]

According to National Guard laws, the officer and noncommissioned officer corps are to be created on a voluntary basis with renewable contracts of two to five years. Male citizens between the ages of eighteen and twenty-five are to be drafted for two years compulsory military service except for individuals in alternative service. Those servicemen "who have voluntarily left the ranks of the Soviet Army" are also allowed to enlist in the National Guard of Georgia.[124]

It is not completely clear how the National Guard is organized and armed, although the founding documents specify that battalion, regimental, division, and corps commanders will be appointed. The republic's budget is to supply financing and its personnel is to be trained by Georgian and "foreign specialists" from Russia and other FSU republics.

After the collapse of Gamsakhurdia government some units of the national guardsmen moved to Western Georgia near the town of Zugdidi. Others joined a new Georgian army loyal to Eduard Shevardnadze's administration. In July-August 1992 the situation in the autonomous republic of Abkhazia, which declared its independence from Georgia, broke out into open warfare. Gamsakhurdia loyalists kidnapped a number of high-ranking government officials and kept them as hostages. The Georgian government dispatched troops to the area. There is some question of how involved the Russians are in this mini-Georgian civil war.

Edward Shevardnadze's government, having legitimate concerns about the loyalty of the National Guard, advocates creating a regular army. In one of his interviews Shevardnadze said he wants "a centralized, and, by international standards, a professional well-armed and equipped army. While it should not have 100,000 but only 15,000 men, it should be a real army."[125] On 20 March the State Council of Georgia passed the Armed Forces of Georgia law. In spring 1992 Georgia started calling young men age eighteen to twenty-five into its regular armed forces, numbering more than 20,000 conscripts.[126]

Georgian Navy

In 1992 Georgia joined Russia and Ukraine in the quest for the Black Sea Fleet. The Georgians may have a good chance to resolve this problem peacefully. On 29 May 1992 a meeting took place in Sevastopol between representatives of the Georgian

Ministry of Defense and a group of Black Sea Fleet officers headed by its chief of staff Vice Admiral Georgii Gurinov. During this meeting they discussed the transfer of ships of the Black Sea Fleet to Georgia along with training specialists for the Georgian Navy. Both sides went to considerable lengths to stress that all issues will be resolved in a "civilized manner." Today, part of the Black Sea Fleet is based in the Georgian ports of Poti, Batumi, and Ochamchira.

Other Military Formations

In addition to the National Guard Georgia has several armed militia formations. The largest ones are the Mkedrioni, the Tetry Georgy, and the Shevardeni.

The Mkedrioni (Horsemen) is supported by the National Congress Party, and is a military organization that opposes the Gamsakhurdia government. Between 1989-1990 the Mkedrioni were actively involved in the armed conflict in South Ossetia. However, since the spring of 1991 it has not taken an active part in the conflict. Its leader, Dzhaba Ioseliani, claims that the Mkedrioni has 2,000 active duty personnel but another 4,000 can be called quickly. Its arsenal includes automatic weapons, dozens of armored personnel carriers, trucks, and explosives in a network of bases throughout Georgia. The Mkedrioni formed the core of the forces that ousted President Gamsakhurdia in January 1992. In payment for his support Ioseliani was appointed a deputy chairman of Georgia's ruling State Council.

On 22 April 1991, after meeting with representatives of Georgia's Ministry of Defense, Dzaba Ioseliani announced the voluntary disbandment of Mkedrioni members who have chosen to join the regular army. It is unclear whether they will be completely integrated or continue to exist as an independent entity within it.[127]

The group Tetry Georgy (The White George Society) is a military organization that supports the Gamsakhurdia government. Its formations are taking part in the armed clashes in South Ossetia. Tetry Georgy's relationship with the Mkedrioni is hostile. In summer 1990 these hostilities resulted in shootings between the two groups in Tbilisi. After the Georgian parliament passed the law disbanding all military groups, Tetry Georgy formally joined the Georgian National Guard.

Shevardeni (The Legion of the Georgian Falcons) was formed in 1989. It has offices in the Tbilisi Higher Artillery Officers School and is neutral in the conflict between the Mkedrioni and the Tetry Georgy.

Georgia remains the most militarized republic of the former Soviet Union. Besides the above-mentioned military groups there are several others that do not have any formal structure or well-defined political programs. Among these are detachments of the Merab Kostava Society which have been very active in South Ossetia. In the autonomous region of South Ossetia so-called self defense detachment have been formed after repeated attacks by Georgian military bands. It reportedly has about 3,000 men but is not subordinated to any central command. In the republic's unstable political and economic situation several well-armed criminal gangs numbering between twenty and seventy continue to act with impunity in various remote regions.[128]

PROSPECTS FOR THE FUTURE
Azerbaijan

After suffering a major setback in Nagorno-Karabakh, Azerbaijan elected a new and more militant government controlled by the Popular Front. With distribution of the Soviet 4th Army equipment soon to begin, the Popular Front has promised to forge a national army out of troops now subordinated to local guerrilla commanders. The new Azeri official spokesman said that his country will never abandon Nagorno-Karabakh even if it means a defense alliance and army training agreement with Turkey. The political situation in the country makes any attempt to resolve the Karabakh conflict with Armenia by peaceful means extremely difficult, if not impossible.

Armenia

Many observers were taken by surprise when the Armenian military secured control of Nagorno-Karabakh after defeating its much larger neighbor Azerbaijan. This situation may not last long. The conflict with Azerbaijan could grow into a major international conforntation, with Turkey, Iran, Russia, and possibly NATO getting involved. The Armenian Army is likely to inherit if not capture some of the very latest generation weapons and equipment from the CIS 7th Army. Such an event could make this situation more violent in the future.

Georgia

The situation in Georgia will be unstable as long as supporters of Gamsakhurdia continue to try to maintain a political and military infrastructure. The Soviet Armed Forces left substantial military assets in Georgia that could make this state a significant military player in the Caucasian region. Georgia will be primarily preoccupied with domestic affairs, which include potential ethnic conflicts in Adzharia, and the continuing armed conflict in South Ossetia and Abkhazia.

CENTRAL ASIA
Tajikistan

In 1990 the Tajikistan Supreme Soviet adopted a resolution stipulating that the republic's conscripts called into construction battalions must serve in the Turkestan Military District, and primarily in Tajikistan.[129] The resolution, which resembles one adopted by Uzbekistan, placed other restrictions on military service by local draftees. The Tajik government started a process that resulted in the creation of a republican military organization. Military establishments are found throughout Tajikistan.

During the February 1990 violence there were reports about nationalist military formations receiving weapons from fellow-Tajiks in Afghanistan.[130] Another militarized force is the self-defense detachment organized by the Russian-speaking population. If new Russian-Tajik tensions emerge in this country, these detachments could play an important role.

On December 24, 1991 Rakhmon Nabiev, the president of Tajikistan, signed a decree establishing the republic's National Guard. This guard, numbering 700 men, is subordinated directly to the president. The decree also appointed Maj. Gen. Bakhram Takhmonov as the guard's commander and presidential advisor on defense and national security affairs.[131] The National Guard could not protect the conservative president during the massive street protests organized by the opposition in April-May 1992. These events forced Nabiev to disband the National Guard.[132]

After the Tashkent meeting of the CIS heads of states in May 1992, Tajikistan announced the formation of its own armed forces. General Rakhmonov was appointed defense minister of Tajikistan. He disclosed that there are about 20,000 CIS military personnel on the republic's territory and that its armed forces will probably be formed on this basis.[133]

Uzbekistan

Although Uzbekistan had no legislation creating its own military until February 1992, it issued several laws limiting the authority of the USSR Ministry of Defense to conduct a draft.

On 6 September 1990 Islam Karimov, the Uzbek president, issued a decree banning the recruitment of Uzbeks into military construction units deployed outside Uzbekistan.[134] The decree also called for the drafting of Uzbeks based on treaties between Moscow and Uzbekistan and instructed the Uzbek government to conclude such treaties before the spring 1991 draft. As an indication of increasing concern over the number of servicemen who died while serving, the decree also included a provision that forbade the drafting of young men whose brothers died while serving in the Soviet Army. In the fall of 1991 the draft in Uzbekistan was based on quotas the government negotiated with the CIS military leaders. As a result, the number of Uzbeks who served in the CIS forces outside their republic decreased dramatically. In October 1991 the Ministry of Defense Affairs was created and, in January 1992, the Uzbek National Guard. Major General Rustam Akhmedov was appointed to head both the ministry and the National Guard.[135]

In January 1992 President Karimov signed a decree subordinating to him all CIS military units stationed in Uzbekistan with the exception of some space and intelligence activities. In February 1992 Uzbekistan declared at the CIS meeting in Minsk that it intended to form its own military within two to three years. According to some estimates, the armed forces of Uzbekistan will include ground forces, an air force (so far they have "privatized" about 300 military airplanes), and some special units. They will have between 25,000 and 30,000 men. Uzbekistan also took under its jurisdiction all USSR Border Troops, which became an integral part of the new Border Troops Directorate in the Uzbekistan National Security Service, the successor to the KGB.

Kyrgyzstan

Kyrgyzstan, along with the other Central Asian republics, resisted the idea of forming its own armed forces. In February 1992 the republic signed a treaty with

Russia on defense cooperation. There were also unconfirmed reports that Kyrgyzstan approached Russia about having joint Kyrgyz-Russian military forces on its territory. Kyrgyzstan maintained that it can only finance internal troops, civil defense, and small National Guard units.

However, on 29 May 1992 Kyrgyz President Askar Akaev issued a decree taking all CIS units stationed in the republic under its jurisdiction. This was obviously a reluctant step taken only after a special request was made by the CIS Forces commander-in-chief, Marshal Shaposhnikov.[136] Despite its strong opposition to the idea Kyrgyzstan will be forced like most of its Central Asian neighbors to have its own armed forces. Although a special investigative team of the republic's KGB could find no military formations, there is some evidence pointing to their existence.[137]

During the clashes between the Kyrgyz and the Uzbek populations in the city of Osh in summer 1990 special Kyrgyz cavalry detachments were very active. There is very little information available about these detachments except that cavalry is a traditional form of organization in Central Asia. As one newspaper points out, "the rapid emergence of this strong militarized formation and its rapid disappearance leads one to consider its re-appearance a high probability during future conflicts."[138]

Uzbek members of Kyrgyz detachments are preparing for future contingencies. According to some reports, self-defense formations have been formed and the Uzbek adult male population has been assigned to them in the manner similar to Abkhazia. There are also reports of weapons being sent to Osh from Andizhan, Fergana, and other cities in Uzbekistan.

Turkmenistan

This republic has no military formations of its own. However, on 27 January 1992 a ministry of defense affairs was created and Lt. Gen. Danatar Kopekov was appointed its first head.[139] In May 1992 Turkmenistan began talks with the Russian and CIS military authorities about the possible structure of its armed forces. By late May 1992 an agreement seemed possible between Russia and Turkmenistan on military forces that could pave the way to similar treaties between Russia and other Central Asian republics. According to Turkmen President Saparmurad Niyazov, Russia and his country were negotiating a bilateral agreement on military affairs. On 14 July 1992 the Turkmen Cabinet of Ministers officially announced formation of the republic's armed forces. The government also decided to create a national guard with an initial strength of 1,000 men.[140]

PROSPECTS FOR THE FUTURE
Tajikistan

The political situation in Tajikistan will remain unstable in coming years. Since the fall of 1992 none of the opponents of the conservative government led by President Nabiev have been strong enough to form a stable government. The political coalition between the democrats and the Islamic nationalists, who form the two major groups in the opposition, has little chance for survival. Fighting for power and influence between various ethnic and tribal groups will continue.

While the Tajik government has announced that it will take control of former Soviet troops stationed on its soil, it is unlikely that it will have enough money to support a 20,000-strong force. A more plausible scenario calls for a National Guard of 1,000 and several thousand border guards to patrol the border with Afghanistan.

Uzbekistan

Several factors will influence Uzbekistan's defense and security policies. First, the country shares a common border with two states which have very unstable political situations, Afghanistan and Tajikistan. This will compel Uzbek authorities to strengthen their border troops and place newly-created military units close to the country's southern border. Secondly, complicated internal political and economic situations and growing inter-ethnic tensions may result in military forces being used against the opposition. Finally, because of a serious shortage of ethnic officers in the republic's armed forces, almost 90 percent of officers are Slavs while about 80 percent of the enlisted personnel are Uzbeks. Although Uzbekistan has three officer training schools, it may take up to ten years before the army becomes Uzbek and not Soviet or Russian.

Uzbekistan has declared that it will have its own armed forces in the next two to three years. Having the largest Muslim population in the FSU, this republic could form armed forces with up to several hundred thousand men. It also has enough Soviet military equipment to arm them. However, Uzbekistan has only a very small defense industrial base to sustain modern military forces. It is dependent on others for supplies and equipment modernization. A profound economic crisis makes it unlikely that this country will amass any serious military capabilities in the near future.

Turkmenistan and Kyrgyzstan

These impoverished Central Asian states cannot afford to form and maintain full-fledged armed forces in the near future. Despite official announcements about the creation of the armed forces, both Turkmenistan and Kyrgyzstan will not be able to support much more than national guard or the riot police-type paramilitary units with 2,000-3,000 men. The protection of their external border will continue to be of greatest concern. Turkmenistan may enter into an agreement with Russia to share expenses in return for its help in controlling this border. Russia likely will accept this arrangement since drug and firearms smuggling from Afghanistan through Turkmenistan is becoming a serious problem.

Kazakhstan

Kazakh President Nursultan Nazarbaev has been one of the strongest supporters of the CIS joint armed forces. After Russia announced the creation of its own armed forces, Nazarbaev changed his position. He said that "it is clear that Russia will have its own armed forces. Naturally then we have to create a national military in Kazakhstan as well. The issues of common defense need to be discussed."[141] Kazakhstan has its own Committee on Defense headed by Lieutenant General Sagadat Nurmagambetov and National Guard units.

On 8 May 1992, President Nazarbaev issued a decree creating the republic's armed forces. According to this decree, all military installations on the territory of Kazakhstan will be transferred to its jurisdiction, Nazarbaev becoming the Kazakh Armed Forces commander-in-chief, and the Committee on Defense being transformed into the Ministry of Defense.[142]

The bulk of the country's military will consist of the 40th Army, which was transferred to Kazakhstan from Afghanistan in 1989. The armed forces of Kazakhstan are expected to have about 50,000 men and include the Ground Forces, the Air Force, Air Defense, and the Navy.[143] For FY 1992 Kazakhstan allocated 22 billion rubles for its military budget.[144]

Kazakhstan has 104 ICBMs based on its territory. Under the START Treaty provisions 80 percent of those have to be dismantled and liquidated. According to expert analysis, most of these ICBMs will be scrapped in the next two or three years because their guaranteed service life expires.[145] While Kazakhstan joined the START Treaty in May 1992 and announced that it would join the NPT as a non-nuclear state,[146] it maintains that none of the nuclear weapons will be moved from its territory without the republic's consent.[147]

The collapse of the Soviet military machine and the attendant creation of military forces in the newly-independent former republics of the Soviet Union do not necessarily make the world a safer place. The disappearance of the USSR faces the new independent states with the challenge of forming their own military-political structures and with formulating national security policies. This challenge, in turn, raises the issue of defining national interests and goals. So far, none of the CIS member states have succeeded in doing this. Most of their military doctrine documents are rather vague and appear to be political declarations rather than concrete programs for building a military and security infrastructure.

Various economic, political and purely military factors mean that none of the former USSR republics except for Russia can conduct its own independent policy leading to political and military alliances. The new states will have a number of alternatives to consider ranging from creating new military-political alliances to joining more stable existing military-political alliances or individual states, to reestablishing old, familiar military-political ties. This process has begun and may take different forms in different republics. For example, on 15 May 1992 in Tashkent, Russia, Armenia, Kazakhstan, and the three Central Asian republics agreed to support some form of a joint military force structure and signed a mutual defense treaty. This treaty formally confirmed that the CIS armed forces will continue to be supported only by Russia and those republics which cannot afford their own armies.

In creating their own military-political structures and formulating national security policies the republics will have to deal with a series of military and political factors. The mechanical parceling of the former Soviet Armed Forces resulted in discrepancies and disproportional division of the weapons, equipment, and related military stock. With the exception of Russia, the republics will need to try various solutions in financing their armed forces and purchasing modern weapons and equipment. There are several options.

• Curtail military programs in response to domestic political pressure.

• Search for "inexpensive" weapons and equipment, with the corresponding lowering of standards.

• Search for "sponsors" and/or influential (and rich) military allies.

• Reestablish the old military-political ties, primarily for joint research and production of military equipment.

• Divide and barter Soviet military equipment among themselves including tanks for airplanes, mortars for shells, etc.

• Buy more arms from abroad.

Political factors have so far played a decisive role in formulating the republican armies. After all, it was their political drive for sovereignty and national statehood rather than external threats that compelled the new governments to create their armed forces. Internal instability, present in almost all of the new states, also makes political leaderships pay particular attention to the loyalty of their militaries. This situation creates the threat of politicizing the armed forces, rival political factions trying to influence the military and even using it in their political struggle. The most extreme cases of such a development have occurred in Armenia, Georgia, and Moldova where various political forces either created their own armed formations or tried to split existing ones.

One of the most disturbing consequences of the Soviet collapse is the use of stolen equipment in inter-ethnic conflicts. This has led to bloodshed in some places, like Karabakh, where there have been hundreds of civilian casualties. Growing civilian casualties correspond to the increased numbers and sophistication of the military equipment and weapons that each of the fighting sides possesses. If this process of dismembering the former Soviet Armed Forces continues, the Azeri and Armenian militaries could obtain hundreds of tanks, modern artillery systems, gunships, and other destructive equipment now under the control of the 4th and the 7th Armies located on their territories. A similar situation can occur in the ethnic trouble spots in Moldova, Ukraine, Central Asia, and even Russia.

The issue of the control of the thousands of nuclear weapons and other means of mass destruction, which will continue to be stored on the territory of the former Soviet Union, also remains of paramount concern. Although all CIS members who have nuclear weapons on their territory signed the START Treaty in May 1992, the question of what will happen to their nuclear arsenals is far from resolved.[148] The tensions that accompanied the transfer of tactical nuclear weapons from Ukraine to Russia may be just the tip of the iceberg. With the CIS General Staff transferred to the Russian Ministry of Defense, Russia effectively assumed control of all other assets including the strategic nuclear formations. The future of the nuclear forces will become the subject of negotiations between Russia, Ukraine, Kazakhstan, Belarus, and the world's other nuclear powers. It is hard to predict the outcome of such negotiations, but control of the remaining nuclear arsenal likely will pass to Russia eventually.[149]

While the CIS Armed Forces high command has lost operational control of the FSU conventional forces, it is still premature and unwise to dismiss the CIS military as an institution. Even in the absence of a center the states of the FSU are still linked to each other by a multitude of economic ties. The states still use an old communication infrastructure, their oil and gas come from the same sources in Russia, and most of them still use the ruble as their currency. In addition, a forum such as the CIS, despite all its problems and imperfections, seems for now to be the only alternative to total Russian domination.

1. In fact, military and paramilitary forces have existed in the FSU republics well before the Minsk declaration in February 1992. As early as 1990, former KGB Chief General Kriuchkov complained that "(t)here are already over 20 nationalistic, politicized associations in the country which have in their make-up paramilitary units or armed detachments of guerrillas." See TASS, 22 December 1990.

2. See Army General Vladimir Lobov's interview for the program "Military Forces of the CIS," Moscow TV-1, 6 January 1992. This situation began to change somewhat when Russia announced the formation of its own armed forces.

3. See Novosti 1, Moscow TV Service, 28 April 1992.

4. See, for example, K. Kobets, "Prioritety voennoi politiki Rossii," NG (hereafter NG), 5 February 1992. Interview with the chairman of the Russia's Committee on Defense, Colonel General Pavel Grachev, Krasnaia zvezda (hereafter KZ), 1 April 1992. For the alternative approaches, see Lt. Col. A. Dokuchaev, "Eksperty, prognozy, protsenty...," KZ, 8 May 1992.

5. This chapter deals with all kinds of military formations known to exist in the former USSR regardless of their subordination and official status. The term "former Soviet Union" or FSU is used instead of CIS because the armed formations of the non-CIS countries are examined as well. The FSU republics can be divided into two groups: those that chose to become part of CIS and those that did not. The second group includes Latvia, Lithuania, Estonia, and Georgia.

6. The full title of this position was changed several times and was finally set as "Chairman of the State Committee for Defense and National Security." On 16 March 1992 Yeltsin signed a decree on forming the Russian Ministry of Defense, giving himself the function of minister. On 18 May 1992, he appointed Army General Pavel Grachev to be Russia's Minister of Defense.

7. Boris Yeltsin's press conference, Moscow TV-1, 25 June 1990.

8. TASS, 6 February 1991.

9. Kobets' former job as chief of the General Staff Main Communications Directorate obviously helped.

10. His official title was State Councillor for Defense Affairs.

11. Grachev is forty-three years old, and most of his deputies are under fifty, an unprecedented case in the post-World War II Soviet history.

12. The 1992 military budget is only 4.5 percent of Russia's GNP compared to 20-25 percent in pre-perestroika era. Allocations for military procurement have been cut even more drastically.

13. See "Osnovy voennoi doktriny Rossii," Voennaia mysl (May 1992), 3-9, and "O voennoi doktrine SSSR," Voennaia mysl (November 1990), 24-28.

14. See Voennaia mysl (July 1992), 12 and 108.

15. For a comparative analysis of the two doctrines, see Mary C. FitzGerald, "Russia's New Military Doctrine," Hudson Institute, Washington, D.C., 15 July 1992.

16. See Voennaia mysl (July 1992), 8.

17. See ITAR-TASS report on Kolesnikov speech, 30 July 1992 and Pavel Felgengauer, "Voennye ozhidaiut vmeshatel'stva Zapada," NG, 1 August 1992.

18. See Pavel Grachev's press conference reported in Los Angeles Times, 23 May 1992.

19. See P.G. Grachev, "Osnovnoe soderzhanie voennoi doktriny Rossii i kontseptsia stroitelstva ee Vooruzhennyk Sil," *Voennaia mysl* (July 1992), 108-117.

20. Ibid., 111-112.

21. Ibid.

22. Former Soviet Baltic MD (with forces still deployed in Lithuania, Latvia, Estonia and Kaliningrad oblast).

23. It is important to call this entity the Guard of Russia or Russia's Guard rather than Russian National Guard. As one of the menbers of the future Guard Organizing Committee pointed out, "Unlike in Georgia or Moldova where only the titular nationalities are allowed to serve in their guards units, Russia's Guard will include along with the Russians, Belorussians, Ukrainians, Jews...i.e., all those who would like to dedicate themselves to service for Russia." See *Voennyi vestnik*, No. 12 (1991), 73. In today's highly politicized atmosphere this distinction is becoming very important. Thereafter in this paper the Guard of Russia is termed "The Guard." The draft of the new Russian Constitution refers to it as Russia's Federal Guard, see *Voennaia mysl*, No. 1 (1992), 24.

24. Ibid.

25. For a good discussion see Lt Col. V.P. Vorozhtsov, "Natsionalnaia gvardiia Rossii. Za i protiv," *Voennaia mysl*, No. 1 (1992), 21-25.

26. See Natalie Gross, "Defense Establishments of the Independent States," *Jane's Intelligence Review*, February 1992, 93.

27. Ibid.

28. *Komsomolskaia pravda*, 13 March 1991.

29. *Moskovskie novosti*, 12 July 1992.

30. See *Voennaia mysl* (July 1992).

31. Quoted in Kathleen Mihalisko, "USSR—Ukrainians Ponder Creation of a National Army," *Report on the USSR*, 14 February 1991.

32. As quoted in Taras Kuzic, "Ukraine—A New Military Power?" *Jane's Intelligence Review*, February 1992, 86.

33. *Kommersant*, No. 6 (February, 1991), 12.

34. Radio Kiev-3, 4 February 1991. Quoted in Kathleen Mihalisko, "USSR—Ukrainians...." Ibid.

35. *Kommersant*, No. 6 (February, 1991), 12.

36. See *Demokratychna Ukraina*, 23 October 1991.

37. See *Moskovskie novosti*, 9 August 1992.

38. See *Golos Ukrainy*, 10 January 1992.

39. *Demokratichna Ukraina*, 18 October 1991.

40. See *Moskovskie novosti*, 9 August 1992.

41. Ibid.

42. In his interview in *Izvestiia* on 16 January 1992 Ukraine's Minister of Defense General Morozov said that Ukrainian armed forces will have between 250,000 and 400,000 men.

43. As quoted by TASS, 28 January 1992.

44. National Guard and Border Guard Troops are not subordinated to the Ukrainian Ministry of Defense.

45. See KZ, 8 May 1992.

46. Ibid.

47. *Golos Ukrainy*, 29 February 1992.

48. See KZ, 15 February 1992. By August 1992 only 10,000 officers refused to take an oath and chose to return to Russia. See *Moskovskie novosti*, 9 August 1992.

49. Ukraine still has more than 80,000 homeless officers according to the Ukrainian Ministry of Defense Information.

50. See Col. V. Rudenko, "Nesanktsionirovannyi perelet," KZ, 18 February 1992.

51. See, for example, "Experty, prognozy, protsenty," KZ, 8 May 1992.

52. TASS, 4 November 1991.

53. *Za vilnu Ukrainu*, 28 November 1991.

54. Ibid.

55. See Kathleen Mihalisko, "Laying the Foundation for the Armed Forces of Ukraine," *Report on the USSR*, No. 45, 6 November 1991, 21.

56. As quoted in *Los Angeles Times*, 3 December 1991.

57. An agreement has been reached with Russia on the air leg of the Ukraine's nuclear triad. The only active regiment of Tu-160 "Blackjack" bombers in the CIS air force will be moved to Russia from its base in Priluki when a new airfield is available. According to the spokesmen for CIS Strategic Aviation, the Ukrainian government agreed to the regiment transfer. But Ukrainian officials are demanding that the Tu-22 Backfire-C bombers stationed in the republic be transferred under their command. See *Jane's Defense Weekly*, 25 January 1992, 101.

58. *Los Angeles Times*, 5 February 1992.

59. *Los Angeles Times*, 13 March 1992.

60. "Kak tebe sluzhitsia," Moscow TV-1, 26 January 1992.

61. *Narodnaia armiia*, 20 March 1992.

62. *Kommersant*, No. 32 (1992), 3.

63. *Los Angeles Times*, 14 January 1992.

64. According to media reports, there are about 400 plants in Ukraine that are involved in the production of different elements of the Strategic Rocket Forces.It also has several nuclear power reactors and strong military R&D assets. See NG, 25 March 1992.

65. KZ, 10 January 1992.

66. See Kathleen Mihalisko, "Belarus Moves to Assert Its Own Military Policy," *Radio Liberty Research Institute Reports*, 28 February 1992.

67. Sovetskaia Belorussiia, 13 December 1991.

68. On 6 May 1992 the Belarusian Military District was liquidated and General Kostenko was appointed Belarus Deputy Minister of Defense. See *Postfactum Report*, 8 May 1992.

69. *Znamia yunosti*, 26 October 1991.

70. On 22 April 1992 Lt. Gen. Pavel Kozlovskii was appointed Minister of Defense of Belarus. His previous position was the Chief of Staff of the Belorussian Military District. General Chaus became one of his nine deputies. See ITAR-TASS, 22 April 1992.

71. The precise figures for the Belarusian armed forces have not yet been finalized.

72. Interfax, 23 May 1992.

73. *Molodezh Estonii*, 7 March 1991.

74. See "Baltic Raise Defense Issues for Discussion," *Izvestiia*, 2 May 1991, in FBIS-SOV-91-085, 2 May 1991, 45.

75. Ibid.

76. Ibid. The talks the Russian government team conducted with the representatives of the Baltic states in May 1992 brought no tangible results.

77. General Mironov obviously included in this number troops stationed not only in the three Baltic states but also the 11th Guards Army staioned in the Kaliningrad oblast.

78. Radio Riga, 8 September 1990; *Sovetskaia molodezh*, 23 August 1990.

79. TASS, 26 September 1990.

80. In a compromise reached between the military and Latvian authorities some conscripts who chose alternative service were eventually drafted into the units located in Latvia. As a result of this agreement, starting with 1991 all conscripts from Latvia will serve within the republic's borders. See TASS, 18 February 1991.

81. RFE/RL Daily Report, No. 69, 10 April 1991.

82. Ibid.

83. Alda Starpane and Janis Domburs, "Policing the Militia," *Awakening*, No. 13 (31 March 1991), 2.

84. Interview with Latvia's Minister of Defense Talavs Jundzis in *Za Rodinu*, 5 December 1991. Also, author's interview with Latvia's Deputy Minister of Defense, Valsis Pavlovskis, July 1, 1992, in Riga.

85. Ibid. Mr. Jundzis probably meant "of the total GNP." The republic's military budget for the first six months of 1992 is 3.6 percent of the republic's budget and amounts to 248 million rubles.

86. For example, even the first deputy minister of Defense of Latvia, Dainis Turlajs, is a former colonel of the Soviet Army.

87. "Lithuanian to Form Economic Border Protection Force," *Report on the USSR*, 5 October 1990, 60.

88. KZ, 23 April 1991. Another Soviet source said that a factory order has been placed for 30,000 uniforms. See *Za Rodinu*, 4 December 1990.

89. KZ, 23 April 1991.

90. Ibid.

91. As of July 1992.

92. Author's interview with the Lithuania's deputy defense minister Ignas Stankovicius, Vilnius, 17 October 1991.

93. *Rabochaia tribuna*, 5 July 1990. This report is unconfirmed.

94. See "Law of the Lithuania Republic on Liability for Alternative (Labor) Service, *Ekho litvy*, 27 October 1990, in JPRS-UMA-91-001, 4.

95. Interview with Col. Vladimir Fedirko, deputy military commissar of Estonia, *New York Times*, 18 December 1990.

96. "Kaitseliit" was the first organization in the Soviet Union which began to sign up volunteers to fight Saddam Hussein in the Gulf War. See "Estonian Kaitseliit Calls for Volunteers to Serve in Kuwait," *Nedelia*, No. 38, 17 September 1990, 4, in JPRS-UMA-1-001, 1.

97. *Estonian radio*, 27 June 1991.

98. BNS, 11 November 1991.

99. BNS, 8 December 1991.

100. RFE/RL Daily Report No. 83, 30 April 1991.

101. Vladimir Socor, "Moldova Resists Soviet Draft and Seeks Own National Forces," *Report On the USSR*, 26 October 1991, 22.

102. See interview with Col. Nicolae Chirtoaca, head of Moldova's State Department of Military Affairs, *Moldovapres*, 13 April 1991.

103. TASS, 11 April 1991.

104. MOLDOVA-PRESS-TASS, 30 December 1991.

105. ITAR-TASS, 21 February 1992. Since that time the situation with the 14th Army grew very complicated. It found itself in the middle of two fighting parties—Moldova's government and the Trans-Dniester administration. Its future is to be decided in negotiations between Moldova, Russia, and Trans-Dniester. In the meantime many 14th Army officers and noncommissioned officers who have families in Moldova do not want to leave. For a good analysis of the 14th Army, see Michal Orr's article "14th Army and the Crisis in Moldova," *Jane's Intelligence Review*, Vol. 4, No. 6, 1992. Also note the interesting and controversial interview with the 14th Army's new commander, Maj. Gen. Aleksandr Lebed, in *Literaturnaia Rossiia*, 31 July 1992.

106. See "Chi voiska silnee?," *Moskovskie novosti*, 9 August 1992.

107. *Komsomolskaia pravda*, 12 March 1991.

108. On 29 July 1992, representatives of Moldova, Trans-Dniester, and Russia reached an agreement about forming a joint peacekeeping force in the region and creating the "safety zones" dividing the fighting parties. The 14th Army units that were temporary charged with this mission were returned to their bases. There is a hope that this joint action under the umbrella of the CIS can serve as a good precedent for resolving the internal conflicts.

109. See Alexandr Kakotkin, "Kazhdoi respublike—svoi Karabakh?" *Moskovskie novosti,* No. 11, 1991; Efim Bershin, "Pogiblo bolshe, chem zakhoroneno," *Literaturnaia gazeta,* 11 March 1992. A number of reports suggested that Trans-Dniester received aid from defecting units of the 14th Army. In May-June 1992 according to some reports one tank company (10 tanks) and one motorized company (10 BTRs) went over to the Dniester Republic. According to General Alvert Makashov, who visited the region in June 1992, they were joined by some other 14th Army units. See "Otvety Generala Makashova," *Den,* No. 24 (1992), 2.

110. See Maj. Gen. Stefan Kigak's interview, ITAR-TASS, 18 June 1992. The president of Trans-Dniester, Igor Smirvov, at a meeting with officers of the 14th Army, announced that the republic would have a 12,000-man-strong regular army. See *Nezavisimaia gazeta,* 22 April 1992.

111. *Kommersant* No. 5 (1992), 22.

112. At his press conference on 4 July 1992 Lebed declared that 32 Romanian pilots were fighting on the side of Moldova against Trans-Dniester. This charge has been denied by Moldova's Ministry of Defense. See ITAR-TASS, 4 July 1992, and MOLDOVA-PRESS-TASS, 5 July 1992.

113. Author's interview with a refugee from Azerbaijan, January, 1990.

114. *Los Angeles Times,* 12 January 1992.

115. *Los Angeles Times,* 7 June 1992.

116. As of August 1992.

117. *Moscow News,* No. 28, 1992.

118. The Nagorno-Karabakh Republic press center would not reveal the real number. This is author's estimate based on the total number of the Nagorno-Karabakh population according to the 1989 Census results.

119. Most of the mercenaries come from Russia and the Armenian diaspora in Lebanon, Syria, and France. Recently, some mercenaries began arriving from Ukraine and Lithuania. See *Moskovskie novosti,* 12 July 1992.

120. *Moskovskie novosti,* 12 July 1992.

121. This information is dated May 1991.

122. See E. Agapova, Lt. Col. A. Dokuchaev, Capt. 2nd Rank G. Dianov, "Vzgliad iz Armenii," KZ, 29 May 1992.

123. According to the later reports, by spring 1992 the Georgian National Guard's strength reached this level. See, for example, *Moskovskie novosti,* 9 August 1992.

124. Unlike some other former Soviet republics, Georgia's National Guard has not been formed on the basis of the existing MVD troops and is a real military formation.

125. NG, 19 March 1992. On 7 June 1992 the chief of the Georgian Defense Ministry personnel department, Tornike Papava, said that Georgia would build an army of some 20,000 men. See Interfax, 7 June 1992.

126. *Krasnaia zvezda,* 21 March 1992.

127. "Novosti-1," Central Television (Moscow), 22 April 1992.

128. *Moskovskie novosti,* 12 July 1992.

129. *Kommunist Tadzhikistana,* 9 October 1990.

130. *Komsomolskaia pravda,* 12 March 1991.

131. See TASS, 24 December 1991.

132. See Interfax, 2 May 1992, and *Los Angeles Times,* 3 May 1992.

133. On 21 July Tajikistan signed an agreement with Russia that all CIS forces stationed in this republic wil be transferred to Russian jurisdiction. It also gave Russian border guard forces the right to control the Tajik border with Afghanistan. This agreement aimed at curbing increasing drug and arms flow across the Tajik-Afghan border and into Russia. See *Kommersant,* No. 30 (1992), 21.

134. Radio Moscow, 6 September 1990.

135. See TASS, 10 October 1991, and *Frunzevets,* 15 May 1992.

136. See KZ, 5 June 1992. Kyrgyzstan has about 15,000 CIS/Russian troops on its territory.

137. *Komsomolskaia pravda*, 12 March 1991.

138. Ibid.

139. ITAR-TASS, 27 January 1992.

140. Interfax, 15 July 1992.

141. As reported by ITAR-TASS, 10 April 1992.

142. As reported by KAZTAG, 8 May 1992.

143. See Lt. Gen. El Alibekov, "Kakoe byt' armii Kazakhstana," *Kazakhstanskaia pravda*, 1 May 1992, and *Nezavisimaia gazeta*, 15 May 1992.

144. As reported by KAZTAG-TASS, 25 December 1991.

145. *Nezavisimaia gazeta*, 19 March 1992.

146. *Nezavisimaia gazeta*, 19 May 1992.

147. See the statement made by Burkutbul Ayanov, an official from the Office of the President of Kazakhstan, *Krasnaia zvezda*, 26 February 1992.

148. Russia already effectively assumed control of the CIS strategic nuclear forces. Strategic Rocket Forces, as well as the nuclear assets of the Navy and the Air Force, are under operational control of the Russian Ministry of Defense.

149. For an analysis of Russian-Ukrainian nuclear debate, see Rose Gottemoeller and Eugene Rumer, *Ukraine's Nuclear Game. In Search of Sovereignty and Statehood*, Santa Monica. RAND, May 1992.

THE RUSSIAN MILITARY AND THE OCTOBER 1993 CRISIS

Brian Taylor

In October 1993 a violent and bloody showdown on the streets of Moscow resolved a protracted political conflict between Russian President Boris Yeltsin and the Supreme Soviet. The Russian Armed Forces played a key role in ending the crisis and the images of tanks attacking the country's parliament building were a dramatic symbol of the fragility of the country's new democracy. The October crisis marked the end of the "romantic period" of Russia's post-independence efforts at political change.[1] It also represented a dismal and inauspicious beginning for the recently created Russian Armed Forces.

This chapter examines the role of the Russian Armed Forces in the events of October 1993. The focus is on the armed forces and not the other military and security bodies from related agencies (Ministry of Internal Affairs, Ministry of Security, Presidential Security Service, etc.). After a brief overview of political events the bulk of the chapter is divided into two sections, the first discussing the army's role and stance in the initial phase of the crisis (21 September-2 October) and the second concentrating on the army's behavior once the political conflict became violent. The conclusion discusses the aftermath of the crisis and consequences of the October 1993 events for the Russian military.

POLITICAL BACKGROUND

The Russian political system was under severe stress throughout most of 1992-1993. After the euphoria following the August 1991 coup waned, the collapse of the Soviet Union and the launching of radical economic reform quickly polarized the political landscape. President Yeltsin fell out with two key former allies, his vice president, Air Force General Alexander Rutskoi, and speaker of the Russian Supreme Soviet, Ruslan Khasbulatov. In March 1993 Yeltsin stepped to the brink of open confrontation by threatening to introduce direct presidential rule thereby suspending the legislature. The Russian president's next gambit was more successful; in April 1993 a nation-wide referendum was conducted in which the voters expressed their support for Yeltsin and his policies, and also voted for early parliamentary—but not presidential—elections.[2]

The political conflict over government policies was exacerbated greatly by the lack of clear rules of the game and the contested nature of political institutions. The Russian constitution was based on the heavily amended and internally contradictory Constitution of the Russian Federation from 1978. The political system combined both an executive presidency, created in 1991, and a parliamentary system. The constitution stated that Russia's governmental order was based on the separation of powers while at the same time asserting that the Congress of People's Deputies was the "highest organ of state power." The congress was able to amend the constitution virtually at will, which it did over 300 times in 1992-1993 alone. Parliamentary speaker Khasbulatov had set himself the goal of either impeaching Yeltsin or reducing him to a mere figure-head.[3]

Yeltsin took the fateful step in September 1993 when he issued a decree (No. 1400) disbanding the parliament and calling for a new constitution and fresh elections. He based this decision on his election to the presidency in 1991, the results of the April 1993 referendum, and his constitutional responsibility for the security of the country. Yeltsin did not have the constitutional authority to dismiss the parliament, however, and the Constitutional Court, led by Khasbulatov-supporter chairman Valery Zorkin, quickly declared Decree 1400 unconstitutional and concluded that there were grounds for removing Yeltsin from the presidency. The Supreme Soviet did not wait for the Constitutional Court's ruling and moved to displace Yeltsin from the presidency and swear in Rutskoi as "acting president" only a few hours after Decree 1400 was released.[4]

The constitutional crisis of September 1993 placed the armed forces in an extremely difficult position. They were faced with two political leaders who claimed the role of commander-in-chief. The Russian minister of defense, General Pavel Grachev, initially sought to walk a fine line between supporting his boss and commander-in-chief, Boris Yeltsin, and indicating that the army had no role to play in an internal political crisis. Unfortunately for Grachev and the military, the eruption of violence made this balancing act untenable which led ultimately to the army's direct involvement in the bloody October events.[5]

THE CRISIS OF SEPTEMBER 21-OCTOBER 2

The first officer to learn of Yeltsin's plan to dismiss the parliament was defense minister Grachev. Yeltsin informed Grachev, along with several other top ministers, on 12 September. According to Yeltsin, Grachev had been in favor of such a step for a while. Grachev insisted that the army was ready for a possible confrontation although he had taken no concrete steps to prepare for various contingencies, believing that the troops of the Ministry of Internal Affairs (MVD) should be responsible for internal order.[6]

The rest of the military leadership, the Military Collegium, apparently was only informed of Yeltsin's plans on 20 or 21 September (Decree 1400 was issued on the twenty-first). Grachev kept the topic from the chief of the General Staff, Colonel General Mikhail Kolesnikov, and First Deputy Minister of Defense Andrei Kokoshin. Kolesnikov later remarked, "maybe Yeltsin discussed it [the decree] with the Minister, but he did not discuss it with us."[7]

News of the Collegium meeting immediately leaked to the Supreme Soviet leadership. Indeed, Rutskoi and Khasbulatov already were aware that Yeltsin was planning to dismiss the parliament and were planning their counter-reaction. Apparently Khasbulatov was informed of the Collegium meeting by Deputy Minister of Defense Colonel General Konstantin Kobets. Kobets was also a Supreme Soviet deputy which apparently explains why he went to Khasbulatov. Still, the episode is mysterious, since Kobets was a Yeltsin loyalist. Regardless, Kobets told Khasbulatov and the deputy speaker of the Supreme Soviet, Yury Voronin, that the Military Collegium had met and that Yeltsin had asked for the support of the Russian Army. The Collegium, however, had decided to take a neutral stance in the political conflict.[8]

Khasbulatov summoned General Staff chief Kolesnikov to the Supreme Soviet building, known colloquially as the White House. According to the Law on Defense, not only the president as commander-in-chief but also the Supreme Soviet and the government were responsible for managing the armed forces. Kolesnikov apparently confirmed that the Collegium had decided to adopt a stance of neutrality in the conflict between Yeltsin and the parliament.[9]

Rutskoi made a fatal blunder the first night (21-22 September) of the conflict. At a session of the Supreme Soviet he announced that he was appointing the former deputy minister of defense, Colonel General (retired) Vladislav Achalov, his "Minister of Defense" and that Grachev was to be dismissed. Rutskoi also appointed new ministers of security and internal affairs (MVD). The appointment of Achalov had several negative consequences for Rutskoi. Most important, it raised the possibility of a split in the armed forces, an outcome that the military leadership was most intent on avoiding. The appointment of Achalov, consequently, drove the high command into Yeltsin's arms. There was no chance that the military leadership would subordinate themselves to Achalov. From an operational point of view the step was meaningless since Achalov had no means available to communicate or control forces outside the walls of the White House. The move was also a personal affront to Grachev, who had served under Achalov in the Airborne Forces in the past. Achalov later claimed that he knew the move was a mistake and that Rutskoi had not asked him in advance about the appointment.[10]

Once Rutskoi appointed his own defense minister, Grachev and the military leadership had to make clear that Yeltsin was the lawful commander-in-chief and only Grachev had the authority to give orders as minister of defense. Neutrality would have raised doubts in the minds of commanders about whose orders should be obeyed and would have led to the very split in the officer corps that Grachev and the high command were attempting to avoid. Grachev announced that the entire command staff had affirmed that they followed only the orders of Grachev and Yeltsin. Kolesnikov, who only a few days before had told Khasbulatov that the military would remain neutral, stated on 23 September, "I obey the

Minister of Defense, the Minister of Defense obeys the Supreme Commander. The army is strong and mighty because of its linchpin, and its linchpin—unity of command."[11]

Rutskoi, Khasbulatov, and others in the parliament called for officers and soldiers to come to the defense of the White House. On 22 September Rutskoi sent an order to the head of the Airborne Troops and the commander of the Moscow Military District demanding that units be sent to the White House. He also appealed to the commanders of four of the five military services (Army, Navy, air force, and air defense forces—evidently he was not yet in need of the help of the strategic rocket forces) not to remain "outside politics" and take an "active position." He continued to send appeals to various units throughout the crisis, and called on officers not to fulfill orders of Yeltsin and Grachev. Khasbulatov and other parliamentarians claim to have expected that the army would be on their side and that units loyal to them would arrive within a day or two.[12]

There was some reason to think that Rutskoi and the Supreme Soviet might be successful in their efforts to gain the support of the officer corps. Rutskoi was a general and a Hero of the Soviet Union due to his service in Afghanistan. Rutskoi and the parliament had shown their support for the armed forces by blaming Yeltsin for the collapse of the Soviet Union and impoverishing the army. The military correspondent of Moscow News, Aleksandr Zhilin, cited polls showing that 62 percent of officers supported Rutskoi. Other polling data from the spring and summer of 1993 found that 60-70 percent of officers and warrant officers were for Rutskoi, while only 12-14 percent were for Yeltsin. But 70 percent of generals were pro-Yeltsin. Regardless of the exact accuracy of this polling data—as is often the case with Russian military polling data, the complete results were not published—there was certainly reason to believe that Rutskoi might be able to bring some units over to his side.[13]

In fact, the White House had almost no active support from the Russian Army. Pro-parliamentary forces claimed backing from about 200 active officers. Rutskoi later admitted that these statements were disinformation and not a single unit came to their defense. In the aftermath of the affair Rutskoi was criticized by pro-parliamentary hard-liners for not accepting the support of military units that offered it, to which Rutskoi replied by asking them to name one unit that offered help and Rutskoi refused. Rutskoi's support was limited to individual officers and private armed organizations such as Cossacks and the fascist Russian National Unity. There is a dispute over 200 officers. Grachev claimed only fifteen officers went to the White House, Lieutenant General (retired) V.V. Serebriannikov, an adviser to Khasbulatov, put the number at sixty, and during the crisis itself Achalov said the White House had the support of eighty officers. The Union of Officers, led by Lieutenant Colonel (retired) Terekhov, also supported Rutskoi, but many of these officers were retired, and less than one hundred of them were present at the Supreme Soviet building. Clearly these numbers were a minuscule amount of support in a multi-million man army.[14]

Rutskoi and Achalov had colleagues throughout the armed forces including in the high command and the two leaders worked to gain additional support during the October crisis. Rutskoi claimed that both air force commander Petr Deinekin and Deputy Minister of Defense Boris Gromov had offered moral support but were unwilling to go further. Voronin states that Kolesnikov and deputy defense minister General Valery Mironov took a similar stance. Yeltsin and Grachev later claimed that Deinekin and other members of the high command who spoke with Rutskoi rebuffed his appeals for help and told him that there was only one president (Yeltsin) and one minister of defense (Grachev). Rutskoi also maintained that he had two meetings with a representative from the Moscow Military District who said that they were thinking about sending units to support the White House. Allegedly on October 2 Rutskoi was told that a regiment would arrive on 3 October. Elsewhere in his account Rutskoi states that in response to his appeals to the army the only reply he received was that officers promised to "consider the matter." Achalov's assistant Ivanov was sent to a brigade based on the outskirts of Moscow to ask for support. Ivanov was initially rebuffed, according to his version, but said he would not support Yeltsin if the MVD stormed the White House.[15]

Despite these intensive efforts and considerable public bluster Achalov had no illusions about his prospects in private. He told his associates on the second night of the October crisis that they could not count on the army if the conflict became violent. Khasbulatov blamed the failure of the pro-parliamentary forces to bring units to the White House on the incompetence of Achalov. On 25 September Khasbulatov asked Achalov where the promised military units were, to which Achalov sarcastically replied, "the same place your promised workers' collectives are." The desperation felt by the pro-parliamentary forces in terms of relations with the military is evident from Rutskoi's order to Achalov to take up his post at the Ministry of Defense headquarters, an order that Achalov obviously had no hope of carrying out.[16]

The one active step involving armed force taken by pro-Rutskoi forces in the early days of the crisis was attacks on various targets throughout Moscow. The attacks took place the night of 23 September and were organized by Terekhov from the Officer's Union. Rutskoi, Khasbulatov and Achalov denied any involvement in the attacks and said they had not been sanctioned by the White House. Indeed, Terekhov himself later bragged about his role in planning the attacks as did the hard-line leader of "Worker's Russia," Viktor Anpilov. Moreover, government sources reported that Achalov's "deputy minister of defense," the retired colonel general Albert Makashov who was a vociferous supporter of the August 1991 coup, had taken an armed group to the State Committee on Emergency Situations on 23 September and demanded that it be turned over to the White House. It is probably true that Rutskoi and Khasbulatov had not sanctioned these efforts. Rutskoi's former aide Andrei Federov maintains that Terekhov thought up the attacks himself, but they were indicative of the extremist orientation of some of their supporters. Khasbulatov later castigated those who attacked CIS military headquarters as "light-headed" people who, while claiming to defend the constitution, had caused great damage to the pro-parliamentary side.[17]

While Rutskoi and Achalov were making efforts to gain support from the officer corps, Yeltsin and Grachev stressed that the army must not be involved. Yeltsin appealed to the armed forces on 22 September to remain calm and to stay focused on military training and the defense of the state. He urged them not to respond to provocations that tried to draw them into politics. On 25 September Yeltsin issued an order that officers making political speeches would be dismissed. Throughout the period after 21 September Grachev reiterated his oft-stated maxim that the army should be "outside politics." He emphasized that the MVD had responsibility for internal order, that the army would stick to its own affairs, and that military units would not be introduced to Moscow. Grachev stated, "the army will not meddle in political activity.... Leave the army alone." To curtail Rutskoi's and Achalov's attempts to drag the army in, Grachev shut off most telephones in the MOD building. He ordered military units to reinforce their security, not allow unauthorized personnel on their territory, and prevent distribution of weapons to personnel. Only orders from Grachev and Kolesnikov were to be obeyed.[18]

A large majority of officers hoped that the political crisis could be resolved peacefully, without military involvement. In an opinion poll conducted on 25 September eighty percent of military personnel surveyed maintained that the army should remain neutral in the conflict. The figure for the general population on the same question was sixty-two percent for army neutrality, twenty percent for military support for Yeltsin, and only five percent for army support for the parliament.[19]

Khasbulatov and his deputy Voronin maintained that much of the officer corps supported the so-called "zero option" which involved a return to the pre-21 September status-quo of simultaneous presidential and parliamentary elections. An unidentified "highly placed General Staff officer" maintained that most officers expressed their support for a return to the status-quo and that all officers were hoping for a peaceful resolution of the conflict. Interestingly, the Ministry of Defense received many letters and telegrams from forces around the country urging restraint on both sides of the conflict. On the eve of the outbreak of violence, 2 October, officers from the key Moscow, Taman, and Kantemirov divisions were adamant that they would not get involved. Analysts for the paper Kommersant Daily argued early in the crisis that neither side could count on military support.[20]

The main political commentator of the army newspaper Krasnaia zvezda, Aleksandr Golts, articulated the military's hopes for a peaceful solution on 2 October. Golts invoked the experiences of the Soviet Army during the late-Gorbachev period in Tbilisi, Baku, Vilnius, and the August 1991 coup attempt as proof that the military wanted to be "outside politics," as it is in "civilized" states.[21] Due to these episodes, Golts argued, the military had "developed an immunity to political games." Russian soldiers understood that their political views could only be expressed "in the voting booth" and that opinions were not relevant to the carrying out of one's military duties. Army commanders, Golts stated, should not have to "work out political riddles" or "analyze legal details regarding the legitimacy of this or that person." The military, he asserted, was very fearful of a split in the armed forces and civil war. The president, Golts concluded, had won a "definite moral and political victory" by asking the military to remain calm and go about its business. Golts hoped that both sides would continue to show such restraint.[22]

BLOODSHED IN MOSCOW AND THE ARMY. OCTOBER 3-4

The armed forces were determined not to get involved directly in the political confrontation between Yeltsin and the Supreme Soviet. Why, then, did the military leadership agree to attack the White House on 4 October? Only the outbreak of widespread violence in Moscow the night of 3-4 October was seen as sufficient cause to bring in the army and the military leadership wavered considerably before agreeing to send in several units. It took a personal visit from President Yeltsin and Prime Minister Viktor Chernomyrdin to the Ministry of Defense, and a direct, public, and written order from Yeltsin, to persuade Grachev and the military leadership to storm the White House. Ultimately the military's subordination to the commander-in-chief trumped their extreme reluctance to be dragged into a domestic political dispute.

Violence in Moscow broke out on the afternoon of 3 October. There had been were sharp clashes between the police and several thousand pro-parliament demonstrators at a meeting not far from the White House called by "Worker's Russia" and the National Salvation Front. The demonstrators had built barricades and lit several fires. On 3 October it was a Sunday and unseasonably warm, and a large crowd of around four to ten thousand demonstrators gathered at October Square, several miles from the White House. The crowd marched toward the White House and overwhelmed the special police units that tried to block their way. The demonstrators continued toward the White House and succeeded in breaking through the police encirclement of the building that had been put in place on 24 September, after the attack on CIS headquarters.[23]

Rutskoi, after having been isolated in the White House for almost two weeks, reacted rashly to this apparent turn in his fortunes. At about four in the afternoon on 3 October Rutskoi addressed his supporters from the balcony of the White House, asking them to form fighting detachments "to take by storm the Mayor's office and Ostankino [the television center]." The mayor's office was located across the street from the White House and the crowd and pro-parliamentary forces succeeded in driving out the remaining police and taking control of the building. Ostankino was several miles across Moscow, and the pro-parliamentary demonstrators set out for their next goal, led by General Makashov. Khasbulatov also addressed the crowd, declaring, "I call on our valiant soldiers to bring troops and tanks here in order to take the Kremlin by storm, where the usurper is holding power, former president Yeltsin, the criminal."[24]

Rutskoi, Khasbulatov, and their supporters claimed that the failure of the police to stop the crowd en route to the White House on 3 October was a planned provocation by the authorities. The purpose of this alleged provocation was to make it possible for Yeltsin to suppress the opposition with force and strengthen his dictatorship. There is much that remains murky about the violence in Moscow on 3-4 October. Both sides claim to have given orders not to open fire first and stated that they have video footage proving that the other side started the shooting. These arguments apply, in particular, to the storming of the mayor's office and Ostankino on 3 October, but also to the storming of the White House on 4 October. Journalists and other eyewitnesses provide contradictory testimony on all of these episodes. What remains undisputed is that the two leaders of the opposition, Rutskoi and Khasbulatov, called on their supporters to storm key government buildings, and that Rutskoi's "deputy minister of defense," Makashov, played a key role in the attack on both the mayor's office and Ostankino. Yeltsin's alleged conspiracy would not have worked if Rutskoi, Khasbulatov, and Makashov had not taken these actions.

The Yeltsin conspiracy theory also looks ridiculous in light of the army's stance during the affair. Yeltsin could not have known in advance what position the army would take if violence erupted and thereby would have been running a huge and unnecessary risk by escalating the conflict. Finally, some of the arguments made by Rutskoi and his supporters are so patently absurd as to completely undermine their credibility. Rutskoi, for example, argues that the United States government instructed Russian Premier Chernomyrdin on how to bring about the disintegration of Russia and "the method of carrying out a coup d'état." Ivanov is even more entertaining with his claims about the role of Mossad agents and Israeli special forces in carrying out Yeltsin's conspiracy.[25]

Even if the conspiracy theory propounded by Rutskoi and his supporters were true, the behavior of the army leadership still has to be explained in light of the information that was available at the time. The military high command believed that the MVD had been unable to control the situation in Moscow and that the White House had launched attacks on the mayor's office and Ostankino and called for a storming of the Kremlin. This was the situation they faced on the night of 3-4 October.

Yeltsin had been taking the day off at his dacha outside Moscow when the violence broke out in the city. He signed a decree introducing emergency rule in Moscow and returned to the Kremlin around six in the evening. The governments of Russia and Moscow, in conjunction with the ministers of internal affairs, security, and defense, were instructed to restore order in the city.

When the Ministry of Defense first introduced troops into Moscow is unclear. According to Grachev, orders went out to units around 5:00 p.m. and the first groups arrived at the General Staff, Ground Forces staff, and Airborne Troops staff around 9:00 p.m. The commander of the Taman Division, Major General V.G. Yevnevich, stated that he received an order from Grachev at 18:00 and arrived at the Ministry of Defense at 23:30. A high-ranking General Staff officer also maintained that a decision to bring in military units was made that afternoon. At this point no decision had been made about using the army. It makes sense that, given the outbreak of violence in the city, Grachev would bring in units to protect Ministry of Defense buildings. However, Yeltsin and his chief bodyguard Aleksandr Korzhakov claimed that they checked with the head of the Moscow traffic police after midnight to verify Grachev's statements that military units were in the city and were told that there were no military forces in Moscow and that they were all waiting at the edge of the city. Indeed, Grachev asserted that troops from the Kremlin regiment were initially sent to defend the Ministry of Defense building because Grachev had no troops of his own.[26]

The failure of the Russian Army to come out promptly and decisively to suppress the parliamentary forces apparently caused panic among members of the Yeltsin administration. An operational staff for putting down the uprising was created under the presidential administration headed by deputy defense minister

Kobets, with Yeltsin's adviser on military affairs, retired General Dmitrii Volko-gonov, as his deputy. Kobets allegedly called Yeltsin several times to argue that the White House be stormed during the night. Kobets' operational staff ultimately played no role in planning and carrying out the attack on the White House but it did organize the defense of other key objects in the city. Kobets' staff also sent emissaries to military units near Moscow. Several presidential representatives allegedly were turned away by the commanders. This is not surprising given that Grachev had sent out special instructions not to allow unauthorized personnel on bases.[27]

The first deputy prime minister, Yegor Gaidar, was alarmed by what he saw as "the foot-dragging and inactivity of the power structures." Gaidar appealed to Muscovites via radio and television to come to the support of President Yeltsin at the Moscow City Council building in the center of the city, a few blocks from the Kremlin. Thousands of Muscovites responded to his appeal. He also talked with Sergei Shoigu, the head of the State Committee on Emergency Situations, to find out what weapons were available to him in Moscow's civil defense system. Gaidar requested 1,000 automatic weapons with ammunition, which Shoigu apparently was willing to provide if necessary. Gaidar later claimed that if the MVD and the army had not been able to reassert control in Moscow that the city government would have been able to defeat the pro-parliamentary forces by distributing weapons to pro-Yeltsin volunteer militia (druzhinniki).[28]

Such extreme measures were not required. The MVD was able to defeat the efforts of Makashov and the pro-parliamentary forces to take control of the Ostankino television center at a cost of forty-six deaths. At that point Makashov returned with his forces to the White House although many of the demonstrators and onlookers had gone to Ostankino. Rutskoi and his allies then prepared for a government storming of their headquarters at the White House.[29]

Why did the army hesitate the night of 3-4 October? Both civilians and officers point to the military's belief that it should not be involved in domestic political disputes as the source of the armed forces' vacillation. Yeltsin wrote in his memoirs that they all (the government, the military, and society) "had become hostages of a pretty formula: the army is outside politics." Gaidar made the same point.

> In the course of recent years we repeated many times that the army is outside politics, that it should never be used to decide internal political aims. It had become in a certain sense an article of faith, convincingly confirmed in August 1991 and from that time acquiring a special durability. None of us had ever discussed the possibility of using the army in an internal political struggle.[30]

Members of the opposition also recognized that the army's institutional culture, which stressed the impermissibility of being involved in a domestic political struggle, was a barrier to military action. Khasbulatov noted that Grachev was hoping to the end that the army would not have to be used. The general mood in the armed forces the night of 3-4 October, writes Khasbulatov, was "do not get involved, avoid bloodshed."[31]

Officers pointed to the military's norms about internal politics as an explanation for their reluctance to get involved. General Volkogonov, who was communicating with officers in Moscow and around the country, noted, "until the last moment, literally until Monday night (4 October), this slogan was heard everywhere, that the army is outside politics." Deputy Minister of Defense Mironov observed that the slogan "the army is outside politics...undoubtedly, made a definite imprint both on societal perceptions and on the psychology of soldiers." Krasnaia zvezda ran a long piece responding to complaints in the liberal press that the army had been slow to act during the crisis. Vladimir Leonidov asserted that the maxim "the army is outside politics...is the law by which the armed forces live in all civilized states." Leonidov stated:

> "The army outside politics" is the formula which, if you like, has entered into the souls of the military, sincerely accepted by them. Taught by the bitter experience of August 1991, the military, frankly speaking, came to believe that never again do they need to send their tanks and BTRs [armored personnel carriers] along the streets of Moscow. And if a dramatic spiral of events leads to that, then an extremely responsible and detailed explanation is necessary.[32]

These behavioral maxims had acquired the force of law. General Leonid Ivashov noted that after Tbilisi, Vilnius, and the August 1991 coup "there were heard demands to call to account soldiers who carried out criminal orders. This norm was even written into the draft military regulations." Moreover, Ivashov observed, the Law on Defense permitted the use of the army inside the country only on the basis of a law or decree adopted by the Supreme Soviet. Segodnia's military correspondent, Pavel Felgengauer, noted that according to the Law on Defense the military leadership was not certain it had the legal right to attack the White House.[33]

The decisive moment that determined the conduct of the armed forces was the visit of President Yeltsin and Prime Minister Chernomyrdin to the Ministry of Defense at 2:00 a.m. on 4 October.[34] At this meeting Grachev and the Ministry of Defense leadership agreed to use the Russian army to storm the White House.[35]

Yeltsin and Chernomyrdin were received in awkward silence by Russia's top generals. The officers had no concrete proposals on the operation until a member of Yeltsin's own Presidential Security Service was introduced by Korzhakov. This officer suggested a plan for storming the White House. Chernomyrdin asked if there were any objections. Grachev turned to Yeltsin and asked, "Boris Nikolaevich, are you giving me sanction to use tanks in Moscow?" Chernomyrdin exploded at Grachev, asking why the president should have to decide exactly how Grachev would carry out the operation. Yeltsin promised to send Grachev a written order, and had one drawn up as soon as he returned to the Kremlin. The order was hand-delivered to Grachev shortly thereafter.[36]

The direct authorization of the commander-in-chief tipped the scales in favor of military involvement. Yeltsin had to issue a second decree on the state of emergency at 4:00 a.m. on 4 October. This decree underlined Yeltsin's responsibility for the decision and authorized the use of the Russian military in a domestic conflict. Retired Colonel Vladimir Lopatin stated, "Yeltsin took on himself the responsibility for going outside the law in the name of putting down mass disorder and securing the stability of the state."[37] When asked what it was that eventually moved the military leadership, General Volkogonov replied without hesitation, "the order of the Commander-in-Chief, which was given in the presence of the Prime Minister." Yeltsin later reflected, "I took the view that the defense minister should have acted himself, but he did not. That is why I had to give the order." Clearly, when push came to shove, the military leadership's unwillingness to be involved in a domestic political conflict was trumped by the need to carry out the orders of the legitimate head of state.[38]

This is not to say that the military leadership would have carried out any order of Yeltsin's. If it took one blunder of Rutskoi's, the appointment of Achalov, to drive the military into Yeltsin's arms, it was Rutskoi's catastrophic mistake of ordering the storming of Ostankino and the mayor's office that was decisive on 3-4 October. The Krasnaia zvezda commentator Leonidov argued, "[the] fact that we were already talking not about political competition, but the threat of bloody chaos, fearsome unlimited criminality, marauding, civil war in the country, in the end, was the single legal basis for the introduction of forces into Moscow." The last Soviet minister of defense, Marshal Yevgeny Shaposhnikov, drew a sharp distinction between events like Tbilisi, Vilnius, and the October 1993 episode. Shaposhnikov maintained that "the army was not sent against a peaceful demonstrating people, but against armed thugs. There is a big difference."[39]

Grachev delegated command of the White House operation to Deputy Minister of Defense Colonel General G.G. Kondratev. Units were brought in from the Taman and Kantemirov divisions, the 119th Airborne-parachute Regiment, the 27th Motorized Rifle Brigade, the Tula Airborne Division, and a company of separate Airborne Troops special forces (spetsnaz). Reportedly some officers from the Kantemirov division refused orders to participate. The operation began around 7:00 a.m. by which point there were very few people in front of the White House. Tank fire was used against the building and the fighting lasted until that afternoon when Rutskoi and Khasbulatov finally capitulated. MVD units and presidential security forces (Main Guard Directorate and Presidential Security Service) were also involved. A key role in the operation was played by members of the Union of Afghan Veterans who were substituted for conscripts in several units and rode in on the top of armored personnel carriers, cleared the barricades, and participated in the firing on the White House.[40]

Yeltsin had more trouble with his own Kremlin guard than he did with the armed forces. Two special anti-terrorist units, "Alpha" and "Vympel," which previously had been part of the secret police (KGB/Ministry of Security) and were now part of the Main Guard Directorate, resisted participating in the storming of the White House. At five a.m. on 4 October Yeltsin was asked to meet with about thirty officers from the group. Yeltsin addressed them directly: "Are you ready to carry out the order of the president?" None of the officers replied. Yeltsin tried again. "Then I will ask you in a different way—do you refuse to carry out the order of the president?" Again there was no response. Yeltsin stormed out, telling their commander that the order must be carried out. Eventually several volunteers from Alpha were persuaded to approach the White House for "reconnaissance." One of them was shot according to the opposition, by a government sniper, and only at that point did the entire unit agree to participate. Alpha and Vympel did not storm the White House but entered into negotiations with Rutskoi and Khasbulatov who agreed to capitulate. Alpha and Vympel did not fire a single shot.[41]

The operation to storm the White House was hindered by the presence of thousands of onlookers in the area. One brigade commander stopped the movement of his unit and said that they were leaving because the people had come to defend the White House and the army would not go fight Muscovites. Only when he found out that the crowd was by and large supportive of the army or neutral did he agree to continue. The military was upset with the militia for not keeping the area near the White House free of onlookers. Many of the 101 deaths and wounded were apparently those in the crowd who got too close to the events.[42]

Rutskoi continued to appeal for military support up to the moment when he surrendered. In one radio transmission, Rutskoi yelled, "I implore military comrades!.... Immediately to the aid of the Supreme Soviet building! Pilots, if you hear me! Bring out combat vehicles!" He was shown on CNN that afternoon cowering under a desk, yelling into a transmitter, "I appeal to military pilots, I implore you, I demand: send the planes into the air!" Khasbulatov stated that until the end Rutskoi and Achalov kept insisting that forces would come to rescue them. Makashov argued against surrendering even after Alpha and Vympel entered the building and agreed with Khasbulatov and Rutskoi on their surrender. In fact, hardly any military officers tried to bring units over to the White House on 4 October. A colonel and a naval captain-lieutenant tried to bring over small groups of soldiers numbering around 17-18 men but the group was intercepted en route. Another lieutenant colonel also tried to organize a group to defend the White House but received no support. There were also a handful of students from Moscow-area military academies who supported the White House on an individual basis. As one of Achalov's deputies put it, "in Moscow there was not one battalion that remained faithful to its oath [i.e., to 'President Rutskoi']." Rutskoi noted how he appealed to the army, the police, and the workers, but "no one came to our defense."[43]

On 5 October, the day after the storming, defense minister Grachev claimed that the armed forces had "rallied like never before, become more united and manageable." This statement was obvious hyperbole. It must be stressed that despite the fears of a split in the armed forces and some hesitation the night of 3-4 October, the army participated in blockading and storming the White House less than 24 hours after Yeltsin had declared a state of emergency in Moscow. This took place at a time when over 20,000 soldiers in the Moscow Military District were away from their units harvesting potatoes. The Russian Armed Forces successfully carried out one of its first domestic missions, one for which it was not designed, not prepared, and had no desire to carry out.[44]

AFTERMATH

In the aftermath of the October 1993 events many observers argued that since the military had saved Yeltsin's regime the Russian Armed Forces, according to this argument, would see a resurgence in their political influence, would receive fiscal and political concessions from the political leadership, and a policy of recreating the Russian empire would soon begin. Some commentators even argued that Russia had become "Latin Americanized," and that the military would play an important if not decisive role in deciding "who rules?" in Russia in the future. Even Vice Premier Sergei Shakrai stated in November 1993, "I am very afraid that Russia could slide into a military-police state."[45]

These fears proved to be misguided and reflected both a misunderstanding of the nature of the military's decision in October 1993 and the Russian Army's basic political outlook. The Russian Armed Forces had no desire to become involved in domestic politics and saw the October 1993 events not as a strategic opportunity but as a shameful day in the army's history, one which the officer corps would prefer to forget.[46]

The October 1993 events were far from the classic military coup that armies in some states use to advance their interests. Otto Latsis, political commentator for the newspaper Izvestiia, noted after the October events:

> The **use** of the army in internal conflicts is no gift, it signifies the failing of politics.... But this in principle shouldn't be confused with the **intervention** of the army in politics, that is an independent political decision of the military.... It would have been intervention if the army had **not** stormed in October 1993, having an order from the legal president and commander-in-chief.[47]

The fact that the military did not gain significant political leverage due to its performance in October 1993 is obvious from the continued sharp decline in its fortunes since 1993.[48] Even the adoption of a new military doctrine shortly after the October crisis was not the straightforward victory it seemed. The Russian Army was forced to accept a version of the doctrine that mandated an internal role for the army in the event of domestic political disturbances, a provision which the high command objected.[49]

For many officers the entire October 1993 episode was a black day for the Russian Army. This was true even for many liberal and moderate officers. Major General Aleksandr Tsalko, the head of the Presidential Commission for the Social Protection of Soldiers and their Families, who made his name as a pro-reform deputy in the Soviet parliament, was critical of the military's behavior in October 1993. Tsalko said that both the president and the army acted unlawfully and that the crisis should have been resolved with other methods. He declared, "one cannot do such things." Retired General V.V. Serebriannikov, although he worked for Khasbulatov, was seen as relatively liberal on civil-military relations issues and wrote several important pieces on the strengthening of civilian control. Serebriannikov argued that the Russian Army's storming of the White House was a violation of its oath to uphold the constitution, and that the military should have supported neither side. Serebriannikov maintained that "an army that only follows the order of its commander is a criminal army" adding that the military needs to be taught respect for the law and the constitution.[50]

More hard-line officers were critical of the military's behavior in October 1993. Colonel A.N. Ivanov (presumably a pseudonym) wrote an open letter to the newspaper Nezavisimaia gazeta denouncing the Yeltsin regime in the strongest terms. He called the shelling of the White House "monstrous" and asserted that the main feeling of the army toward the government was "hatred, all-consuming blunt hatred, hatred." Ivanov said he was "ashamed" for the army and embarrassed to wear his uniform in public.[51]

Other officers felt ashamed to wear their uniforms after 4 October. Most officers, according to several General Staff officials, opposed the storming of the White House and argued that the conflict should have been resolved peacefully. Of course, none of these officers were in the position of Grachev and the military leadership who received a direct order of the commander-in-chief. Nor were they in the position of those unit commanders who had to bring in their troops. Those who had to carry out such orders, such as General Yevnevich, the commander of the Taman Division, remarked later that it was "emotionally and morally difficult," but that "no one has the right to not carry out" an order of one's commander. Similarly, Krasnaia zvezda observed on the first anniversary of the October 1993 events, "the military, as befits it, carried out the order. The tragedy of the events many men in uniform felt more sharply and painfully than anyone else." The sense of shame felt by many officers was certainly genuine and alluded to even by those who supported Grachev's decision. Shaposhnikov stated, "It seems to me that a normal officer or soldier regrets that he was drawn into this conflict and now desires only one thing, that it not be repeated. This is a black mark on the White House, and a mark on all of us, on Russia."[52]

The October 1993 events in Moscow were indeed a black mark on Russia. The army's role, although arguably necessary after violence broke out in Moscow on 3 October, was a tragedy for the new Russian Army and its officer corps. In hindsight, October 1993 seems to fit into a more general picture of organizational decline, from Afghanistan to the failed August 1991 coup, the collapse of the Soviet Union, and the Chechen debacle.

1. On this point, see David Remnick, *Resurrection. The Struggle for a New Russia* (New York, 1997), 80-83.

2. The exact results of the April 1993 referendum were 58 percent support for Yeltsin, 53 percent for his policies, 67 percent for early parliamentary elections, and 49.5 percent for early presidential elections. These figures, and an overview of the political situation in 1992-1993, are in Remnick, *Resurrection*, 37-56.

3. A good short discussion of the internal contradictions in the constitution is Leonid Poliakov, "Otzovite svoe reshenie, poka ne pozdno...," *Nezavisimaia gazeta* (hereafter NG), 30 September 1993. For more background on these points, see Remnick, *Resurrection*, 47-53; Robert Sharlet, "Russian Constitutional Crisis. Law and Politics Under Yeltsin," *Post-Soviet Affairs*, Vol. 9, No. 4 (October-December 1993), 314-327; Archie Brown, "The October Crisis of 1993. Context and Implications," *Post-Soviet Affairs*, Vol. 9, No. 3 (July-September 1993), 183-190. A good collection of materials on the conflict between Yeltsin and Khasbulatov is M.K. Gorshkov, V.V. Zhuravlev, and L.N. Dobrokhotov, eds., *Eltsin-Khasbulatov. Edinstvo, kompromiss, borba* (Moskva, 1994).

4. In fact, the Russian Supreme Soviet did not have the constitutional authority to remove Yeltsin. This authority resided with the Congress of People's Deputies. For the text of Yeltsin's decree and the decisions of the Supreme Soviet and the Constitutional Court, see A.P. Surkov, ed., *Moskva. Osen-93. Khronika protivostoianiia* (Moskva, 1994), vii-xii, 7-17.

5. I know of no comprehensive, scholarly book on the October 1993 events. Two very different journalistic accounts are Remnick, *Resurrection*, 54-83; Jonathan Steele, *Eternal Russia.*

Yeltsin, Gorbachev, and the Mirage of Democracy (Cambridge, Mass., 1994), 371-387. Two thorough chronicles of the affair, with accompanying interviews and articles, are Surkov, ed., *Moskva. Osen-93*, and a special issue of the journal *Vek XX i Mir*, released under the title *93-Oktiabr, Moskva. Khronika tekushchikh sobytii,* 1993. The Surkov volume presents the view of the Yeltsin administration while the *Vek XX i Mir* compendium encompasses a range of views. The most important memoirs are Boris Yeltsin, *Zapiski prezidenta* (Moskva, 1994); R.I. Khasbulatov, *Velikaia rossiiskaia tragediia,* 2 vols. (Moskva, 1994); Aleksandr Rutskoi, *Krovavaia osen. Dnevnik sobytii 21 sentiabria – 4 oktiabria 1993 goda* (Moskva, 1995); Aleksandr Korzhakov, *Boris Eltsin. Ot rassveta do zakata* (Moskva, 1997); Egor Gaidar, *Dni porazhenii i pobed* (Moskva, 1997). Another publication of Rutskoi's on these events, the protocols of his examinations while in prison, is less useful. Aleksandr Rutskoi, *Lefortovskie protokoly* (Moskva, 1994). A similar account to Rutskoi's and Khasbulatov's, although even more hard-line, is Ivan Ivanov (pseudonym), *Anafema. Khronika gosudarstvennogo perevo-rota. Zapiski razvedchika* (Sankt-Peterburg, 1995). For other accounts in English of the military's role, see Brian D. Taylor, "Russian Civil-Military Relations After the October Uprising," *Survival*, Vol. 36, No. 1 (Spring, 1994), 3-29; James H. Brusstar and Ellen Jones, *The Russian Military's Role in Politics*, McNair Paper 34 (Washington, January 1995), 23-29; Robert V. Barylski, *The Soldier in Russian Politics* (New Brunswick, N.J., 1998), 245-269.

6. Yeltsin, *Zapiski prezidenta*, 349-352; Korzhakov, *Boris Eltsin*, 155-157; Viktor Baranets (former General Staff colonel), *Eltsin i ego generaly. Zapiski polkovnika genshtaba* (Moskva, 1997), 201-202.

7. Baranets, *Eltsin i ego generaly*, 201; Author's interview with Pavel Felgengauer, defense correspondent for the newspaper *Segodnia* and a "personal friend" of Kolesnikov, 7 July 1994.

8. The accounts of this Collegium meeting come mainly from the anti-Yeltsin opposition and were contradictory about when the meeting took place and when Kobets came to the White House to meet with the Supreme Soviet leadership. According to Khasbulatov and Voronin, Yeltsin called Grachev while the meeting was in progress. Voronin states that Kobets told them only what Grachev said, while Khasbulatov claims that the entire Collegium could hear the conversation, and gives a fantastic account of the dialogue between Grachev and Yeltsin, and between Grachev and the members of the Collegium. For the different versions, see Khasbulatov, *Velikaia rossiiskaia tragediia,* Vol. 1, 186-189; Iurii Voronin, *Svintsom po Rossii* (Moskva, 1995), 183-184; Ivanov, *Anafema*, 15; Ravil Zaripov, interview with General (retired) Vladislav Achalov, "Po tu storonu 'barrikadnoi,'" *Komsomolskaia prc ⁄ 'a* (hereafter KP), 7 October 1994. A contemporary press story that refers to this Collegium meeting is Unattributed, "Silovye vedomstva ne khoteli by vmeshivat'sia v konflikt," *Kommersant Daily* (hereafter KD), 23 September 1993.

9. Khasbulatov, *Velikaia rossiiskaia tragediia,* Volume I, 189-190; Voronin, *Svintsom po Rossii*, 187-188. Reports about Kolesnikov's visit to the White House also appeared in the press at the time. Veronika Kutsyllo, "V Rossii vvedeno prezidentskoe pravlenie," KD, 22 September 1993.

10. The Supreme Soviet decree appointing Achalov is in *Moskva. Osen-93*, 40. Achalov told me himself that he knew at the time it was a mistake, but that he felt obligated to accept because the Supreme Soviet had protected him from prosecution for his role in the August 1991 coup attempt by refusing to revoke his parliamentary immunity. Author's interview with Vladislav Achalov, 26 July 1994. Ivan Ivanov, a pseudonym for someone who worked directly for Achalov during the crisis, writes that Achalov told him during the crisis that it had been a mistake to appoint new power ministers (defense, security, and internal affairs) and that he had not been consulted in advance. Ivanov, *Anafema*, 40-41, 70. Achalov also told a reporter at the time that he could not "betray" his colleagues in the Supreme Soviet after their previous support for him. Stepan Kiselev et. al., "Moskva. Subbota, 2 Oktiabria. Khronika smutnogo vremeni (den pervyi)," *Moskovskie novosti* (hereafter MN), 10 October 1993. Pavel Felgengauer told me the appointment of Achalov was Rutskoi's crucial error that essentially "decided the issue"; author's interview with Felgengauer. See also Fred Hiatt, "The Army's Crucial Role," *Moscow Times*, 6 October 1993.

11. Pavel Felgengauer, "Rukovodsto armii sdelalo vybor. 'Prezident Yeltsin ne sovershil nichego antikonstitutsionnogo'," *Segodnia*, 23 September 1993; Petr Karapetian, "Tamantsev ispytyvaet poligon," *Krasnaia zvezda* (hereafter KZ), 24 September 1993.

12. Rutskoi, *Krovavaia osen*, 31-34, 184-186, 231, 232-233, 286-287, 302; Khasbulatov, *Velikaia rossiiskaia tragediia*, Volume I, 184-185, 194, 297. For more on Rutskoi's and the parliament's appeals to the armed forces, with examples, see *Moskva. Osen-93*, 58, 99, 101-102; *93-Oktiabr, Moskva*, 12, 50; *Listovki belogo doma. Moskovskie letuchie izdaniia 22 sentiabria – 4 oktiabria 1993* (Moskva, 1993), 14, 20.

13. Zhilin's data are in Alexander Zhilin, "Who is to Blame," *Moscow Guardian*, 15 October 1993. The other data are from Iu.I Deriugin, I.V. Obraztsov, and V.V. Serebriannikov, *Problemy sotsiologii armii* (Moskva, 1994), 82, 122.

14. For Rutskoi's admission that they had no support, and that their claims were disinformation, see Rutskoi, *Krovavaia osen*, 156-157, 218, 514-517; Aleksandr Gamov, interview with Major General Aleksandr Rutskoi, "Nadeius, chto na etot raz moi parashiut raskroetsia," KP, 20 May 1994. For the varying estimates reported here, see Dmitrii Kholodov, "Oktiabr tsveta khaki," *Moskovskii komsomolets* (hereafter MK), 8 October 1993; Aleksandr Pelts, "Armiia byla vynuzhdena deistvovat reshitelno," KZ, 8 October 1993; Deriugin, Obraztsov, and Serebriannikov, *Problemy sotsiologii armii*, 82; Kiselev et al., *Moskva. Subbota, 2 Oktiabria*; Nikolai Burbyga, "Tragediia u shtaba OVS SNG. Novye podrobnosti," *Izvestiia*, 29 September 1993; Aleksandr Gorbunov and Andrei Kolesnikov, "Iz 'belogo doma'—chernym khodom," MN, 31 October 1993.

15. Rutskoi, *Krovavaia osen*, 211, 232-233, 381; Kiselev et al., *Moskva. Subbota, 2 Oktiabria*; Voronin, *Svintsom po Rossii*, 190; Yeltsin, *Zapiski prezidenta*, 373; Igor Cherniak, "Ministr Grachev utverzhdaet," KP, 8 October 1993; Ivanov, *Anafema*, 72-73. Baranets states that Gromov and Kolesnikov supported army neutrality in the conflict. Baranets, *Eltsin i ego generaly*, 325-326, 352.

16. Ivanov, *Anafema*, 40-41; Khasbulatov, *Velikaia rossiiskaia tragediia*, Vol. 1, 297; Rutskoi, *Krovavaia osen*, 157, 331-332.2

17. On the attack on CIS headquarters and Makashov's visit to the State Committee on Emergency Situations, see Pavel Felgengauer, "V gorod vvedeny dopolnitelnye sily," *Segodnia*, 25 September 1993; Vladimir Zainetdinov, Igor Cherniak and Olga Saprykina, "V vooruzhennoi predvybornoi skhvatke navsegda poteriany dva golosa—Very Malyshevoi i Valeriia Sviridenko," KP, 25 September 1993; Burbyga, "Tragediia u shtaba OVS SNG"; *Moskva. Osen-93*, 100, 102-104, 109-110; *93-Oktiabr, Moskva*, 48, 54, 70-72. For Rutskoi's and Ivanov's versions, see Rutskoi, *Krovavaia osen*, 91-101, 173; Ivanov, *Anafema*, 58-61. For Terekhov's admission of his role, besides the quotes in Rutskoi, see Aleksandr Shadrin, "Ya ne ponimaiu...," *Argumenty i fakty*, No. 40, October 1994. Khasbulatov's version is in Khasbulatov, *Velikaia rossiiskaia tragediia*, Vol. 1, 233-235. Federov's statement is based on author's interview with Andrei Federov, December 1997.

18. On Yeltsin's statements, see Boris Yeltsin, "Obrashchenie Prezidenta Rossiiskoi Federatsii—Glavnokomanduiushchego Vooruzhennymi Silami Rossii," KZ, 24 September 1993; *93-Oktiabr, Moskva*, 100. For Grachev's statements and actions, see "Parlament kliunul na prezidentskuiu blesnu," MN, 17 October 1993; "'Vertushki' Minoborony uzhe vkliucheny. Khorosho by sdelat eto i u nas v redaktsii...." KP, 6 October 1993; Felgengauer, "Rukovodsto armii sdelalo vybor"; Felgengauer, "V gorod vvedeny dopolnitelnye sily"; Vladimir Mariukha, "General armii Pavel Grachev. U armii zadacha odna—zashchita otechestva," KZ, 23 September 1993; Zainetdinov, Cherniak and Saprykina, "V vooruzhennoi predvybornoi skhvatke..."; *93-Oktiabr, Moskva*, 5, 14, 16, 50.

19. The polling data for September 1993 is in *93-Oktiabr, Moskva*, 129.

20. Khasbulatov, *Velikaia rossiiskaia tragediia*, Vol. 1, 337; Voronin, *Svintsom po Rossii*, 190; Sergey Turchenko, "Chernaia pobeda. Ispoved ofitsera generalnogo shtaba," *Sovetskaia Rossiia*, 18 December 1993; Baranets, *Eltsin i ego generaly*, 189, 399; Deriugin, Obraztsov, and Serebriannikov, *Problemy sotsiologii armii*, 82; Unattributed, "Silovye vedomstva ne khoteli...."

21. For details on these internal uses of the military from the late Soviet period, see Brian D. Taylor, "The Soviet Military and the Disintegration of the USSR" in Mark Kramer, ed., *The Collapse of the Soviet Union* (Boulder, Colo., 1999).

22. Aleksandr Golts, "Armiia ostaetsia garantom grazhdanskogo mira. Mozhet byt, edinstvenno nadezhnym," KZ, 2 October 1993.

23. On the October 2 and 3 demonstrations, see *93-Oktiabr, Moskva,* 211-212, 224-225; *Moskva. Osen-93,* 302-305, 359-363, 424-430; Vadim Belykh, "Moskva, 3 Oktiabria. Krovavoe voskresene," *Izvestiia,* 5 October 1993; Kolya Kachurin, "Ministry Admits Troops Were Poorly Prepared," *Moscow Times,* 5 October 1993. See also the chronicles in Vladimir Larin, ed., *Vse o chernom oktiabre* (Moskva, October 1993); MN, 10 October 1993; *Kuranty,* 5 October 1993. Ivanov estimated the crowd to be one-third to half a million. See Ivanov, *Anafema,* 208.

24. *Moskva. Osen-93,* 365; Khasbulatov, *Velikaia rossiiskaia tragediia,* Vol. 2, 112. Yeltsin claimed that all the events of October 3 were a planned uprising by the pro-parliament forces, but there is little evidence for this view. For Yeltsin's claim, see *Moskva. Osen-93,* 526-529.

25. The literature on the details of the fighting of 3-4 October that bears on the conspiracy question is enormous. I cite only a few major sources here. For the pro-Yeltsin treatment, see *Moskva. Osen-93.* For the version of the pro-parliament forces, see Khasbulatov, *Velikaia rossiiskaia tragediia;* Rutskoi, *Krovavaia osen;* Ivanov, *Anafema.* The specific points from Rutskoi and Ivanov are Rutskoi, *Krovavaia osen,* 449; Ivanov, *Anafema,* 46-50, 398. The conspiracy theory has been endorsed by one Western journalist; see Steele, *Eternal Russia,* 371-387. For the conventional (pro-Yeltsin) account, see Remnick, *Resurrection,* 54-83. For a short piece that does an effective job of ridiculing this conspiracy theory, see Maksim Sokolov, "Novopravozashchitniki i starochekisty," *Segodnia,* 6 November 1993.

26. For Grachev's account, see Kholodov, "Oktiabr tsveta khaki"; Pelts, "Armiia byla vynuzhdena deistvovat reshitelno." Yevnevich's testimony is in *Moskva. Osen-93,* 595. The anonymous General Staff officer's version is Turchenko, "Chernaia pobeda." For Yeltsin's and Korzhakov's accounts, see Yeltsin, *Zapiski prezidenta,* 382; Korzhakov, *Boris Eltsin,* 163-168. See also Baranets, *Eltsin i ego generaly,* 26-27, 352; Nikolai Burbyga, "Belyi dom ia videl skvoz pritsel," *Izvestiia,* 6 October 1993; Pavel Felgengauer, "Army's Role. Less Than Certain," *Moscow Times,* 12 October 1993; Zhilin, "Who is to Blame"; *93-Oktiabr, Moskva,* 229; *Moskva. Osen-93,* 435, 451.

27. For reports on alarm in the Yeltsin administration about the army's stance, and the role of Kobets and the operational staff that he headed, see author's interview with Colonel A.A. Volkov, assistant to Dmitrii Volkogonov, 20 July 1994; Turchenko, "Chernaia pobeda"; Baranets, *Eltsin i ego generaly,* 26, 202; Stepan Kiselev et. al., "Moskva. Voskresene, 4 Oktiabria. Khronika smutnogo vremeni (den tretii)," MN, 10 October 1993; Unattributed, "Tragicheskie sobytiia v Moskve. Srazhenie za Belyi dom," KZ, 5 October 1993; Igor Cherniak, "Gde byla armiia? Vyiasniaia, za kogo narod," KP, 5 October 1993; Dmitry Kholodov, "Rokovoi urozhai," MK, 6 October 1993; Mikhail Sokolov, "Dazhe ministr pod podozreniem," KP, 7 October 1993; Dmitry Volkogonov and Yevgeny Kiselev "Itogi," NTV, 17 October 1993; Dmitry Volkogonov, "U posledney cherty," in *Moskva. Osen-93,* 605-607.

28. For Gaidar's account, see Gaidar, *Dni porazhenii i pobed,* 284-294; Egor Gaidar, "Krasnaia osen 93-go," *Izvestiia,* 28-29 September 1994; Egor Gaidar, interviewed by Mikhail Gurevich, "'Eta noch' pokazala, kto chego stoit," MK, 4 October 1994; Irina Savvateeva, "Egor Gaidar. Vse eto moglo by stat' temoi dlia obsuzhdeniia v kontslagere," KP, 9 October 1993; Elena Tregobova, "Egor Gaidar. Silovye struktury veli sebia neadekvatno," *Segodnia,* 9 October 1993; Nadezhda Zheleznova, interview with Egor Gaidar, "Ostanovit' grazhdanskuiu voinu" in *Moskva. Osen-93,* 565-567.

29. The total of forty-six deaths at Ostankino is the official figure. For the government version of events at Ostankino, see *Moskva. Osen-93,* 381-415, 530-531, 582-590. For the opposition's version, see Rutskoi, *Krovavaia osen,* 406-431; Ivanov, *Anafema,* 234-305, 467-468. See also Thomas de Waal, "Elite Unit Key to TV Victory," *Moscow Times,* 7 October 1993; Igor Andreev, "Oborona teletsentra. Vzgliad iznutri," *Izvestiia,* 12 October 1993; Vladimir Novikov, "Vystrel iz granatometa reshil vse," MK, 3 October 1995.

30. Yeltsin, *Zapiski prezidenta,* 384; Gaidar, "Krasnaia osen 93-go"; Gaidar, *Dni porazhenii i pobed,* 286. See also Aleksei Arbatov, "Fashizm ne proshel, no demokratiia poterpela porazhenie," NG, 22 October 1993.

31. Khasbulatov, *Velikaia rossiiskaia tragediia*, Vol. 1, 341, 344.
32. Volkogonov and Kiselev, "Itogi"; Col. Gen. V.I. Mironov (deputy Minister of Defense), interviewed by Aleksei Surkov, "Raskol armii ne grozil" in *Moskva. Osen-93*, 591; Vladimir Leonidov, "Okazyvaetsia, Rossiiu spasla Akhedzhakova!" KZ, 7 October 1993.
33. Lt. Gen. Leonid Ivashov, interviewed by Igor Cherniak, "Kogda nad 'Belym domom' rasseialsia dym," KP, 20 October 1993; Felgengauer, "Army's Role. Less Than Certain."
34. Some sources claim that on the evening of 3 October there had been a meeting of the top military leadership (the Military Collegium). According to an anonymous General Staff officer, at this meeting "the military leadership did not want to drag the army into the conflict...no concrete operational decisions were taken." However, a highly placed Russian government official told the author that no meeting took place the evening of the third because Grachev was "too nervous." Author's interview (off the record comment). The General Staff officer is cited in Turchenko, "Chernaia pobeda." Pavel Felgengauer also reported that the Collegium met the evening of the third. Pavel Felgengauer, "Armiia vse-taki sdelala svoe delo," *Segodnia*, 5 October 1993; Pavel Felgengauer, "Po otsenkam spetsialistov, voiska deistvovali bezukoriznenno," *Segodnia*, 7 October 1993.
35. There are several different accounts of the decisive meeting at the Ministry of Defense. Sources disagree about both the time of the meeting and the participants. According to Yeltsin, he and Chernomyrdin met with the Military Collegium. According to Chief of Staff Kolesnikov, the meeting was a Security Council meeting with the following individuals present: Yeltsin, Chernomyrdin, Grachev, Kolesnikov, Yerin, Security Minister Nikolai Golushko, head of the Foreign Intelligence Service Yevgeny Primakov, and the chairman of the Security Council, Oleg Lobov. According to Ivanov, the following individuals were present: Yeltsin, Chernomyrdin, Grachev, Yerin, head of the Presidential Administration Sergei Filatov, Moscow mayor Yury Luzhkov, and Moscow militia head Vladimir Pankratov. Later, according to Ivanov, other military officers joined them. Baranets also describes the meeting as a Collegium meeting, and notes that Deputy Minister of Defense Gromov refused to attend. For these accounts, see Yeltsin, *Zapiski prezidenta*, 384-386; Pavel Felgengauer, interview with Col. Gen. Mikhail Kolesnikov, chief of the General Staff, "Mikhail Kolesnikov. Realnoe sokrashchenie armii operezhaet zaplanirovannoe," *Segodnia*, 29 December 1993; Ivanov, *Anafema*, 317-323; Baranets, *Eltsin i ego generaly*, 26, 202-203, 326. Other sources on this meeting are Korzhakov, *Boris Eltsin*, 168-170; Turchenko, "Chernaia pobeda"; Burbyga, "Belyi dom ia videl...."
36. Yeltsin, *Zapiski prezidenta*, 385-386; Baranets, *Eltsin i ego generaly*, 202-203; Korzhakov, *Boris Eltsin*, 168-170. According to Korzhakov, Grachev stated he refused to participate without a written order. The officer from Korzhakov's staff who came up with the plan was Naval Captain First Rank G.I. Zakharov. For his account, see *Moskva. Osen-93*, 601-605.
37. Vladimir Lopatin, "O roli sily v ispolnenii zakona," NG, 19 October 1993. For Yeltsin's decree on the morning of 4 October, see Boris Yeltsin, "Sem blizhaishikh dnei," NG, 5 October 1993. According to Baranets, Yeltsin's written order to Grachev was cleverly crafted in a way to allow the Russian president to deny responsibility for the use of tanks if necessary. Baranets, *Eltsin i ego generaly*, 203-204.
38. As Igor Cherniak, the defense correspondent for Komsomolskaia pravda remarked, it was "rather strange" for the commander-in-chief to complain that Grachev had not acted without orders. See Volkogonov and Kiselev, "Itogi"; Unattributed (AFP-Reuters), "President Criticizes Grachev on TV," *Moscow Times*, 13 November 1993; Igor Cherniak, "Konei i generalov na pereprave ne meniaiut," KP, 25 November 1993.
39. Leonidov, "Okazyvaetsia, Rossiiu spasla Akhedzhakova!"; Yevgeny Shaposhnikov, interviewed by Elena Dikun, "The Army in the City—The Final Argument of the President," *Obschchaia gazeta*, 15-21 October 1993, translated in Joint Publications Research Service, *Central Eurasia Military Affairs*, JPRS-UMA, No. 93-045, 22 December 1993, 1-2. This view also was endorsed by Major General (retired) Vladimir Slipchenko, the former head of scientific research at the General Staff Academy, and Colonel Sergei Yushenkov, who was head of the Duma Defense Committee from 1993 until 1995. Author's interviews, 1994.

40. On the units involved, see Pelts, "Armiia byla vynuzhdena..."; Kholodov, "Oktiabr tsveta khaki"; Zhilin, "Who is to Blame"; Colonel General G.G. Kondratev (deputy Minister of Defense), interviewed by Aleksei Surkov, "Armiia ostalas predannoi svoemu narodu, svoe-mu verkhovnomu glavnokomanduiushchemu!" in *Moskva. Osen-93*, 598. The rumor about officers from the Kantemirov Division refusing to participate is in Turchenko, "Chernia pobe-da." On the role of Afghan veterans, see Nikolai Burbyga, "V armii predatelei shchitaiut na edinitsy," *Izvestiia*, 7 October 1993; Elena Korotkova, "Afghantsy otpushcheniia," MK, 3 October 1995; Interview with General Evnevich (commander of Taman Division), "Pust sudiat politikov," MK, 3 October 1996; Major General V.G. Evnevich, interviewed by Alek-sei Surkov, "Nerzberikha nenuzhnoi voiny," in *Moskva. Osen-93*, 596.

41. Yeltsin, *Zapiski prezidenta*, 11-13; Korzhakov, *Boris Eltsin*, 171-176, 193-196; Aleksandr Gorbunov and Andrei Kolesnikov, "Shturm 'belogo doma'. 'Alfa' ne khotela krovi," MN, 7 November 1993; Leonid Nikitinskii, "Katia i 'Alfa,'" *Izvestiia*, 19 October 1993. For the opposition account of Alpha and Vympel's behavior, see Rutskoi, *Krovavaia osen*, 462-464, 505-509; Khasbulatov, *Velikaia rossiiskaia tragediia*, Volume I, 397-399, 401-403; Ivanov, *Anafema*, 383-407.

42. Burbyga, "Belyi dom ia videl..."; *Moskva. Osen-93*, 452-455, 532-534; Cherniak, "Ministr Grachev utverzhdaet."

43. For Rutskoi's radio appeals, see *Moskva. Osen-93*, 461; "Posledniaia komanda Aleksandra Rutskogo," KP, 6 October 1993; Remnick, *Restoration*, 78. Khasbulatov's recollections are in Khasbulatov, *Velikaia rossiiskaia tragediia*, Vol. I, 389, 398. On the officers that tried to support the White House, see Burbyga, "V armii predatelei shchitaiut na edinitsy"; Pelts, "Armiia byla vynuzhdena..."; Vasilii Starikov, "Starshii leitenant Ostapenko zastrelilsia tak. Zazhal avtomat mezhdu nog i vystrelil sebe v rot," *Novaia ezhednevnaia gazeta*, 24 March 1994; Ivanov, *Anafema*, 416. For Rutskoi's and Ivanov's statements on the absence of mili-tary support, see Rutskoi, *Krovavaia osen*, 500; Ivanov, *Anafema*, 416.

44. Grachev's quote is in Igor Cherniak, "Vliianie krupnogo kalibra," KP, 7 October 1993. On the influence of the autumn harvest on the military in October 1993, see Felgengauer, "Po otsenkam spetsialistov..."; Kholodov, "Rokovoi urozhai"; Yeltsin, *Zapiski prezidenta*, 385; Korzhakov, *Boris Eltsin*, 156, 169.

45. Sergei Chugaev, interview with Sergei Shakrai (vice premier), "Sergei Shakrai. Dlia menia glavnye tsennosti—semia, sobstvennost, gosudarstvo," *Izvestiia*, 17 November 1993. For these predictions of greater military influence see, for example: Stephen Foye, "Updating Russian Civil-Military Relations," RFE/RL Research Report, Vol. 2, No. 46 (19 November 1993), 44-50; Adi Ignatious and Claudia Rosett, "Russian Army's Assault on Parliament Forces Holdouts to Yield to Yeltsin," *Wall Street Journal Europe*, 5 October 1993; William Odom, "Yeltsin's Faustian Bargain," *Moscow Times*, 27 October 1993; Aleksandr Kuz-mishchev, "Import politicheskoi kultury. Rossiia skvoz latinoamerikanskuiu prizmu," NG, 3 November 1993; Andranik Migranian, "Avtoritarnyi rezhim v Rossii," NG, 4 November 1993.

46. This issue is dealt with extensively in Taylor, "Russian Civil-Military Relations After the October Uprising."

47. Otto Latsis, "U drakona ne odna golova. O prirode zagovora, terzaiushchego Rossiiu," *Iz-vestiia*, 13 October 1993. Emphasis in original.

48. For general overviews of the many problems facing the Russian Army, see Anatol Lieven, "Russia's Military Nadir. The Meaning of the Chechen Debacle," *The National Interest*, No. 44 (Summer, 1996), 24-33; US Department of State, *Annual Report on Military Expenditures, 1998*, submitted to Congress on February 19, 1999; Sergei Rogov, *Military Reform and the Defense Budget of the Russian Federation* (Alexandria, Va., August 1997); *Voennaia reforma v Rossiiskoi Federatsii. Tezisy Soveta po vneshnei i oboronnoi politike* (Moskva, 1997); Alexei G. Arbatov, "Military Reform in Russia. Dilemmas, Obstacles, and Prospects," *International Security*, Vol. 22, No. 4 (Spring, 1998), 83-134; Stephen M. Meyer, "The Devolution of Rus-sian Military Power," *Current History*, Vol. 94, No. 594 (October 1995), 322-328; Benjamin

S. Lambeth, "Russia's Wounded Military," *Foreign Affairs*, Vol. 74, No. 2 (March/April 1995), 86-98; Dale R. Herspring, "The Russian Military. Three Years On," *Communist and Post-Communist Studies*, Vol. 28, No. 2 (June 1995), 163-182.

49. Baranets, *Eltsin i ego generaly*, 204; Ilia Bulavinov, "Proekt voennoi doktriny ne udovletvoril Kreml," KD, 19 October 1993; Igor Cherniak, "Tak chto zh, na zimnie kvartiry?" KP, 2 November 1993; "Segodnia," NTV, 3 November 1993. For the text of the fundamental postulates of the military doctrine, see "Osnovnie polozheniia voennoi doktriny Rossiiskoi Federatsii," KZ, 19 November 1993.

50. Author's interview with Maj. Gen. Aleksandr Tsalko, 28 July 1994; Author's interview with Lt. Gen. (retired) V.V. Serebriannikov, 6 July 1994. Tsalko stressed that his views were his "personal opinion." For more on Serebriannikov's views, see Deriugin, Obraztsov, and Serebriannikov, *Problemy sotsiologii armii*, 55-130.

51. Col. A.N. Ivanov, "K neschastiu, ostalas sovest (letter)," NG, 2 November 1993. For a reply to Ivanov from a junior officer, see Jr. Lt. V.D. Tarasov, "Gde priatalas sovest?" NG, 16 November 1993.

52. Turchenko, "Chernaia pobeda"; Baranets, *Eltsin i ego generaly*, 206, 399; Interview with Evnevich, "Pust sudiat politikov"; Vladimir Gavrilenko, "Nasha pamiat i bol. Chto donosit do nas veter iz proshlogodnego oktiabria," KZ, 4 October 1994; Shaposhnikov, "The Army in the City...."

FSU NUCLEAR WEAPONS AND THE WEAPONS INDUSTRY NEAR COLLAPSE

David Beachley

INTRODUCTION

After the collapse of the Soviet Union unprecedented opportunities arose for the dramatic yet regulated reduction of the world's two largest nuclear arsenals. The end of the Cold War and the ideological struggle between East and West reduced the requirement for such huge inventories. But nearly two years later the early optimism of arms control enthusiasts on both sides was muted, and in some cases had become pessimistic as the sobering realities of the realpolitik of the post-Cold War era set in.

Arms control assumed that each country would maintain centralized control and sustain a viable nuclear industrial infrastructure to implement reductions. What happened in the former Soviet Union (FSU) in the first two years shook this assumption and put into question the ability of arms control treaties. Questions regarding the deteriorating status of the nuclear weapons industry, the falling physical and technical security of weapons, roadblocks to ratification of arms control treaties and the possible dissolution of the FSU arsenal for the first time in the nuclear age, have greater impact on global security than the strategic and operational use of nuclear weapons.

Responsible Russian authorities recognize that the probability of a nuclear accident has significantly increased while the potential for any premeditated massive nuclear strike against Russia or other members of the FSU has been equally reduced. There are greater chances for the decentralization of the FSU nuclear arsenal than ever before due to claims by competing parties and the threat of slow economic and political disintegration of the Russian Federation itself.

Although the Russian leadership recognizes that nuclear weapons are the foundation of Russian defense in the near-term, the Strategic Rocket Forces has become the one branch of the armed forces which has suffered most since the fall of the Soviet Union. Compounding the problem, nuclear industry workers and the nuclear industrial base have become increasingly unstable and are approaching collapse.

To understand the current status of FSU nuclear security, the subject will be addressed on several levels. These include the enhanced value of nuclear weapons in FSU/Russian national security, the debate over the stewardship/control over nuclear weapons and the role of arms control (i.e., START-2), the status of nuclear weapons R&D, production and testing complex, the status of the physical and technical security of weapons systems, and the impact of the political and economic disintegration of Russia on the Russian nuclear arsenal.

NUCLEAR WEAPONS' CONTINUED ROLE IN RUSSIAN NATIONAL SECURITY

Since the collapse of the Soviet Union and the rapid deterioration of conventional armed forces capability in the FSU, nuclear weapons played an even larger role in national security, acting as the only force offering a credible threat to large-scale aggression against Russia. As stated by General Makmut Gareev, a famous military theoretician of the late Soviet period, "nuclear weapons are the most reliable and cheapest means of deterring aggression."[1]

In April 1993 Minister of Atomic Energy Mikhailov stressed the continuing value of nuclear weapons for Russia's national security. According to Mikhailov, the world still has "many regions which are characterized by an unstable political situation, much extremism and aggressive moods, including those in direct proximity to our borders." He also observed that several "third countries" are developing nuclear weapons.

In short, Mikhailov argued, the continued viability of the Russian nuclear arsenal helps achieve three main Russian national security objectives: 1) deterrence of military adventurism against Russia by neighboring states; 2) deterrence of nascent Third World nuclear powers; and 3) insurance that Russia will be treated on an equal level with the US during arms control negotiations and negotiations to halt nuclear testing. Thus, "in this difficult time for our country, the development of the nuclear potential and its constant maintenance at a modern scientific-technical level is a guarantee of the stability of peace on our planet...."[2]

Russian military theoreticians recognize that the end of Soviet-American rivalry introduced a requirement to reassess the role of nuclear weapons in Russian military thought and to search for new paradigms. The concept of a potential enemy would be eliminated, thus further complicating planning and requiring a response to a larger number of contingencies.[3] Instead of missiles targeted mainly at the United States, the old ideological enemy and, in the USSR's worse-case planning, its most dangerous opponent, weapons would be to defend on "all azimuths," implying a requirement to parry or respond to nuclear strikes from any potential opponent, at any range and on any scale. One author said that Russia's strategic nuclear defense should be modeled on the French force under De Gaulle.[4]

As a result of the potential proliferation of nuclear weapons among a large number of nations, Russian military planners are preparing for a wide variety of contingencies including limited nuclear options. Gen. Sergiev, chief of the Strategic Rocket Forces, stated in the June issue of Voennaia mysl that by the year 2000 nearly twenty states would have the technical potential to possess nuclear weapons. Russia must be prepared to counter a nuclear attack under any "conditions of the situation." The April 1993 issue of Voennaia mysl argued that Russia should study options to counter such limited strikes with a comparable "limited, by scale, counter-force nuclear strike."[5]

Thus, it appears that Russia may be preparing new contingencies against China, as well as other contingencies to answer the new and evolving threat from the south (a thinly veiled reference to the threat from Islamic countries, i.e., Iran).[6]

Due to fiscal constraints, changing targeting priorities and reductions in force which require more flexible armed forces, Russia appears to have initiated a process of preparing for the most likely scenarios rather than for the worst case scenarios which so dominated nuclear planning in the Soviet period. Significantly Russia will continue to refine limited use options and study various scenarios which may require a nuclear response. The continued fall in conventional capabilities, indicated most recently by the dramatic manpower shortages in the spring call-ups, indicates that for the foreseeable future nuclear weapons, for better or worse, will continue to be the foundation of Russia's defensive power.[7]

Although declaratory statements concerning "all azimuth defense" are being made, nuclear use guidelines have not been laid down. According to Yevgeny Avrorin of Cheliabinsk-70, the role of nuclear weapons in Russia's future has not yet been defined. More specifically, a "concept for nuclear weapons needs to be worked out" which would be especially applicable if the country, like the United States, is to rely on a sea-based nuclear force.[8]

Even after nuclear use guidelines are defined, it seems that Russian nuclear planners, changing targeting priorities and the increasing requirements for limited nuclear options could not come at a worse time. Limits on nuclear testing suggest that Russia may be forced to use warheads with higher yields, dirtier payloads, and greater collateral damage effects than would be advantageous for a limited counter-force response. While pressure mounts for Russia to consider limited nuclear use in planning scenarios, the windows to enhance the surgical nature of these strikes have practically closed.

STEWARDSHIP/CONTROL OVER NUCLEAR WEAPONS AND THE IMPACT OF ARMS CONTROL

Russia's claim to the FSU nuclear arsenal was under continuous challenge by Ukraine in 1993. Evidence suggests that Ukraine, already a de facto nuclear power, may announce its intentions to retain the nuclear arsenal on its territory and not turn over its potent weapons to Russia.

Ukraine's interest in retaining its arsenal is generated by several factors. First, there is a growing paranoia regarding Russian intentions towards Ukraine and a belief that some powerful circles in Moscow do not accept Ukrainian independence. The Russian parliament's claim to the Crimean port of Sevastopol is only one indicator of this growing distrust. Second, Ukraine has come to realize that ownership of nuclear weapons equates to respect for Kiev in international affairs.[9] Third, it appears that Ukraine increasingly believes that it can not only retain the arsenal, at least the SS-24 solid-fuel portion, but also maintain these missiles at combat ready status and service them and their warheads with a nascent nuclear industrial infrastructure.

Regarding the latter point, many of the nuclear scientists and technicians at Arzamas-16 were Ukrainian nationals. One source indicated that Slavic nuclear scientists and technicians have begun to leave Kazakhstan and return to their homes in the European part of the FSU, further suggesting that Ukraine may be augmenting the sector of its scientific cadres needed to maintain the arsenal.[10] In addition, during the Soviet period, the land-based rockets of the Strategic Rocket Forces were designed and built in Ukraine. Yevgeny Avrorin, science chief of Cheliabinsk-70, remarked that Ukraine retains the best designers of land-based rocket systems, while Russia hosts the best sea-based missile designers.[11]

Evidence suggests that despite public denials Ukraine has been fervently working to circumvent the permissive action links of the nuclear weapons on its soil, currently controlled by Russia, and will soon achieve positive control over these systems. By early 1992, the first evidence surfaced that Ukraine was actively working to achieve positive control of the nuclear weapons located there and that it would be one or two years before they were able to achieve this goal. A recent Interfax report contends that Ukraine has been performing preparatory work to retarget the SS-19 inventory and that complete retargeting of the 172 missile complexes on Ukrainian soil might take no less than two years. Another source indicates US concern that Ukraine could gain control over missiles and warheads there in 12-18 months.[12]

Meanwhile, its seems that Kazakhstan has been watching Ukraine's actions with interest, indicating that the fate of the Kazakh nuclear arsenal may only be resolved when Ukraine makes a final decision regarding its own weapons. The desire to retain nuclear weapons may be more problematic for Kazakhstan since many of the skilled nuclear cadres are returning to the European part of the FSU and there is no inherent Kazakh nuclear industrial infrastructure there.[13]

As a result of the divisiveness of arsenal ownership the status of the signed but not ratified START-2 Treaty is in serious jeopardy. It seems that timelines will be pushed back and, most likely, parts if not all of the treaty may be renegotiated. For Ukraine and Kazakhstan, the fate of START-2 hangs on their decisions to retain part if not all of their current arsenals. For Russia, with the largest portion of the existing weapons stocks and its sense of responsibility for the nuclear security of at least most of the FSU, the question of START-2 implementation is much more problematic.

Opposition to START-2 ratification in Russia is surprisingly wide and is based on a number of considerations. Conservatives contend it is a sell-out to the US and they voice no confidence in mono-block mobile missiles to ride out a surprise strike. They contend that the US is forcing Russia to move its capability to sea where Russia is weak and the US is strong. As one source argues, by the year 2000, the deadline for treaty implementation, Russia's strategic forces will completely lose their deterrent potential.[14]

From the Russian view, the future nuclear threat includes many powers which are not subject to the strictures of START-2. This includes the growing Third World nuclear threat. In March 1992, Deputy Chairman of the Supreme Soviet, Nikolay Ryabov, argued that by the year 2000 there will probably be 500-600 warheads distributed among countries that did not sign the treaty.[15]

Centrist and liberal opposition cite both the severe economic impact and the serious ecological threat posed by a weapons dismantlement industry already overtaxed by existing demands. Deputy Yevgeny Kozhokin, signer of the "Democratic Russia" policy documents and currently chairman of the subcommittee on international security and intelligence, opposes the treaty on the grounds that workers in the military-industrial complex will loose their jobs. Ratification will be difficult, Kozhokin predicted in early January 1993, since START was signed without taking into consideration all the financial, economic, ecological and technical complications which could result from its implementation.[16] The financial and economic costs of the treaty have created significant repercussions across the political spectrum. In late January one author asked if Russia would be able to "withstand the disarmament race" since no figures had been submitted on its cost. He warned that this process would result in the mass migration of personnel and the destruction of the "infrastructure for strategic bases and military production."[17]

Captain 1st Rank Malyshev, writing in a "green" ecology newspaper, argues that implementation of START-2 would have a potentially disastrous environmental impact and present an enormous financial and materiel burden on the Russian economy in general and the disarmament and dismantlement infrastructure in particular. Malyshev's argument is a particularly devastating blow against START-2 since it attempts to enlist center and left blocs against the treaty using the warning of potential ecological disaster.

Malyshev suggests that Russian military security cannot be ensured under conditions of radical arms reductions, if all reductions are conducted simultaneously, as the treaty specifies. He asks readers to ponder the impact of START-2 implementation on the problem of financing disarmament, ensuring ecological security, and the social and economic security of service personnel and defense industry workers who find themselves prematurely unemployed. In a jab at promises of Western aid, Malyshev condemns the "hasty" decision-making in the disarmament process which was designed to attract foreign "investors." Such actions could increase the "monetary-financial slavery of our country," he contends. In conclusion, Malyshev argues that it is necessary "at this moment, to abstain from the ratification of the START-2 Treaty and to reexamine its positions...."[18]

As a result of the struggle over the FSU nuclear arsenal and the anticipated disastrous economic impact it seems likely that modifications to the START-2 Treaty will be sought. The complete scuttling of the treaty is an equally compelling scenario which may happen if Ukraine and possibly even Kazakhstan retain the nuclear forces on their territory. Such actions would, in effect, make the treaty null and void and set nuclear arms negotiations into a tailspin for years to come as new nuclear states assess the need and role of nuclear weapons in their national security strategy.

STATUS OF NUCLEAR WEAPONS PRODUCTION COMPLEX

At the very time when Russia and even Ukraine have become more dependent on nuclear weapons for national security, all evidence suggests that the infrastructure which develops, produces, tests and maintains the nuclear devices is nearing collapse. In recent months the situation has become more acute, although some evidence in early 1993 suggested that the nuclear weapons complex was returning to fiscal solvency and to some degree of normalcy.

In April 1993 a renewed optimism by some of those closest to the nuclear weapons industry seem to appear. Yevgeny Avrorin revealed that for the last two to three years Arzamas-16 and Cheliabinsk-70 had been threatened with closure. He noted that there was a realistic threat of their disappearance. Three factors were to blame for this situation: 1) insufficient financing; 2) uncertainty and malaise in nuclear policy; and 3) no directives or plans for future research and development, what Avrorin described as the "absence of future work."

Avrorin contends the situation has improved and there is no fear of lab closures. He suggests that President Yeltsin's visit to Arzamas-16 in early 1992 helped turn the situation around. As a result of the visit a "decision was taken" which confirmed that "Russia needed the nuclear centers of Arzamas-17 and Cheliabinsk-70." Yeltsin issued assurances on the importance of the federal nuclear centers and was willing to back these with financing and support. As explained by Avrorin, "it became clear" that "we were needed for the security of Russia."[19]

Also in April, Minister of Atomic Energy for the Russian Federation V. Mikhailov tried to put a positive spin on the funding reductions for the nuclear weapons centers, noting that recent changes towards "defensive sufficiency" had forced Russia's military-industrial potential to focus on "qualitative parameters regarding armament," a thinly veiled remark suggesting that the nuclear industry would be forced to maintain S&T levels with less. In a more direct comment Mikhailov reveals that for 1991 actual expenditures on scientific research and experimental design work at the Russian national laboratories fell 40 percent from 1990 levels due to reduced financing and rising costs. Mikhailov also discussed a twenty-year program to update the nuclear weapons industry, pointing out areas targeted for financing and improvements.[20]

Woven throughout the writings of both Avrorin and Mikhailov are less optimistic snapshots of an industry in the throes of profound and fundamental change. Both Avrorin and Mikhailov admit that a significant number of scientists and personnel have left the industry for more lucrative work in the private sector. "Unfortunately," Avrorin reveals, "among those numbers were very active cadres," most of whom were looking for "new paths in life," suggesting the disinterest that has similarly overcome many "cold warriors" in the United States after the fall of the Soviet Union. Mikhailov also admitted that a serious hemorrhage of personnel had occurred. The "most qualified and active scientific personnel, designers and workers have been forced to stop weapons work and go to cooperatives or into small enterprises."[21]

By mid-June any optimism regarding the situation in the nuclear weapons industry had gradually withered away. On 11 June scientists at Arzamas-16 told leaders in an open letter that "nuclear incidents with consequences comparable to Chernobyl cannot be ruled out" if the country's scientific potential, and particularly its nuclear industrial potential, is destabilized. Low wages and poor working and living conditions were destroying morale and putting scientists in a degrading position, the letter said. A month later, on 13 July, the directors of Arzamas-16 warned of unpredictable consequences if the government failed to pay workers and provide financial support to the lab. Workers were on the verge of a general strike, the directors warned. Director Vladimir Belugin revealed that at least 700 personnel, mostly young people, recently quit their positions for more lucrative commercial positions. Despite these pleas, a parliamentary leader, Alvin Yeremin, lamented that the "treasury is empty and we are in debt up to our ears."[22]

Even allowing for overzealousness by the nuclear weapons industry, it seems clear that the situation is bad and rapidly getting worse. Yeltsin's well-meaning but now hollow promises to the industry during his visit to Arzamas-16 in early 1992 seem to have only heightened the industry's sense of betrayal. The hemorrhage of skilled personnel into the private sector, and possibly out of the country, is continuing in increasing numbers with no end in sight for the salvation of the real nerve center of the nuclear weapons industry.

TECHNICAL AND PHYSICAL SECURITY OF WEAPONS SYSTEMS

As a result of the slow collapse of the nuclear weapons industry, increasing alarm has been voiced over the physical and especially the technical security of warheads within the FSU inventory. As early as August 1992 there were warnings that falling security standards and the growing shortage of qualified personnel would gradually place the inventory at risk. Academician Petr Korotkevich explained that "we are witnessing the collapse of the administrative and production structures of the [controlling apparatus] that arranged for manufacturer's [oversight of the operation of strategic nuclear arms] in the past and which should continue to do [so] in the future.... Over decades in the USSR, a normative and technical base was established and perfected, the appropriate documentation was prepared, teams of experts were formed to take charge of these tasks, and practical experience was accumulated.... Today, however, we have to admit that we are rapidly losing our experts and that work regulations are being violated. If this process is not stopped as soon as possible, by tomorrow we may not have anyone to guarantee the proper oversight."[23]

Korotkevich's warnings were published in mid-1992, nearly nine months before those of Avrorin and Mikhailov. Evidence suggests that the situation is approaching a breaking point and may soon destabilize not only the industry but the safety of the warheads themselves. In early April Izvestiia reported increasingly dangerous conditions at nuclear warhead storage sites in Ukraine. Accidental explosions and/or radiation leaks are risked by poor maintenance regimes and improper storage techniques, the story relayed.[24] To date, there is little published evidence to suggest that the physical security of nuclear weapons in the FSU has improved.

Combined with falling technical security is fear of the decreasing physical security of the weapons systems, especially for mobile systems, the ground-based backbone of the Strategic Rocket Forces. P. Belov, formerly an ABM designer, warned that mobile missiles are "more dangerous to us than to the enemy since they are more susceptible to accidents and sabotage with disastrous consequences." Academician Yury Trutnev relayed that the missiles should be "more secure, especially in our country, and new and more reliable and secure types" should be developed. In late 1992 Deputy Minister of Defense Andrei Kokoshin acknowledged concern about terrorist attack against nuclear weapons or with the objective of seizing them. He claimed that one of the objectives in future missile design would be to enhance the defense of launchers against such terrorist attacks.[25]

To enhance the deteriorating physical security of the warhead inventory the Russian nuclear weapons industry has been pressing for a resumption of testing. For nearly two years Russia has been poised to resume testing the moment the US ended its moratorium and conducted its first test. Given President Clinton's recent proclamation of "no first test" for the US nuclear program, political pressures may preclude testing by Russia unless the strategic necessity to improve the technical security of the warheads becomes so great that resumption of testing is demanded.

From the vantage point of the nuclear weapons industry there is little to be optimistic about. Budgets are falling with no end in sight, skilled personnel are leaving in alarming numbers and lab activity has nearly ground to a halt. A once proud, unified and supremely powerful nuclear weapons complex is now rent by split allegiances and filled with demoralized personnel, pitting Russian scientists against their Ukrainian colleagues. There is no doubt that the technical and physical security of the warheads and their launchers have suffered. It is difficult to judge whether the deterioration is still within an acceptable range of risk or whether it has slipped beyond the safety point to a potential radioactive leaks, accidental explosions and sabotaged or missing weapons.

THE EVOLUTION OF THE FSU NUCLEAR ARSENAL AND FEDERATION DISINTEGRATION

The future for FSU nuclear forces is difficult to predict. A number of scenarios could be postulated ranging from Russia becoming the de facto sole inheritor of the inventory, to Russia, Ukraine and Kazakhstan establishing their own nuclear universes, independent of one another and outside the boundaries of traditional bilateral arms control treaties with the United States.

One scenario which has received little attention in the Western press is the increasing potential for the disintegration of the Russian Federation, and the disintegration of the Russian armed forces and nuclear arsenal to the regions. The debates over the draft constitution and the subsequent declaration of "republic" status by the Volgograd region, Sverdlovsk region and Primorskii district has only exacerbated the issue and heightened the debate about the future of the federation.

Since early 1992 the Russian press has been filled with discussions warning of the disintegration of the federation. As an indication of how serious the situation has become, only recently has the official army daily, Red Star, addressed the issue. Writing on 8 July, Red Star, in a front-page commentary, challenged the new "republicanization" of the federation, asking if nothing had been learned from disintegration of the USSR. The article raised fears of fracturing the armed forces into regional and district allegiances and called upon Russia and the Russian leadership to maintain a unified federation.[26]

Disintegration of the federation is fraught with dangers for the nuclear forces. Not only is it possible that the nuclear inventory may be divided among Russia, Ukraine and Kazakhstan, it is also possible that these systems may fall under the control of various regional authorities if Russia continues to splinter, creating a multi-headed nuclear hydra where once a single power stood. It is also possible that some may not be inclined to return these weapons to responsible authorities or else these systems may be viewed as a commodity for sale to the highest bidder, creating proliferation nightmares. The dismantlement of a large part of the nuclear inventory, envisioned by START-2, would halt. A Pandora's box of dangerous and even unthinkable scenarios would open.

In August 1992 First Deputy Minister of Defense Kolesnikov warned that there is a "real danger" of a "Yugoslav sovereignty process" in the FSU which could lead to Western intervention.[27] One of the most pressing reasons for intervention in a disintegrating state would be to secure or destroy nuclear weapons where centralized authority over the systems had collapsed or was severed. A few short years ago such ideas would have been dismissed out of hand. Now they appear to receive more serious consideration.

At present there are few bright spots for the FSU nuclear forces as further deterioration and the potential for both military and industrial accidents occur. Moreover, compliance with arms control treaties is even more difficult as the infrastructure responsible for weapons dismantlement and destruction continues its down-turn and even collapse in certain sectors. Even missile crews and combat support structures are stretched to their limits. Currently, combat readiness has been seriously affected and personnel shortages are at the chronic stage with combat missile crews now at only 50-60 percent manning levels.[28]

The nuclear industrial complex is in disarray, while the nuclear workers remaining are threatening strikes and dire consequences to the nuclear arsenal and to national security if their requests for more and stable funding levels are not met. Even the key facilities of Arzamas-16 and Cheliabinsk-70 have not been immune from fiscal reductions and the general malaise which has enveloped the industry and the forces themselves.

START-2 appears headed to a slow death or else radical amendment since it seems that Ukraine soon will declare its intentions to keep its most potent and technically stable nuclear systems and the possibility that Kazakhstan may follow. Also, wide-scale opposition to START-2 in Russia threatens treaty ratification, criticism ranging from its alleged surrender to US interests to the threat of serious financial burdens. The fear of serious ecological dangers posed by the dismantlement and destruction of both warheads and missiles has been raised further, expanding the scope of criticism beyond that voiced by conservative military men and parliamentarians.

The specter of federation disintegration, recently manifest in declarations by the new "republics" in recent weeks and the slow dissolution of centralized authority over the past year, casts a dark shadow over the fate of the arsenal. Potential scenarios abound, ranging from the potential for nuclearized regional powers to the possible sale of weapons to Third World powers looking for shortcuts to their own nuclear force. Even combat-crew stability appears on the verge of collapse, as soldiers and officers must certainly be working near levels of physical and mental exhaustion. A serious compromise of the unified command of Russian nuclear forces may occur if disintegration continues and crew reliability plummets. At the moment, there is little good news to suggest otherwise.

1. Makmut Gareev, "What Russia Needs Is a Military Doctrine." *Rossiiskie vesti*, 4 March 1993.

2. V. Mikhailov (Minister of Atomic Energy for Russian Federation, Professor), "The Nuclear Shield of Russia," *Armiia*, No. 7 (April 1993), 22-25.

3. Ye. Shaposhnikov, "The Military Danger for the Commonwealth is Located Within It," *Izvestiia*, 16 November 1992.

4. Yury Alekseevich Trutnev, "The Bomb—the Least Expensive Method to Avoid War," *Izvestiia*, 18 August 1992. For a recent and brief discussion of "all azimuth defense" see Sergei Ovsienko, "Where Are the Missiles Aimed?" *Rossiiskie vesti*, 5 May 1993.

5. I.D. Sergeev (Gen. Col., Glavkom of the Strategic Rocket Forces of the Armed Forces of the Russian Federation), "The Strategic Rocket Forces. Problems of Their Construction and Re-Formation," *Voennaia mysl*, No. 6 (June 1993), 12-18 and Col. V.F. Grinko and Lt. Col. S.I. Kokhan, "The Concept of Deterrence and Strategic Stability in Modern Conditions," *Voennaia mysl*, No. 4 (April 1993), 14-21.

6. Tai Ming Cheung, "Quick response. Military Planners Focus on External Threats," *Far Eastern Economic Review* (14 January 1993), 19-21. For a discussion of the threat from the south, see Y.A. Kosolapov, "The Internal Troops District—An Absolutely New Structure," *Krasnaia zvezda*, 20 April 1993, and A. Aderekhin, "The Kuban is Becoming Russia's Southern Outpost," *Izvestiia*, 28 May 1993.

7. Lt. Gen. Vladimir Bondartsev, first deputy chief of the defense ministry's organization-mobilization directorate, was quoted by ITAR-TASS on 15 July as saying that the army's enlisted ranks are still only 51 percent manned, leaving a total shortfall of more than 700,000. It is estimated that following the demobilization of some 320,000 draftees this fall manning levels among enlisted men would fall to 30-35 percent of the required number, a level at which normal functioning of the army would be impossible. See Stephen Foye, "More on Army's Manpower Problems," *RFE/RL Daily Report*, No. 134, 16 July 1993.

8. Yevgeny Nikolaevich Avrorin (scientific head of Cheliabinsk-70), "We Look to the Future With Optimism. The Scientific Chief of Cheliabinsk-70, Akademik Ye.N. Avrorin on the Fate of the Federal Nuclear Center and the 'Fate of Those People Who Work There,'" *Rossiiskaia gazeta*, 7 April 1993.

9. A poll conducted in March 1993 in Kiev showed that the proportion of those favoring nuclear status for Ukraine had doubled since May of the previous year. Fifty percent think that Ukraine should be non-nuclear, a figure that remains essentially unchanged. However, only about 11 percent of those supporting a non-nuclear status think that Ukraine should yield its nuclear armaments unconditionally. Almost 90 percent say that Ukraine should be given international security guarantees and financial compensation. See Roman Solchanyk, "What Kievites Think About Nukes," *RFE/RL Daily Report*, No. 79, 27 April 1993.

10. Unattributed, "There Are No Wars. But Nuclear Workers are Needed," *Rabochaia tribuna*, 21 May 1993.

11. Avrorin, "Look to the Future," 7 April 1993.

12. Pavel Felgengauer, "Ukraine Seeks Nuclear Independence. This Could Lead to Its International Isolation," *Nezavisimaia gazeta*, 14 March 1992. Translated in FBIS Daily Report/Central Eurasia, 16 March 1992, 4-5, FBIS-SOV-92-051. Also see RFE/RL Report, "Ukrainians have Technical Ability to Retarget Missiles," 3 June 1992. NCAJS and Interfax. "Russian 'Expert' Says Kiev to Retarget Missiles," 30 June 1993. In FBIS-SOV-93125-A, 1 July 1993, 1-2. For

a discussion of US fears over Ukraine gaining positive control, see John Lepingwell, "US Intelligence Concerned Over Ukrainian Nuclear Weapons Control," RFE/RL Daily Report, No. 103, 2 June 1993.

13. Unattributed, "Nuclear Workers Needed," 21 May 1993. The source indicates that "Slavs" are returning to the European part of the FSU because the best educational and working facilities exist there and not in Kazakhstan. No mention is made of possible discrimination against native Slavs which is reported to be increasing throughout the newly independent Central Asian states. For concerns over Kazakhstan, see John Lepingwell, "Stepashin Claims Ukraine Trying to Retarget Nuclear Weapons," RFE/RL Daily Report, No. 95, 19 May 1993.

14. Oleg Georgiev, "START-2. There Are No Analogs," *Nezavisimaia gazeta*, 5 February 1993. For another example of conservative opposition, see Petr Belov, Col. (retired), "A Note to the President. You Must Answer to the Fatherland," *Pravda*, 31 December 1992. For a recent discussion opposing START-2 ratification, see Grigory Kisunko, "Disarming But With Intelligence Plus Nuclear Diktat of the US," *Pravda*, 9 June 1993. For a recent discussion supporting START-2 ratification, see Igor Sergeev (Col. Gen., Glavkom of the SRF of Russia), "START-2. Parity Is Possible and Achievable," *Rossiiskie vesti*, 16 June 1993.

15. Vladimir Yermolin, "A Hearing on START-2 Occurred in the Supreme Soviet of the Russian Federation," *Krasnaia zvezda*, 3 March 1993.

16. Anatoly Shabad (coordinator of the Radical Democrats parliamentary faction), Iona Andronov (member of the Supreme Soviet and deputy chairman of the Supreme Soviet Committee for International Affairs and Foreign Economic Relations) and Lev Ponomarev (member of the Supreme Soviet and co-chairman of the Democratic Russia movement), "START II. The Presidents Have Reached Agreement. The World Public Has Given Its Backing. It Is Now Up to the US Congress and the Russian Parliament," *Rossiiskie vesti*, 6 January 1993, and Hal Kosiba, "Doubts in Russian Parliament About START-2," RFE/RL Daily Report, No. 2, 5 January 1993.

17. S. Ivanov, "Ball in Parliament's Court," *Komsomolskaia pravda*, 28 January 1993.

18. L. Malyshev, Capt. 1st Rank (Retired), "START-2 and the Ecological Security of Russia," *Zelenyi mir*, No. 11 (March 1993), 1, 7, 10. Other writings have suggested that Russia should not expect significant aid from the West. In the words of Izvestiia political observer Stanislav Kondrashov, it is commonly understood that the US "will not bust a gut for the Russians." See Stanislav Kondrashov, "Old Prescriptions of Glasnost Applied to New Treaty." *Izvestiia*, 12 January 1993.

19. Avrorin, "Look to the Future," 7 April 1993, 3.

20. Mikhailov, "Nuclear Shield," April 1993.

21. Avrorin, "Look to the Future," 7 April 1992 and Mikhailov,"Nuclear Shield," April 1993.

22. Reuters, 11 June 1993 and P. Orlov, "The Meeting By the Bombs. The Ultimatum of the Nuclear Scientists of Arzamas-16," *Sovetskaia Rossiia*, 26 June 1993, and Mikhail Rebrov, "Disturbing Events at Arzamas-16," *Krasnaia zvezda,* 23 June 1993. For extensive exploration of events at Arzamas-16, see Vladimir Gubariev, "Nightmares Are Born Into Reality. Thoughts About the Crisis in the Federal Nuclear Centers of Russia, Its Sources and Potential Variants for the Development of Events," *Delovoi mir*, 1 July 1993.

23. Petr Korotkevich, "We Need a New Global Strategy, but Few Members of the Governing 'Team' Realize This," *Nezavisimaia gazeta*, 15 August 1992.

24. Viktor Litovsky, "Nuclear Warheads in Ukraine Present a Danger," *Izvestiia*, 7 April 1993.

25. P. Belov, "Missiles in SDI Sauce. Will We See the Day When Our Parliament Gives Bush a Standing Ovation?" *Komsomolskaia pravda*, 20 August 1992. Trutnev, "The Bomb," 18 August 1992, and Yury Mamachur and Aleksandr Dolinin, "Russia Will Keep Its Nuclear Shield. And It Will Be Reliable Enough," *Krasnaia zvezda*, 14 November 1992.

26. Unattributed, "Is It Possible That We Did Not Learn From the Hard Lessons of the Disintegration of the USSR?" *Krasnaia zvezda,* 8 July 1993. For some sources on federation disintegration, see Council on Foreign and Defense Policy, "The Disintegration of Russia? Thesis of a Report by the Council on Foreign and Defense Policy," *Nezavisimaia gazeta*, 10 December 1992; A. Ugalanov, "Is Russia Breaking Into Pieces?" *Argumenty i fakty*, No. 2, January 1993, and V.N.

Leksin, et al., "The Territorial Disintegration of Russia," *Rossiiskie ekonomicheskii zhurnal*, Pt. 1, No. 8 (August 1992), 32-41, and Pt. 2, No. 9 (September 1992), 34-43.
27. P. Felgengauer, "Military Men Anticipate Intervention from the West," *Nezavisimaia gazeta*, 1 August 1992.
28. For a detailed assessment of the deteriorating situation in the Strategic Rocket Forces, see Igor Sergeyev (Col. Gen., Glavkom of the SRF), "All of Us Stand Watch—From the Soldier to the Glavkom," *Krasnaia zvezda*, 9 July 1993.

THE RETURN OF THE RUSSIAN GENERAL STAFF AND THE FUTURE OF MILITARY REFORM

Kenneth M. Currie

INTRODUCTION

After a period of uncertainty following the August coup and the creation of the CIS military command structure the General Staff is once again gaining its traditional pride of place as the principal operational command and control entity within the military. In the process we have witnessed the rebirth of the Russian General Staff. Not remarkably, this institution bears a significant resemblance to its Russian-dominated Soviet predecessor. This continuity will affect the way the Russian General Staff looks at the world around it. It will also affect the way the Russian military leadership approaches the issue of military reform.

This review looks at the circumstances surrounding the demise of the Soviet General Staff and its Russian successor. These were, and are, trying times for the General Staff officer who strives to regain some degree of the stability and security he knew under the old system, as well as a sense of loyalty to the new state he serves.

The review then examines Russian military reform at two levels. It briefly looks at the changes taking place at the military-technical level, to borrow a useful taxonomy from Soviet and now Russian doctrinal thought, by focusing on the changes occurring at the political level of military doctrine; i.e. the relationship between the military as an institution and the rest of society.

Some Western commentators who focus on the changes taking place at the military-technical level assert that traditionalists are still in control of the military and, consequently, there is little difference in thinking between Soviet and Russian military leaders. Based on this assumption, the assertion is then made that there has been no meaningful reform of the Soviet military in terms of how it envisions the threat and the necessary responses to deal with it.

As Western commentators view the changes taking place at the political level in Russia, they often charge that the military is becoming more assertive, that it has done little to reform itself internally, and that it represents an omnipresent danger to the stability of the new Russian state. What is missing to date is the development of a relationship between the Russian government and the military which is "conflict prone," and thus represents a "perennial threat" to the Russian state's political stability.[1]

THE RETURN OF THE INSTITUTION

The General Staff has been at the core of the evolution of Soviet military politics since the coup. A battle for control of the post-Soviet military was fought out between Soviet Minister of Defense Shaposhnikov and Chief of the General Staff Lobov, a contest which Shaposhnikov eventually won. At issue were two very different views of the role of the General Staff in the operational control of the armed forces. Lobov envisioned the General Staff as a largely independent body, directly under the union president and parallel rather than subordinate to the Ministry of Defense, in direct control of the operational forces. The General Staff would tend to "strictly military things" and the "civilian" Ministry of Defense would coordinate the activity of the various republic defense ministries, "resolve questions of military development, and run the defense industry."[2] Counterpoised to this argument was Shaposhnikov's vision of the General Staff as one of several military departments directly subordinate to the defense minister.[3]

Lobov clearly was at a disadvantage in the turf war with the new Minister of Defense, who had been one of the key leaders of the anti-coup resistance among the military. Although Lobov was in no way implicated in the coup, having been head of the Frunze's Academy, he could not compete with the charismatic, non-traditional Shaposhnikov, who clearly had Gorbachev's and, more importantly, Yeltsin's ear. Lobov attempted to counter rumors of a conflict with Shaposhnikov by asserting that he had been working "in close contact" with Shaposhnikov and that his references to the "preferential role" of the General Staff in troop management were not designed to enhance his personal position.[4] Finally, in early December Lobov was dismissed from his post and accused of pushing reform ideas which did not "coincide" with the decisions of the USSR State Council and the country's leadership.[5]

Lobov refused to go peacefully, arguing that he had submitted no resignation request, that his health was fine (contrary to press reports), and that since he was appointed by the State Council he could not be removed by the USSR president. He also claimed immunity from removal by virtue of his status as a People's Deputy.[6]

Shaposhnikov moved quickly to put forth his version of the events surrounding Lobov's dismissal. He asserted that Lobov had "verbally" accepted the decision of the State Council on the reorganization of the military along the lines advocated by Shaposhnikov, but then continued to implement his own plan by "splitting the higher echelons of the military administration into two parallel structures," a step which Shaposhnikov argued violated the principle of "unified management." The result, according to Shaposhnikov, was "increasing disorganization" in the General Staff's work and growing "disorientation" among the officer corps. These developments made Lobov's dismissal "necessary."[7] The letter of indictment against Lobov also included the charge that he had sought to expand the size of the General Staff and his personal staff.[8]

Lobov's dismissal marked the nadir of the General Staff. Lobov's previous service on the General Staff, including a stint as its first deputy chief, and his public prominence as a military theorist and advocate of military reforms based on the experience of the 1920s, seemed to suggest the General Staff in the post-coup era would retain its pride of place in the military hierarchy. Instead, Sha-poshnikov secured the staff's complete subordination to him by appointing the unassuming and, by most accounts, unimpressive Col. Gen. Viktor Samsonov, commander of the Leningrad Military District, as the new General Staff chief.[9]

The conflict between Shaposhnikov and Lobov also reflected the struggle for control of resources and the overall direction of military development. That contest largely pitted the views of senior air force officers, led by Marshal of Aviation Shaposhnikov, against the ground force officers who had dominated the pre-coup Ministry of Defense and General Staff. Shaposhnikov had moved quickly to bring a number of air force officers into prominent positions within the Ministry of Defense. Lobov's removal brought control of the General Staff and its planners under the control of an air force officer dedicated to pushing reforms that would favor the future of the Soviet air power.

The demise of the USSR and the creation of the Commonwealth of Independent States (CIS) presented the General Staff with a different set of problems than being headed by a relative unknown. Although Shaposhnikov was designated commander-in-chief of the CIS forces, he soon discovered that his inheritance was growing smaller by the day. Shaposhnikov's efforts to accommodate emerging republic armies within the framework of a unified Commonwealth command structure came to naught as Ukraine opted out of the joint military structure and Belarus made its participation conditional on the transition to its own independent armed forces.[10] Shaposhnikov found himself in nominal control of a force which was becoming increasingly Russian. This position was also under siege by ground force officers who were advocating a separate Russian ministry of defense. Shaposhnikov, aware that this constituted a clear challenge to his control of the armed forces, resisted these proposals.

The failure to tackle the question of a separate Russian army left the armed forces lurching about in confusion, with soldiers wondering to whom or to what state they owed their loyalty. This confusion was reflected in the "war of the oaths" that broke out between Ukraine and Russia as Kiev sought to ensure the allegiance of the former Soviet Army officers serving on its soil. Compounding this uncertainty was the matter of the rapidly declining welfare of the soldiers and their perception that the leadership cared little about their plight except when it needed their "votes." The failure of the CIS states to reach agreement on funding of the armed forces, a question postponed through repeated summits in early 1992, left the former Soviet military in a state of limbo.

Certainly in such an environment the morale of the General Staff officers, like that of the officer corps in general, was suffering. The staff had been hit by economically driven manpower cuts and personnel turnovers precipitated by the coup, although the turnover at the lower levels of the General Staff appears to have been limited. The collapse of the Warsaw Pact and the politically mandated demise of the Western threat had thrown the General Staff's carefully crafted plans into disarray. With the republics organizing their own armed forces and Ukraine challenging Moscow for control of strategic assets, the General Staff must have wondered exactly what their mission was, other than planning for the next round of budget cuts. These difficulties constituted a direct challenge to the

General Staff's status and the prestige which an assignment to its ranks had previously bestowed upon the recipient.

A few General Staff officers found relief from their predicament by jumping ship. Maj. Gen. G. Zhivitsa, formerly of the Operational Strategic Research Center, found gainful employment in Ukraine, where he became the chief of the Ukrainian General Staff. But for most General Staff officers their plight constituted an imminent threat to their military professionalism, the factor that ensures the military's cohesiveness and its neutrality in politics.[11]

The creation of the Russian Armed Forces and their general staff is a necessary step to restoring this military professionalism and in defusing the potential danger of military intervention in Russian politics. The continued existence of a force of several hundred thousand stateless and homeless officers was a far more troubling phenomenon, one which posed a long term threat to Russian stability and the growth of Russian democracy. Its creation reestablished clear lines of authority in place of the confusion which existed under Shaposhnikov's command. Shaposhnikov is the clear loser in all of this, his staff is exiled to the lodgings of the former Warsaw Pact command, whereas the rest of the military and Russia emerged as the potential winners as the armed forces struggle to bring order.

The Russian General Staff appears poised to regain the stature of its Soviet predecessor. It has been accorded pride of place in the operational chain of command of the Russian Armed Forces. The May 1992 "Special Edition" of the journal Voennaia mysl appears to accept Lobov's view of how the military should be organized by making the Ministry of Defense responsible for developing and carrying out "military, military-technical, and cadres policy, financial and logistic support of the Armed Forces, and other administrative functions."[12] On the other hand, the commander-in-chief of the armed forces, the Russian president, "exercises control of the Russian Armed Forces through the General Staff."[13] Shortly after his appointment as defense minister on 18 May 1992, General Pavel Grachev told an interviewer that the functions of the Ministry of Defense and the General Staff would be "strictly" separated, with the semi-civilian MOD responsible for "political-administrative" functions and the General Staff tasked with "operational-strategic planning and lead[ing] the troops."[14] Grachev also described the Russian General Staff as the "supreme executive body in the military command system" and noted its tasks.

It is to "implement strategic and operational planning; direct the leadership of the Armed Forces in peacetime and wartime; maintain the combat and mobilization readiness of the troops (forces); determine the Armed Forces requirements with regard to personnel, material resources, arms, and military hardware in peacetime and wartime; and organize strategic and operations support."[15]

This list essentially replicates the description of the functions of the once-powerful Soviet General Staff,[16] and reflects the strong desire of General Staff officers for as much continuity and stability as possible in an era of traumatic change.

The new chief of the General Staff, forty-nine-year-old Col. Gen. Viktor Dubinin, is an example of the generational change that has taken place in the post-coup military. An armor officer who formerly commanded the Northern Group of Forces in Poland, Dubinin has asserted that his job is to develop a new structure for the General Staff, one that is "small in number, but powerful, effective, and modern." The first task of this new General Staff, according to Dubynin, is to "draw up in the quickest possible time a new military doctrine for the Russian state" so that Moscow can then "talk boldly with any state on an equal footing" instead of being treated as a "second- and third-class power."[17]

Despite the positive signs from the General Staff's perspective, things are still very much in a state of flux as the new Russian military institutions set up shop and attempt to gather the personnel and material resources they need to do business. Although Russian military spokesman have repeatedly stated that the new Russian General Staff will be drawn from the body of the Soviet General Staff, the process is off to a slow start. According to the new first deputy chief of the Russian General Staff, Col. Gen. Mikhail Kolesnikov, the General Staff "physically" seems to exist but in legal terms it consists of only Dubinin and his first deputy. The heads of the main directorates and their deputies are serving in an "acting" capacity and, according to Kolesnikov, this is "impeding" their ability to function normally. Kolesnikov also echoed his superior's comments on the future of the General Staff by stating that its structure will be "simplified" and its personnel cut by a third. Stressing the theme of continuity, Kolesnikov asserted that he was "by no means certain that the new army" had to differ "fundamentally" from its Soviet predecessor, since "modern armed forces in any country do not differ 'fundamentally' from each other." Driving the point home, he argued that the new Russian Army "must in no way forget the traditions of either the old Russian Army, or the Soviet Armed Forces."[18]

MILITARY-TECHNICAL REFORM OF THE MILITARY

Driven by economic realities which have dictated a drawdown in the size of the armed forces and created enormously difficult problems of providing for the social welfare of service members, and compelled by a desire to create smaller, but more effective armed forces, the Russian military leadership has introduced a series of measures which will significantly transform the structure and employment of the armed forces. These steps build upon the reforms begun in the Soviet Armed Forces under Yazov and Moiseev, but they also represent a qualitatively different approach to future military requirements. These proposed changes are not universally accepted, however. They are decried by military leaders as ignoring current world realities and by political activists as only a half-hearted attempt at reforming military and security policy.

The key area of change has been in the area of threat perception. Public statements by Grachev and others strongly enunciate the view that the period of the traditional threat posed by the West is over. Indeed, the draft military doctrine notes that "Russia does not consider a single state or coalition of states to be its enemy."[19] But while the threat of nuclear war has receded and the West is no longer considered a direct military threat, the Russian military leaders hold that there are a number of uncertainties in the world which create the potential for military dangers as well as threats, including instability on Russia's borders as well as the violation of the rights of Russian citizens living abroad.[20]

Some members of the high command appear to be taking exception to the more benign interpretation of the traditional Western threat. First Deputy chief of the Russian General Staff Col. Gen. Mikhail Kolesnikov believes that while the threat of nuclear war "no longer exists," Russia's overall security position "could not be worse." In a speech to the Council on Foreign and Defense Policy in Moscow Kolesnikov warned that disputes between the former Soviet republics contained the danger of degenerating into the "Yugoslav precedent" which could lead to "direct intervention" by the West under the guise of "ensuring 'international control' over the nuclear potential" of the former USSR. He asserted that Russia's emergence as a regional power "does not accord with the long-term interests of United States, the NATO bloc as a whole, or Japan." Kolesnikov also criticized "inadequately considered disarmament initiatives."[21]

Despite the persistence of elements of "old thinking" among some members of the high command, or perhaps because of it, the Russian military leadership is pushing ahead with plans to restructure the armed forces to make them, in Grachev's words, smaller, more mobile, and capable of "performing limited tasks in any region of Russia" and eventually "repelling aggression in local and regional wars and military conflicts."[22] But these military-technical reforms will not come as quickly as some would like. According to the Russian defense minister, for the next few years the MOD will rely mainly on the exiting military structure not because it is conservative, rather because the "radical destruction of the existing structures would necessitate considerable expenditure." During this period MOD will create "mobile forces as a new operational-strategic formation" drawing upon the airborne forces, the naval infantry, light ground force units, military transport aviation, and related units." After this brief transitional period the armed forces will move toward a recruiting system "based on the draft and voluntary entry into military service on contract," will make "drastic cuts" in the number of "large strategic formations and combined units," will move from an army/division to a corps/brigade structure, will "radically" review and transform the military procurement system, will separate the "functions of operational and administrative control," and will "radically" restructure "all command and control organs, above all the Defense Ministry." These are ambitious plans, given the continuing tumult within the Russian Armed Forces, but Grachev asserts that they will be carried out with "unswerving consistency and determination."[23]

One area where military-technical reform, which also touches on political reform of the military, does not appear to be moving ahead is in the area of "radically" restructuring the defense ministry. After much speculation that Yeltsin would appoint a civilian defense minister, he instead opted for Grachev. He argued that appointing a civilian seemed to be the "last word in fashion" at present, but a step replete with problems because a civilian would "not be able to handle the tasks that went with the job. He would not have enough knowledge of the military."

Grachev conceded that a civilian defense minister might be possible at some future date after the "strong army organism that our Russia so badly needs has been created."[24] Grachev failed to grasp the point of those of his countrymen who had argued for the appointment of a civilian. The purpose was not to appoint someone who would continue to serve as an advocate of the uniformed military's parochial interests, but someone who would assure civilian control of the military agenda and the military leadership.

Nevertheless, even the Russian democrats who are most keen on reforming the military concede that a military man could continue to lead the MOD. The leaders of Democratic Russia have stated that such an appointment would be acceptable, on the "condition that following a six-month transition period they [the military appointees] hand in their [officers'] stripes."[25]

POLITICAL REFORM OF THE MILITARY

Political reform in the Russian military has been much more problematic, and has been the aspect of military reform that has caused the most concern in the West. Continued coup rumors in Russia reflect the uncertainties about an institution several of whose senior members were active participants in the August events. Although the military has fallen on severely hard times, there is still a perception among many Western students of Soviet military politics that it may be cohesive enough to mount a challenge to Yeltsin or the evolving democratic order in Russia.

Because of Gorbachev's failure to take measures to add to the stability of civil-military relations, the key element of political reform of the Russian military is missing.[26] Obstacles include the continued presence of party organs within the military, overt political activity on the part of military personnel, open questioning of state policy by senior military leaders, and allowing active duty military officers to serve as members of legislative bodies.

The disappearance of party organs within the military was achieved with alacrity in the wake of the coup, although the fate of many former political officers remains unclear. Many have been reassigned to serve as unit welfare officers supervising morale, welfare, and social needs of the troops, certainly a thankless task given the limited resources available to meet these needs. The loyalty of many of the former political workers remains uncertain. Those who are not retired, reassigned, or cashiered represent a reservoir of potential opposition to the current Russian leadership. Military personnel were screened to determine their suitability for continued military service, but the specific nature of any political litmus test to be applied during this process has not been made public. Indeed, one prominent critic of the Soviet and Russian government's military policies has asserted that party membership is still a part of the officer's personnel files and is "still taken into consideration during their promotion."[27]

Although the current military leadership does not bemoan the disappearance of the party and its organizational network in the military, it is very concerned about the need to develop a new source of ideological or spiritual commitment necessary to motivate the troops. Talk of introducing a corps of chaplains into the military is viewed by some as one means of providing servicemen the motivation to ensure discipline and loyalty to the Russian state.

The persistence of overt political activity within the military is arguably a necessary by-product of the chaos associated with the building of the new Russian state. At the same time it reflects a failure on the part of the military and civilian leadership to come to grips with the political reform of the military necessary to ensure its subordination to the civil authority.

The most prominent example of organized overt political activity by military officers has been the officers' assemblies organized in various military units.

These advocacy groups have been very active in the post-coup period, and their platforms have been critical of the government's failure to halt the collapse of political authority and the decline in the military's status. Some 5,000 representatives of these assemblies, selected at meetings held in "units, on ships, at military training institutions, and in other military collectives,"[28] gathered in Moscow in mid-January in a session attended by senior members of the CIS high command as well as Russian President Yeltsin and Kazakhstan President Nazarbaev. Nevertheless, the meeting was heavily weighted with senior military officers and representatives of the politically active, and presumably conservative, Moscow Military District.[29]

Although Yeltsin acquitted himself well in front of this skeptical group, he finished third in the polling of the delegates behind Nazarbaev and Vice President Rutskoi.[30] The delegates overwhelmingly felt that the military, not the civilian politicians, should decide issues pertaining to the armed forces future. Most also favored restoration of a unified state within the former borders of the USSR,[31] a troubling prospect for the newly independent states on whose territory thousands of former Soviet troops were still located.

The convening of the assembly, although it may have helped defuse tensions in the military by letting its spokesmen air their grievances, touched off alarm bells among political circles in Moscow. The Defense Committee of the Russian Supreme Soviet issued a statement that noted the "negative" outcome of the assembly since it revealed the "aggressiveness" of "military circles." The committee members argued that the meeting "further aggravated" the situation by the military's "wish to bring pressure to bear on the country's authorities."[32] An effort to bring the officers' assemblies under control, or under the high command's purview, was made on 11 February when Shaposhnikov issued a provisional regulation governing the Coordinating Council of the Officers' Assemblies.[33] Defense minister Grachev also restricted them to the garrison level and below. According to Grachev, he will not allow the continuation of the coordinating council or "structures of its ilk."[34]

Despite these efforts to control the officers' groups they remain the wild card in the new regime's efforts to bring the military firmly under its control. In what has become a pattern for local officers' assemblies the group in Tajikistan took issue with the republic parliament's decision to bring forces on its territory under Tajik control, arguing that such a step would "deprive the republic of stability and lead to civil war." In that event, the officers warned, the military would take the appropriate steps to protect "their own interests" and reserved "the right to make its own decisions" and to inform the CIS heads of state about them.[35]

Former chief of the General Staff Lobov warned of the danger of the officers' assemblies. He argued that these groups serve only to "rub salt in the wounds. And thereby drag the officer corps, which is already politicized, into a dangerous game." He argued that the military's problems demand a "political solution, one adopted not by the military but by politicians."[36]

Although the danger of local military units taking matters into their own hands is a very real concern for the Russian leadership, it does not pose as direct a threat to ensuring civilian control of the military as the failure to prohibit open questioning of the government's policies. This fact became a pervasive problem during the period prior to the August coup, and Gorbachev's failure, or inability, to discipline those who openly criticized his policies almost certainly emboldened some senior military leaders to push even harder and directly challenge the Soviet leader's control.

Determining when senior military leaders have crossed the line from policy advocacy to policy criticism is often difficult in the Russian context. The problem is also compounded by the Yeltsin government's failure to specify publicly what its policies are in certain areas, an oversight which invites the military and other institutions to enter what appears on the surface to be a still open debate. Despite these cautions, there have been some clear-cut examples of senior military leaders disputing their civilian leaders. Unlike his Soviet predecessor, Yeltsin appears more attuned to the implications of transgressions of the civil-military boundary and has taken some steps that are essential if political reform of the military is to succeed.

Defense minister Grachev has skated perilously close to the edge of acceptable criticism. In an appeal to Russian servicemen stationed abroad he asserted that the armed forces had been turned into a "lightning rod for discontent by the actions of certain politicians" and attempts had been made to "embroil the Army in conflicts." He warned that "sooner or later it will be necessary to respond to all of this."[37] Publicly he has been careful not to cross the line. The same cannot be said for all of his subordinates.

The most notable example concerns the commander of the Russian 14th Army in Tiraspol, Moldova, Maj. Gen. Aleksandr Lebed. Sent to the Dniester region to restore order and discipline in the 14th Army, Lebed instead leaped into national politics during his first news conference. He described the CIS as an "assemblage of abnormal states," asserted that the Dniester region was part of Russia, and claimed that the Russian Army's "retreat from nearby foreign parts" would soon come to an end.[38] Lebed also criticized Yeltsin's Western-oriented foreign policy by decrying the practice of "going with outstretched hands to the world's cabinets, instead of building up a great power capable of imposing its will."[39] Lebed purportedly told a Russian correspondent that his appointment was connected "with strong shifts in the policy of the Russian Government."[40]

Yeltsin apparently moved quickly to bring the new commander in line, certainly more quickly than his predecessor did in a similar situation.[41] The commander of the Russian Ground Forces was dispatched to Moldova amid reports that he was being sent to "investigate the consequences" of Lebed's statements.[42] A gag order apparently was issued to Lebed, although this was subsequently denied by an MOD spokesman.[43] In the final expression of his displeasure, and a clear warning to others who might attempt to emulate Lebed's example of taking oratorical liberties, Yeltsin reportedly struck the general's name from a flag officers promotion list, the only officer to merit that distinction.[44]

Grachev also has taken steps to ensure discipline among the ranks. He reportedly issued an executive order authorizing only him and his deputies to make "political statements."[45]

While this may put a stop to "shoot-from-the-lip" generals like Lebed, it will not halt the larger problem of senior leaders' making statements at variance with the government's policies, such as Grachev and his deputies did.

The General Staff has provided one of the most recent examples of public statements openly questioning government policies. Although the statement was a response to a Russian Supreme Soviet inquiry on a specific issue, the publication of the General Staff's arguments gives the impression once again of a military not fully under the control of the civilian authorities. In language reminiscent of "Cold War" threat analysis, the General Staff argued that the return of the Kurile Islands to Japan would be "highly dangerous" from a national security standpoint because it would split the Russian Pacific Fleet and provide "free access for the likely enemy's forces." The General Staff also urged a reexamination of the question of unilateral Russian troop withdrawals from the islands, where their presence served to restrain "Japan's wish to resolve the territorial question by force." The statement noted that acceding to Japan's claims would spawn a "'chain reaction' of territorial claims against Russia."[46]

These interventions by the military on behalf of or against Russian government policy have elicited a strong reaction from those who are engaged in their own battles with the Russian high command. In an interview which drew a strong response from a military spokesman and a rebuke from the Russian Security Council, Foreign minister Kozyrev excoriated the practice of the "KGB and the military departments" of providing "suitably leaked" information to advance their agendas. Kozyrev noted that this was not completely distorted information, but "suitably cooked and biased." He viewed this pattern as evidence of the rise of a "war party, the party of neo-Bolshevism," although he declined to associate specific members of the high command with this right-wing opposition.

Kozyrev argued that giving into the arguments of this opposition would mean that the "power structures...will be out of control and sooner or later they will shed the democratic skin that is unnecessary, that is a nuisance to them."[47]

In a final indicator that the Russian government has not yet come fully to grips with the problem of military reform, active duty military officers still sit on local and national-level legislative bodies where they are free to question openly the policies of the government and their senior officers. This practice not only undermines civilian control of the military, it imperils military discipline as well.[48] The Russian leadership appears finally to be coming to grips with the problem. According to Article 94 of the Draft Constitution of the Russian Federation, deputies to the Russian Supreme Soviet may not hold a position in the "civil or other service" or receive "any other regular compensation," a provision that would appear to exclude the election of military officers on active duty.[49]

THE FUTURE OF MILITARY REFORM

The future of military reform in Russia will depend on Yeltsin's political strength and his willingness to push reform. Gorbachev's support for military reform appeared to wax and wane in time with his political powers. Yeltsin has let the new defense ministry establish the parameters of military reform although it has resisted the pace and scope of the force and budget cuts imposed upon it. The Russian military leadership has accepted the necessity of the drawdowns and has shaped its reform plans accordingly. Although Yeltsin may take issue with some of the more abrasive comments of his military commanders, there appears to be little in their reform proposals that should cause him discomfort. Given the fact that Yeltsin's attention is focused on preserving the Russian Federation and securing Russia's economic recovery, it is not surprising that he has devoted little attention to detailed military reform issues.

Should the military reforms fail to produce the results that will let Yeltsin address his principal concerns, he is likely to play a more active role. During a meeting in July 1992 with military commanders and local government leaders, Yeltsin criticized the military for its failure to implement order and allowing the "squandering of military equipment and property, the abuse of official status, corruption, and swindling."[50] Clearly, there are limits to his patience in dealing with the high command.

1. The reference is to Roman Kolkowicz's assessment of Soviet party-military relations. See his *The Soviet Military and the Communist Party* (Princeton, N.J., 1967), 11.

2. "We Are Not Going to Divide Up the Army," Lobov's interview with V. Tkachenko and A. Cherniak, *Pravda,* 9 September 1992. What was also significant in the interview is that Lobov had conceded the Ministry of Defense to civilians, although given his vision of future military organization the MOD would clearly be the less important of the two military organs subordinate to the union president as supreme commander-in-chief. Also see "The New Chief of the Soviet General Staff. General Lobov on the Armed Forces' Structure During the Transitional Period," *Nezavisimaia gazeta,* 3 September 1991.

3. Vladimir N. Lobov, "The Army on the Brink of Reform. The Chief of the General Staff Tells Military Attaches What It Will Be Like," *Izvestiia,* 28 September 1991.

4. *Komsomolskaia pravda,* 10 September 1991.

5. TASS, 9 December 1991, reported in *Foreign Broadcast Information Service, Daily Report. Soviet Union* (hereafter FBIS-SOV), FBIS-SOV-91-237, 10 December 1991, 35.

6. *Pravda,* 13 December 1991.

7. TASS, 13 December 1991, in FBIS-SOV-91-241, 16 December 1991, 29.

8. *Krasnaia zvezda,* 17 December 1991.

9. "What Brought About the Changes in the General Staff?" *Izvestiia,* 10 December 1991.

10. Ukraine's decision was clearly foreshadowed in Kravchuk's announcement in late 1991, while the USSR was still in existence, that Ukraine would form its own armed forces. See *Nezavisimaia gazeta,* 24 October 91. Prior to the dissolution of the USSR Shaposhnikov expressed alarm over Ukraine's decision to move ahead with creating its own army. He noted that he had discussed the issue with the Ukrainian defense minister "to no avail," and objected to the "haste" with which Kiev was moving on the issue "without having asked the Army." *Moscow News,* No. 44, 3-10 November 1991.

11. For a discussion of the General Staff and its role in promoting military professionalism as a bulwark against military intervention in politics, see Kenneth M. Currie, "Soviet Military Politics. Contemporary Issues" (New York, 1992), especially Chapter 5.

12. *Voennaia mysl, Spetsialnyi vypusk* (May 1992), 9. Emphasis added.

13. Ibid.

14. "Officers to Be Appointed on a Competitive Basis." *Kuranty,* 20 May 91.

15. "Army General Pavel Grachev. Clear Calculation and Common Sense Are Required in Forming the Russian Army," *Krasnaia zvezda,* 21 July 1992.

16. Currie, "Soviet Military Politics," Chapter 3.

17. "Thanks, Poles, for Putting Up with Us for 47 Years," *Novoe vremia,* No. 26 (23 June 1992), 28, 29.

18. "General Kolesnikov. The Armed Forces Are Only a Tool in the Hands of the Government," *Nezavisimaia gazeta,* 3 July 1992.

19. *Voennaia mysl, spetsialnyy vypusk*, 4.
20. Ibid., 3-4.
21. Pavel Felgengauer, "Military Expects Intervention by the West. Grim Prospects for Russian Foreign and Defense Policy," *Nezavisimaia gazeta*, 1 August 92.
22. "Army General Pavel Grachev. Clear Calculation and Common Sense Are Needed in Forming the Russian Army," loc. cit.
23. Ibid.
24. "The Army. Overcoming Arrhythmia," *Rossiiskie vesti*, 29 May 1992.
25. Interfax, 28 March 1992, in FBIS-SOV-92-062, 31 March 1992, 31.
26. Currie, "Soviet Military Politics," 224-226.
27. "Do the Generals Hate Urazhtsev?" *Kuranty*, 25 June 1992. Urazhtsev is the head of the well-known officers' union *Shchit* (Shield).
28. "Decision Made to Hold All-Army Officers' Meeting," *Krasnaia zvezda*, 7 January 1992.
29. "Real Support for Army Reform. This Most Likely Will Come from the 'Middle Echelon' of the Officer Corps and the Young Officers," *Nezavisimaia gazeta*, 20 February 1992.
30. *Nezavisimaia gazeta*, 5 February 1992.
31. Ibid.
32. Radio Moscow, 21 January 1992, in FBIS-SOV-91-014, 59.
33. *Postfactum*, 12 February 1992, in FBIS-SOV-92-031, 14 February 1992, 17.
34. "Officers' Meetings Will Operate," *Krasnaia zvezda*, 17 June 1992; "Officers to Be Appointed on a Competitive Basis," *Kuranty*, 20 May 92.
35. ITAR-TASS, 25 June 1992, in FBIS-SOV-92-123, 25 June 1992, 72.
36. "Will There Be a Unified Army on the Territory of the Eleven States?" *Izvestiia*, 14 January 1992.
37. "Appeal to the Personnel of Military Units Performing Service in the States of the Baltic, Transcaucasus, and Moldova," *Krasnaia zvezda*, 30 June 1992.
38. A. Kakotkin, "Lull for the Time Being on the Fronts," *Moskovskie novosti*, No 27, 5 July 1992.
39. Vladimir Socor, "14th Army Commander Criticizes Yeltsin...," Radio Free Europe/Radio Liberty Daily Report, No. 127, 7 July 1992.
40. Kakotkin, "Lull on the Fronts."
41. But not fast enough for some of Yeltsin's critics. Former Gorbachev aide Aleksandr Yakovlev argued that Lebed's continuation in his post reflected an indecisiveness of the Russian president that would lead him to repeat the same mistakes as Gorbachev and thus "repeat the sad path of the Union." Yakovlev wondered whether a "power which does not know how to control the 'personal initiative' of gallant generals [is] powerless," or whether Yeltsin was just playing a "complex game, unafraid of jeopardizing human lives?" See Yakovlev's article, "Repeat of the Past," *Moskovskie novosti*, No. 28, 12 July 1992.
42. ITAR-TASS, 7 July 1992, in FBIS-SOV-92-131, 8 July 1992, 20.
43. "Lebed Permitted to Speak," *Komsomolskaia pravda*, 10 July 19921.
44. "He Went Too Far," *Moskovskii komsomolets*, 18 July 1992.
45. Interfax, 30 July 1992, in FBIS-SOV-92-147, 30 July 1992, 31.
46. "General Staff. Troop Cuts in the Southern Kuriles Must Be Halted. Russian Armed Forces Leadership Conclusion Signed by General Dubynin Adopts a Hardline Position," *Nezavisimaia gazeta*, 30 July 1992.
47. "Andrey Kozyrev. 'War Party on the Offensive.' Foreign Minister Warns of the Danger of a Coup d'Etat," *Izvestiia*, 1 July 1992.
48. Currie, "Soviet Military Politics," 226.
49. *Argumenty i fakty*, No. 12, March 1992, in FBIS-SOV-92-063, 1 April 1992, 16.

50. ITAR-TASS, 21 July 1992, in FBIS-SOV-92-141, 22 July 1992, 20. What is interesting about the report is that Krasnaia zvezda failed to mention Yeltsin's criticisms of the military in its account of the 21 July meeting in the Kremlin, although it did note his criticism of local government leaders for failing to fulfill their commitments to help resolve the military's social problems. See "Servicemen and Their Families Should Not Be the Victims of Unsettled Lives. The Russian President Examines Questions of Social Protection for Servicemen," *Krasnaia zvezda*, 23 July 1992.

RUSSIAN REGIONAL DEFENSE CONVERSION, 1992–1993

Sonia Ben Ouagrahm

The dissolution of the USSR and the economic reforms launched in 1992–1993 stripped the military complex of its homogeneity, economic power and organized political influence. Military industry became the arbitrator of political battles and continued to receive a great amount of financing from the state. This renewed influence did not allow the military complex to become a political force able to exert an efficient influence on political and economic decisions. Although its influence clearly was evident in the softening of shock therapy as soon as mid-1992, the military complex was distributed among conflicting groups which used defense enterprises as allies in their bureaucratic battles. The military complex also lost cohesion after the dissolution of the Committee for Military Industry (Voenno-Promyshlenyi Komitet—VPK) and creation of a multitude of departments, services and administrations within the executive and legislative branches in Moscow and the regions. Though palpable, the influence of the military complex was unable to better organize the conversion process and showed little success. Defense directors became disillusioned with the new order.

The disillusion of 1992–1993 stemmed from unrealistic expectations that the defense enterprises would nest in the conversion process. They viewed the hardships they endured as a lesser evil inasmuch as their newly acquired independence would allow them to compensate for the loss of political and economic clout through intensified international cooperation. However, foreign investors' interest in Russian defense technology materialized only in a few instances of real cooperation. The quick, easy and cheap conversion that defense directors expected did not occur. To the contrary, these first few years of conversion revealed all the obstacles and problems the defense enterprises must solve before they could convert. The Soviet legacy in terms of production organization and mentalities was one of them. It also became clear that conversion of the defense industry was only one aspect of the restructuring of the Russian economy. Conversion proved more complex than originally estimated and its extent revealed greater problems since it embraced not only weapons producers but also all regional enterprises. As the reforms splintered the Russian economy, the impact on the regional defense enterprises appeared and proliferated.

GREAT EXPECTATIONS AND DISILLUSIONS

In the beginning defense enterprises were rather supportive of a new approach to conversion.

In 1992 the new government conceived of conversion in very liberal terms. No conversion policy or even an industrial policy had been designed and the defense enterprises had to conceive their own conversion programs according to their local technical and financial means. Simultaneously, military expenditures dropped by 68 percent.[1] This decline translated into deregulation of most prices and privatization and commercialization of public enterprises. A law on conversion was signed on 20 April 1992 which defined the framework for conversion by the federal government, VPK, branch ministries, and the Communist Party.

Defense enterprises welcomed these measures since they sharply contrasted with those of the previous government and because they expected to derive quick and substantial profits from the process. In the late 1980s Gorbachev handled the conversion process in a very authoritative way. The objective was to reverse the scale of military and civilian production which accounted for 60 percent and 40 percent of the total production respectively. In order to reach that goal two tactics were used. The first consisted of transferring civilian enterprises to VPK to increase their productivity and to shift to civilian producers the work of defense enterprises.

Both tactics were unsuccessful since they were based on the belief that defense enterprises would be efficient. Of 120 new products that the defense industry was to produce, only 23 were released.[2]

The conversion program to civilian products was planned with little attention to the need for certain types of goods. Some enterprises of the aviation sector were to produce equipment for fruit and vegetable processing, and packaging equipment.[3] No inventory of existing facilities was conducted. The planners also paid little attention to the enterprises' social and economic role in their regions. While military orders remained compulsory, no additional resources were planned to finance the new civilian production. The realization of this program was entrusted to VPK, the Ministry of Defense and Gosplan, which had no real interests in making reform successful. Many defense directors opposed the effort and refused to cooperate. Instead they tried to develop cooperation with foreigners on the basis of their expertise outside government supervision.

Decentralization affected the defense industry. Instead of executing orders issued by federal agencies which knew little about the strengths and weaknesses of each facility, defense enterprises pursued their own conversion programs based on their own technical and financial means. The privatization process allowed them to reinforce their cooperation with foreigners and attract foreign investment. They deemed this would decrease their dependence on the government. They expected to derive important profits from the sale of their equipment and technologies after deregulation of prices, and to compensate for their losses of military orders and subsidies.

Although foreign investors showed great interest in Russian technologies and equipment, the economic and political instability that resulted from the USSR collapse and the reforms that followed discouraged them from cooperating with Russians during the conversion process. They expected a legal framework to protect their investments. No insurance for repatriating profits nor a law on intellectual property were in force. There was no guarantee that an appeal to the courts could be filed. But Russian directors prevented greater commitment from foreign investors since they were reluctant to give information about their enterprises and technologies, and admit a lack of knowledge of commercial trade and negotiation techniques.

In mid-1992 defense enterprises experienced the backlash of liberalized policy. They lost their main source of financing when military orders decreased by two-thirds and they were unable to find new outlets for their production. Inflation reached unprecedented levels, some 2,510 percent in 1992 and 847 percent in 1993. The liberalization of prices resulted in a sudden and uncontrolled increase in prices. Defense enterprises increased their prices by 200 percent overnight without considering the negative effect on the production system. Such inflation levels should have paralyzed the production system. Although the decrease in production was important, 19 percent in 1992 and 15 percent in 1993 were still low compared to the level of inflation. Defense enterprises maintained their production levels by supplying each other with goods and services often without paying each other or their employees. This resulted in the emergence of barter networks that forced decentralization.

Defense enterprises also faced growing liquidity problems. One cause was the newly created commercial banks and their ability to withhold clients' funds for speculation purposes thereby depriving enterprises of the use of their own money. Banks also rarely granted credit owing to high risks, and when they did credit was very short-term with very high interest rates. The state also was a major source of illiquidity when it sequestrated funds voted in the budget to control inflation. In December 1993 such withholding accounted for 1,000 billion rubles or about $800 million at December 1993 exchange rates, of which about R700 million were destined to defense enterprises.[4] The government debt owed its suppliers had a high multiplier effect inasmuch as the total debt generated by government borrowing was estimated at 2,000 trillion rubles.[5]

The growing indebtedness and liquidity problems translated into late payment of salaries that ranged from several months to a year. Some defense enterprises closed their doors for several months while others decreased the working week to three or four days. This caused a decrease in the fiscal revenues of local and regional budgets, and a high federal budget deficit owing to the inability of the Russian state to collect taxes. In 1992 the monetization index decreased from 62.4 percent in 1990 to 4.1 percent in 1993.[6] In summer 1993 barter accounted for a whopping 45 percent of industrial exchanges.[7]

This financial crisis occurred in the context of public enterprise privatization. Although the first privatization program mostly concerned small and medium-size enterprises, some defense enterprises also received instructions to start preparing a privatization program. In St. Petersburg defense enterprises developed privatization programs before the end of 1992 since otherwise they risked an auction sale.[8] This privatization program was in fact a conversion program in disguise because defense enterprises described their planned future activities, production, outlets, and means of financing.[9] We now know that the threat of an auction sale was not used due to the intervention of local leaders who wanted to avoid social unrest in their regions. But defense directors had no guarantee that local leaders would intervene or be successful. Therefore privatization, which first was well greeted because it was a promise of greater freedom and independence, became a major problem that needed to be solved urgently.

This fact generated opposition directed at the process rather than privatization itself.

Defense directors criticized the privatization process on three main points. The first criticism concerned the pace and scope of the privatization process, which endangered their production and conversion plans. The directors also considered the privatization law too rigid since it proposed only three privatization variants that did not take into account the diversity and specificity of the defense industry.[10] Their third criticism was that the privatization regulations were either unavailable or too often modified for local implementation. As a result defense enterprises faced very high uncertainty and designed their own privatization rules, which often differed from the regulations promulgated by the Committee for Federal Property (Gosudarstvennyi Komitet Imushchestvo).

The conversion process from 1992 to 1993 was different from what defense directors originally expected. Indeed, conversion had to take place in a very volatile environment, without proper funding or guidelines. This generated a rapid evolution of the way directors conceived conversion, which translated into specific adjustment models, and combined various conversion and restructuring strategies.

THE EVOLUTION

Conversion was mostly a "technology-push" phenomenon. This approach was one of the main reasons why defense enterprises concentrated their efforts on foreign investment. Sales of technologies to foreign enterprises were preferred conversion strategies. Even though defense enterprises kept on designing their projects according to their Russian technologies, their expectations led to four important results.

First, defense directors came to understand that the total conversion of their enterprises was an impossible task. Various civilian and military products and the size of their social infrastructures made them too rigid to change. The idea of a partial conversion then began to gain favor.

Defense directors also realized that relying on foreign markets for conversion was a mistake. Not only did a lack of incentives for foreign investors fail to commit to the conversion process in Russia, it was also clear that defense directors did not really understand the needs and demands of foreigners. A change in thinking was needed for cooperation between defense enterprises and local enterprises.

The reorganization of regional defense production appeared to be an unstable trend. Even if some enterprises tried to maintain production links with their former Soviet partners, the sharp increase in communication and transportation costs made this option unsustainable for most of them. They therefore started to find new clients and new partners nearby.

Finally, not all defense enterprises were able to convert. This was due to the characteristics of each branch and the Soviet legacy in terms of management and production organization. Some enterprises were indeed too specialized and could not use their technologies, facilities and personnel in civilian sectors. Others were poorly located or too important to local economies in terms of labor and contributions to local and regional budgets. The introduction of the market colluded with the Soviet legacy of conversion.

These evolutions generated a conversion process where defense enterprises had to use their resources to ensure their survival. This required them to maintain a sufficient labor force and to contemplate production that might have no direct connection with their specific defense technologies.

Some defense technologies and "technological culture"[11] had to be preserved. This could not endanger the integrity of the parent company because production links existing between the various elements had to be maintained, even when Moscow tried to implement privatization.

These principles generated three adjustment models by regional and local defense enterprises.[12]

First, defense enterprises designed new products either simultaneously (A) or successively (A'). The multiplication of activiues was based on existing technologies aimed at determining which activity was the most adapted to the new environment. In other words, defense enterprises tried to identify new sources of profit. They acted like sonar to locate and define objects in a strange, unknown environment. If new activities generated a profit, defense enterprises could choose to concentrate their resources on them. Otherwise they would design new products until one of them obtained positive results. New activities appeared and others disappeared rapidly according to shifting environments.

Second (B), defense enterprises concentrated their activities on civilian products based on dual-use technologies. They often maintained their former other activities at a lower level either because they were obliged to do so under military orders or because they planned a slow decline of these activities to stretch out their work and responsibilities.

Third (C), defense enterprises concentrated their resources on military activities and abandoned their other activities either slowly or immediately. This decision might be motivated by the existence of demand on the domestic or international arms markets. It also might be the result of the director's assuming that there would be increased demand in the future.

RUSSIAN DEFENSE ENTERPRISE ADJUSTMENT STRATEGIES, 1992–1993

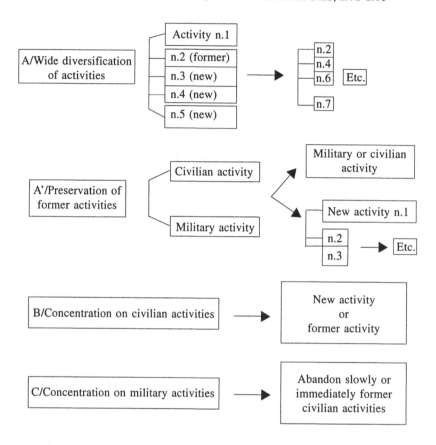

Defense enterprises also designed several restructuring strategies. Many defense enterprises divided into smaller entities based on various existing departments or factories. This restructuring model gave birth to new entities based on a coherent technological chain. The aim of the restructuring was to decrease the cost of their maintenance by allowing them to find new clients while participating in the parent company's main activity.

The various defense entities had separate and unrelated activities and were supposed to develop, adapt and convert independently.

Many enterprises also added new activities through joint ventures. Sometimes they created financial institutions (pocket banks) whose functions were to channel Central Bank credits directly to enterprises.

Other enterprises decreased the level or abandoned altogether their civilian production to reinforce their military profile. These enterprises usually preserved their Soviet structure and organization and even enlarged their social infrastructures.

Very few enterprises transferred their social infrastructures to local authorities. Social infrastructures were offered as a payment in kind to employees. In some cities, like Moscow and St. Petersburg, social infrastructures were a source of wealth since the price of real estate was rising.

Defense enterprises used all these strategies as a function of their needs and the possibilities offered to them. The charts above give some examples of the combinations used by various enterprises.[13]

ST. PETERSBURG LENINETZ ELECTRONICS DIVERSIFICATION

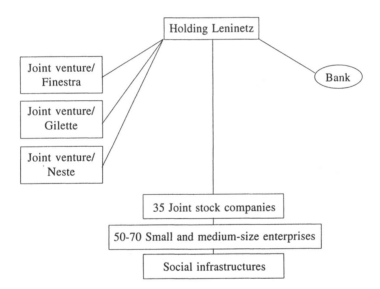

SARATOV AVIATION FACTORY CIVILIAN CONVERSION

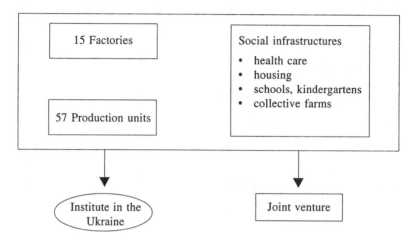

VYMPEL MILITARY CONVERSION

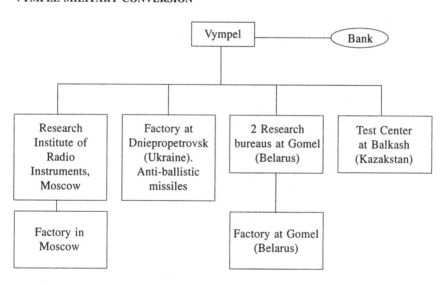

Each strategy had advantages and drawbacks but no clear correlation may be drawn between a specific strategy and conversion success or failure. The analysis of case studies revealed also an important difference because some enterprises tried to understand their environment better and evolved according to incentives and/or limits of their environment. The motivations behind these varied approaches greatly influenced future defense enterprises to convert and to implement useful strategies.

The conversion process in 1992–1993 has been considered a failure. Instead of creating a sound foundation it paved the way for an uncontrolled and counterproductive restructuring of industry. The financial situation deteriorated so much that many defense enterprises were bankrupted. The increasing uncertainty that resulted from the destruction of the former potential economic institutional framework dramatically limited conversion. Defense industries lacked finances, time and organization, enterprises mainly aimed at ensuring their survival, and this led them to make contradictory and apparently irrational decisions. Many believed that, if such conditions were to endure, the industry must eventually disappear. Even though the situation worsened in many respects in following years, defense enterprises resisted these obstacles.

RESISTING THE SHOCK OF CONVERSION

Defense directors in 1992–1993 increased their economic and political clout in their regions and in Moscow. The impact of defense enterprises on regional policies is revealed by their growing social functions. Russian defense enterprises employed from 2,000 to 100,000 people to whom they provided medical care, schooling, daycare, housing, and leisure activities. These social services were created and maintained by individual enterprises. The new government did not liberate defense enterprises from their social functions after the Soviet collapse. No federal social system existed to replace those organized by defense enterprises. Enterprises remained as production units and as social administrations. These two functions contradict each other in Russia's new economy. The absence of adequate funding for conversion and the rapid rhythm of privatization endangered the social milieu. One reaction was creation of alliances which unified local directors, employees and local authorities against federal rules.

The transformation of defense enterprises into joint stock companies gave directors a major role in these new alliances. Outside control of defense enterprises could lead to layoffs and dramatic changes in corporate social policy. But, often on the advice of directors themselves, employees opted for control of 51 percent of the shares according to privatization laws.[14] Directors were thus confirmed in their role of "protectors" of their employees and became "leaders" of an electorate local authorities could not ignore.

One of directors' priorities was therefore to maintain their enterprises' workforce since their political and economic influence was measured by the number of employees. In spite of sharp decreases in production the official unemployment rate remained low. On 1 January 1994 the number of registered unemployed was 835,500. Instead of laying off personnel, directors negotiated departures, salaries and working time. This allowed them to decrease wage costs while maintaining employees on the payroll and allowing them to use social infrastructures.

Consequently, the privatization process and disorganization of the economy allowed the emergence of local interests which eventually evolved into organized alliances that challenged the decisions of the federal government. This was the first factor which allowed defense enterprises to resist the shock of conversion.

THE FEDERAL DEFENSE SECTOR

Defense directors also exerted a strong impact at the federal level. Their influence was channeled through industrial associations, lobbies, and even parties that took advantage of the power struggle between the federal executive and legislative branches.

The collapse of the USSR enhanced the influence of VPK, and defense enterprises were placed under the Ministry of Industry. Privatization, economic reforms and the consequent confusion completed the destruction of the cohesion of the military complex at the federal level.

But by 1992 the defense sector reemerged through a cabinet reshuffling. The Ministry of Industry, which proved unmanageable, was dissolved and defense enterprises were placed under the Russian Committee for Defense Industry (Roskomoboronprom). Roskomoboronprom was to coordinate state orders and supervise research and development and export control. Later this committee became the State Committee for Defense Industry (Goskomoboronprom). Thereafter the defense sector influenced government bodies. The defense directors were still considered influential individuals.

The consequences of the directors' growing influence was generally negative for the conversion process. As early as mid-1992 defense enterprises realized that conversion was not an easy process and began lobbying for an increase in military orders. Many of the competing administrations and individuals supported them. President Yeltsin encouraged defense enterprises to intensify exports of military hardware by promising they would be allowed to keep 80 percent of the profits.[15] At this time Mikhail Malei, former advisor to President Yeltsin for conversion issues, launched an "economic conversion" program which consisted of financing conversion with the profits derived from arms exports. The Ministry of Foreign Economic Relations also announced that it had received orders for military hardware amounting to R37.1 billion at 1991 prices. In March 1992 Yegor Gaidar signed a decree ordering $5.4 billion worth of military hardware, approximately four times 1991 exports.[16] Unfortunately, all these promises were not realized because of the surplus of unsold military hardware.

Federal funding to defense enterprises changed too. After military orders were cut defense enterprises were financed in new and different ways. For instance, they received loans from the state at a 10 percent interest rate.[17] They also received subsidies from ministries and other federal agencies engaged in defense and economic affairs. In 1993 defense enterprises received one trillion rubles to finance their conversion and these funds paid late salaries.[18] In 1992 the government decided to cancel the huge R3.5 trillion inter-enterprise debt, which greatly benefited defense enterprises.[19]

Defense directors were able to soften reform policy to ensure their survival. This produced a paradoxical situation. While the impact of defense enterprises on economic decisions increased at both the regional and federal levels, it did not allow a better organization of the conversion process. Directors took advantage of the situation to advance their own or their enterprises' interests but their activity was disorganized and resulted in greater uncertainty. No coherent armament and conversion policies were designed due to "bureaucratic competition."

CREATION OF REGIONAL AND INDUSTRIAL ASSOCIATIONS[20]

Defense industrial and regional associations emerged due to federal weakness and the shifting of funds. These associations had the virtue of stabilizing the environment and allowing the restructuring and conversion of defense enterprises.

In the late 1980s St. Petersburg began creating industrial associations. They were often a response to the government's authoritative approach to conversion but their aim was to promote a conversion process based on expertise and technologies and not to resist conversion.

Defense associations, in order to solve financial problems and maintain their production, created new economic relationships called production networks. The participating enterprises were linked to each other through debt and production. Barter was the means of exchange. The participating enterprises canceled their mutual debts on a regular basis by providing each other with services and goods. Although these networks could not work efficiently without a sufficient number of enterprises, they were associated with other enterprises.

For instance, in Vladivostok defense enterprises created industrial associations and production networks to make up for the lack of funding and organization. They launched this process very early. One of the first industrial associations, known as "Red Pine," was created in 1989 by the famous helicopter producer Progress, and included local civilian and military enterprises as well as the local branch of "Sberbank" (National Savings Bank).

In 1993 another association was created to harmonize the conversion process, avoid duplication, design common production projects, and promote defense enterprises productions abroad.

Unfortunately, these associations remained empty shells. Their inefficiency was mainly due to the extreme specialization of local enterprises prior to the dissolution of the USSR. Local enterprises produced or assembled parts of a weapon or system that were sent to end producers in European and Central Russia. Since the local economy was not diversified, local defense enterprises could not find substitutes for their former Soviet partners.

Omsk employed industrial associations under the auspices of the regional association's Siberian Agreement (Sibirskoe soglashenie). The Siberian Agreement was created in 1990 with its main objective to preserve links between Siberian enterprises and protect them against the consequences of poorly designed conversion.

After the break-up of the USSR the association's role evolved. A policy for Siberian economic reorganization was created. Because Siberian enterprises were very dependent on the Soviet organization of production, the dissolution of the USSR deprived most of them of their partners. For example, power plants in Omsk used coal from Kazakhstan while Siberian gas and oil producers received their equipment from Azerbaijan, Ukraine and Moldavia. To limit the effect of the dissolution of the USSR on their economies, the Siberian regions created production associations which united various Siberian enterprises to create coherent production chains unlike other parts of the Russian Federation.

RUSSIAN FEDERATION CONVERSION BY REGION

One of the issues that intrigued many observers between 1992 and 1993 was how the defense enterprises made their choices and what factors determined the failure or success. The use of a specific conversion or restructuring strategy is not a valid explanation because different enterprises could use the same strategy with varying success. The branch factor was an inadequate explanation. Although we cannot deny the fact that some branches, such as the aviation and space industries, had more chances to succeed in their conversion, case studies showed that there was great differentiation among enterprises within each branch.

But the most important question is how to measure the success and failure of conversion. Conversion in Russia was much different than in Europe and the United States. The simultaneous change in the economic, political and geostrategic environments created so many obstacles to conversion that it was difficult to determine what impact director decisions had on conversion results.

There was no clear regional differentiation at the beginning of the conversion process but it started to emerge by the end of 1993. The struggle for federal power, the weakening of the Russian state, and Yeltsin's reforms resulted in fragmentation of the economy. These events reduced the perimeter of conversion to regions where defense enterprises were located. The result of their conversion was very dependent on regional characteristics.

At the beginning of the conversion process defense enterprises generally began by diversifying production. Diversification is a Soviet tradition. Defense enterprises in the Soviet era planned both military and civilian production. They also developed a certain level of self-sufficiency and thereby increased their power and reduced the impact of the failing supply system. Diversification was a logical continuation of a Soviet tradition.

The main drawback of this strategy is that it dispersed resources. Most defense enterprises launched new products destined for different markets and requiring differing expertise. They seldom learned whether there was sufficient demand for their new products and therefore rarely derived a profit. This is quite understandable inasmuch as they were in the process of learning market rules.

Such strategy proved sustainable only in regions where there were sufficient sources of financing and a sufficient variety of clients and partners. It also required an economic environment allowing the learning process so directors could distinguish between successes and failures.

These were the characteristics of Northwest Russia. It attracted the greatest number of foreign investors, foreign enterprises, and international organizations, including embassies, consulates and foreign banks. The banking system developed quickly in this region. The presence of Moscow officials allowed defense enterprises to use their connections more easily and regularly to obtain extra-budgetary funds. The Northwest was also the birthplace of Russian and foreign consulting firms that rendered a number of services to defense enterprises, including audits, networking and assistance with the privatization process. In short, they helped defense enterprises to learn market rules more quickly. St. Petersburg is a good example of this evolution. In 1992-1993 consulting firms were the main architects of conversion and privatization.[21]

The Northwest also had a very diversified military complex that allowed defense enterprises to set contacts with new partners to design new products or continue their former production.

Enterprises could use a wide range of conversion and restructuring strategies. They diversified with new production while maintaining their former production. They often adopted activities unrelated to their area of expertise. Some enterprises derived profits from assembly of equipment for a foreign partner, or from leasing their unused production space to local enterprises. A large number of joint ventures were created thanks to presence of numerous research institutes. Local defense enterprises were also among the first to create pocket banks and other financial institutions.

In central Russia and the Far East the wide diversification strategy could not be maintained in the long term without endangering the survival of defense enterprises. These regions were much less diversified than the Northwest. They attracted fewer foreign investors. The distance that separated them from Moscow did not allow them to obtain extra-budgetary funds on a regular basis. Local economies were often dependent on a few economic sectors badly hurt by the crisis, such as the defense industry and agriculture. A wide diversification program was too costly in 1993 when the government started using public funds to decrease inflation. A concentration of resources on military or civilian production was necessary for the survival of defense enterprises. The economic specialization of local economies limited the ability of defense enterprises to develop new clientele and new partnerships. This led defense enterprises to maintain their former civilian or military production and links. Some enterprises tried to develop agricultural equipment for the other local economic sectors or they cooperated with local authorities to modernize municipal and regional transportation and telephone systems. Regional differentiation translated into a variety of possible conversion strategies. The Northwest region allowed defense enterprises to choose between wide diversification and a concentration on military or civilian activities. The other regions had a smaller range of potential strategies.

Conversion did not concern arms producers only. It affected all civilian enterprises that had direct connections with weapons production. They were hit by the decrease in defense expenses just as badly as defense enterprises, and they also needed to adjust to decrease in demand. Further, the regionalization of the economy increased the extent and the difficulty of conversion in the regions having many defense enterprises and a specialized economy. In these regions failure of conversion could entail the complete collapse of local economies. This explains why the enterprises located in these regions reinforced their rigidities as a means of survival.

The importance of the notion of survival and the ability of defense enterprises to survive in a very uncertain environment have been generally underestimated. This led many observers to consider the process a failure. There is no doubt that the process was unsuccessful in the sense that it did not allow transformation of defense enterprises into profit-driven enterprises producing quality goods. But it was successful in the main objective, to survive.

The underestimation of the importance of survival also led to a number of miscalculations and assumptions in the evolution of the conversion.

In 1992 Russian leaders and their foreign advisors failed to recognize that the Russian economy was structurally mobilized. The military complex was at the heart of the economy; it constituted the greatest part of Soviet industry, and it had imposed its mode of operation on the civilian sector. A great number of civilian goods were produced according to military standards. The over-development of the military complex also resulted in a structural deficit. The communication and transportation systems were underdeveloped, and there was an insufficient number of big power plants. These facts deprived the civilian sectors of the means to develop. Russia inherited an economy where exchanges could not take place and where the civilian sector was not developed enough to replace the military sector in the economy. No conversion and no reform could take place in such conditions. A demobilization of the economy was, and still is, required. This implies a decrease in military expenditures and the creation of a civilian economy to allow exchanges to take place without obstacles.

It appears that between 1992 and 1993 the main conversion restructuring and strategies had been designed. The choices made by defense enterprises oriented them on trajectories that some found difficult to modify. It was also the period when the military sector ceased being an homogeneous group with sufficient common interests to exert an efficient political influence, and was transformed into a heterogeneous set of actors with conflicting interests and objectives whose influence, although real, was disorganized and inefficient as far as conversion was concerned.

Finally, it was the period when the regional aspect of conversion emerged. As regionalization and regionalism "trapped" defense enterprises in their regions, the regional economic, political and social environment became one of the main factors influencing the success or failure of conversion.

1. "Conversion of Defense Industry Changes Concepts," *Military Technology* (March 1993) 54.
2. *La reforme de l'industrie de defense sovietique,* ICPSI, July 1991.
3. Sonia Ben Ouagrahm, *Le desarmement et la conversion de l'industrie militaire en Russie,* UNIDIR, Research Paper No. 24, (New York, 1993).

4. Jacques Sapir, *Le secteur militaro-industriel dans la desintegration russe,* Centre d'Etude des Modes d'Industrialisation, Ecole des Hautes Etudes en Sciences Sociales (Paris, Feb 1994).

5. Sapir, *Le secteur militaro-industriel.*

6. It is worth noting that the monetization index of 1990 has been calculated on the basis of regulated prices, and it may not reflect reality. Source: Yevgeny Yasin, "L'economie de la Russie et sa politique economique," *Politique Etrangere,* Vol. 4 (Paris, 1997), 525.

7. Sapir, *Le secteur militaro-industriel.*

8. Interviews with local directors conducted by the author.

9. Idem.

10. For a detailed description of the privatization program, see Ouagrahm, *Le desarmement.*

11. By "technological culture" is meant the set of explicit and implicit knowledge shared by members of a team or company which allows them to approach and solve a problem in a specific way. For a detailed discussion of this issue, see Sapir, "Les bases futures de la puissance militaire russe," *Cahiers d'Etudes Strategiques,* No.16; CIRPES, Ecoles des Hautes Etudes en Sciences Sociales, 1993.

12. The three models presented here are constructed for the purpose of this paper. Even if we can find in the real world cases of enterprises whose evolution is very similar to these models, they are nonetheless not as clear-cut as presented here.

13. The flow charts presented here do not aim at giving a complete description of the enterprises' activities. They only aim at presenting the various restructuring trends of the 1992-1993 period.

14. Katharina Pistor, *Privatization and Corporate Governance in Russia. An Empirical Study* (n.d., n.p.).

15. V. Shlykhov, "Economic Readjustment Within the Russian Defense-Industrial Complex," *Security Dialogue,* Vol. 26, No. 1 (1995), 19-34.

16. Ibid.

17. Ouagrahm, *Le desarmement.*

18. V. Shlykhov, "Economic Readjustment."

19. Ibid.

20. Ouagrahm, *La conversion des entreprises de defense en Russie. Une analyse regionale,* (Ph.D. diss., Ecole des Hautes Etudes en Sciences Sociales, Paris, 1999).

21. Ouagrahm, *Le desarmement.*

THE END OF THE WESTERN GROUP OF FORCES

Randall E. Newnham

INTRODUCTION

On 31 August 1994 the last soldiers of the former Western Group of Soviet Forces left Germany. The final troop train departed from Karlshorst, outside of Berlin, the very spot where the unconditional surrender of the German Wehrmacht was signed on 8 May 1945. This departure brought to an end a fascinating four-year period in which the Western Group of Forces (WGF) gradually and peacefully was disbanded.[1] A force which, at the end of the 1980s, was still seen as

the most threatening of all Soviet armies—poised to invade Western Europe—
was suddenly no more.

How could the end of this powerful army have come about so quickly and
quietly? One of the most critical factors was German economic influence. In
1990, as part of the negotiations leading to German unification, the West German
government agreed to pay the USSR billions of Deutsche Marks in aid, which aid
was linked explicitly to the prompt withdrawal of the WGF. Yet the aid package
not only influenced Gorbachev and top Soviet political leaders and, later, the
Yeltsin leadership, it also affected Soviet military leaders and rank-and-file members of the WGF. The impact of the official aid program was only heightened by
the effects of German monetary unification (1 July 1990) and full German unification (3 October 1990). Suddenly WGF soldiers found themselves living in a
capitalist environment. By 1992-1993 the WGF had virtually ceased to exist as
a fighting force and it many of its members were more concerned with personal
gain than military duty. Crime, espionage, and desertion flourished. The economic
influence of the West, both in the form of direct German government payments
for housing, salaries, and transport, and in the indirect form of the temptations
of Western lifestyle, seemed to have dissolved the WGF like a sugar cube in a
hot cup of coffee.

This chapter traces the process of the dissolution of the WGF through several
key stages. First, the vital role of the WGF in the postwar European order is discussed as a legacy of the Second World War. Next, an examination of top-level
negotiations which led to the Soviet decision to withdraw the WGF demonstrates
that German economic aid played a key role in facilitating this decision. There
were two stages in this process. The initial withdrawal timetable was hammered
out in a dramatic series of meetings in the summer and fall of 1990, most notably the July 1990 Kohl-Gorbachev meeting held in Moscow and the Caucasus.
Later, at a December 1992 meeting between Kohl and Boris Yeltsin, Germany
was able to use a new aid package to further accelerate the original withdrawal
timetable agreed to by the Gorbachev government. Finally, the chapter surveys
the effects of the aid package on both the Russian military leadership and the
WGF rank and file. Economic factors were important in turning a number of top
officers from skeptics to advocates of German unification and this in turn had a
noticeable impact on the eventual Soviet decision to accept German unity. Meanwhile, the officers and men of the WGF began to rush to secure their share of
the benefits made available by reunification in a variety of legal and illegal ways.
In the end, it will become clear that this case stands as a striking example of an
elite military force defeated by political and economic factors more easily than
by military power.

THE ROLE OF THE WGF

From the moment the Berlin Wall fell, signaling that German unification was no
longer a remote impossibility, the fate of the WGF was to be a central issue in
the reunification process. Many analysts have concluded that the collapse of East
Germany and the withdrawal of the WGF were inevitable. But many of the same
analysts argued that the USSR, even under a reformist government, would never

sacrifice its foothold in Germany. Gorbachev had advanced such new foreign policy concepts as the notion of a common European home and some US government analysts asserted the clarion call for a free and united Europe as largely a maneuver designed to weaken NATO ties.[2] The Soviets were by no means eager to leave Germany quietly. Even after the fall of the Berlin Wall the threat of some form of Soviet military intervention in East Germany seemed a real possibility. The negotiations over the pullout of the WGF were long and tense and bringing them to a successful conclusion required both great skill and Western concessions, particularly German economic concessions.

In order to understand the difficulties involved in negotiating the pullout of the WGF it is first necessary to understand the special nature of the WGF as a powerful force central to the Cold War balance of power, and deeply tied to the legacy of the Second World War in both legal and emotional terms.

At the time of the Berlin Wall's fall the WGF consisted of nineteen Soviet combat divisions with 400,000 men. This force was comparable to the entire West German Bundeswehr and larger than the Soviet presence in all of Eastern Europe.[3] The WGF also was equipped with modern weaponry and kept at full battle strength, unlike many Soviet units. Soviet tactical nuclear weapons stationed in the German Democratic Republic (GDR) included some 166 aircraft bombs and missiles, 50 nuclear artillery projectiles, and 284 ballistic missiles.[4] Even as late as 1992 the WGF's remaining reputation for strength and readiness was such that the Russian minister of defense, Pavel Grachev, regarded it as the logical nucleus around which the newly-founded Russian Army would be formed.[5]

The WGF's strategic significance in the Cold War cannot be overestimated. Its military importance in the balance of power was clear. The army group represented the largest and most threatening Soviet force outside of the USSR. Defending against the WGF was NATO's central preoccupation for over forty years. Yet the WGF also played a political role in the Cold War. Its presence ensured Soviet control over East Germany, a state which Moscow regarded as the Kremlin's most important ally. Control over East Germany kept Germany divided and weak, directly removing a key potential rival to the USSR. But control over East Germany also anchored Soviet rule in Eastern Europe and maintaining control ensured that Moscow would be taken seriously not just as a major power, but as a superpower. In short, the WGF embodied Soviet power and the Cold War. Hence it was not surprising that, at the time, most observers believed that it would be nearly impossible to induce any Soviet government, even Gorbachev's, to withdraw this force and would mean the death knell for the USSR's role as a superpower.

The view that the USSR would find it nearly impossible to withdraw the WGF was only strengthened by the army group's legal and emotional links to the legacy of the Second World War. It must be remembered that the presence of the WGF in Germany was not legitimized by an agreement between the USSR and the GDR. The legal fig leaf of a status of forces agreement between the two countries did not exist until 1957. Instead, the WGF grew directly out of the Soviet occupation forces which entered Germany at the end of WWII. The continued presence of Soviet forces was legitimized under the Potsdam Treaty and other post-war agreements. The Soviet Military Administration in Germany ruled East Germany directly until 1949. Thereafter the WGF continued to behave as though it was still occupying the country, most notably in suppressing the uprising of 17 June 1953. It was not coincidental that West Germans continued to routinely refer to the GDR as "the zone" (i.e., the Soviet zone of occupation) until at least the late 1960s.

The USSR retained key legal rights as an occupying power until German re-unification. These rights were not extinguished until 15 March 1991, when the USSR formally delivered documents confirming its ratification of the Two Plus Four Treaty on unification to the German government.[6] After the Second World War the USSR, along with Great Britain, the United States, and France, was explicitly granted the right to be involved in matters pertaining to "Germany as a whole," i.e., to any decision on possible German reunification. The USSR, along with the Western allies, still retained special rights in Berlin, which remained formally under Four Power rule. The right of the WGF to exercise its occupation rights by intervening in the GDR's internal affairs, as it had in 1953, was affirmed in the 1957 USSR-GDR status of forces agreement. This accord gave the commander of the WGF the right to impose a state of emergency in the GDR if he felt it was necessary to protect Soviet troops.[7] In all, this strong legal position made it very difficult for the Germans to negotiate the WGF's withdrawal. The army group could not simply be told to leave Germany. Legal norms dictated that the WGF had every right to stay until the USSR agreed to renounce its occupation rights. Indeed, due to Four Power legal rights, German reunification could not proceed without Soviet approval.

In addition to this extraordinary legal status WWII also gave the WGF a strong emotional legacy. This fact greatly increased the difficulty of persuading the USSR to withdraw these troops. The core of the WGF consisted of the Eighth Guards Army and the First and Second Guards Tank Armies which fought to Berlin at the end of WWII as part of Marshal Zhukov's First Belorussian Front. Thereafter, the force remained in East Germany for fifty years. This institutional and emotional legacy was carefully maintained in the WGF in ways similar to events in Soviet society. In short, most Russians believed that the WGF's presence in Germany was fully justified by the USSR's suffering in WWII. This view was clearly shared by the older Soviet military and political leaders, especially those who had participated in the war. Any attempts by Germans or Soviet liberals to argue otherwise were met with accusations that the sacrifices of the heroes of the "Great Patriotic War" were being betrayed. It is hardly surprising that Col. Viktor Alksnis, a leader of the conservative Soiuz Union bloc in the Supreme Soviet, called 2 April 1991 the day the last treaties related to German reunification were finally ratified, "a day of mourning...it is the day the USSR lost the Second World War."[8]

NEGOTIATING THE WGF WITHDRAWAL

Given the enormous complications stemming from the role of the WGF as a powerful military force, a vital strategic asset, and a crucial part of the USSR's

WWII gains, German success in inducing Moscow to agree to remove its forces was far from inevitable. In fact, many analysts questioned whether the Gorbachev government would be able to agree to such a massive concession and remain in power. Few in the West realize how dangerous the situation was at this time. Nikolai Portugalov, at the time second-in-command of the CPSU International Department, noted during the GDR collapse that Gorbachev had to use all of his powers of persuasion repeatedly and forcefully to prevent some sort of armed intervention from occurring. If he had reacted passively or indecisively, the intervention would have happened.[9] This path is certainly the way German insiders regarded the situation. At each stage when the USSR made a crucial concession, top German leaders reacted with a mixture of joy and disbelief—showing that they knew the outcome was uncertain.[10] Nonetheless, the German government was successful both at negotiating a withdrawal agreement with the Gorbachev regime and, later, inducing the Yeltsin government to improve the terms of the agreement for Germany. In both cases economic incentives apparently played a vital role in influencing Russian decision-makers.

From November 1989 when the Berlin Wall fell, until July 1990, the USSR refused to agree to a timetable for WGF withdrawal. With the help of massive economic aid the Germans were able to win Gorbachev's agreement to pull out the troops. Even then, though, several months of hard bargaining remained until the exact terms of the "army for Deutsche Marks" deal were finalized.

In February 1990 the Soviet Union agreed that the "internal" aspects of German reunification could be decided by the German people, but the Kremlin firmly maintained that the Four Powers must play a leading role in determining the "external" aspects of reunification. Hence they took a hard line during the early sessions of the Two Plus Four negotiating process, thereby committing the two Germanys and the Four Powers to Germany's borders and determining Germany's future alliance status.

As late as May and June 1990, despite the looming collapse of the GDR and the March election of Kohl allies to head the new East German government, the Soviet leadership continued to negotiate the external conditions of German unification. At the 5 May meeting of the foreign ministers of the Two Plus Four group, ironically held the day after he had met with Kohl to request a large German credit package, foreign minister Shevardnadze insisted that German membership in NATO was still not acceptable. He asserted that the "inner" and "outer" aspects of German unification did not have to be solved simultaneously. Perhaps Germany could reunify internally yet remain subject to Four Power controls for some time, until all external aspects of reunification were settled.[11] The German side did not react positively to these suggestions. In late May, at a meeting with French President Francois Mitterrand, Gorbachev also held to a hardline position. The Soviet president made clear that Soviet troops would not be withdrawn from the GDR unless Moscow accepted German reunification.[12] Soon thereafter Gorbachev traveled to Washington for a meeting with George Bush. The Kremlin leader made clear that he was unwilling to accept a united Germany in NATO.[13]

At the second meeting of the Two Plus Four foreign ministers held in East Berlin on 22 June, Shevardnadze surprised the assembled delegates by presenting another hard-line plan for German reunification. He suggested that following reunification the new country might remain a member of NATO and the Warsaw Pact for five to seven years. He also demanded that a united German army be reduced to 250,000 men, about half the size of West German force. Finally, he suggested that foreign forces be withdrawn from a united Germany, Western forces in Berlin being removed only six months after unification. Such withdrawal would be long before the Soviet forces surrounding Berlin could be removed.[14]

The Federal Republic, supported by its Western allies, firmly rejected the Soviet plan. Soviet hard-liners tried to influence the reunification negotiations. Gorbachev and Shevardnadze apparently needed to show their domestic opponents that the Kremlin had tried to obtain a neutral Germany, particularly in view of the fact that the 28th CPSU Party Congress was about to open in Moscow. Many were still not sure if the USSR would ever agree to leave Germany. The Germans stepped up their extensive efforts to influence the Soviets with economic aid.

In the months after the fall of the Berlin Wall West Germany offered generous economic aid to the USSR. Indeed, West Germany's effort began before the fall of the wall. In the fall of 1988 Germany granted the Soviets a credit of three billion DM. In the winter of 1989-1990 Germany increased aid. German aid eventually included food and medical aid, technical assistance, generous export credit guarantees, a direct loan of five billion DM, and arrangements to ensure that GDR-USSR trade would be maintained after unification. Total aid offered amounted to DM 87 billion, over half of the total world aid offered to the USSR and its successor states until 1993.[15] At first the aid seemed to be designed to generally improve German-Soviet relations. As 1990 wore on, it became clear that aid was tied to Soviet political concessions on German reunification including withdrawal of the WGF. Shortly before German monetary unification took effect on 1 July 1990, Bonn decided to assume temporarily the stationing costs of the WGF which the GDR had paid. Upon abolition of the East German mark soldiers' salaries and base operating expenses had to be paid in hard currency. This decision represented a huge windfall for the WGF and the Soviet Army and government.

The economic-political "package deal" between the USSR and Germany was sealed at the July 1990 meeting between Chancellor Kohl and Gorbachev. The meeting began in Moscow, where the two leaders agreed on the broad outlines of the Soviet-German deal. The meeting then continued at a mountain resort in the Caucasus Mountains, where additional details were finalized.

During the meeting in Moscow Kohl reminded Gorbachev of the economic and political linkage underlying the economic "carrots," stating that "all efforts for financial and economic cooperation are part of the package deal," i.e., they sought Soviet cooperation on reunification.[16] Gorbachev agreed to all of the crucial German political demands. Germany could remain in NATO, the USSR would renounce its Four Power rights over Germany as soon as reunification occurred, and Soviet troops would be withdrawn from the GDR. In making these concessions Gorbachev was careful to note that they were not unconditional. He insisted, for example, that a treaty be drafted providing German support for Soviet troops in the former GDR until their withdrawal and German help in resettling those troops in the USSR. The Soviet protocol showed that Gorbachev bargained with Kohl specifically.

> *Kohl.* We could provide help with the retraining of members of the army for civilian professions, particularly for those which will be needed for the transition to a market economy.
> *Gorbachev.* And housing.[17]

The link to German economic aid forced Gorbachev to admit openly that:

> Some have implied that we are selling the victory which we won at such a high price and with so much sacrifice [in the Second World War] for German marks. One should not oversimplify the connection, but we must also see that this is a reality.[18]

After their initial meetings in Moscow Gorbachev and Kohl traveled to the mountain resort of Arkhyz in Georgia to finish their bargaining over the economic-political "package deal" between their countries. As in Moscow, Gorbachev mentioned the importance of German financial support for the Soviet troops left in the former GDR.[19] As noted above, the German side was already providing temporary financial support for the Soviet forces. Germany agreed to fund the GDR until they were withdrawn, and also agreed to a massive program for housing troops in the USSR. The Soviets hinted for several months that the USSR's housing shortage could delay the withdrawal of the troops from Germany.[20] At Arkhyz the Germans succeeded in accelerating the withdrawal of troops by promising financial support. When Gorbachev told the German delegation that the troops could only be withdrawn in five to seven years, Kohl promptly stated his offer of help for the retraining and housing of returning troops. Gorbachev then reduced his time required for WGF withdrawal to "three or four years."[21]

The two sides also discussed details of the German plan to ensure that GDR's obligations to the USSR for the Soviet army in East Germany were met. The GDR had long covered costs for Soviet troops on its territory. Thus the West German agreement to do the same was in formal terms merely an extension of the East German commitment. Clearly both sides were aware that the West German commitment to subsidize the Soviet forces was in reality much more beneficial than the old GDR-Soviet arrangement. The Soviet troops would be receiving the same number of marks as before, except that now they would be West German rather then East German. The flow of hard currency to the WGF had affected both the army group itself and the Soviet high command.

The agreements reached at the July 1990 Kohl-Gorbachev meeting were not the end of the difficult bargaining over the "price" of the WGF pullout. The July agreements did seem to clear the way for the crucial Two Plus Four Treaty to be signed, which in turn allowed German unification to proceed. Later in July the Two Plus Four foreign ministers met in Paris and agreed to meet one more time, in Moscow in September, to sign the final Two Plus Four Treaty, essentially on the West's terms. Between July and September the Soviet Union tried to use its remaining bargaining power to induce West Germany to pay for the WGF withdrawal. If Germany refused, the Soviets threatened, the Two Plus Four accord could still be scuttled and German unity delayed.

The USSR and Germany decided that two separate treaties should be negotiated: one on Soviet conditions in the former GDR after reunification, and one for Soviet withdrawal (the Überleitungsvertrag, or Transitional Treaty). The agreement for the presence of Soviet troops in the former GDR[22] was mainly a technical agreement. There were a number of provisions which were beneficial to the Soviet side and costly to the German government.[23] Perhaps most notably, the Soviet forces in East Germany shipped goods into and out of Germany without customs inspections or paying tariffs. This provision soon allowed Soviet soldiers and officers to carry out an array of semi-legal and illegal activities, including shipment of stolen German cars to Russia in sealed army trains. The Soviet forces also were exempted from all internal German taxes, including the gasoline tax. Many other treaty provisions would added significant costs for the German government.

It was the more costly Überleitungsvertrag which caused the most German-Soviet friction in the days leading up to the final meeting of the Two Plus Four process, and almost caused that meeting to be aborted. At the July summit the Germans promised to pay for the maintenance and withdrawal of the Soviet troops in Germany and to build housing for returning troops in the USSR. In return, the Soviet leadership agreed to withdraw the troops within four years. However, the Germans had not discussed the specific amount of money required to meet their commitments. This was to prove a costly oversight. For some weeks after the Arkhyz meeting the negotiations over the Überleitungsvertrag were stalled, the Germans offering an aid package totaling only about six billion DM while the Soviets insisted on at least 18 billion. With the 12 September Moscow Two Plus Four meeting fast approaching, the Soviets showed that they could be fierce negotiators. A letter from Shevardnadze to West German foreign minister Genscher on 27 August called the German offer "totally insufficient" and pointedly noted that the Soviet commitment to withdraw its troops depended on the size of German financial support.[24] The Germans were still hesitant as they wanted to shape the economic package carefully. Their strategy was to be generous in the question of support for the Soviet troops after their withdrawal—in housing and retraining—but less generous in subsidies for the troops while they were still in Germany. Consequently, Soviet forces would have a financial incentive to withdraw quickly.

On 7 September in their first direct contact since the Arkhyz summit Chancellor Kohl telephoned Gorbachev in an attempt to resolve the impasse over funding the troop withdrawal.[25] The chancellor offered eight billion DM. Gorbachev reacted harshly, pointedly reminding Kohl that the conclusion of the Two Plus Four talks could be endangered if the "solution to the financial questions" was not found. The two leaders could only agree to hold another telephone conversation on Monday, September 10, less than forty-eight hours before the opening of the Moscow Two Plus Four meeting. The Germans realized that Gorbachev's "surprisingly hard" effort to pressure the chancellor showed clearly that "the financial packet is a central part of the entire result" of the unification package. When Kohl again telephoned

Gorbachev, he had a much better offer ready—DM 11 to 12 billion. Gorbachev again insisted on more, claiming that at least DM 15 billion would be needed to ensure that German unification could proceed. Under this pressure the chancellor agreed to give the Soviets an interest-free loan of DM 3 billion on top of the 12 billion he was already offering, bringing the total payment to DM 15 billion. In the end, this DM 3 billion loan was to cost the Germans some DM 1.5 billion in interest payments alone, with no guarantee that the loan itself would ever be repaid. Thus the real cost of the package was probably closer to DM 16.5 billion, almost three times greater than the initial six billion offer. In the end, two short telephone calls cost the German government DM 10 billion.

The final text of the Überleitungsvertrag contained these provisions.[26] For the housing program for returning Soviet troops Bonn would commit DM 7.8 billion, retraining the troops for civilian occupations, DM 200 million, and one billion was allocated for the transport costs involved in returning the army to Russia. Finally, DM 3 billion was earmarked to support the Soviet troops during their stay in the former GDR. The troop withdrawal package thus totaled DM 12 billion, as agreed to by Kohl during his telephone negotiations with Gorbachev. To these sums must be added the interest-free DM 3 billion credit agreed to by Kohl, which was supposedly to be used by the Soviets to fund their share of the troop withdrawal costs but in reality disappeared quickly into the Soviet treasury. The agreement was costly, yet the Germans still regarded this price as well worth paying to free their country peacefully from the Soviet troops.

The impact of German aid on the Gorbachev leadership was clear. As the July 1990 summit and the July-September German-Soviet negotiations made obvious, the decision to withdraw the WGF and the timing of the withdrawal were directly linked to the German financial package. Even after the treaties on German reunification and the withdrawal of the WGF were signed, Germany still faced many hurdles before the WGF pullout was complete. The treaties still had to be ratified by the Supreme Soviet, a body which contained many Communist Party hard-liners hostile to Germany. The pullout process itself was fraught with difficulties. Was the WGF still a threat? Could it be used against Germany if the Gorbachev regime was overthrown? The attitude of the Soviet military, both the leadership in Moscow and the troops in the former GDR, played a crucial role in ensuring both the ratification of the treaties and their peaceful implementation.

Upon the collapse of the USSR at the end of 1991 Russia assumed the role of the main Soviet successor state. While the WGF at first was to be placed under the command of the joint armed forces of the Commonwealth of Independent States (CIS), it soon became clear that this organization would be largely powerless. The army group passed into Russian control in the spring of 1992. Thus Russian President Boris Yeltsin became Germany's new partner in managing the withdrawal of the WGF.

In December 1992 Chancellor Kohl met with Yeltsin. Kohl was eager to win Russian agreement to two important political issues to accelerate withdrawal. The 1990 treaty regulating the troop departure had not specified what was to become of the property left behind. The Russians had demanded massive German compensation for the military bases they were abandoning, while Germany, concerned that the bases were contaminated by toxic wastes which would be expensive to clean up, demanded that the bases be conveyed without compensation, the so-called Null Lösung or Zero Solution. Kohl was also anxious to speed the Russian withdrawal if at all possible. It was originally scheduled to be completed at the end of 1994. Kohl must hold national elections in Germany before that time, and was anxious to have the troop withdrawal finished first.[27]

In the end Russia agreed to complete the troop withdrawal four months before schedule, by the end of August 1994, and also agreed to give back military lands in the former GDR without additional compensation. In return Germany agreed to add DM 550 million to the amount it would spend to build housing for officers of the ex-Soviet forces, bringing the total amount invested to DM 8.35 billion. It was planned to build some 9,000 additional housing units with the money, bringing the total constructed to shelter some 45,000 soldiers. Germany also agreed to delay discussion of repayment of hard currency debts which Russia accumulated in trade with the former GDR after German monetary union.[28] It was clear that the Yeltsin government was at least as vulnerable to economic linkage as the Gorbachev regime. In fact, given the ongoing collapse of the Russian economy in succeeding years, economic aid became an even more valuable policy tool for the West since 1992.[29]

THE IMPACT OF AID ON THE MILITARY

German economic aid also influenced the Soviet and Russian Army directly. During 1990-1991 the position of the Red Army leadership on the Two Plus Four agreement and the accompanying bilateral Soviet-German treaties was shaped by fears of losing the generous support which Bonn was providing to the Soviet Army. Also, the WGF itself was greatly affected by both the direct impact of German aid and the indirect impact of life in a capitalist society. Taken together, the effect of aid on the top leadership of the military and on WGF helped to ensure the prompt departure of the army group and to hollow its morale and fighting capacity sufficient to render it unusable. In both ways German aid advanced the security interests of Germany and, indeed, of the West as a whole.

During the 1989-1991 period, as Soviet control of Eastern Europe was weakening and the USSR itself was teetering towards collapse, the Soviet military loomed as the key force which might try to reverse these trends. The army was regarded, along with the KGB and old-style party apparatchiks, as the core of the potential "conservative" opposition to Gorbachev. The army leadership was motivated by loyalty to the communist system, by an underlying Russian patriotism, which included great pride in the country's achievements in WWII, and also by concern for the military's own institutional interests—its budget, prestige, and influence. Given these understandable concerns, it seemed obvious that the military leadership would strenuously oppose the reunification of Germany and the withdrawal of the WGF. Indeed, in a variety of statements during the period many top Soviet generals voiced their opposition to these plans. For example, at the congress of the newly-formed hard-line Russian Communist Party on 19 June 1990 General Makashov of the Urals Military District bluntly stated that a unified Germany would surely be a military threat, and that analysts who asserted otherwise were speaking in "formulas which are calculated to appeal to the feeble-minded.... Only a blind person or a criminal can fail to see this." He also condemned the fact that "the Soviet Army is being driven without a fight out of countries which our fathers liberated from fascism."[30] Gorbachev reportedly worried that some small incident in Germany could provoke the military to "send in the tanks" without direct authorization from the Kremlin.[31] In early 1991 special forces units acting to suppress independence movements in the Baltic states often seemed to be out of Gorbachev's control. By mid-1991 rumors of a possible military coup swirled through Moscow and eventually, in August, a coup attempt indeed took place.

Despite the key Supreme Soviet debates in early 1991 on ratifying the Two Plus Four accords and related German-Soviet bilateral treaties, the military leadership gave its support to the agreements. The army also cooperated in a myriad of ways in implementing the practical details of the accords. Given the military leadership's obvious hostility toward German unification and withdrawal of the WGF, and given the fact that the generals were clearly not hesitating in 1990-1991 to act on their political views, to the point that some were plotting to overthrow the Soviet government, how can one explain their willingness to back down quietly when they had a real opportunity to disrupt Germany's plans seriously? A large part of the explanation lies in the German economic aid package.

The first of two crucial Supreme Soviet debates over the ratification of the bilateral treaties with Germany and the Two Plus Four final agreement took place on 4 March 1991. Deputy foreign minister Kvitsinsky led the defense of the agreements by stressing their benefits to the USSR. To the surprise of some, he was strongly supported by General Yazov, the Minister of Defense, who was usually known as a conservative on foreign policy issues. Yazov argued that the army could not afford to renounce the German-financed housing program and other aid linked to the treaties. His support, Kvitsinsky believed, "influenced many doubters and fence-sitters."[32] Still, some ambiguity remained since the Two Plus Four accord and two other bilateral treaties were ratified immediately, whereas the Supreme Soviet delayed its final vote on the ratification of the two treaties related to the Soviet army in the former GDR for several weeks. Yet with the firm support of the Soviet military General Moiseev stated at the second, final debate that "any delay is detrimental to the interests of the Soviet army," when the last two treaties were approved on 2 April 1991.[33] Germany's package of generous aid for the Soviet Army, which was specifically designed to ensure that the army have a vested interest in German unification, appeared to have paid off.

It is striking that even the most conservative Red Army generals soon no longer questioned the notion of withdrawing the WGF. Instead, their complaints about the process increasingly focused merely on raising the payoff to the Soviet military. As one author noted, "it is worth pointing out how far the priorities of the [post-]Soviet Armed Forces have shifted from the military/strategic to the social and economic side. In early 1991 General Lobov still feared that the left-behind facilities [in the former GDR] could be used by the enemy for a military buildup against the Soviet Union, and he even recommended dismantling them. Today WGF official argue that the gains from equipment and real estate sales are needed to provide additional funding for military housing programs."[34]

A variety of military leaders called loudly for large German payments in return for the property being vacated by the departing WGF. In a typical statement General Burlakov, the last commander of the Soviet forces in Germany, called for Germany to pay DM 10.5 billion for the property being vacated by the departing troops and also build 19,000 more apartments in the USSR for the Soviet Army.[35] These demands continued unabated until December 1992 when, as noted above, President Yeltsin decided to allow the Germans to take over the bases without payment.

While it now seems apparent that the Soviet military leadership was influenced by the prospect of German economic aid, all levels of the WGF itself were also affected. By 1992-1993 it seemed that the army group's main preoccupation was not military preparedness but making money. Russian officers and men were increasingly willing to resort to any means to obtain hard currency including corruption, theft, desertion and even espionage.

The WGF's collapse in discipline was not due to inherent immorality on the part of Russian soldiers. Much of the collapse is explained by the difficult and confusing circumstances of the WGF during the four years of the withdrawal period. The main problem was simple: the end of the GDR meant that the troops were now surrounded by a sea of capitalist wealth, while at the same time the USSR and, later, Russia was in a state of economic collapse. As the economic gap between the two countries grew, so too did the temptation to obtain Deutsche Marks by any means necessary. The standard of living of the former GDR already was noticeably higher than that of the USSR. Assignment to the WGF, particularly as an officer, was always seen as a relatively desirable posting since it was possible to obtain some small luxuries to bring back to the Soviet Union. German unification vastly increased the range of temptations surrounding the men of the WGF.

Many of these "temptations" were provided directly by the West German government. Previously it was nearly impossible for members of the WGF to obtain hard currency. After July 1990, when the monetary union between the two Germanys came into effect, all Soviet soldiers were paid in Deutsche Marks by the Bonn government. This financial decision served to put the entire Soviet military leadership in Germany's debt and influenced its attitude toward reunification. Common recruits received DM 25 per month, lieutenants received 700 and colonels DM 1,200. Especially for the officers, this was truly a princely sum. As Der Spiegel noted in 1991, "1,000 marks are equivalent on the black market to about 12,000 rubles. A single month's salary is thus worth four years worth of average wages in the USSR."[36] It is not surprising that monthly paydays led to chaos in many WGF units. Young recruits were robbed of their modest payments by older soldiers as part of the Red Army's tradition of "hazing" new soldiers. Veterans about to return home pressed young soldiers to "contribute" to funds for a "going-home party" or for presents for family members waiting in the USSR. Those with larger DM windfalls, particularly officers, would go on spending sprees in nearby German towns or at flea markets which quickly sprang up at the gates of Soviet barracks, offering electronic goods, used cars, and various luxury goods.[37]

The program providing housing for returning Red Army soldiers also was a rich source for morale by destroying competition and corruption among WGF troops. Despite Germany's best efforts housing was available only for a limited number of soldiers and not every officer of the WGF was guaranteed a space. Officers of other army units already stationed in locations in the former USSR where the new apartments were being built were eager to gain access to the housing. Hence a covert battle ensued in many WGF units where bribery, connections, and any other means necessary were used to gain access to desirable housing after each unit's return to the former USSR. The losers in this competition often found themselves living with their families in drafty, collapsing barracks, or even in tents.[38]

Given the limited amount of Deutsche Marks available the temptation to steal army property for resale was almost irresistible. In May 1991 WGF defector Yuri Teplykov reported in a German newspaper that "anything that can be unscrewed or removed is stolen."[39] The German-Soviet treaty on WGF conditions in the former GDR allowed the Soviet Army the right to export and import supplies freely with no tax or customs inspections. This right was soon abused with trainloads of German luxury goods and even stolen cars shipped to the USSR and, later, Russia for resale. The competition to obtain an automobile became so intense, with theft, drunk driving, and accidents in uninsured vehicles mounting steadily, that the WGF soon decided to allow soldiers to purchase cars only in the last month of their tours in Germany.[40] Corruption was spread through contacts with both Western firms and Russian traders, many affiliated with the Russian Mafia. In a typical scheme German firms installed video games and video poker machines in many officers' clubs in WGF bases and then quietly split the profits with the Russian officers in charge of the clubs.[41]

Allegations of theft and corruption soon reached the very top of the WGF. The army group's last commander, General Matvei Burlakov, was accused of a scheme to transfer Soviet military property to a real estate company of which he was a co-owner.[42] These allegations prompted the Defense Committee of the Congress of People's Deputies to launch an investigation. While no charges were filed, a cloud remained over Burlakov. With the completion of the WGF withdrawal he was given the post of deputy Defense Minister. Only two months later, in October 1994, a Russian journalist who was researching the corruption allegations was killed in a car bombing. Although suspicions of his involvement could not be proven, Burlakov was forced to resign his new post in disgrace.

Like theft and corruption, desertion from the WGF also often was motivated by economic factors. Previously, with a closed inner-German border and tight discipline in the ranks, desertion was all but impossible. After 1989 desertions increased. As with other problems in the WGF its true extent was not known for some time, as both the German and Russian sides had strong reasons to downplay its significance. The Russians did not want to admit to the embarrassing collapse of their army's discipline. The Germans wanted to prevent an international incident which could slow the WGF pullout. Their agreement with the USSR called for the WGF to maintain full disciplinary jurisdiction over its own troops, but Germany's willingness to shelter deserters seemed to break that pledge.

Initial reports in 1990-1992 suggested that between 150 and 250 WGF soldiers had deserted to the West.[43] Occasionally a desertion would make the headlines. In late 1990 a Soviet regimental commander defected to the West and took some secret Soviet weaponry with him. In response the then-commander of the WGF, General Boris Snetkov, was fired along with three of his deputies on 10 December 1990, and General Burlakov assumed command.[44] Gradually it became obvious that more Russian soldiers had defected than was officially admitted. More recent reports speak of about a thousand deserters about 600 of whom are still living in Germany.[45] Many of the rest were resettled in the US by the CIA. Recently the Russian government attempted to lure the deserters home by offering amnesty. The offer was generally ignored since the amnesty covered only desertion itself, leaving the former soldiers open to prosecution for other crimes such as espionage.[46]

Given the general collapse of morale in the WGF and the appearance of various forms of corruption and theft it should not be surprising that Western intelligence agencies found the army group amazingly easy to penetrate. Soviet hard-liners had warned loudly of this danger as early as 1989.[47] The true extent of the West's espionage success did not become apparent until years later. Although the WGF command persistently denied such "rumors,"[48] spies were easily able to obtain even advanced weapons. The West German Bundesnachrichtendienst (BND or Federal Intelligence Service) and the CIA hastily established a joint center in Berlin to manage the massive flow of military goods and information, camouflaged as the "Federal Agency for Military Technology and Procurement."[49] BND and CIA spies scored the most "incredible successes" by offering cash and goods such as used cars in exchange for weapons and secrets. The Berlin headquarters reportedly maintained a stable of several dozen used Russian Lada cars which could be even be customized in any color desired by WGF soldiers.[50] By 1992-1993 the process had advanced to the point where whole T-80 tanks were available for the right price. As one article reported, "sometimes the tank would only remain in the barracks because the spies could not arrange quickly enough for a tank transporter to haul it away."[51] In the end, the list of secrets and technology obtained was impressive.

> [Technology obtained ranged] from the on-board computer of the most modern fighter plane, the MiG-29, to the "Friend-Foe" identification system of the Mi-24 helicopter to chemical weapons detectors. Hundreds of secret documents were taken from the barracks by Soviet soldiers: disciplinary statistics, code books, strategy papers of the Moscow General Staff and detailed personnel lists. Through obtaining the hardware or detailed technical descriptions [the BND] learned the details of the latest Soviet

weapons: the laser guided anti-tank weapons of types 9K116 and 9M117 as well as the most modern fire direction and rocket systems.[52]

Even examples of Soviet encryption machinery were obtained, allowing the Germans to read all of the top secret messages sent by the WGF in its final years of existence.[53]

The collapse of the WGF is indeed an impressive case of the ability of economic factors to influence and even defeat military power. Top Soviet and, later, Russian political leaders agreed to withdraw the army group in return for generous German economic aid. The leaders of the Russian military were influenced by the prospect of economic gain, for the army and, in some cases, for themselves personally. Finally, the WGF itself was permeated from top to bottom by greed to the point where its morale and fighting ability were seriously compromised.

In all, Germany's use of economic aid paid dramatic dividends for the security of both Germany and the West as a whole. The USSR was persuaded to peacefully withdraw a force which was the largest security threat to Western Europe. The withdrawal was kept on schedule by German economic carrots such as the housing built for returning officers in the former USSR. The readiness of the WGF itself was steadily undermined by deliberate Western efforts and by the capitalist environment in which it found itself. Finally, intelligence agencies were able to score dramatic coups with the help of economic inducements. In sum, a major threat to Germany and the West had been neutralized. Yet not a drop of blood was shed and, perhaps best of all, the Russians were largely left feeling grateful to the Germans for their generosity despite some lingering resentment that generosity came with strings attached.

1. The term Western Group of Forces (WGF), the name adopted on 29 June 1989, is used here. Previously these forces were known as the Group of Soviet Occupation Forces in Germany (1945-1949) and as the Group of Soviet Forces in Germany (1949-1989). See Ulrich Brandenburg, "The 'Friends' Are Leaving. Soviet and Post-Soviet Troops in Germany," *Aussenpolitik*, Vol. 44, No. 1 (1993), 77.

2. Cited in the US Department of Defense publication *Soviet Military Power. Prospects for Change, 1989* (Washington, 1989), 26. Ironically, this volume, with its view of Soviet strategic plans, was sent to press in September 1989, only weeks before the fall of the Berlin Wall.

3. The USSR maintained two divisions in Poland (Northern Group of Forces), five in Czechoslovakia (Central Group of Forces), and four in Hungary (Southern Group of Forces), for a total of eleven divisions. David Cox, *Retreating from the Cold War. Germany, Russia, and the Withdrawal of the Western Group of Forces* (New York, 1996), 1. Specifically, in the late 1980s the WGF consisted of the First and Second Guards Tank Armies, the Third Shock Army, and the Eighth and Twentieth Guards Armies. It contained nineteen motor-rifle and tank divisions, one artillery division, two surface-to-surface and two surface-to-air missile brigades, an air assault brigade, a spetsnaz brigade, and was supported by an entire Air Army. See John Erickson, Lynn Hansen, and William Schneider, *Soviet Ground Forces. An Operational Assessment* (Boulder, Colo., 1986), 37-38, 42.

4. 1989 figures from *Armed Forces International Journal* (December 1991), 30. Cited in Brandenburg, "The 'Friends' Are Leaving," 81.

5. Grachev interview on Russian television, 7 June 1992, as cited in FBIS-SOV-92-110, 8 June 1992, 25.

6. These documents can be found in *Deutsche Aussenpolitik 1990/91. Auf dem Weg zu einer europäischen Friedensordnung* (Bonn, 1991), 364-366.

7. David Childs, *The GDR* (London, 1988), 272.

8. Quoted in Yuli Kvitsinsky, *Vor dem Sturm. Errinnerungen eines Diplomaten* (Berlin, 1993), 100-101.

9. Author's interview with Nikolai Portugalov, Moscow, April 1994. Portugalov echoes these comments in Ekkehard Kuhn, *Gorbatschow und die Deutsche Einheit* (Bonn, 1993), 9-10.

10. Two such key turning points were the February 1990 Kohl-Gorbachev meeting at which the Soviet leader first agreed that unification could, in theory, take place, and the July meeting at which Gorbachev agreed to remove the key obstacles to unification by withdrawing the WGF and allowing Germany to remain in NATO. See the accounts of these meetings by Horst Teltschik, Chancellor Kohl's top aide. Horst Teltschik, *329 Tage. Innenansichten der Einigung* (Berlin, 1991), 138-141, 321-337.

11. For a complete text of Shevardnadze's statement, see *Pravda*, 6 May 1990. Extensive excerpts can also be found in Karl Kaiser, *Deutschlands Vereinigung. Die internationalen Aspekte* (Bergisch Gladbach, 1991), 212-217.

12. John-Thor Dahlberg, "Gorbachev Warns West on German Role in NATO," *Los Angeles Times*, 26 May 1990.

13. See the accounts of the Washington summit in Stephen Szabo, *The Diplomacy of German Unification* (New York, 1992), 85-88. Teltschik reports that the American secretary of state, Jim Baker, told the press bluntly after the meeting that no progress was made on the key issues related to German unification. Teltschik, *329 Tage,* 255.

14. This plan was worked out by such conservative thinkers as Yuli Kvitsinsky, who was summoned from his post as Soviet ambassador in Bonn to become deputy foreign minister in May. For a copy of the plan, see Kvitsinsky, *Vor dem Sturm,* 41-46. For an account of the East Berlin meeting, see Fred Oldenburg, "Die Deutschlandpolitik Gorbatschows 1985-1991," *Berichte des Bundesinstituts für ostwissenschaftliche und internationale Studien,* No. 17 (1992), 30, and Serge Schmemann, "Shevardnadze Seeks Curbs on Forces in New Germany," *New York Times,* 23 June 1990. Shevardnadze's speech at the meeting was printed in *Pravda,* 23 June 1990.

15. For a summary of the overall German aid to the USSR and Russia from 1989-93 see "Antwort der Bundesregierung auf die Große Anfrage der Fraktionen der CDU/CSU und F.D.P. (Drucksache 12/5046). Unterstützung der Reformprozesse in den Staaten Mittel-, Südost- und Osteuropas (einschließlich der baltischen Staaten) sowie in den neuen unabhängigen Staaten auf dem Territorum der ehemaligen Sowjetunion," *Deutscher Bundestag*, Drucksache 12/6162 (12 November 1993), 55-56.

16. Teltschik, *329 Tage,* 321. See also Szabo, *German Unification,* 100.

17. Mikhail Gorbachev, *Gipfelgespräche. Geheime Protokolle aus meiner Amtszeit* (Berlin, 1993), 175.

18. Ibid., 171.

19. Teltschik, *329 Tage,* 324-325.

20. On 25 May 1990, for example, Soviet officials confirmed that they had halted the partial withdrawal of their forces from the GDR, then taking place under the terms of Gorbachev's December 1988 offer to unilaterally cut Soviet forces, due to the shortage of housing in the USSR for returning soldiers. See Dahlberg, "Gorbachev Warns West."

21. Teltschik, *329 Tage,* 336.

22. This agreement was formally called the "Treaty Relating to the Conditions for the Limited Stay and Modalities for the Planned Withdrawal of Soviet Troops."

23. The text of the treaty and its associated appendices (Anlage) can be found in *Bulletin of the German Federal Press and Information Agency,* No. 123 (1990), 1284-1300.

24. Teltschik, *329 Tage,* 352.

25. Ibid., 359-363. The two crucial telephone conversations are recounted in detail.
26. The text of the treaty is found in *Europa-Archiv*, No. 3 (1991), D63-D67. See also Timothy Aeppel, "Friendship Treaty and Troop-Related Aid Deepen Bonn's Economic Ties With Soviets," *Wall Street Journal* (European Edition), 14 September 1990.
27. Under the German Basic Law elections for the Bundestag must be held at least once every four years. Kohl was last re-elected in December 1990.
28. Author's interview with Herr Lambach, foreign ministry, Bonn, June 1994, and with Georg Boomgaarden, German embassy in Moscow, March 1994. For the text of the agreements reached at the meeting, see *Bulletin*, 22 December 1992. For an updated report on the housing program for returning ex-Soviet troops, see the publication "Information zum Wohnungsbauprogramm für die aus dem Gebiet der ehemaligen DDR zurückkehrenden Soldaten der GUS-Streitkräfte," Bundesministerium für Wirtschaft, May 1994.
29. For instance, the Nunn-Lugar plan enabled the US to use aid to significantly speed Russian disarmament. See Jason Ellis, "Dollar Diplomacy and Nuclear Non-Proliferation. The Case of Nunn-Lugar." Paper presented at International Studies Association conference, San Diego, 1996.
30. "Makashov Addresses 19 June Russian Conference," FBIS-SOV-90-120, 21 June 1990, 92-93.
31. Author's interview with former CPSU International Department official Nikolai Portugalov, Moscow, April 1994.
32. Kvitsinsky, *Vor dem sturm*, 98. For the text of Kvitsinsky's statement in support of the treaties, see ibid., 86-96. For more details on the March 4 debate see "Parlamentarisches Muskelspiel im Obersten Sowjet," *Stuttgarter Zeitung,* 5 March 1991.
33. For details on the final debate over the two military treaties see Kvitsinsky, *Vor dem sturm*, 100-101.
34. Brandenburg, "The 'Friends' Are Leaving," 78. Lobov is cited in *Voennaia mysl*, No. 2 (1991).
35. See, for example, the discussion in Brandenburg, "The 'Friends' Are Leaving," 84-85. See also "More Cash Wanted for Withdrawal from FRG," Berlin ADN report, reprinted in FBIS-SOV-91-039, 27 February 1991, 23-24, and the examples cited in Suzanne Crow, "Germany. The 'Second Crisis' of Soviet Foreign Policy," *Radio Liberty Report on the USSR* (15 March 1991), 9-12. For a Soviet view, see Igor Maksimychev, "Cossacks Riding Through Berlin," *International Affairs* (Moscow), June 1991, 52-60.
36. "Den Rückzug nicht gelernt," *Der Spiegel*, No. 10 (1991), 151.
37. Ibid., 144-145.
38. "Es Sind Wunderbare Wohnungen," *Der Spiegel*, No. 13 (1992), 126-130.
39. Yuri Teplykov, "Quiet as a Church Mouse, Heads Down Low," *Der Morgen*, 21 May 1991. Reprinted in FBIS-SOV-91-108, 5 June 1991, 26-27.
40. "Den Rückzug nicht gelernt," 144-145.
41. Ibid., 145.
42. See John Lloyd, "Corruption Charges Threaten Yeltsin's Referendum," *Financial Times*, 23 April 1993. Cited in Cox, *Retreating from the Cold War*, 120. A similar complaint was made in a military memorandum pubished in Komsomolskaia pravda, 1 April 1992. The memorandum notes that "some officials of the CIS armed forces" have been illegally transferring military property to various partnerships and joint-stock corporations. It specifically singled out the Conversion Housing International Concern which received 200 facilities on German territory from the army without payment.
43. The lower figure is the estimate of Soviet military representatives as to the number of deserters at the end of 1990. Cited in "Den Rückzug nicht gelernt," 145. The figure of 250 was an estimate as of April 1992 cited in Brandenburg, "The 'Friends' Are Leaving," 82.
44. "Den Rückzug nicht gelernt," 145.
45. "Kopf ab und Schluß," *Der Spiegel*, No. 44 (1998), 104-106.
46. Ibid., and "Helfende Hand," *Der Spiegel*, No. 52 (1998), 60.

47. See "Instead of Aid—Espionage?" *Pravda*, 27 December 1989. Reprinted in FBIS-SOV-89-248, 29 December 1989, 25.

48. Nikolai Burbyga and Sergei Mastovshikov, "Matvei Burlakov, Commander of the WGF. 'We Are Not Trading in Weapons,'" *Izvestiia*, 30 March 1992. Reprinted in FBIS-SOV-92-065, 3 April 1992, 11.

49. "Suche Panzer, biete Lada," *Der Spiegel*, No. 49 (1997), 70.

50. Ibid., 71.

51. Ibid.

52. Ibid.

53. Ibid., 74.

THE COSSACK BROTHERHOOD AS A POLITICAL-MILITARY FORCE IN A DISINTEGRATING RUSSIA

Lt. Col. Lester W. Grau

Uniformed personnel are not an uncommon sight on the streets of Moscow, Volgograd, Alma-Ata, Rostov or other cities of the former Soviet empire. Uniformed military and police mingle freely with the crowds and join in the perpetual hunt for food, drink and other scarce commodities. However, another distinctive and unusual uniformed force has emerged and become a fairly common street sight since 1990. Early twentieth-century uniforms are now freely worn by swaggering Cossacks carrying sidearms and lead-weighted whips (nagaika). A people and a way of life which was systematically destroyed by the Soviets have risen from the ashes, and they are playing an ever-increasing role as both a military and law enforcement force and "king-maker."

HISTORICAL BACKGROUND

To a Westerner the word "Cossack" usually conjures an image of a dance troupe or choir, a body of light cavalry ruthlessly suppressing a street demonstration against the tsar or a close-knit community. Defining a Cossack is much more difficult. Cossacks were neither a racial group nor a nationality. While there were thirteen Slavic Cossack "hosts" in Russia and the Ukraine, there were also tribes and subtribes of Mongols, Turkic-Tatars, Caucasians, Persians, Lithuanian Tatars, and Poles who were Cossacks. Cossacks were not bound by a single religion and included Muslims, Russian Orthodox and Old Believers, Lamaists, and Shamanists.

Cossacks were groups of Slavic peasants who migrated to the borders to escape the repressive hand of governments, serf owners and the tax collectors. They are described as freemen, oppressive tools of an oppressive tsar, gallant warriors, earthy libertines, pioneer adventurers, ruthless conquerors, champions of downtrodden serfs, infamous plunderers, defenders of the faith, leaders of every significant revolt against the tsar from 1600 to 1800, light cavalrymen, pirates, fishermen, trappers, herdsmen and farmers.

Philologists trace the origin of the word "Cossack" to Asia several centuries before the birth of Christ.[1] The term Cossack followed Genghis Khan's conquering armies and described Tatar raiders who roamed the southern Russian plain. The Turko-Tatar word from which the Russian version of Cossack is derived meant "free adventurer".[2] Cossacks apparently are descended from Tatars, Turks, Russians, Ukrainians and any number of other people who passed through or settled on the traditional southern invasion route from Asia to Europe. Beginning in the 1400s Russian-speaking Cossacks appeared regularly in the chronicles of the day, normally in connection with border security. With the collapse of the Golden Horde the southern and southeastern borderlands of Russia and the Ukraine were fortified to prevent Tatar incursions. These fortifications were anchored on the Dnieper, Don and Yaik (Ural) rivers. The vast expanses between the forts were patrolled by mobile Cossack guard detachments.[3] The tradition of using Cossacks for hazardous duty such as guards and border patrols had begun.

The Cossacks of the fifteenth and sixteenth centuries were of two distinct groups including the "free" light irregular horsemen who provided guides, escorts and steppe patrols and the "town" Cossacks, who were cavalry-based in frontier towns and outposts. The latter were individual mercenaries recruited for full- or part-time service. Many were farmers who were granted plots of land, often for life. Town Cossacks were found in all frontier areas but the southern flank.[4] The free Cossacks' way of life created a separate identity.

Cossacks were originally seeking sanctuary from serfdom, taxation, penury, starvation or justice. They were of Russian stock with little respect for tsarist law and custom. Once refugees were accepted by the Cossack community, they were never delivered to the tsar's emissaries, no matter how serious their crime. Cossacks proved to be a source of contention between the Crimean and Tatar khanates, the prince of the Nogai Horde, and the tsar of Muscovy. Each blamed the other for Cossack depredations while they secretly attempted to subvert or control the Cossacks for their own purposes. Tsar Ivan the Terrible was particularly adept at disowning the Cossacks and publicly condemning their forays while secretly arming and inciting them.[5] The Cossacks, however, conducted an independent foreign policy and maintained their own government and court system.[6]

Cossack administrative units or "hosts" such as the Don, Volga, Cherkass, Grebinsk and Yaik were established during the fifteenth and sixteenth centuries. Simultaneously, Polish Cossacks appeared in Poland and the Zaporozhian, Ukrainian and Slobodsk hosts were established in Ukraine. The rapid conquest and subsequent expansion of the Russian empire into Siberia and the Far East was on the heels of Cossack mercenaries hired by powerful Muscovite political and economic interests.[7]

Cossacks were a mixed blessing for Russia's rulers. They provided a buffer force between Russia and the Ukraine and Turkey. They were a source of inexpensive warriors and good light cavalry yet their lack of discipline and propensity to loot during vital phases of the battle limited their value. During the seventeenth and eighteenth centuries Cossacks led or supported every revolt against the throne. Bogdan Khmelnitskii, Stenka Razin, Kondraty Bulavin and Yemelian Pugachev all led major Cossack-backed revolts which threatened to topple the tsarist throne. This led Peter the Great and Catherine the Great to launch campaigns which eventually brought the Cossacks to heel.[8] The Zaporozhe Cossack host was disbanded, and the Yaik Cossacks were renamed the Ural Cossacks and resettled. Cossack military colonies were moved to the very edges of the empire and loyalty to the throne was assured through a system of watchful army officers and governors empowered to use any means to prevent further Cossack uprisings. New Cossack hosts, obliged to be loyal to the throne, were formed.[9]

The relation of the Cossacks to the tsar fundamentally changed. The Cossacks, who previously answered only to the Cossack elders, now were firmly controlled by the tsar, becoming tools of the tsar and an extension of the tsar's might. They were responsible for military service to the tsar with each Cossack furnishing his own uniforms, mount, saber, saddle and horse furniture. The government gave the Cossacks rifles, but charged the host for half the cost of each weapon. Each able-bodied male Cossack was liable to military call for up to a twenty-five-year term of service, later reduced to twenty and then eighteen years. Cossack forces and their families were ordered to the far-flung frontiers of the expanding Russian empire as military colonists where they served as border guards and the first line of defense. In return, Cossacks were paid during their time of service and could receive up to thirty desiatins or eighty-one acres of land.[10] Cossack forces were used extensively to combat all of Russia's external and internal enemies. The history of Russian Siberia, Russian Central Asia, Russian Caucasia, Russian Crimea and the Russian Far East is basically a history of Cossack political will and warfare tactics.[11]

The Cossacks lived in Cossack towns, called stanitsa (sing.), farms and garrisons. Military service began at age eighteen, when every able-bodied male was enrolled into service. The first three years of service were spent in basic training, the first two years conducted in the Cossack town while the last year was spent in a Cossack garrison training center. The youth's family had to arm and equip the "fledgling warrior" themselves. Twelve years of active service and five years of reserve service followed this training period. Of the twelve years' active service, only the first four years were actually with the colors. For the remaining two four-year periods the soldier returned home and was called up only for seasonal refresher training or emergency service.[12] In terms of manpower, over sixty percent of the Cossack male population served, compared with an average of thirty-one percent of the rest of the tsar's subjects.[13]

The basic Cossack military unit was the sotnia (100 men) which was the base of the cavalry squadron and the infantry company. The sotnia was divided into four platoons and each platoon was divided into two squads. Four to six cavalry sotnia were in a cavalry regiment and two-three cavalry regiments made up a cavalry brigade. Cossack cavalry divisions and corps were fielded. Cossack infantry or plastun units were also employed. Three or four infantry sotnia made up a battalion while two or three battalions made up a regiment. Cossack horse artillery originally had twelve guns per sotnia. In 1834 this was reduced to eight guns in an artillery battery. By the turn of the century a Cossack battery consisted of six guns.[14]

Cossack forces were fierce irregulars during the Seven Years War of 1756-1763, the War of 1812, the Crimean War, 1853-1856, the Russo-Turkish wars of the seventeenth, eighteenth and nineteenth centuries, and the First World War.

In 1897 there were 3.5 million Cossacks in the Russian empire.[15] By 1916 the Cossack population stood at 4,434,000 and included twelve Cossack hosts: the Don, Kuban, Terek, Ural, Siberian, Amur, Semirecheniye, Astrakhan, Ussuri, Yenisei, Irkutsk and Yakutsk Cossacks. During the first World War the hosts fielded 474,000 combatants and held title to 63,000,000 desiatins (1,701,000,000 acres) of land.[16] During the war the Cossacks fielded 164 cavalry regiments, 119 of which were organized into twenty-eight cavalry divisions. In addition, they fielded 35 separate, 142 general purpose and 4 home guard cavalry companies and seventy-eight convoy security cavalry half-companies. The Cossacks contributed two separate infantry divisions comprising thirty infantry battalions organized into five separate infantry brigades. They further fielded twenty-seven horse artillery battalions consisting of a total of sixty-three batteries, plus an additional fifteen separate horse artillery batteries. Reserve Cossack forces consisted of sixteen cavalry regiments, three cavalry battalions, eight cavalry companies, three infantry battalions, eight infantry companies, one horse artillery battalion, two horse artillery batteries, two horse artillery platoons and a command structure.[17] Cossack military contribution to the war effort was clearly significant.

DEATH OF THE BROTHERHOOD

Tsar Nicholas II's rule ended when Cossack loyalty to the tsar dissipated. In March 1917 the war-weary populace of Petrograd was striking and demonstrating against food shortages. These may have been suppressed or dispersed by the Cossacks who were detailed to support the police. As revolution broke out the 1st, 4th, and 14th Don Cossack regiments and the Guards Cossack Regiment went over to the rebel side. The Cossacks could have conquered the revolution but chose not to and the reign of the tsars ended.[18]

At first the Cossacks welcomed the revolution with fervor and elected a "Union of Cossack Hosts" or SVRK. The Union sent representatives to the March preliminary All-Russian Congress of Soviets, where they extracted a promise from the Provisional Government guaranteeing "the rights of the Cossack to their land."[19] A second Cossack congress was held in June 1917. Don, Terek and Kuban Cossacks held their own assemblies and began to form a union of the three hosts. A small group preferred a radical, leftist orientation. They formed the "Central Soviet of Cossacks," chaired by a Kuban Cossack named Kostenetskii. The Central Soviet of Cossacks followed Lenin's Bolshevik line of opposition to Kerenskii's provisional government.[20]

A propaganda battle ensued between the Union of Cossack Hosts and Kostenetskii's group, which became known as the Party of the Working Cossacks. When the communists attempted to seize power, the Petrograd Cossack units crushed the attempt and then raided the offices of Pravda and Kostenetskii's Cossack Bolsheviks.[21]

While statesmen tried to create the first Cossack state, war-weary Cossack soldiers fought to preserve order for Kerenskii's provisional government. The Kerenskii government's insistence on continuing the war with Germany and Austria created disaffection among the Cossack soldiers. On the night of 6 November (new calendar) the Union of Cossack Hosts called on Kerenskii and insisted on a showdown with Lenin's supporters in the Smolny Institute. Kerenskii agreed, and General Krasnov, a Don Cossack serving at the front, was ordered to the capital. The 1st, 4th and 14th Don Cossack regiments were ordered to move against the communists but chose to abstain. Krasnov was arrested and the Bolsheviks seized power. The second revolution also succeeded due to the Cossacks refusal to act.[22]

The Cossacks found the Bolsheviks no more to their liking than the tsar or the Social Revolutionaries. The Bolsheviks had clear designs on Cossack lands and property. The Cossacks represented an organized, armed military group which could threaten the existence of the communist state. Lenin saw the Cossack borderlands as a base for counter-revolution and disbanded the Union of Cossack Hosts. Armed communist columns were sent south to seize control of the Cossack lands. Many of the poorer Cossacks joined the communist ranks. The Cossack authorities, on the other hand, saw the communists as a threat to the Cossack way of life and vowed to save Moscow and the motherland during this "time of troubles."[23]

Although Cossacks fought both with the "Reds" and the "Whites" during the civil war, the majority supported the Whites. Those Cossacks who supported the Bolsheviks soon found Bolshevik rule oppressive. The Bolsheviks stabled their horses in Novocherkassk cathedral, the spiritual center of the Don Cossacks, pulled down the statue of Yermak, the Don Cossack conqueror of Siberia, and pillaged Cossack villages indiscriminately.[24]

When the civil war ended, the Cossacks were clearly among the losers. The war had ravaged their lands and Bolshevik scavengers were determined to transfer grain and goods to supply loyal Bolshevik regions. Thousands of Cossacks immigrated to Paris, Tunis, Egypt, Turkey, China, England and America. Those who stayed behind were subject to industrialization and agricultural collectivization programs.[25] The communist sought to eliminate every vestige of Cossack life. Their property and livestock were confiscated, over two million Cossacks were repressed, more than 1.5 million were killed and over 53 million desiatins or 1,431 million acres of their land was confiscated.[26] Cossack institutions, laws, self-government and customs were abolished. By the late 1920s the Cossack brotherhoods had ceased to exist.

Stalin maintained a few Cossack trappings. Before World War II he established a "Cossack" cavalry division in the Soviet Army.[27] It appears that Cossack ancestry was not a prerequisite for membership in the division. When Germany invaded the Soviet Union some 100,000 soldiers of Cossack parentage were in the Red Army. Many fought for the Soviet Union but others supported the Germans in hopes of future Cossack autonomy. During World War II the Soviets raised a "Cossack" cavalry corps and several other "Cossack" units but there was no effort to place Cossacks in these units. Instead "Cossack" uniforms were designed and issued to 17th Cavalry Corps soldiers and the corps was redesignated a Cossack Cavalry Corps.[28]

The German Army also raised some "Cossack" units from among their POWs, Red Army deserters and the Russian émigré population of occupied Europe. The Wehrmacht formed a Cossack division which eventually became a Cossack cavalry corps and fought in Yugoslavia. After the war its members were forcibly repatriated to the Soviet Union by British forces, where many of them were executed.[29]

After the war the Cossack uniform again disappeared from the Soviet Army as Stalin and his successors again attempted to bury the very memories of a Cossack past.

REVIVAL

The impetus behind the present Cossack movement in the 1990s came from singers and dancers in folk ensembles, not from a warrior clan. In the late 1970s folk ensembles in Moscow discussed a revival of Cossack culture but nothing occurred until the spring of 1989 when a chapter of Cossack countrymen in Moscow was created under the auspices of the All-Union Historical and Cultural Monument Preservation Society Central Propaganda House, which itself was officially registered at the start of 1990. This led to the founding of countrymen chapters, community clubs and Cossack political movements countrywide.[30]

In the Don region in the spring of 1990 the first Cossack assembly was held in the Starodonye Club. Lawyer Samsonov was elected as ataman or chieftain.[31] The local Communist Party committee did its best to destroy this and other "unofficial" groups but due to political turmoil the Party failed to wield the same power it exerted in the past.[32] The Rostov Oblast Communist Party Committee received secret instructions to keep the Cossack movement away from the democrats. The Party did not wish to lose control of the Cossacks at any cost. Party members were instructed to leave the Party publicly if this was necessary for them to gain leadership positions within the Cossack movement.[33] Party apparatchiks began attending Cossack assemblies, and the First Assembly of the Don Cossacks, held in November 1990, elected many Party functionaries to leadership positions. This process was repeated among other Cossack groups and the Cossack movement began to split among "Reds" and "Whites."[34]

In Moscow the Communist Party's attempt to control from within the original Moscow Countrymen's chapter failed. A group of pro-communist Cossacks separated from the chapter at the end of May 1990. On 29 June a Grand Krug (circle) was convened under the leadership of the Communist Party Central Committee. The krug announced a Union of Cossacks.

Relations between the Moscow Countrymen's Chapter and the Union of Cossacks was stormy at best. The "Red" Union of Cossacks supported former Premier Nikolai Ryzhkov while the "White" Countrymen's Chapter plus ten other Cossack organizations signed an open letter of support for Boris Yeltsin. The final break came when the Union of Cossacks publicly announced its orientation toward the Russian Communist Party.[35]

During July 1991 more than thirty "White" Cossack organizations met in Moscow. Sponsors for the krug included the Cossacks in the Moscow Countrymen Chapter, the Rostov Dolomanovskaia Cossack stanitsa, the Cherkassy region of the Don Host, the Siberian Host, Kuban Host and Yenisei Host. The krug resurrected the Union of Cossack Hosts of Russia (SVRK), which was abolished by the Bolsheviks.[36]

Cossack communities and hosts began to appear all across the former Soviet Union. By 1992 they occupied a belt stretching across the width of the land mass of the former Soviet empire and, ominously, across borders of newly independent republics. It became readily apparent that the Cossack movement was concerned with reclamation of Cossack lands, establishment of Cossack self-government and protection of Russians who suddenly found themselves living in newly independent republics as "strangers and outsiders." Cossacks took over local government or established parallel organs of power to that of local government, including courts.[37] Accepted, but by no means all-inclusive, hallmarks of the Cossack movement are Cossack land ownership, maintenance of Cossack military forces, Cossack self-rule, preferential tax treatment for Cossacks based on their military readiness and agrarian/production role, and Orthodoxy.[38]

Although the Cossack movement shares many goals, it is hardly monolithic.[39] Independent regional associations such as the Union of Cossack Republics and the Cossacks of Southern Russia have formed. The Kuban Cossacks have resurrected and combined two civil war-era political parties, the Greens and the Anarchists, into the Anarcho-Green Cossack Union.[40] Despite their multiple factions Cossacks formed a powerful political element in Russia, Ukraine, Kazakhstan, Moldova, Armenia and Georgia. They represent a potential organized, coherent polity which can rapidly generate discontent within their geographic areas. They have recognized leaderships which state their political demands. The hosts also carry a popular appeal to ethnic Russians who see Cossacks as far more willing to defend their interests than the Russian government.

Most Cossacks claim to hate the Communist Party and everything for which it stood.[41] Prominent Cossack leaders, especially in the communist camp, were ranking Party functionaries and although most of them have denounced the Party, old allegiances die slowly. Local opposition parties are quick to accuse local atamen of being part of the Party nomenclature. A. Marynov, a former communist, is the ataman of the Union of Cossacks. Sergei Meshcheriakov, his bitter opponent and also a former communist, is ataman of southern Russia and ataman of the Don Cossack Host.[42] Prominent ultra-right-wing Red-Brown leaders, such as the former KGB general Aleksandr Sterligov, leader of the National-Patriots, and Aleksandr Barkashov of the Russian National Unity are paying avid court to Meshcheriakov and by extension, to the Don, Kuban and Terek Cossacks.[43] Russian politicians see the Cossacks as an organized, armed, potentially coherent force which, if harnessed, could assure the ascendancy of a political bloc. The politicians wish to make the Cossacks their pawns.

LAW ENFORCEMENT

Participation in and control of local law enforcement has always been high on the Cossack agenda.[44] In some regions volunteer Cossack auxiliaries help maintain order. In Rostov Oblast they patrol the streets, maintain order on public transportation and during mass events, help in the fight against hooliganism, drunkenness, illegal alcohol production, and drug addiction, and assist prosecutors, the courts and the tax inspectorate.[45] In other regions Cossacks have assumed law enforcement and maintenance of public morality entirely. This event has led to over-zealous behavior and public floggings.[46] Cossacks in Chita gave a vote of no confidence to their ataman and his aides because of the ataman's use of public flogging, creation of his own intelligence service and morality patrols, and maintaining files on all the members of the Cossack community.[47]

COSSACK BORDER GUARDS AND MILITARY UNITS

Cossacks have actively sought to reestablish their traditional border guard role and, based on their current locations, are well positioned to perform this duty. A Cossack border guard is based at the Cossack stanitsa of Nezlobnaia as a guard unit near Northern Ossetia.[48] In the Transbaikal area a Cossack border guard regiment is replacing the internal security border guards and establishing a traditional military colony which will combine military duties with agriculture and local industry.[49] The regiment will guard the border with Mongolia.

As early as spring 1991 the Don Cossack Krug petitioned then Chief of Staff Moiseev to allow formation of Don Cossack units within the Soviet Armed Forces. They proposed establishment of mounted Cossack cavalry regiments, Cossack spetznaz brigades, separate infantry divisions, mounted border guard companies and ship crews. They also asked to receive the Novocherkassk Higher Military Command Signal School and use it as a Don Cossacks school to teach combined arms, artillery, signal, service support, and military medicine.[50] Serving generals and officers began accepting the office of ataman or other military positions with Cossack hosts.[51]

In May 1992 President Yeltsin signed legislative acts which restored Cossack regiments to the Russian Army. Each Cossack host was to raise its own units and pay expenses for maintenance of the units. Military chaplains were to be reintroduced into these Cossack units.[52] The first Cossack regiment in the Russian Army is stationed in Transbaikal near the Chinese border.[53] Decree 632, entitled On Measures to Implement the Russian Federation Law On the Rehabilitation of Repressed Peoples in Relation to the Cossacks, dated 15 June 1992, further states:

> The Russian Federation Defense Ministry and the Russian Federation Ministry of Internal Affairs, in conjunction with other interested organs, should submit proposals on the procedure for and special features of the military service performed by Cossacks, and also safeguard the state borders and public order.[54]

In addition to Cossack units in the armed forces formed in 1992, there are large, armed Cossack units whose allegiance is nominally to their Cossack host.[55] In the current, unsettled political and economic crisis gripping Russia there is ample opportunity for free-booting gangs. There are many parallels between modern Russia and Germany following the Thirty Years War or Germany following World War I. Armed semi-military forces of brigands loosely controlled by various warlords or Freikorps frustrated German recovery and created conditions for authoritarian central government. Such parallel developments among the Cossacks are a distinct possibility and could play havoc with Russia's recovery.

COSSACKS AND INTERNATIONAL RELATIONS

Russian Cossacks have created problems with Russia's neighbors, including Ukraine, Moldova, Armenia, Chechen-Ingush, Georgia, Kazakhstan, and Japan, as well as Muslims and Jews in general.

The Ukrainian government has seen fit to raise its own Cossack forces, apparently not by a popular movement but rather by government sponsorship. This has been in response to the oath of allegiance taken by Krasnodon Cossacks who live in Ukraine and the Don Cossacks, who live in Russia and Ukraine, to the Don Republic and Russia.[56] This threat to Ukrainian sovereignty has led to the spectacle of Ukrainian Cossacks solemnly abjuring the oath of loyalty sworn to the tsar of Muscovy in 1654. Hetman Viacheslav Chornovil stated that this was not done to break the friendship between Russia and Ukraine. Rather, it was to correct the mistake of national hero, Bogdan Khmelnitskii, and "to expiate the involuntary sin committed by our Cossack forbears 388 years ago." Ukrainian Cossacks then swore a loyalty oath to Ukraine.

In Moldova armed Don, Kuban and Terek Cossacks, a large number of them former paratroopers, spetznaz, reconnaissance specialists and Afghanistan veterans, volunteered to fight as Cossack units in defense of the break-away Russian Dniester Republic and the Russian Black Sea Cossacks. By most reports, the Cossacks fought well, at least ten died, and they were important to the morale of ethnic Russian defenders. They were finally withdrawn following a visit by Vice President Rutskoi that they saw as a vindication and a sign of Russian government support for extraterritorial adventures.[57]

In the Caucasus one hundred Cossacks, backed by two armored personnel carriers, seized the town hall of Kurganinsk in the Krasnodar region on 22 June 1992. This was their reaction to the refusal of the local government to clear Krasnodar region of ethnic Armenians.[58] In Chechnya fighting between Cossacks and Chechen-Ingush people has been going on since April 1991. Numerous deaths on both sides have resulted. Terek Cossacks are sending sotnia into the area since "only Russians can defend Russians in the Northern Caucasus."[59] In Georgia fighting in Northern Ossetia has involved Cossack forces and Sunzha Cossacks are emigrating from the area. A thousand Terek Cossacks were reportedly preparing to fight in Northern Ossetia.[60]

In Kazakhstan many Russian Cossack communities are located in the northern and eastern sectors of the republic. Cossacks established a Union of Cossacks of the Volga and Ural whose boundaries include large portions of Kazakhstan.[61] During September 1991 some 700 Cossack "volunteers" crossed into Kazakhstan to help local Cossacks "liberate" Cossack lands. They were driven back by some five thousand Kazakhs. The 1992 New Year issue of the Cossack newspaper, Stanitsa, discussed the Cossack lands in Kazakhstan.

> "[T]he land is temporarily under Kazakhstan control, and a well-founded struggle is being waged for bringing about its annexation to Russia, the historical homeland. We offer our caring hands to Ural Cossacks, Siberian Cossacks and Semirechenie Cossacks." Articles in the Kazakh press call for arming the citizenry against brigands and Cossack depredations.[62]

Cossacks also conduct foreign relations. Japan has asked for return of the Kurile Islands as part of Japanese aid to Russia. South Sakhalin, Ussuri and Amur Cossacks are loudly protesting and claiming that the Kuriles have always been Russian. The Cossacks' protests seem to have bound Russia's hands on negotiating for the return of the islands. In addition, Cossacks have been anti-Turkish and anti-Semite and frequently led pogroms against Jewish settlements. The Don Cossack leadership continues to incite social tension and extremist tendencies through anti-Muslim, anti-Jewish and anti-Caucasian pronouncements and proposed segregation measures.[63] In January 1992 Don Cossacks actively participated in a pogrom against Jews.

The Cossacks seek land, power and restoration of a lost way of life. Political forces of all persuasions are trying to bend them to their will and some have been very successful. President Yeltsin is attempting to curry their favor but is accepting politicized units into his armed forces in doing so. Loyalty to the leader in Moscow has never been the Cossacks long suit. The price of Cossack support may be more than Yeltsin can pay. If so, the forces of demagoguery may be able to find the necessary capital.

1. G.B. Gubarev, "Kniga o kazakakh" (Book about Cossacks), *Voenno-istoricheskii zhurnal* (Military History Journal, hereafter cited as VIZh) (February 1992), 82. VIZh has published a part of Gubarev's book, published in Paris in 1957. VIZh has incorporated a new feature entitled "Kazachestvo. V proshlom, nastoiashchem i budushchem" (Cossackdom. Past, Present and Future). This is the first article under this rubric and is an attempt to undo the Sovietized history of the cossack hosts.

2. Albert Seaton, *The Cossacks* (London, 1972), 7. There are several English-language books on the history of the cossacks. Since this study is mainly concerned with the contemporary cossack movement, the following are also recommended for additional historic background reading. Albert Seaton, *The Horsemen of the Steppes* (London, 1985); Philip Longworth, *The Cossacks* (London, 1969); H.N.H. Williamson, *Farewell to the Don*, ed. by John Harris (London, 1970); Samuel J. Newland, *Cossacks in the German Army, 1941-1945* (London, 1991); Maurice Hindus, *The Cossacks* (London, 1946); and C.E. Bechhofer, *In Denikin's Russia and the Caucasus, 1919-1920* (London, 1921).

3. A.P. Pronshtein and K.A. Khmelevsky, "Kazachestvo" (Cossackdom), *Bolshaia sovetskaia entsiklopediia* (The Great Soviet Encyclopedia), Vol. 11 (Moscow, 1973), 175.

4. Ibid.

5. Seaton, *The Cossacks*, 8.

6. "Kazachestvo" (Cossackdom), *Sovetskaia voennaia entsiklopediia* (Soviet Military Encyclopedia, hereafter cited as SVE), Vol. 4 (Moscow, 1977), 32.

7. Pronshtein and Khmelevsky, 175.

8. Ibid.

9. New Cossack hosts formed: Astrakhan-1750, Orenburg-1755, Black Sea-1787, Siberian-1808, Caucasus Line-1832 (repositioned with Kuban and Terek Cossacks in place of the Black Sea Cossacks in 1860), Baikal-1851, Amur-1858, Semirechnie-1867 and Ussuri-1889. See Pronshtein and Khmelevsky, 176.

10. SVE, 33.

11. G.V. Glinka, *Aziatskaia Rossiia* (Asiatic Russia), Vol. 1 (St. Petersburg, 1914), 361.
12. SVE, 34.
13. Seaton, *The Cossacks*, 23.
14. SVE, 34.
15. Pronshtein and Khmelevsky, 176.
16. SVE, 33.
17. "Godovshchina soiuz kazakov" (Anniversary of the Union of Cossacks), *Sovetskaia Rossiia* (Soviet Russia), 29 June 1991.
18. Longworth, 285-286.
19. Ibid., 288.
20. Ibid., 288-289.
21. Ibid., 289.
22. Ibid., 290-291.
23. Ibid., 292-297.
24. Ibid., 298.
25. Ibid., 299-329.
26. V. Medvedev, "Terpi, kazak..." (Patience, Cossack), *Komsomolskaia pravda*, 2 April 1992; and V. Perushkin, "Kazachi krug" (Cossack Assembly), *Argumenty i fakty* (Arguments and Facts), 15 April 1992.
27. SVE, 35.
28. A. Ya. Soshnikov, P. N. Dmitriev, and A.S. Arutynov, *Sovetskaia kavaleriia* (Soviet Cavalry) (Moscow, 1984), 214.
29. Newland's book provides an excellent overview of Cossacks in the German Army. Maurice Hindus' book provides a more-biased look at Cossacks under Soviet rule.
30. Yuri Averianov, "The Present-Day Russian Cossacks. Political Portrait," *Nezavisimaia gazeta*, 19 May 1992, in FBIS-USR-92-067, 5 June 1992, 70.
31. Russian Cossack chieftains are atamans, while Ukrainian Cossack chieftains are hetmans.
32. Alexander Andrusenko, *Moscow News*, No. 3, 19-26 January 1992.
33. Vladimir Zharinov, "The Sin of Old Grievances," *Rossiiskaia gazeta*, 9 January 1992, in FBIS-USR-92-016, 18 February 1992, 43-44.
34. Andrusenko, 47.
35. Averianov, 71.
36. Ibid.
37. L. Mazirin, "Kuda kazak skachet" (Where are the Cossacks Galloping?), *Sovetskii patriot* (Soviet Patriot), No. 13 (March 1991), 7.
38. Vladimir Kiselyov's interview of Sergei Meshcheriakov, *Moscow News*, No. 22, 31 May-7 June 1992.
39. A. Ganelin, A. Khantsevich, and A. Khokhlov, "Hetman's Squadron. Some Call Cossacks in Dniester Region Mercenaries, Others Call Them Saviors. So What Are They?" *Komsomolskaia pravda*, 21 March 1992, in FBIS-SOV-92-058, 25 March 1992, 67.
40. Averianov, 71.
41. The apparent disconnect of Reds claiming to hate the former Communist Party of the Soviet Union (CPSU) is that the Reds are Bolsheviks who publicly claim that the CPSU strayed far from the Bolshevik line and failed to bring true communism to the state. This approach also allows the Reds to avoid being blamed for the ills of the old system, while maintaining ideological purity should the march toward communism resume.

42. Galina Mashtakova, "On the Cossack's Quarrel", *Rossiiskaia gazeta,* 25 June 1992, in FBIS-USR-92-088, 15 July 1992, 28. Of course, there are often more than one claimant to the title of ataman. G. Moiseev of Canada proclaims that he is ataman of the Don Cossack Host.

43. Ibid.

44. *Moskovskiie novosti,* No. 19, reporting on the aftermath of the clash between Ingush and Cossacks on 28 and 29 April 1992.

45. RFE/RL Report on the USSR, No 42, 18 October 1991, 40.

46. An ataman is empowered to order five strokes of the nagaika for infractions of Cossack morality. Additional strokes for more serious infractions are usually dictated by actions of the rada (council). A. Orlov, "Kazachata" (Cossackdom), *Komsomolskaia pravda,* 29 February 1992.

47. *Moscow News,* 10-17 November 1991.

48. A. Aleksandrova, *Na boievom postu,* October 1991.

49. Moscow All-Union Radio Maiak, 12 October 1991, in FBIS-USR-91-044, 29 October 1991, 50.

50. Mazirin, "Kuda kazak skachet."

51. Lieutenant General V. Bogachev, Far East Military District and chief of the Rear Services, accepted the post of ataman of the Union of Transbaikal and Far East Russian Cossacks. The gold epaulets of a Cossack general and an engraved saber accompanied the appointment. "Kazaki poluchili atamana, ataman, shashku" (The Cossacks Receive an Ataman and the Ataman, a Saber), *Krasnaia zvezda,* 23 March 1991.

52. ITAR-TASS, 5 May 1992, in FBIS-SOV-92-088, 6 May 1992, 19.

53. Conversations with a serving Russian officer during July 1992.

54. *Rossiiskaia gazeta,* 18 June 1992, as cited in FBIS-SOV-92-122, 28.

55. Alexander Luganskii, ataman of the Naur district of the Terek Cossacks, said that the Cossacks would set up their own military units and that five sotnia were already formed in Vladikavkaz. A thousand Cossacks from Arkhonskaia of the Mozdok district have volunteered to serve in Northern Ossetia. Interfax, 22 February 1992, in FBIS-SOV-92-036, 24 February 1992, 59.

56. Interfax, 25 March 1992, in FBIS-SOV-92-059, 59; and Kiev Radio Ukraine World Service, 1 April 1992, in FBIS-SOV-92-064, 2 April 1992, 66. In an interview Hetman Chornovil of the Ukraine Cossacks stated that the Don Cossacks' oath of loyalty to Russia, while living in the Ukraine, is an attempt to restore the Soviet Union and the totalitarian order. Yuri Pryhornytski, *Literaturna Ukraiina,* No. 20, 21 May 1992, in FBIS-SOV-92-080.

57. Mashtakova, 29.

58. *Postfactum,* 23 June 1992, in FBIS-SOV-92-123, 25 June 1992, 54.

59. Aleksandr Simonov, "Zashchitit' russkikh na Severnore Kavkaze toogut tolko russkiie" (Only Russians can Defend Russians in the Northern Caucasus), *Situatsiia,* No. 21 (1992), 6-7.

60. Interfax, 22 February 1992, in FBIS-SOV-92-036, 24 February 1992, 59.

61. Radio Moscow, 2 December 1991, in Radio Liberty Report on SOVSET, 4 December 1991.

62. Nuri Muftakh, "Uralsk incidents: 1. What MeansAre There for Resistance? 2. A Dog Barks, the Caravan Moves On. 3. Kazakhs Need Weapons" (three part series), *Yegemendi Qazaqstan* (in Kazakh), 20, 21 and 24 March 1992, in FBIS-USR-92-090, 20 July 1992, 93.

63. V. Zubkov, "Kazachestvo pered litsoe istorii" (Cossackdom Before the Face of History), *Izvestiia,* 21 March 1992.

APPENDIX

CHRONOLOGY OF COSSACK MEDIA COVERAGE, 1989–1992

Spring, 1989. Creation of the chapter of Cossack Countrymen in Moscow under the auspices of the All-Union Historical and Cultural Monument Preservation Society Central Propaganda House.

29 June 1990. Founding of the Union of Cossacks, a Communist front organization.

30 November 1990. Declaration of Russia's Cossack movement by the first council of atamans at Krasnodar.

19 January 1991. *Komsomolskaia pravda.* Ataman of Kuban Cossacks forming an officers' cossack "100" organization. Reserve and active duty officers being registered. Commander is an elective position. Priority task is to conduct military-patriotic training of youth in preparation for Soviet Army service. Rostov-on-Don Don Cossacks recently held a krug calling for the establishment of Cossack power on the Don. Kuban Cossacks to hold a krug on 24 January, 72 years to the day when the Red Army was ordered to annihilate all cossacks.

March 1991. *Sovetskii Patriot.* Commentary on the Don Cossack krug and the general Cossack movement. Don Cossacks are establishing parallel organs of power to that of local government. Cossack courts are called for. The Cossacks wish to become an ethical, cultural and economic force in the region. The krug decided to petition the Minister of Defense to allow the formation of Don Cossack units within the Soviet Armed Forces. They propose establishment of cossack mounted chasseur regiments, spetsnaz regiments, separate infantry (plastun) divisions, mounted border guard companies, and complete ship crews. Don Cossacks also wish to take over the Novocherkassk Higher Signals School and use it as the Don Cossack Junkers School to teach combined arms, artillery, signal, service support, and military medicine. Author is not a strong supporter of the Cossack movement.

23 March 1991. *Krasnaia zvezda.* Military chaplain Father Tikhon consecrated the banner of the Ussuri Cossack Forces (voiska) in the Khristorozhdestvenskii Church in Khabarovksk. Then a large Cossack gathering, attended by the atamans and representatives of all Cossack forces being revived east of Lake Baikal, was held in the okrug officers' club. Lieutenant General V. Bogachev, Far East Military District chief of Rear Services, Major General Gurinovich, Military District prosecutor; and Lieutenant General V. Butenko, chief of the Far East border district, and leaders of the districts attended the gathering.

Participants adopted a decision to divide the Ussuri Cossack forces into two districts, the Maritime and Khabarovsk, and to form a union of Transbaikal and Far Eastern Cossacks with its center in Khabarovsk. The participants decided to depart from tradition by electing the first official ataman of the union with a vote of military atamans, rather than appointing him. Lieutenant General Bogachev was elected. He was presented a Cossack general's shoulder boards and an engraved saber.

29 April 1991. TASS. Eight people were killed in clashes on April 28 between Chechen-Ingush and Cossacks in a Cossack settlement 80 kilometers from Grozny in the Chechen-Ingush ASSR. Sixteen others received stab or bullet wounds. The incident reportedly took place outside a hospital where two Chechen-Ingush youths were recovering from injuries received in a fight with Cossacks the previous day.

30 April 1991. *Moskovskie novosti.* Following the clash between Ingush and Cossacks in Troitskaia stanitsa on April 28/29 the local rural soviet decided that Cossacks be resettled outside the republic. The Kuban Cossacks and Stavropol expressed readiness to receive them, but attempts are now being made to discourage their departure for fear of precipitating a mass resettlement throughout the North Caucasus. The Cossacks are being promised a Cossack okrug, which they have been demanding for two years, and access to jobs in retail trade and law enforcement agencies.

May 1991. *Voenno-istoricheskii zhurnal.* Articles on Cossacks in history begin appearing regularly in this right-wing publication.

10 May 1991. Radio Moscow Russia Network. The Don military-historical club has proposed creating Cossack formations in the Soviet Army. They propose restoring Cossack military names and changing the text of the military oath in that section which refers to the Communist Party. As reported by the Postfactum agency, Vladimir Popov, chief of the Rostov Cossack district stated that according to available data USSR Minister of Defense Dmitry Yazov has approved the idea of creating Cossack units.

24 May 1991. TASS. Cossack atamans of south Russia met in Moscow for a two-day assembly 22-23 May. They were addressed by RSFSR presidential candidate Albert Makashov, and vice-presidential candidates Ramazan Abdulatipov and Aleksei Sergeev. Presidential candidate Nikolai Ryzhkov also discussed his program with some of those attending the assembly. Representatives of a number of the mountain people of the North Caucasus attended the assembly, which was called to discuss ways of avoiding further inter-ethnic clashes in the North Caucasus. The assembly proposed that a congress of the peoples of the North Caucasus be held.

26 May-2 June 1991. *Moscow News.* Full page article on Ural Cossacks in Kazakhstan. Of 250,000 inhabitants 70,000 are of Cossack ancestry. Dues-paying membership in the Ural Cossack movement, Vozrozhdenie (Rebirth), is 2,500. They can easily put 7,000 people on the streets for a rally or demonstration whenever needed. There has been a battle for control of the Ural Cossacks between Ataman Alexandr Kachalin and Valery Shukov. Shukov pushes for the establishment of a Yaik republic and abolishment of Soviet rule for Cossack rule. The council of atamans threw out Shukov, who promptly challenged Kachalin to a duel for the position of ataman. Refused, Shukov now calls himself the ataman of the Yaik Army and is searching for allies among the Siberian, Don and Kuban Cossacks.

28 May 1991. *Novoe vremia.* This popular magazine begins carrying full page advertisements for the Kazachok store in Kamensk-Shakhtinskii where Cossack uniforms and accouterments in the style of 1913 are on sale.

29 June 1991. *Sovetskaia Rossiia*. First anniversary of the founding of the (Red) Union of Cossacks. Portrayed as a patriotic organization for teaching youth love for the motherland.

5 July 1991. *Syn otechestva*. Full-page article arguing against Cossack rebirth and the Union of Cossacks.

July 1991. Krug in Moscow of over thirty "White" Cossack organizations. Voted to reestablish the Union of Cossack Hosts of Russia (SVRK).

14-21 July 1991. *Moscow News*. Pika, the first Cossack news agency, opened in Volgograd. Founders include press center of the regional Cossack Union of the Don Army, the military, historical commission of All-Don club named in honor of Ataman Platov, the historical-cultural association Sholokhov assembly, and the Cossack museum.

July 1991. *Vestnik protivovozdushnoi oborony*. Article on the founding of the first organization of the Union of Cossacks in an unnamed air defense missile regiment.

19 August 1991. Coup in Moscow. "White" Cossacks defend the Russian White House.

20 August 1991. *Sovetskaia Rossiia*. The Zelenchukskii-Urupskii Cossack Soviet Republic, as part of the RSFSR, proclaimed at a congress of Cossacks from Zelenchukskii and Urupskii districts of the Karachaevo-Cherkess SSR. The congress requested that the Supreme Soviet of the Russian Federation approve this declaration. The congress stated that a survey of people in the area show that most favor it. The declaration is aimed at the rebirth of the Cossack way of life, communal possession and use of the land, and cultural traditions, and was proclaimed at Zelenchukskaia stanitsa. This is a "Red" Cossack movement.

8 September 1991. Moscow Radio Russia Network. Cossacks of the lower Volga elect Aleksandr Zabolotnev from Bunino, Novonikolaievsk district, Volgograd region ataman. Zabolotnev, a farmer, declared that all Cossacks remained loyal to Boris Yeltsin, the legitimate president of Russia, during the coup. Cossacks assisted Volgograd democrats during the coup by guarding rallies against the junta. The republic must be able to defend itself against future putsches and Cossack youth must be an inalienable and most reliable part of the Russian national guard.

October 1991. *Na boyevom postu*. Pictorial article on visit to Cossack sotnia of Nezlobnaia stanitsa. Ataman is V. Kireev.

October 1991. Elections for ataman in Don Cossack capital of Novocherkassk replace Mikhail Sholokhov with Meshcheriakov—a former Party secretary and "Red" Cossack.

3 October 1991. *Krasnaia zvezda*. Major General (Ret) L. Bublik headed a collective which wrote *The History of the Transbaikal and Far East Cossacks* at the Frunze Academy. The book covers the opening of the Amur in the seventeenth century, the founding of the Transbaikal, Amur and Ussuri Cossacks, Russian-Chinese relations, the Russo-Japanese War, and Cossack ways and traditions. The book has yet to be published, and the military publishing house is in no hurry to do so.

12 October 1991. Moscow All-Union Radio Maiak Network. During a meeting between the economic association of Transbaikal Cossacks and Major General Aleksei Rusanov, head of the Transbaikal border district, an agreement was reached to replace the border guards with a Cossack regiment. The Cossacks will combine their border duty with agricultural work, upgrading villages and working the land.

18 October 1991. RFE/RL Report on the USSR. The executive committee of the Rostov region Soviet decided to create volunteer Cossack units (druzhiny) to maintain public order in Don villages and cities. Cossacks will help patrol streets, maintain order on public transportation and during mass events, fight hooliganism, drunkenness, illicit liquor and drug addiction, and assist the prosecutor's office, the courts and the tax inspectorate.

24 October 1991. *Izvestiia.* During the night of 20-21 August the Sverdlovsk city Soviet building was the site for registration of volunteers for Cossack sotnias and people's militia. They were enrolled to go to Moscow to defend the Russian White house during the coup. They were never sent.

10-17 November 1991. *Moscow News.* Cossacks in the area of Chita (Eastern Siberia) have voted down their chief and his aides. The Cossacks refused to accept his decisions on public whippings, creation of a intelligence branch, creation of a police force for public morality, and maintenance of files on members of the Cossack community.

10 November 1991. TASS. The second All-Russian Great Cossack Krug, the congress of the Union of Cossacks of Russia, ended in Stavropol today. The krug declared that the Union of Cossacks and its regional structures are the rightful successors of Cossack national and state formations which were illegally abolished in the past, and discussed plans to bring about the historic and spiritual rebirth of the Cossacks. The krug sent an appeal to Dzhakhar Dudaev, president of the Chechen republic, calling on him to avoid bloodshed and protesting "the intolerable nature of human rights violations and of all manifestations of national oppression." The krug also passed resolutions on events in South Ossetia and the Dniester Republic. The creation of a Don republic was approved.

13 November 1991. *Sovetskaia Rossiia.* The second congress of the Cossack Union was held in Stavropol and involved 563 delegates and 200 guests. Ataman Boris Alamazov of Nevskaia (city of St. Petersburg) instructed the delegates on the traditions and rules of a Grand Assembly. The Don Cossacks were best prepared for the congress. The regional atamans' council recently proclaimed the Don Cossack Republic and drafted supporting documents on self-government and land use. The Grand Assembly supported the proclamation of the Don Republic. Other highlights included

The announcement of the impending migration of the 12,500 Sunzha Cossacks from war-torn Northern Ossetia to the Stavropol district. Stavropol district Soviet Chairman I.S. Boldyrev was present.

Cossacks in Chechen-Ingush feel threatened. N.A. Liashenko, ataman of the Zelenchukso-Ugup Republic and V.N. Tkachev, ataman of Batalpashinsk (both in Karachaevo-Cherkessia), complained that Russia does not care and will not protect them.

P.S. Sazonov (Dubasary City, Dniester Republic) echoed fears for Dniester Republic Cossacks. Seven were killed and many were wounded in October fighting. The Dniester Republic has appealed to both Ukraine and Russia for help and for incorporation. There has been no support.

The Grand Assembly voted

1) not to allow private ownership of Cossack land and to restore traditional communal Cossack land use;

2) to call for prudence and prevention of bloodshed in Chechen-Ingush, and guarantee assistance for brother Cossacks;

3) to establish an association of Cossack writers and a Cossack cultural fund;

4) to work on economic reform and restoration of Cossack traditions and way of life.

15 November 1991. *Literaturnaia Rossiia.* Front page picture spread on the Second All-Russian Great Cossack Krug.

November 1991. *Sobesednik.* Feature on Ataman Georgy Galkin in Chechen-Ingush. Chechen-Ingush wants to establish a Muslim republic and ban the use of Russian. This makes Cossacks second-class citizens and has resulted in a mass migration from the area. Moscow does nothing to support the Russian Cossacks. Dudayev is a smart, pleasant man, but he has to deal with the problems of ultra-nationalism.

November 1991. *Agitator armii i flota.* The foundation of the Union of Cossacks is the true sign of the rebirth of Russia.

27 November-3 December 1991. *Rossiia.* On 17 November in the capital city of the Don Cossacks, Novocherkassk, a Grand Ataman Council of the Southern Russian Cossacks met and formed the Union of Southern Russian Cossacks. They chose Sergei Meshcheriakov, ataman of the Union of Cossacks of the Oblast Army of the Don, as its ataman. The council further proclaimed the establishment of a Union of Republics and Southern Russian Cossacks and defined its legislative and executive organs. The council appointed a legation to Moscow entrusted with extraordinary, plenipotentiary powers. The council further appointed a transitional government for the new union. They sent a demand to the president of Russia and the president of the USSR for an executive order, within 24 hours, authorizing the formation and arming of a national Cossack guard.

When no executive order was given the Grand Krug of the Union of Southern Russian Cossacks met in Novocherkassk on 20 November and declared registration open for a National Cossack Guard. One hundred men were immediately registered. President Yeltsin was informed of the formation of this unit, directly subordinate to his command, and the request for the withdrawal of the Don sotnia spetsnaz division from the Caucasus to Southern Russia, to further strengthen this National Cossack Guard. Yury Galushkin, ataman of the legation to Moscow, is conducting negotiations with Russia.

2 December 1991. Radio Moscow. A constituent congress in Samara set up a Union of Cossacks of the Volga and Urals. The union includes Cossack communities along the Volga from Astrakhan to Ioshkar-Ola, the capital of the Mari Republic, and two Cossack hosts, the Ural and the Orenburg. One of the chief aims of the union is to preserve the sovereignty and integrity of Russian historical frontiers. Colonel Gusev, a deputy of the Samara region Soviet, was elected ataman. The inclusion of Ural Cossacks, who live in Kazakhstan, is bound to cause concern in Kazakhstan.

14 December 1991. *Sovetskaia Rossiia.* The rehabilitation of the Cossacks is a powerful national, political movement. It is concerned with the restoration of territorial rights, self-government, readjustment of borders. The central idea is that seventy years of communist rule must be disregarded and all borders and lands must be returned to the way it was before the revolution. The only exception is that Finland and Poland should go their own way. This will create difficulties in those areas where the new Cossack republics (Don and Terek) borders overlap with the borders of the breakaway national republics. The Caucasus, Dniester, Chechen-Ingush, and Ossetia all present problems. The Cossack movement is based on defending the interests of Russian-speaking people, yet Cossacks are uniquely multinational. The Don, Kuban, Stavropol and Terek Cossacks have formed a Union of Southern Russia to protect their interests.

19 December 1991. Moscow Central Television First Program. Cossack detachments have begun arriving in Dubasary to defend the Dniester Republic. The Moldovan parliament has declared the Dniester Republic illegal.

1 January 1992. End of the Soviet Union. Birth of the Commonwealth of Independent States.

9 January 1992. *Rossiiskaia gazeta.* The CPSU gave secret instructions to the former Rostov region Communist Committee not to allow the democrats to come together with the Cossacks. The communists must not lose control of the Cossacks at any cost. CPSU members should publicly quit the Party in order to gain positions with the Cossack movement.

14 January 1992. *Lesnaia gazeta.* The revision of Cossack traditions, culture and way of life is natural. The Republic of the Cossacks of the Don, the Kuban and Stavropol wants to give special rights to land, natural resources and property at the expense of others. The Democratic Party of Russia calls for the spiritual and cultural rebirth of Cossacks, the unity of Russia and the observance of the rights and freedoms of Russians everywhere. The Democratic Party opposes breakaway republics of every nature.

19-26 January 1992. *Moscow News.* History of the Cossack movement and the split between "Red" and "White" Cossacks.

23 January 1992. *Sovetskaia Rossiia.* Kuban Cossacks send protest to Boris Yeltsin concerning the actions of district administration head V. Diakonov. His activities in economic reform, land reform and price liberalization are seen as ruinous to the populace. Kuban Cossacks did not select Diakonov and other executive representatives. There are over 250 Cossack organizations functioning on the Kuban, yet Diakonov has refused to recognize the law On the Rehabilitation of Repressed Peoples and has openly suppressed the Cossack movement. He is trying to set non-Cossacks against Cossacks and has misrepresented the Cossack movement to President Yeltsin. He reported the 18 December 1991 meeting between the Kuban Cossack council and deputies of the district soviet as an attempted military coup using the servicemen of the Krasnodar garrison. As a result of this false report discharge proceedings were initiated against V. Belousov, chief of the Krasnodar Higher Military Command-Engineering School for Missile Forces and Colonel P. Muzhikov, a senior instructor at this school and Ataman of the Yekaterinodar division of the Kuban Cossack council. The atamans of the Kuban give a vote of no confidence to V. Diakonov and request that he be relieved.

28 January 1992. *Sovetskaia Rossiia.* Ataman Aleksandr Martynov of the South Sakhalin Cossacks called for the economic revival of the Kurile Islands, "lands discovered by our ancestors, the early pioneers of these parts." The call was at the Great Krug of the Sakhalin Island Okrug. The Great Krug was organized a year ago and unites nine villages and 450 families.

5 February 1992. *Komsomolskaia pravda.* Stavropol marketplace is experiencing very real difficulties as the Cossacks attempt to take over the market.

February 1992. *Syn otechestva.* The Don Cossack Host has petitioned to establish a military academy in Novocherkassk in an old signal school. The new academy would have a combined arms, artillery, rear services and military-medicine faculty. Don and Kuban Cossacks wish to raise all-Cossack subunits for service in the armed forces of the CIS.

21 February 1992. Moscow Radio Russia. The Grand Krug of the atamans of Cossack Troops, meeting in South Sakhalin, have demanded that the Kurile Islands be handed over to its jurisdiction. The Cossacks discussed the agenda for economic development of Sakhalin and the Kurile Islands and the possibility of opening a branch of the Central Cossack Trade House there. Exploitation of the Kurile Islands' natural resources was discussed with the goal of becoming independent of fuel deliveries from the mainland by 1995.

22 February 1992. Interfax. A krug of the Kuban Cossack Assembly (Rada) and Union of Stavropol Region Cossacks met in Vladikavkaz in response to Chechen violence, felonious assaults, murders and arson. Terek Cossacks declared that "Cossacks have exhausted all legal remedies and will have to take up arms should Russia fail to defend them." They demanded that Cossacks be rehabilitated as an estate, Cossack autonomy be created in the territory of the Chechen Republic, ataman rule of villages be instituted and that Cossack lands be publicly owned by the Cossacks. Alexandr Luganskii, ataman of the Naur district of the Terek Cossacks, said that Cossacks would set up their own military units and that five sotnia were formed in Vladikavkaz. A thousand Cossacks from Arkhonskaia of the Mozdok district have volunteered to serve in Northern Ossetia.

25 February 1992. Moscow Radio Russia. The first edition of Stanitsa, new Cossack non-ideological newspaper, published.

27 February 1992. Interfax. Anatoly Plugaru, the minister of National Security of Moldova, charged that the presence of Cossacks on Moldovan territory constitutes interference in the affairs of an independent state. He charges that many of the armed Cossacks are known criminal fugitives and are there to make money.

29 February 1992. *Komsomolskaia pravda.* Discussion of school children's attitude toward the Cossack movement and the Cossack practice of flogging. The children generally favored public flogging for lying, drunkenness and thievery. The Union of Cossacks wants the right to carry sabers and kinzhal daggers publicly, and to maintain a Cossack militia. The Cossack ataman is empowered to order five strokes of the nagaika for infractions of Cossack morality.

March 1992. *Voenno-istoricheskii zhurnal.* Four-page article on Guards Cossacks history.

2 March 1992. Postfactum. Cossacks and Dniester Republic militia surround Moldovan police station. Fighting breaks out which leaves two killed and three wounded (one Cossack killed and one Cossack severely wounded). Cossacks are reportedly from the Don and Volga.

2 March 1992. Moscow Maiak Radio. The press service of the Union of Cossacks has accused the Moldovan secret services of subversive actions and of dressing saboteurs in the uniforms of Dniester militia and Cossacks. The saboteurs then attack guards, civilians and officials.

2 March 1992. *Izvestiia.* The two Cossack casualties from the fighting in Moldova have been identified as Don Cossacks from Volgodonsk. Don Cossack Field Chief V. Rateiev explains that the Don Cossacks are there at the request of local Cossacks who do not wish to be under Romanian rule.

4 March 1992. Moscow Radio Russia. A council of atamans of the Black Sea Cossacks in Tiraspol, Dniester Republic, has placed key installations under guard. Kuban, Don and Ural Cossacks are arriving in Tiraspol to aid the Dniester Republic.

5 March 1992. *Krasnaia zvezda.* Six guardsmen and Cossacks have died and 25 have been wounded in recent fighting. Forces around the embattled village of Kochiyery include up to 1,000 guardsmen and Cossacks.

11 March 1992. *Krasnaia zvezda.* Ataman of the Regional Union of Don Cossacks, Sergei Meshcheriakov, declared that Cossacks were in the Dniester Republic combat zone voluntarily. Don Cossacks who live in Moldova have no wish to become part of Romania. Don Cossacks will leave only when the complete safety of the local populace is guaranteed.

13 March 1992. *Nezavisimaia gazeta.* The Union of Cossack Hosts of Russia (Whites) are opposed to the dispatch of Don Cossacks to Moldova by Ataman Meshcheriakov because "the red flag is flying over Tiraspol." Further, they stated that Moldova could easily use the Cossacks to fan anti-Russian sentiment. The Ministry of Defense originally approached the Union of Cossack Hosts with the idea of sending volunteers to Dniester and offering to pay, arm and equip the volunteers. The Union of Cossack Hosts rejected the offer and the ministry then approached the Don Cossack atamans. The Union of Cossack Hosts rejects adventurism and prefers the incorporation of Cossack units within the Russian Army. The Russian government, however, is dragging its feet in forming Cossack units.

14 March 1992. *Sovetskaia Rossiia.* The Cossacks have fought bravely and well at Dubasary and Kochiyery. Their arrival in the Dniester is the first example of a decisive response to an appeal for aid from Russia. Russians no longer will silently endure the mockery of nationalists. Most of the Don Cossacks in the Dniester were former career military men. The Dniester is Russian land and the people want to stay Russian. The Russian government is doing nothing to stop this civil war. Although Cossacks defended the White House during the coup, they would not do so today.

18 March 1992. *Literaturnaia gazeta.* The Kurile Islands are Russian, returned to Russia after World War II, and the Cossacks are ready and willing to guard them and ask that they be put under the jurisdiction of the Cossack Union. The Kuriles are now under a virtual economic blockade from the mainland, which is denying fuel and raw materials and overcharging for transportation fees.

19 March 1992. Moscow Radio Television Network. Interview with the CIS minister of defense, Air Marshal Yevgeny Shaposhnikov, in which he states that although he is of Cossack ancestry he is not in favor of incorporating Cossack units in the armed forces.

19 March 1992. Moscow Ostankino Television First Program. Ukrainian authorities confiscate four hand grenades and three submachine guns from three Kuban Cossacks en route to the Dniester. Ataman Meshcheriakov of the Regional Union of Don Cossacks stated that "the Don Cossacks are not defending socialism in the Dniester region but are defending the Russian and Slav population from genocide." We appeal to President Yeltsin and to Chairman of the Supreme Soviet Khasbulatov not to close their eyes to the situation, and to state their position on the protection of the Russian people and Slavs along the Dniester.

21 March 1992. *Komsomolskaia pravda.* There is a high proportion of former paratroopers, spetsnaz and reconnaissance personnel in the Cossack forces on the Dniester. Not all of them are as pro-communist as is the government of the Dniester Republic. Yet the Cossacks see their role as defending Russians.

23 March 1992. TASS. Interview with the CIS minister of defense, Air Marshal Yevgeny Shaposhnikov, in which he again states that he is opposed to incorporating Cossack units into the armed forces.

24 March 1992. *Washington Post Foreign Service.* Cossacks have become a real political force, but their numbers are uncertain. Active Don Cossacks are over 10,000. Cossacks offer protection to the thirty million Russians who live outside the boundaries of Russia. The Don Cossacks recently called for a ban on "Zionist organizations" and strict controls on the movement of Muslims on Don territory. The ataman of the Don Cossacks is a former communist.

25 March 1992. Interfax. Two hundred Cossacks of the city of Krasnodon in the Lugansk region of Ukraine have taken an oath of allegiance to the Don and Russia at a local Orthodox church. The ceremony was witnessed by Cossacks from Lischansk, Schastye and Lugansk.

March 1992. *Situatsiia.* Interior Troops newspaper prints positive interview with Ataman Meshcheriakov and his assistant ("First Comrade") Aleksei Ozerov.

1 April 1992. Kiev Radio Ukraine World Service. Interview with Viacheslav Chornovil, Ukrainian leader and hetman of Ukrainian Cossacks, on the "provocation" of Krasnodon Cossacks swearing allegiance to the Don Cossacks and Russia. Several days ago the Don Cossacks, who claim part of Ukraine, swore allegiance to Russia. This political game is at variance with the interests of the Ukrainian state. The Ukrainian Cossacks are organized with many sotnia and regiments all over Ukraine.

1-7 April 1992. *Rossiia.* Ataman of Black Sea Cossack troops, Aleksandr Vasilevich Kucher, interviewed. Hero of the Soviet Union, Ivan Vasilevich Pashchenko appears to be in charge of the Cossack staff. Pashchenko received his HSU in 1945 for aerial combat. He retired from the Air Force in 1973 as a colonel. He retired in Tiraspol. Other Cossacks who live in the region include those in Tiraspol, Dubasary, Dniester and Slobodz. Cossacks are assigned to the most dangerous sector close to the Dubasary bridge.

2 April 1992. *Komsomolskaia pravda.* Lengthy article on Cossack movement, the "Red" and "White" counter-movements and the fragmentation of effort. Interview with Ataman Vladimir Kosianov, Orenburg Cossack Host. Cossack history, religion, classic krug democracy need to be taught to the people. Over two million Cossacks were repressed and over 1.1 million Cossacks were killed during the 1920s and 1930s. Transbaikal Cossacks have had discussions with the Transbaikal Military District regarding stationing Cossack border guard units on the Russian-Chinese border. Interview with Ataman Kachalin of the Ural Cossack Host.

9 April 1992. *Sovetskaia Rossiia.* Eulogy for Starshina Aleksandr Berlizov, killed in the Dniester fighting.

15 April 1992. *Megapolis Express.* Synopsis of Kurile Islands dispute. There are approximately 600 families in twelve villages on four islands. The Cossacks' grand economic plans have no financial backing.

15 April 1992. *Argumenty i fakty.* Bolsheviks killed approximately 1.5 million Cossacks and took 53 million desiatins (1,431,000,000 acres) of their land. Two driving ideas behind the Cossack movement are self-government and return of their lands. Cossacks maintain an iron discipline in their ranks and provide service. They wish to provide all-Cossack units to serve in the armed forces.

16 April 1992. Moscow Radio Russia. Don and Kuban Cossacks begin leaving the Dniester per an agreement with the Don and Kuban atamans and the leadership of the Dniester region.

16 April 1992. Interfax. Descendants of Cossack families living in Kazan intend to create a Cossack community and a local branch of the Orenburg Cossacks to defend the interests of the Russian-speaking population of Tatarstan. Yury Yegorov reported that Kazan Cossacks are establishing ties with the Orenburg, Don, and Irkutsk Cossacks and the staff of the Cossack Forces in Moscow. "Cossack-dom is an international unity. That is why we part from the Tatar and Russian national-patriots and invite under our banner not only the direct descendants of Cossack families, but everybody who cherishes the idea of Cossackdom."

16 April 1992. *Nezavisimaia gazeta.* "Russian Cossacks did not charge Sergei Meshcheriakov, ataman of the Union of Cossacks of the Don Regional Host, to act on their behalf at the Sixth Russian Federation Congress of Peoples Deputies." Russian Union of Cossacks representatives further state that Meshcheriakov did not participate in the work of the Russian Union of Cossacks Atamans Council on the issue of required steps on the Dniester. Instead, Meshcheriakov used his time in Moscow to meet with Russian deputies "who are known for their unpatriotic sentiments and who actively conduct work to create a schism in the Cossack community."

28 April 1992. *Sovetskaia Rossiia.* Article on withdrawal of Don and Kuban Cossacks which reminds readers of the indigenous Cossacks (Black Sea) who remain to man the trenches. Article dwells on the dedication of non-combatant female medical orderlies.

5 May 1992. TASS. The Russian president and parliament intend to issue a range of legislative acts regulating some aspects of Russian Cossack life to convert them into allies of central authority. There will be Cossack regiments in the Russian Army. A law on Cossack rehabilitation and Cossack land use also will be issued. The government commission for drafting these laws is headed by Sergei Shakhrai, who stated that Cossack historic traditions were considered in resolving the issues of land use, local self-government, and military service. The president's decree on Cossack military service is to be issued on 20 May. Each Cossack region will have its own regiment and will bear part of the expense of maintaining the regiment. Military chaplains will be introduced into the regiments per an agreement with the Moscow Patriarch.

13 May 1992. *Nezavisimaia gazeta.* The Council of the Russian National Assembly socio-political movement (right-wing, anti-Yeltsin) calls upon the Cossacks of Russia to take part in their congress on 12-13 June in Moscow. "Cossacks can and should contribute to the Russian people's struggle against everything that transforms Russia into an appendage of Western politicians and deprives it of independence and national identity."

15 May 1992. *Literaturnaia Rossiia.* The dance ensemble Cossack Russia was founded about a year ago in Lipetsk. The purpose of the group is to preserve Cossack culture and propagandize the Cossack movement.

21 May 1992. *Izvestiia.* The goal of the Cossack movement is the rebirth of the rich and famous Cossack lands. Two years ago the Communist Party gained control of Cossack atamans, who danced like puppets to the Party's tune. The Party used the cover of the Cossack movement to entrench itself in southern Russia as a neo-Bolshevik, national totalitarianism. Traditional Cossack values of discipline, respect for law, bravery, hard work, respect for elders, and the strengthening of the family were pushed aside for political ambitions fueled by discrimination against non-Russians.

The ataman of the Union of Cossacks of the Don Cossacks Region is Sergei Meshcheriakov, who was elected in October 1991 and immediately conducted a military mobilization of Don Cossacks. His second order was to register all Cossacks. This order, which was countermanded, would have disenfranchised the majority of the populace. Meshcheriakov used large groups (three hundred) of Cossacks to intimidate and take over meetings of the Council of People's Deputies. He then used this forum to declare the Republic of the Don and to staff all its offices with Communist Party and Komsomol functionaries. Meshcheriakov unilaterally sent Cossack forces to the Dniester, and when the Cossack atamans met in Moscow to discuss the problem, Meshcheriakov absented himself from the proceedings to meet with anti-democrats. Atamans of almost all Cossack groups in Russia joined in sending a telegram of concern to the Don, asking the Cossacks to examine the manner in which Meshcheriakov is fulfilling his duties as ataman. The Don Cossack leadership has issued anti-Semite, anti-Muslim and anti-Kazakh proclamations and has begun measures to segregate various populations in the region.

The Cossacks must banish the political adventurers, rogues and dark forces. Russia needs a law rehabilitating the Cossacks and needs to create Cossack Guards regiments in the Russian Federal Guards and Cossack regiments in the army. Cossack cadet schools need to be founded.

21 May 1992. *Literaturna Ukraina.* Interview with Hetman Viacheslav Chornovil, Ukraine Cossacks. The Don Cossacks' oath of loyalty to Russia while living in the Ukraine is an attempt to restore the Soviet Union and the totalitarian order. We need to take immediate and certain action against them.

27 May 1992. *Komsomolskaia pravda.* Siberian Cossacks near Omsk are building a new stanitsa called Ust-Zaostrovk. Twenty Cossack families are settling on 43 hectares.

7 June 1992. *Moscow News.* Interview with Ataman Meshcheriakov, Cossack Union of the Don Cossack Regional Host. Meshcheriakov renounces the CPSU and accuses it of trying to use the Cossack movement for their own purposes. He admits that he and several other Don Cossacks were Party functionaries, but he quit the Party when that was a hazardous thing. He claims that at least one million of the four million inhabitants of the Rostov region are hereditary Cossacks. Hallmarks of the Cossack movement are

1) Cossack land ownership, private land ownership, but with common land tenure;

2) maintenance of a unique, mobile, inexpensive fighting force;

3) democratic self-rule with an elected leader who fulfills the people's will but maintains rigid discipline;

4) preferential tax treatment due to Cossack willingness to be the first to shed blood for the motherland while also being farmers and producers;

5) Orthodox religion.

The Red-White split on the Don must be healed. Meshcheriakov denies ordering Don Cossacks to the Dniester, and states that they were all volunteers.

June 1992. *Situatsiia.* Interview with the ataman of the Vladikavkaz Detachment, Terek Cossacks, Vladimir Sireakin and first sotnia commander, Vladikavkaz Regiment, Aleksandr Cherniutskii. "Only Russians can defend Russians in the Northern Caucasus.

10 June 1992. *Rossiiskaia gazeta.* Russian international lawyer defends rights of Cossacks to fight on the Dniester.

18 June 1992. *Rossiiskaia gazeta.* Decree No. 632 of the Russian Federation president, On Measures to Implement the Russian Federation Law On the Rehabilitation of Repressed Peoples in Relation to the Cossacks, was signed by President Yeltsin on 15 June 1992.

20 June 1992. ITAR-TASS. Amur Cossacks from Birobidzhan have conducted a rally whose motto was "The Kuriles have always belonged to Russia and we will not surrender them to anyone."

21 June 1992. *Komsomolskaia pravda.* Ukrainian Cossacks solemnly abjure the oath of loyalty sworn to the tsar of Muscovy in 1654. Hetman Viacheslav Chornovil stated that this was not done to break the friendship between Russia and Ukraine. Rather, it was to correct the mistake of Bogdan Khmelnitskii and "to expiate the involuntary sin committed by our Cossacks forebears 338 years ago." Ukrainian Cossacks then swore a loyalty oath to Ukraine.

22 June 1992. Postfactum. One hundred Cossacks, backed by two armored personnel carriers, seized the town hall of Kurganinsk in the Krasnodar region. This was in response to the refusal of the local administration to clear the Krasnodar region of ethnic Armenians.

23 June 1992. Moscow Radiotelevision. The Don Cossacks are prepared to return to the Dniester if requested.

23 June 1992. *Narodnaia Armia.* The 500th anniversary of the founding of the Ukrainian Cossacks was observed in Ivano-Frankovsk.

25 June 1992. Postfactum. The third congress of the Russian population of Chechnia will be held in Grozny in mid-August. The Terek Cossacks are organizing the event which is expected to declare an autonomous republic.

2 July 1992. *Sovetskaia Rossiia.* Position of pro-Yeltsin Krasnodar District administration chief V. Diakonov is challenged by the Kuban Cossack Rada. Krasnodar District's production of meat, milk, eggs, grain and vegetables is falling, prices are higher in the Kuban than in most of the rest of Russia, and the crime rate is rising.

5 July 1992. Kiev Ukraine Radio First Program. Anti-Ukraine forces are creating a fifth column in Ukraine under cover of societies and associations. Ataman Ignatkin is preparing children of the Uzhgorod Cossacks for service in the Don Cossack Host. The transgressor must be punished.

9 July 1992. *Pravda.* Khoperskii Cossacks founded in Volgograd district.

20 July 1992. Kazakh Radio Network. Aleksandr Kachalin, ataman of the Ural Cossacks, denied that there are any Ural Cossacks currently fighting in the Dniester region.

IV DOCUMENTS

START II TREATY, MOSCOW, 3 JANUARY 1993

Full text of the treaty between the United States of America and the Russian Federation on further reduction and limitation of strategic offensive arms. The treaty was signed in Moscow by Russian President Boris Yeltsin and US President George Bush.

"The United States of America and the Russian Federation, hereinafter referred to as the parties,

reaffirming their obligations under the treaty between the United States of America and the Union of Soviet Socialist Republics on the reduction and limitation of strategic offensive arms of July 31, 1991, hereinafter referred to as the START Treaty,

stressing their firm commitment to the treaty on the nonproliferation of nuclear weapons of July 1, 1968, and their desire to contribute to its strengthening,

taking into account the commitment by the Republic of Belarus, the Republic of Kazakhstan, and Ukraine to accede to the treaty on the non-proliferation of nuclear weapons of July 1, 1968, as non-nuclear-weapon states parties,

mindful of their undertakings with respect to strategic offensive arms under Article VI of the treaty on the non-proliferation of nuclear weapons of July 1, 1968, and under the treaty between the United States of America and the Union of Soviet Socialist Republics on the limitation of anti-ballistic missile systems of May 26, 1972, as well as the provisions of the joint understanding signed by the presidents of the United States of America and the Russian Federation on June 17, 1992, and of the joint statement on a global protection system signed by the presidents of the United States of America and the Russian Federation on June 17, 1992,

desiring to enhance strategic stability and predictability, and, in doing so, to reduce further strategic offensive arms, in addition to the reductions and limitations provided for in the START Treaty,

considering that further progress toward that end will help lay a solid foundation for a world order built on democratic values that would preclude the risk of outbreak of war,

recognizing their responsibility as permanent members of the United Nations Security Council for maintaining international peace and security,

taking note of United Nations General Assembly Resolution 47/52k of December 9, 1992,

conscious of the new realities that have transformed the political and strategic relations between the parties, and the relations of partnership that have been established between them, have agreed as follows:

ARTICLE I

1. Each party shall reduce and limit its intercontinental ballistic missiles (ICBMs) and ICBM launchers, submarine-launched ballistic missiles (SLBMs) and SLBM launchers, heavy bombers, ICBM warheads, SLBM warheads, and heavy bomber armaments, so that seven years after entry into force of the START Treaty and thereafter, the aggregate number for each party, as counted in accordance with Articles III and IV of this treaty, does not exceed, for warheads attributed to deployed ICBMs, deployed SLBMs, and deployed heavy bombers, a number between 3800 and 4250 or such lower number as each party shall decide for itself, but in no case shall such number exceed 4250.

2. Within the limitations provided for in Paragraph 1 of this article, the aggregate numbers for each party shall not exceed:

(a) 2160, for warheads attributed to deployed SLBMs;

(b) 1200, for warheads attributed to deployed ICBMs of types to which more than one warhead is attributed; and

(c) 650, for warheads attributed to deployed heavy ICBMs.

3. Upon fulfillment of the obligations provided for in Paragraph 1 of this article, each party shall further reduce and limit their ICBMs and ICBM launchers, SLBMs and SLBM launchers, heavy bombers, ICBM warheads, SLBM warheads, and heavy bomber armaments, so that no later than January 1, 2003, and thereafter, the aggregate number for each party, as counted in accordance with Articles III and IV of this treaty, does not exceed, for warheads attributed to deployed ICBMs, deployed SLBMs, and deployed heavy bombers, a number between 3000 and 3500 or a lower such number as each party shall decide for itself but in no case shall such a number exceed 3500.

4. Within the limitations provided for in Paragraph 3 of this article, the aggregate numbers for each party shall not exceed:

(a) a number between 1700 and 1750, for warheads attributed to deployed SLBMs or such a lower number as each party shall decide for itself, but in no case shall such number exceed 1750;

(b) zero, for warheads attributed to deployed ICBMs of types to which more than one warhead is attributed; and

(c) zero, for warheads attributed to deployed heavy ICBMs.

5. The process of reductions provided for in Paragraphs 1 and 2 of this article shall begin upon entry into force of this treaty, shall be sustained throughout the reductions period provided for in Paragraph 1 of this article, and shall be completed no later than seven years after entry into force of the START Treaty. Upon completion of these reductions, the parties shall begin further reductions provided for in Paragraphs 3 and 4 of this article, which shall also be sustained throughout the reductions period defined in accordance with Paragraphs 3 and 6 of this article.

6. Provided that the parties conclude, within one year after entry into force of this treaty, an agreement on a program of assistance to promote the fulfillment of the provisions of this article, the obligations provided for in Paragraphs 3 and 4 of this article and in Article II of this treaty shall be fulfilled by each party no later than December 31, 2003.

ARTICLE II

1. No later than January 1, 2003, each party undertakes to have eliminated or to have converted to launchers of ICBMs to which one warhead is attributed all its deployed and non-deployed launchers of ICBMs to which more than one warhead is attributed under Article III of this treaty (including test launchers and training launchers), with the exception of those launchers of ICBMs other than heavy ICBMs at space launch facilities allowed under the START Treaty, and not to have thereafter launchers of ICBMs to which more than one warhead is attributed. ICBM launchers that have been converted to launch an ICBM of a different type shall not be capable of launching an ICBM of the former type. Each party shall carry out such elimination or conversion using the procedures provided for in the START Treaty, except as otherwise provided for in Paragraph 3 of this article.

2. The obligations provided for in Paragraph 1 of this article shall not apply to silo launchers of ICBMs on which the number of warheads has been reduced to one pursuant to Paragraph 2 of Article III of this treaty.

3. Elimination of silo launchers of heavy ICBMs, including test launchers and training launchers, shall be implemented by means of either:

(a) elimination in accordance with the procedures provided for in Section II of the protocol on procedures governing the conversion or elimination of the items subject to the START Treaty; or

(b) conversion to silo launchers of ICBMs other than heavy ICBMs in accordance with the procedures provided for in the protocol on procedures governing elimination of heavy ICBMs and on procedures governing conversion of silo launchers of heavy ICBMs relating to the treaty between the United States of America and the Russian Federation on further reduction and limitation of strategic offensive arms, hereinafter referred to as the elimination and conversion protocol. No more than 90 silo launchers of heavy ICBMs may be so converted.

4. Each party undertakes not to emplace an ICBM, the launch canister of which has a diameter greater than 2.5 meters, in any silo launcher of heavy ICBMs converted in accordance with Subparagraph 3(b) of this article.

5. Elimination of launchers of heavy ICBMs at space launch facilities shall only be carried out in accordance with Subparagraph 3(a) of this article.

6. No later than January 1, 2003, each party undertakes to have eliminated all of its deployed and non-deployed heavy ICBMs and their launch canisters in accordance with the procedures provided for in the elimination and conversion protocol or by using such missiles for delivering objects into the upper atmosphere or space, and not to have such missiles or launch canisters thereafter.

7. Each party shall have the right to conduct inspections in connection with the elimination of heavy ICBMs and their launch canisters, as well as inspections in connection with the conversion of silo launchers of heavy ICBMs. Except as otherwise provided for in the elimination and conversion protocol, such inspections shall be conducted subject to the applicable provisions of the START Treaty.

8. Each party undertakes not to transfer heavy ICBMs to any recipient whatsoever, including any other party to the START Treaty.

9. Beginning on January 1, 2003, and thereafter, each party undertakes not to produce, acquire, flight-test (except for flight tests from space launch facilities conducted in accordance with the provisions of the START Treaty), or deploy ICBMs to which more than one warhead is attributed under Article III of this treaty.

ARTICLE III

1. For the purposes of attributing warheads to deployed ICBMs and deployed SLBMs under this treaty, the parties shall use the provisions provided for in Article III of the START Treaty, except as otherwise provided for in Paragraph 2 of this article.

2. Each party shall have the right to reduce the number of warheads attributed to deployed ICBMs or deployed SLBMs only of existing types, except for heavy ICBMs. Reduction in the number of warheads attributed to deployed ICBMs and deployed SLBMs of existing types that are not heavy ICBMs shall be carried out in accordance with the provisions of Paragraph 5 of Article III of the START Treaty, except that:

(a) the aggregate number by which warheads are reduced may exceed the 1250 limit provided for in Paragraph 5 of Article III of the START Treaty;

(b) the number by which warheads are reduced on ICBMs and SLBMs, other than the Minuteman III ICBM for the United States of America and the SS-N-18 [RSM-50] SLBM for the Russian Federation exceed the limit of 500 warheads for each party provided for in subparagraph 5(C)(I) of Article III of the START treaty at any given moment;

(c) each party shall have the right to reduce by more than four warheads, but not by more than five warheads, the number of warheads attributed to each ICBM out of no more than 105 ICBMs of one existing type of ICBM. An ICBM to which the number of warheads attributed has been reduced in accordance with this paragraph shall only be deployed in an ICBM launcher in which an ICBM of that type was deployed as of the date of signature of the START Treaty; and

(d) the re-entry vehicle platform [platforma boyegolovki] for an ICBM or SLBM to which a reduced number of warheads is attributed is not required to be destroyed and replaced with a new re-entry vehicle platform.

3. Notwithstanding the number of warheads attributed to a type of ICBM or SLBM in accordance with the START Treaty, each party undertakes not to:

(a) produce, flight-test, or deploy an ICBM or SLBM with a number of re-entry vehicles greater than the number of warheads attributed to it under this treaty; and

(b) increase the number of warheads attributed to an ICBM or SLBM that has had the number of warheads attributed to it reduced in accordance with the provisions of this article.

ARTICLE IV

1. For the purposes of this treaty, the number of warheads attributed to each deployed heavy bomber shall be equal to the number of nuclear weapons for which any heavy bomber of the same type or variant of a type is actually equipped, with the exception of heavy bombers reassigned to fulfill non-nuclear tasks [pereorientirovannyye dlya vypolneniya neyadernykh zadach] as provided for in Paragraph

7 of this article. Each nuclear weapon for which a heavy bomber is actually equipped shall count as one warhead toward the limitations provided for in Article I of this treaty. For the purpose of such counting, nuclear weapons include long-range nuclear air-launched cruise missiles (ALCMs), nuclear air-to-surface missiles with a range of less than 600 kilometers, and nuclear bombs.

2. For the purposes of this treaty, the number of nuclear weapons for which a heavy bomber is actually equipped shall be the number specified for heavy bombers of that type and variant of a type in the memorandum of understanding on warhead attribution and heavy bomber data relating to the treaty between the United States of America and the Russian Federation on further reduction and limitation of strategic offensive arms, hereinafter referred to as the Memorandum on Attribution.

3. Each party undertakes not to equip any heavy bomber with a greater number of nuclear weapons than the number specified for heavy bombers of that type or variant of a type in the Memorandum on Attribution.

4. No later than 180 days after entry into force of this treaty, each party shall exhibit one heavy bomber of each type and variant of a type specified in the Memorandum on Attribution. The purpose of the exhibition shall be to demonstrate to the other party the number of nuclear weapons for which a heavy bomber of a given type or variant of a type is actually equipped.

5. If either party intends to change the number of nuclear weapons specified in the Memorandum on Attribution, for which a heavy bomber of a type or variant of a type is actually equipped, it shall provide a 90-day advance notification of such intention to the other party. Ninety days after providing such a notification, or at a later date agreed by the parties, the party changing the number of nuclear weapons for which a heavy bomber is actually equipped shall exhibit one heavy bomber of each such type or variant of a type. The purpose of the exhibition shall be to demonstrate to the other party the revised number of nuclear weapons for which heavy bombers of the specified type or variant of a type are actually equipped. The number of nuclear weapons attributed to the specified type and variant of a type of heavy bomber shall change on the ninetieth day after the notification of such intent. On that day, the party changing the number of nuclear weapons for which a heavy bomber is actually equipped shall provide to the other party a notification of each change in data according to categories of data contained in the Memorandum on Attribution.

6. The exhibitions and inspections conducted pursuant to Paragraphs 4 and 5 of this article shall be carried out in accordance with the procedures provided for in the protocol on exhibitions and inspections of heavy bombers relating to the treaty between the United States of America and the Russian Federation on further reduction and limitation of strategic offensive arms, hereinafter referred to as the Protocol on Exhibitions and Inspections.

7. Each party shall have the right to reassign heavy bombers equipped for nuclear armaments other than long-range nuclear ALCMs to fulfill non-nuclear tasks. For the purposes of this treaty, heavy bombers reassigned to fulfill non-nuclear tasks are those heavy bombers specified by a party from among its heavy bombers equipped for nuclear armaments other than long-range nuclear

ALCMs that have never been accountable under the START treaty as heavy bombers equipped for long-range nuclear ALCMs. The party that carries out the reassignment shall provide to the other party a notification of its intent to reassign a heavy bomber to fulfill non-nuclear tasks no less than 90 days in advance of such reassignment. No conversion procedures shall be required for such a heavy bomber to be specified as a heavy bomber reassigned to fulfill non-nuclear tasks.

8. Heavy bombers reassigned to fulfill non-nuclear tasks shall be subject to the following requirements:

(a) the number of such heavy bombers shall not exceed 100 at any one time;

(b) such heavy bombers shall be based separately from heavy bombers with nuclear roles;

(c) such heavy bombers shall be used only for non-nuclear missions. Such heavy bombers shall not be used in exercises for nuclear missions, and their air crews shall not train or exercise for such missions; and

(d) heavy bombers re-assigned to fulfill non-nuclear tasks shall have differences from other heavy bombers of that type or variant of a type that are observable by national technical means of verification and visible during inspections.

9. Each party shall have the right to reassign to fulfill nuclear tasks again heavy bombers that were reassigned to fulfill non-nuclear tasks in accordance with Paragraph 7 of this article. The party carrying out such action shall provide to the other party through diplomatic channels notification of its intent to reassign a heavy bomber to fulfill nuclear tasks again no less than 90 days in advance of taking such action.

Such a heavy bomber reassigned to fulfill nuclear tasks again shall not subsequently be reassigned to fulfill non-nuclear tasks. Heavy bombers reassigned to fulfill non-nuclear tasks which are subsequently reassigned again to fulfill nuclear tasks shall have differences observable by national technical means of verification and visible during inspection from other heavy bombers of that type and variant of a type that have not been reassigned to fulfill non- nuclear tasks, as well as from heavy bombers of that type and variant of a type that are still reassigned to fulfill non-nuclear tasks.

10. Each party shall locate storage areas for heavy bomber nuclear armaments no less than 100 kilometers from any air base where heavy bombers reassigned to fulfill non-nuclear tasks are based.

11. Except as otherwise provided for in this treaty, heavy bombers reassigned to fulfill non-nuclear tasks shall remain subject to the provisions of the START treaty, including the inspection provisions.

12. If not all heavy bombers of a given type or variant of a type are reassigned to fulfill non-nuclear tasks, one heavy bomber of each type or variant of a type of heavy bomber reassigned to fulfill non-nuclear tasks shall be exhibited in the open for the purpose of demonstrating to the other party the differences referred to in subparagraph 8(d) of this article. Such differences shall be subject to inspection by the other party.

13. If not all heavy bombers of a given type or variant of a type reassigned to fulfill non-nuclear tasks are reassigned to fulfill nuclear tasks again, one heavy bomber of each type and variant of a type of heavy bomber returned to

a nuclear role shall be exhibited in the open for the purpose of demonstrating to the other party the differences referred to in Paragraph 9 of this article. Such differences shall be subject to inspection by the other party.

14. The exhibitions and inspections provided for in Paragraphs 12 and 13 of this article shall be carried out in accordance with the procedures provided for in the protocol on exhibitions and inspections.

ARTICLE V

1. Except as provided for in this treaty, the provisions of the START Treaty, including the verification provisions, shall be used for implementation of this treaty.

2. To promote the implementation of the objectives and provisions of this treaty, the parties hereby establish the Bilateral Implementation Commission. The parties agree that, if either party so requests, they shall meet within the framework of the Bilateral Implementation Commission to:

(a) resolve questions relating to compliance with the obligations assumed; and

(b) agree upon such additional measures as may be necessary to improve the viability and effectiveness of this treaty.

ARTICLE VI

1. This treaty, including its Memorandum on Attribution, Elimination and Conversion Protocol, and Protocol on Exhibitions and Inspections, all of which are integral parts thereof, shall be subject to ratification in accordance with the constitutional procedures of each party. This treaty shall enter into force on the date of the exchange of instruments of ratification, but not prior to the entry into force of the START Treaty.

2. The provisions of Paragraph 8 of Article II of this treaty shall be applied provisionally by the parties from the date of its signature.

3. This treaty shall remain in force so long as the START Treaty remains in force.

4. Each party shall, in exercising its state sovereignty, have the right to withdraw from this treaty if it decides that extraordinary events related to the subject matter of this treaty have jeopardized its supreme interests. It shall give notice of its decision to the other party six months prior to withdrawal from this treaty. Such notice shall include a statement of the extraordinary events the notifying party regards as having jeopardized its supreme interests.

ARTICLE VII

Each party may propose amendments to this treaty. Agreed amendments shall enter into force in accordance with the procedures governing entry into force of this treaty.

ARTICLE VIII

This treaty shall be registered pursuant to Article 102 of the charter of the United Nations.

Completed in Moscow on January 3, 1993, in two copies, each in the English and Russian languages, both texts being equally authentic."

START II PROTOCOL ON ELIMINATING ICBMS, MOSCOW, 3 JANUARY 1993

Full text of a protocol to the START II Treaty on procedures governing elimination of heavy ICBMs [intercontinental ballistic missiles] and on procedures governing conversion of silo launchers of heavy ICBMs relating to the Treaty between the United States of America and the Russian Federation on further reduction and limitation of strategic offensive arms.

Pursuant to and in implementation of the treaty between the United States of America and the Russian Federation on further reduction and limitation of strategic offensive arms, hereinafter referred to as the treaty, the parties hereby agree upon procedures governing the elimination of heavy ICBMs and upon procedures governing the conversion of silo launchers of such ICBMs.
I. Procedures for elimination of heavy ICBMs and their launch canisters
1. Elimination of heavy ICBMs shall be carried out in accordance with the procedures provided for in this section at elimination facilities for ICBMs specified in the START Treaty or shall be carried out by using such missiles for delivering objects into the upper atmosphere or space. Notification thereof shall be provided through the Nuclear Risk Reduction Centers (NRRCs) 30 days in advance of the initiation of elimination at conversion or elimination facilities, or, in the event of launch, in accordance with the provisions of the agreement between the United States of America and the Union of Soviet Socialist Republics on notifications of launches of intercontinental ballistic missiles and submarine-launched ballistic missiles of May 31, 1988.
2. Prior to the confirmatory inspection pursuant to Paragraph 3 of this section, the inspected party:
(a) shall remove the missile's re-entry vehicles;
(b) may remove the electronic and electromechanical devices of the missile's guidance and control system from the missile and its launch canister, and other elements that shall not be subject to elimination pursuant to Paragraph 4 of this section;
(c) shall remove the missile from its launch canister and disassemble the missile into stages;
(d) shall remove liquid propellant from the missile;
(e) may remove or actuate auxiliary pyrotechnic devices installed on. the missile and its launch canister;
(f) may remove penetration aids, including devices for their attachment and release; and
(g) may remove propulsion units from the self-contained dispensing mechanism. These actions may be carried out in any order.
3. After arrival of the inspection team and prior to the initiation of the elimination process, inspectors shall confirm the type and number of the missiles to be eliminated by making the observations and measurements necessary for such confirmation. After the procedures provided for in this paragraph have been carried out, the process of the elimination of the missiles and their launch canisters may begin. Inspectors shall observe the elimination process.
4. Elimination process for heavy ICBMs:

(a) missile stages, nozzles, and missile interstage skirts shall each be cut into two pieces of approximately equal size; and

(b) the self-contained dispensing mechanism as well as the front section, including the re-entry vehicle platform and the front section shroud, shall be cut into two pieces of approximately equal size and crushed.

5. During the elimination process for launch canisters of heavy ICBMs, the launch canister shall be cut into two pieces of approximately equal size or into three pieces in such a manner that pieces no less than 1.5 meters long are cut from the ends of the body of such a launch canister.

6. Upon completion of the above requirements, the inspection team leader and a member of the in-country escort shall confirm in a factual, written report containing the results of the inspection team's observation of the elimination process that the inspection team has completed its inspection.

7. Heavy ICBMs shall cease to be subject to the limitations provided for in the treaty after completion of the procedures provided for in this section. Notification thereof shall be provided in accordance with Paragraph 3 of Section I of the notification protocol relating to the START Treaty.

Procedures for conversion of silo launchers of heavy ICBMs, silo training launchers for heavy ICBMs, and silo test launchers for heavy ICBMs

1. Conversion of silo launchers of heavy ICBMs, silo training launchers for heavy ICBMs, and silo test launchers for heavy ICBMs shall be carried out in situ and shall be subject to inspection.

2. Prior to the initiation of the conversion process for such launchers, the missile and launch canister shall be removed from the silo launcher.

3. A party shall be considered to have initiated the conversion process for silo launchers of heavy ICBMs, silo training launchers for heavy ICBMs, and silo test launchers for heavy ICBMs as soon as the silo launcher door has been opened and a missile and its launch canister have been removed from the silo launcher. Notification thereof shall be provided in accordance with Paragraphs 1 and 2 of Section IV of the notification protocol relating to the START Treaty.

4. Conversion process for silo launchers of heavy ICBMs, silo training launchers for heavy ICBMs, and silo test launchers for heavy ICBMs shall include the following steps:

(a) the silo launcher door shall be opened, the missile and the launch canister shall be removed from the silo launcher;

(b) concrete shall be poured into the base of the silo launcher up to the height of five meters from the bottom of the silo launcher; and

(c) a restrictive ring with a diameter of no more than 2.9 meters shall be installed into the upper portion of the silo launcher. The method of installation of the restrictive ring shall rule out its removal without destruction of the ring and its attachment to the silo launcher.

5. Each party shall have the right to confirm that the procedures provided for in Paragraph 4 of this section have been carried out. For the purpose of confirming that these procedures have been carried out:

(a) the converting party shall notify the other party through the NRRCs: [not further identified]

(i) no less than 30 days in advance of the date when the process of pouring concrete will commence; and

(ii) upon completion of all of the procedures provided for in Paragraph 4 of this section; and

(b) the inspecting party shall have the right to implement the procedures provided for in either Paragraph 6 or Paragraph 7, but not both, of this section for each silo launcher of heavy ICBMs, silo training launcher for heavy ICBMS, and silo test launcher for heavy ICBMs that is to be converted.

6. Subject to the provisions of Paragraph 5 of this section, each party shall have the right to observe the entire process of pouring concrete into each silo launcher of heavy ICBMs, silo training launcher for heavy ICBMs, and silo test launcher for heavy ICBMs that is to be converted, and to measure the diameter of the restrictive ring. For this purpose:

(a) the inspecting party shall inform the party converting the silo launcher no less than seven days in advance of the commencement of the pouring that it will observe the filling of the silo in question;

(b) immediately prior to the commencement of the process of pouring concrete, the converting party shall take such steps as are necessary to ensure that the base of the silo launcher is visible, and that the depth of the silo can be measured;

(c) the inspecting party shall have the right to observe the entire process of pouring concrete from a location providing an unobstructed view of the base of the silo launcher, and to confirm by measurement that concrete has been poured into the base of the silo launcher up to the height of five meters from the bottom of the silo launcher. The measurements shall be taken from the level of the lower edge of the closed silo launcher door to the base of the silo launcher, prior to the pouring of the concrete, and from the level of the lower edge of the closed silo launcher door to the top of the concrete fill, after the concrete has hardened;

(d) following notification of completion of the procedures provided for in Paragraph 4 of this section, the inspecting party shall be permitted to measure the diameter of the restrictive ring. The restrictive ring shall not be shrouded during such inspection. The parties shall agree on the date for such inspections;

(e) the results of measurements conducted pursuant to Subparagraphs (c) and (d) of this paragraph shall be recorded in written, factual inspection reports and signed by the inspection team leader and a member of the in-country escort;

(f) inspection teams shall each consist of no more than 10 inspectors, all of whom shall be drawn from the list of inspectors under the START Treaty; and

(g) such inspections shall not count against any inspection quota established by the START Treaty.

7. Subject to the provisions of Paragraph 5 of this section, each party shall have the right to measure the depth of each silo launcher of heavy ICBMs, silo training launcher for heavy ICBMs, and silo test launcher for heavy ICBMs that is to be converted both before the commencement and after the completion of the process of pouring concrete, and to measure the diameter of the restrictive ring. For this purpose:

(a) the inspecting party shall inform the party converting the silo launcher no less than seven days in advance of the commencement of the pouring that it will measure the depth of the silo launcher in question both before the commencement and after the completion of the process of pouring concrete;

(b) immediately prior to the commencement of the process of pouring concrete, the converting party shall take such steps as are necessary to ensure that the base of the silo launcher is visible, and that the depth of the silo launcher can be measured;

(c) the inspecting party shall measure the depth of the silo launcher prior to the commencement of the process of pouring concrete;

(d) following notification of completion of the procedures provided for in Paragraph 4 of this section, the inspecting party shall be permitted to measure the diameter of the restrictive ring, and to remeasure the depth of the silo launcher. The restrictive ring shall not be shrouded during such inspections. The parties shall agree on the date for such inspections;

(e) for the purpose of measuring the depth of the concrete in the silo launcher, measurements shall be taken from the level of the lower edge of the closed silo launcher door to the base of the silo launcher, prior to the pouring of the concrete. And from the level of the lower edge of the closed silo launcher door to the top of the concrete fill, after the concrete has hardened;

(f) the results of measurements conducted pursuant to subparagraphs (c), (d), and (e) of this paragraph shall be recorded in written, factual inspection reports and signed by the inspection team leader and a member of the in-country escort;

(g) inspection teams shall each consist of no more than 10 inspectors, all of whom shall be drawn from the list of inspectors under the START Treaty; and

(h) such inspections shall not count against any inspection quota established by the START Treaty.

8. The converting party shall have the right to carry out further conversion measures after the completion of the procedures provided for in Paragraph 6 or Paragraph 7 of this section or, if such procedures are not conducted, upon expiration of 30 days after notification of completion of the procedures provided for in Paragraph 4 of this section.

9. In addition to the reentry vehicle inspections conducted under the START Treaty, each party shall have the right to conduct, using the procedures provided for in Annex 3 to the inspection protocol relating to the START Treaty, four additional reentry vehicle inspections each year of ICBMS that are deployed in silo launchers of heavy ICBMS that have been converted in accordance with the provisions of this section. During such inspections, the inspectors also shall have the right to confirm by visual observation the presence of the restrictive ring and that the observable portions of the launch canister do not differ externally from the observable portions of the launch canister that was exhibited pursuant to Paragraph 11 of Article XI of the START Treaty. Any shrouding of the upper portion of the silo launcher shall not obstruct visual observation of the upper portion of the launch canister and shall not obstruct visual observation of the edge of the restrictive ring. If requested by the inspecting party, the converting party shall partially remove any shrouding, except for shrouding of instruments installed on the restrictive ring, to permit confirmation of the presence of the restrictive ring.

10. Upon completion of the procedures provided for in Paragraph 6 or Paragraph 7 of this section or, if such procedures are not conducted, upon expiration of 30 days after notification of completion of the procedures provided for in Paragraph 4 of this section, the silo launcher of heavy ICBMs being converted shall, for the purposes of the Treaty, be considered to contain a deployed ICBM to which one warhead is attributed.

III. Equipment; costs.

1. To carry out inspections provided for in this protocol, the inspecting party shall have the right to use agreed equipment, including equipment that will confirm that the silo launcher has been completely filled up to the height of five meters from the bottom of the silo launcher with concrete. The parties shall agree in the bilateral implementation commission on such equipment.

2. For inspections conducted pursuant to this protocol, costs shall be handled pursuant to Paragraph 19 of Section V of the inspection protocol relating to the START Treaty.

This protocol is an integral part of the Treaty and shall enter into force on the date of entry into force of the Treaty and shall remain in force as long as the Treaty remains in force. As provided for in Subparagraph 2(b) of Article V of the Treaty, the parties may agree upon such additional measures as may be necessary to improve the viability and effectiveness of the Treaty. The parties agree that, if it becomes necessary to make changes in this protocol that do not affect substantive rights or obligations under the Treaty, they shall use the Bilateral Implementation Commission to reach agreement on such changes, without resorting to the procedure for making amendments set forth in Article VII of the Treaty.

Done at Moscow on January 3, 1993, in two copies, each in the English and Russian languages, both texts being equally authentic.

START II MEMORANDUM ON WARHEAD ATTRIBUTION
MOSCOW, 3 JANUARY, 1993

Text of the memorandum of understanding on warhead attribution and heavy bomber data relating to the Treaty between the United States of America and the Russian Federation on further reduction and limitation of strategic offensive arms.

Pursuant to and in implementation of the Treaty between the United States of America and the Russian Federation on further reduction and limitation of strategic offensive arms, hereinafter referred to as the Treaty, the parties have exchanged data current as of January 3, 1993, on the number of nuclear weapons for which each heavy bomber of a type and a variant of a type equipped for nuclear weapons is actually equipped. No later than 30 days after the date of entry into force of the Treaty, the parties shall additionally exchange data, current as of the date of entry into force of the Treaty, according to the categories of data contained in this memorandum, on heavy bombers equipped for nuclear weapons; on heavy bombers specified as reoriented to a conventional role, and on heavy bombers reoriented to a conventional role that are subsequently returned to a nuclear role; on ICBMs and SLBMs to which a reduced number of warheads is attributed; and on data on the elimination of heavy ICBMs and on conversion of silo launchers of heavy ICBMs.

Only those data used for purposes of implementing the Treaty that differ from the data in the memorandum of understanding on the establishment of the data base relating to the START Treaty are included in this memorandum.

I. Number of warheads attributed to deployed heavy bombers other than heavy bombers reoriented to a conventional role

1. Pursuant to Paragraph 3 of Article IV of the Treaty each party undertakes not to have more nuclear weapons deployed on heavy bombers of any type or variant of a type than the number specified in this paragraph. Additionally, pursuant to Paragraph 2 of Article IV of the Treaty, for each party the numbers of warheads attributed to deployed heavy bombers not reoriented to a conventional role as of the date of signature of the Treaty or to heavy bombers subsequently deployed are listed below. Such numbers shall only be changed in accordance with Paragraph 5 of Article IV of the Treaty. The party making a change shall provide a notification to the other party 90 days prior to making such a change. An exhibition shall be conducted to demonstrate the changed number of nuclear weapons for which heavy bombers of the listed type or variant of a type are actually equipped:

(a) United States of America		(b) Russian Federation	
Heavy Bomber Type and Variant of a Type	Number of Warheads	Heavy Bomber Type and Variant of a Type	Number of Warheads
B-52G	12	Bear B	
B-52H	20	Bear G	2
B-1B	16	Bear H6	6
B-2	16	Bear H16	16
		Blackjack	12

Aggregate number of warheads attributed to deployed heavy bombers, except for heavy bombers reoriented to a conventional role.

II. Data on heavy bombers reoriented to a conventional role and heavy bombers reoriented to a conventional role that have subsequently been returned to a nuclear role.

1. For each party, the numbers of heavy bombers reoriented to a conventional role are as follows:

*Heavy bombers of the type and variant of a type designated B-52C, B-52D, B-52E, and B-52F, located at the Davis-Monthan Conversion or Elimination Facility as of September 1, 1990, as specified in the memorandum of understanding to the START Treaty, will be eliminated, Under the provisions of the START Treaty, before the expiration of the seven-year reductions period.

(a) United States of America

Heavy Bomber Type and
   Variant of a Type   Number

—   —

—   —

(b) Russian Federation

Heavy Bomber Type and
   Variant of a Type   Number

—   —

—   —

2. For each party, the numbers of heavy bombers reoriented to a conventional role as well as data on related air bases are as follows:

(a) United States of America

Air Bases:
Name/Location   Bomber type and variant of a type

—   —

Heavy bombers reoriented to a conventional role   Number

—

(b) Russian Federation

Air Bases:
Name/Location   Bomber type and variant of a type

—   —

Heavy bombers reoriented to a conventional role   Number

—

3. For each party, the differences observable by national technical means of verification for heavy bombers reoriented to a conventional role are as follows:

(a) United States of America

Heavy bomber type and variant of a type   Difference

—   —

(b) Russian Federation

Heavy bomber type and variant of a type   Difference

—   —

4. For each party, the differences observable by national technical means of verification for heavy bombers reoriented to a conventional role that have subsequently been returned to a nuclear role are as follows:

(a) United States of America

Heavy bomber type and variant of a type   Difference

—   —

(b) Russian Federation

Heavy bomber type and variant of a type   Difference

—   —

III. Data on deployed ICBMs and deployed SLBMs to which a reduced number of warheads is attributed.

For each party, the data on ICBM bases or submarine bases, and on ICBMs or SLBMs of existing types deployed at those bases, on which the number of warheads attributed to them is reduced pursuant to Article III of the Treaty are as follows:

(a) [as received] United States of America

Type of ICBM or SLBM

Deployed ICBMs or deployed SLBMs, on which the
   number of warheads is reduced   —

Warheads attributed to each deployed ICBM or
   deployed SLBM after reduction in the number of
   warheads on it   —

Number of warheads by which the original attribution
   of warheads for each ICBM or SLBM was reduced   —

Aggregate reduction in the number of warheads
   attributed to deployed ICBMs or deployed
   SLBMs of that type   —

ICBM bases at which the number of warheads on deployed ICBMS is reduced:

Name/Location	ICBM Type on Which the Number of Warheads is Reduced
Deployed ICBMs on which the number of warheads is reduced	—
Warheads attributed to each deployed ICBM after reduction in the number of warheads on it	—
Number of warheads by which the original attribution of warheads for each ICBM was reduced	—
Aggregate reduction in the number of warheads attributed to deployed ICBMS of that type	—

SLBM bases at which the number of warheads on deployed SLBMs is reduced:

Name/Location	ICBM Type on Which the Number of Warheads is Reduced
Deployed SLBMs on which the number of warheads is reduced	—
Warheads attributed to each deployed SLBM after reduction in the number of warheads on it	—

Number of warheads by which the
   original attribution of warheads
   for each SLBM was reduced   —
Aggregate reduction in the number
   of warheads attributed to deployed
   SLBMs of that type   —

(b) Russian Federation

Type of ICBM or SLBM
Deployed ICBMs or deployed SLBMs on which
   the number of warheads is reduced   —
Warheads attributed to each deployed ICBM or
   deployed SLBM after reduction in the number
   of warheads on it   —
Number of warheads by which the original
   attribution of warheads for each ICBM or
   SLBM was reduced   —
Aggregate reduction in the number of warheads
   attributed to deployed ICBMs or deployed
   SLBMs of that type   —

ICBM bases at which the number of warheads on deployed ICBMs is reduced:

| | ICBM Type on Which the |
Name/Location	Number of Warheads is Reduced
Deployed ICBMS on which the number of warheads is reduced	—
Warheads attributed to each deployed ICBM after reduction in the number of warheads on it	—
Number of warheads by which the original attribution of warheads for each ICBM was reduced	—
Aggregate reduction in the number of warheads attributed to deployed ICBMS of that type	—

SLBM bases at which the number of warheads on deployed SLBMs is reduced:

| | SLBM Type on Which the |
Name/Location	Number of Warheads is Reduced
Deployed SLBMs on which the number of warheads is reduced	—
Warheads attributed to each deployed SLBM after reduction in the number of warheads on it	—

Number of warheads by which the
   original attribution of warheads
   for each SLBM was reduced   —
Aggregate reduction in the number of
   warheads attributed to deployed
   SLBMS of that type   —

   IV. Data on eliminated heavy ICBMS and converted silo launchers of heavy ICBMs

   1. For each party, the numbers of silo launchers of heavy ICBMs converted to silo launchers of ICBMs other than heavy ICBMs are as follows:

(a) United States of America Aggregate
Number of Converted Silo Launchers

ICBM Base for silo launchers of ICBMs: ICBM type installed in a converted
   silo launcher
Name/Location
Silo launcher group: (designation)
Silo launchers:

Russian Federation Aggregate
Number of Converted Silo Launchers

ICBM base for silo launchers of ICBMs: ICBM type installed in a converted
   silo launcher
Name/Location
Silo launcher group: (designation)
Silo launchers:

   2. For each party, the aggregate numbers of heavy ICBMs and eliminated heavy ICBMs are as follows:

(a) United States of America
Number

Deployed heavy ICBMs
Non-deployed heavy ICBMs
Eliminated heavy ICBMs

(b) Russian Federation
Number

Deployed heavy ICBMs
Non-deployed heavy ICBMs
Eliminated heavy ICBMs

V. Changes
Each party shall notify the other party of changes in the attribution and data contained in this memorandum.

   The parties, in signing this memorandum, acknowledge the acceptance of the categories of data contained in this memorandum and the responsibility of each party for the accuracy only of its own data.

This memorandum is an integral part of the Treaty and shall enter into force on the date of entry into force of the Treaty and shall remain in force so long as the Treaty remains in force. As provided for in Subparagraph 2(b) of Article V of the Treaty, the parties may agree upon such additional measures as may be necessary to improve the viability and effectiveness of the Treaty. The parties agree that, if it becomes necessary to change the categories of data contained in this memorandum or to make other changes to this memorandum that do not affect substantive rights or obligations under the Treaty, they shall use the bilateral implementation commission to reach agreement on such changes, without resorting to the procedure for making amendments set forth in Article VII of the Treaty.

Done in Moscow on January 3, 1993, in two copies, each in the English and Russian languages, both texts being equally authentic.

FBIS-SOV, Moscow, 4 January 1993.

START II PROTOCOL ON BOMBERS, MOSCOW, 3 JANUARY 1993

Full text of protocol to the START-2 treaty on exhibitions and inspections of heavy bombers relating to the treaty between the United States of America and the Russian Federation on further reduction and limitation of strategic offensive arms.

"Pursuant to and in implementation of the Treaty between the United States of America and the Russian Federation on further reduction and limitation of strategic offensive arms, hereinafter referred to as the Treaty, the parties hereby agree to conduct exhibitions and inspections of heavy bombers pursuant to Paragraphs 4, 5, 12, and 13 of Article IV of the Treaty.

I. Exhibitions of heavy bombers

1. For the purpose of helping to ensure verification of compliance with the provisions of the Treaty, and as required by Paragraphs 4, 5, 12, and 13 of Article IV of the Treaty, each party shall conduct exhibitions of heavy bombers equipped for nuclear armaments, heavy bombers reoriented to a conventional role, and heavy bombers that were reoriented to a conventional role and subsequently returned to a nuclear role.

2. The exhibitions of heavy bombers shall be conducted subject to the following provisions:

(a) the location for such an exhibition shall be at the discretion of the exhibiting party;

(b) the date for such an exhibition shall be agreed upon between the parties through diplomatic channels, and the exhibiting party shall communicate the location of the exhibition;

(c) during such an exhibition, each heavy bomber exhibited shall be subject to inspection for a period not to exceed two hours;

(d) the inspection team conducting an inspection during an exhibition shall consist of no more than 10 inspectors, all of whom shall be drawn from the list of inspectors under the START Treaty;

(e) prior to the beginning of the exhibition, the inspected party shall provide a photograph or photographs of one of the heavy bombers of a type or variant of a type reoriented to a conventional role and of one of the heavy bombers of the same type and variant of a type that were reoriented to a conventional role and subsequently returned to a nuclear role, so as to show all of their differences that are observable by national technical means of verification and visible during inspection; and

(f) such inspections during exhibitions shall not count against any inspection quota established by the START Treaty.

II. Inspections of heavy bombers

1. During exhibitions of heavy bombers, each party shall have the right to perform the following procedures on the exhibited heavy bombers; and each party, beginning 180 days after entry into force of the Treaty and thereafter, shall have the right, in addition to its rights under the START Treaty, to perform, during data update and new facility inspections conducted under the START Treaty at air bases of the other party, the following procedures on all heavy bombers based at such air bases and present there at the time of the inspection:

(a) to conduct inspections of heavy bombers equipped for long-range nuclear ALCMs [Air Launched Cruise Missiles] and heavy bombers equipped for nuclear armaments other than long-range nuclear ALCMs, in order to confirm that the number of nuclear weapons for which a heavy bomber is actually equipped does not exceed the number specified in the memorandum on attribution. The inspection team shall have the right to visually inspect those portions of the exterior of the inspected heavy bomber where the inspected heavy bomber is equipped for weapons, as well as to visually inspect the weapons bay of such a heavy bomber, but not to inspect other portions of the exterior of interior;

(b) to conduct inspections of heavy bombers reoriented to a conventional role, in order to confirm the differences of such heavy bombers from other heavy bombers of that type or variant of a type that are observable by national technical means of verification and visible during inspection. The inspection team shall have the right to visually inspect those portions of the exterior of the inspected heavy bomber having the differences observable by national technical means of verification and visible during inspection, but not to inspect other portions of the exterior or interior; and

(c) to conduct inspections of heavy bombers that were reoriented to a conventional role and subsequently returned to a nuclear role, in order to confirm the differences of such heavy bombers from other heavy bombers of that type or variant of a type that are observable by national technical means of verification and visible during inspection, and to confirm that the number of nuclear weapons for which a heavy bomber is actually equipped does not exceed the number specified in the memorandum on attribution. The inspection team shall have the right to visually inspect those portions of the exterior of the inspected heavy bomber where the inspected heavy bomber is equipped for weapons, as well as to visually inspect the weapons bay of such a heavy bomber, and to visually inspect those portions of the exterior of the inspected heavy bomber having the differences observable by national technical means of verification and visible to inspection, but not to inspect other portions of the exterior or interior.

2. At the discretion of the inspected party, those portions of the heavy bomber that are not subject to inspection may be shrouded. The period of time required to carry out the shrouding process shall not count against the period allocated for inspection.

3. In the course of an inspection conducted during an exhibition, a member of the in-country escort shall provide, during inspections conducted pursuant to Subparagraph 1(a) or Subparagraph 1(c) of this section, explanations to the inspection team concerning the number of nuclear weapons for which the heavy bomber is actually equipped, and shall provide, during inspections conducted pursuant to Subparagraph 1(b) or Subparagraph 1(c) of this section, explanations to the inspection team concerning the differences that are observable by national technical means of verification and visible during inspection. This protocol is an integral part of the Treaty and shall enter into force on the date of entry into force of the Treaty and shall remain in force so long as the Treaty remains in force. As provided for in Subparagraph 2(b) of Article V of the Treaty, the parties may agree upon such additional measures as may be necessary to improve the viability and effectiveness of the Treaty. The parties agree that, if it becomes necessary to make changes in this protocol that do not affect substantive rights or obligations under the Treaty, they shall use the Bilateral Implementation Commission to reach agreement on such changes, without resorting to the procedure for making amendments set forth in Article VII of the Treaty.

Done at Moscow on January 3, 1993, in two copies, each in the English and Russian languages, both texts being equally authentic.

FBIS-SOV, 4 January 1993.

RUSSIAN FEDERATION FOREIGN AND DEFENSE
POLICY COUNCIL REPORT, AUGUST 1992

PRELIMINARY REMARKS

The present theses are based on the understanding that the report will be focused, above all, on the traditional problems of national security. Problems of economic, social, and ecological policy are touched upon to the extent to which they refer to the text or else are not discussed at all. It may later become possible to go back to another concept of the report, according to which the strategy of national security would be considered on a broader basis, would include economic, social, and ecological policy, and would coincide as a whole with the government's strategy.

1.2. GENERAL REMARKS

1.2.1. Policy planning requires, above all, a realistic definition of the subject of policy-the Russian Federation-and its possibilities. No such thing has been done so far. Meanwhile, compared to the former USSR, Russia has changed radically. Having retained more than four-fifths of the territory of the USSR, Russia nonetheless accounts for slightly over one-half of the population. It controls (taking into consideration production decline) less than one-half of the Soviet gross national product for 1990. In terms of most parameters (other than the size of its territory and its nuclear potential) Russia has become a middle-sized country. In Europe this is the equivalent of France, Great Britain, and Italy; in Asia, of India, and Indonesia; in America, of Brazil, Argentina, and Canada. Russia has successfully become the principal heir of the USSR and has inherited the psychological baggage of the former power (as well as fear of this power). Gradually, however, this baggage will decrease. It is important to realize this as of now.

1.2.2. Another major question is what type of state will Russia develop into in the foreseeable future and toward the interests of which social strata will its policies be oriented?

It is most likely that in the foreseeable future Russia will be a moderately authoritarian state with a mixed state-capitalist type economy. This kind of state and economy, multiplied by its economic backwardness, would not allow it to fully and rapidly become part of the community of industrially developed capitalist countries with efficient democratic institutions and fully to identify its interests with theirs. A significant portion of the new ruling class—the political and official nomenclature, directors of state enterprises, the new entrepreneurs and the representatives of the power structure—will oppose a totally economically and politically open Russia, believing this to be a threat to their interests. However, this ruling class will be mostly interested in close cooperation with the outside world, realizing that its well-being radically depends on such cooperation.

A semi-democratic development and very likely recurrence of authoritarianism and harsh acts of force against neighbors or even temporary splashes of imperial ambitions do not allow us to hope for cloudless relations with the West even despite the hopefully predominant partnership elements in such relations.

In many respects Russia will be forced to rely on its own possibilities and will go through several stages of improved or worsened relations with the outside world.

It would be better to prepare the strategy and the instruments for such a policy precisely geared to such a moderate-optimistic option.

1.2.3. It is obvious that the interests of Russia, as a state, and those of its people would be most consistent with another development option: a fast 10-year conversion to a Western European type of economy and the creation of a developed and effective democracy as well as close alliance and cooperation with the West. Such an option would require relatively minor strategic corrections.

Russia could also choose a worse option, which is that of disintegration, or else an attempt to launch a semi-fascist and/or imperial revenge, which, once again, would be most likely followed by disintegration. If Russia's development were to take such a path it would be threatened not only by an internal but also by an external catastrophe. The West has not lost its ability quickly to resurrect its containment system in a variant which would be even harsher and qualitatively less advantageous to Russia. The line of confrontation would run not across the center of Europe but along the borders of the Russian Federation, thus including new opportunities for engaging in operations on Russian territory as well. Hostile isolation would be much greater than even that of the 1920-1930s, or the 1940s-1950s. For the first time in its history, Russia would find itself in a position of extreme military weakness, deprived of the possibility to recover from its military and technological lagging. Sooner or later even the nuclear front will become depreciated.

The disintegration and subsequent instability and weakness of the quasi-states which will be formed will leave Russia open to hostile or even "non-hostile" interventions (with a view to preventing incidents including use of mass destruction weapons) and will put an end to Russian statehood.

1.2.4. Another basic issue is that of Russia's geostrategic interests. It is quite clear that financial limitations, economic interests, lack of possibility for any serious export of capital, and high internal resource availability dictate the need for the revival of a continental strategy which is traditional to Russia, and a total rejection of the global involvement of the USSR in the affairs of the entire world, imposed by communist messianism and historical accident. This indicates the need for further reduction, at least for the foreseeable future, of geostrategic ambitions and overseas commitments and the forces and funds needed for their support (an oceangoing fleet above all).

1.2.5. A reduced resource, power, and geopolitical base in defense and foreign policy drastically curtails possibilities of influencing the outside world and all other countries. This progressive reduction of possibilities to defend one's governmental interests abroad will continue for at least the next. few years. This dictates the expediency of a policy of sensible compromises but also sets a certain limit of what is admissible. The position of objective weakness should be compensated by a doubly ingenious diplomacy.

1.2.6. One of the main reasons for Russia's current political weakness is the inability to concentrate its political willpower, the absence of a unified governmental policy and strategic line, and the lack of a clear concept of national interests, as well as bureaucratic confusion and multiplicity of opinions.

1.2.7. So far, as was the case with the USSR in the past, there is a gap in Russia between foreign and military policies (to the extent to which they exist); they are not integrated within a single strategy.

1.3. GEOPOLITICAL ENCIRCLEMENT. CHALLENGES OF THE OUTSIDE WORLD

1.3.1. It is quite obvious that the main challenges to Russia's security are generated within the country, on the territory of the former USSR. However, we begin the study of the challenges to security coming from the traditional foreign area.

1.3.2. Despite all difficulties and the slowing down of this process, in the past few months a powerful subject of international life has been taking shape in Western Europe: the European Union. In eight to 15 years this union could become a quasi-federative formation with a single economic, foreign, and defense policy. Such a union or something similar to it would include virtually all European countries outside the former USSR (except for some republics of the former Yugoslavia, Albania, and, possibly, Romania). Its sphere of influence would include, in addition to the Eastern European countries, the Baltic republics. Only a catastrophic development of events in Eastern Europe could halt the creation of such a union which would become a superpower in a number of areas. The establishment of such a union threatens Russia with isolation and with weakened positions should it be unable during this decade to achieve a rapprochement with it and lay the foundations for mutually profitable although unequal relations.

1.3.3. As was the case in the past, the process of the establishment of such a union will absorb a substantial share of the political energy of the participants and draw them within itself. In the next few years a similar situation of "retreat within itself" will be typical of Germany as well. This will hinder obtaining economic and other aid from Europe. It will require a diversification of policy. "Eurocentrism" may prove to be weak. However, there will exist the influence of premature or groundless fears of German hegemony in Europe. Germany's economic and, respectively, political movement toward the East would be resumed in two to four years.

1.3.4. The processes occurring in the United States and in North America as a whole indicate a growing, albeit slow, trend toward relative neo-isolationism by the United States. The need for profound internal reforms in the United States and the establishment of a single North American market added to a parallel aspiration to ease the burden of commitments abroad, particularly in relatively stable areas in Europe and the Far East, is leading Washington to a new strategy of American participation in world affairs. Despite the fact that the United States has remained, in fact, the only superpower, and despite its intention to maintain its leadership in world affairs, from the economic viewpoint this role will become increasingly burdensome and, in the absence of any threat by the Soviet "evil empire," it will enjoy an ever diminishing domestic support. For that reason, it intends to maintain it, and could allow itself to do so, not on the basis of a strict hegemony or the imposition of a "pax Americana," but through the further reapportionment of the burden with its allies. One way or another, the growth of neo-isolationism in the United States and its domestic difficulties apparently limit the long-term possibilities for its constructive participation in Russia's economic revival. This, therefore, makes any "American-centrist" policy weak. However, interest in preserving its positions in Europe and sharing the burden in settling the situation in Asia and the Far

East and preventing the total disintegration of the geostrategic space of the former USSR and loss of control over the OMP [mass destruction weapons] are urging the United States toward establishing relations of a strategic, even if only for show, partnership with Russia (politically, from the prestige point of view, Russia could benefit more from such a partnership but has far fewer possibilities of defining its conditions).

1.3.5. The drastic change which has occurred in the ratio of military power has not brought about any increased threat on the part of the West. This threat has never been so low. Its reduction is contributing to the new political relations and to the formation in Central Europe of a wide buffer zone of low-armed countries unaffiliated with the Western security system, and a lessening of military efforts in the West which, it is true, is largely compensated by technological improvements in armaments.

Russia's sufficiently powerful nuclear potential actually evens up for the foreseeable future (10 years) the significance of virtually any type of technological breakthroughs and advantages in the sum of military possibilities. The theoretical threat could increase in the case of further reduction in the role of the nuclear factor thanks to a reduction in armaments or the creation of efficient global anti-missile defense systems, as well as a qualitatively new technological advance of the West in the areas of armaments, and communications, intelligence, and control systems.

Even such a theoretical threat could be reduced with the establishment of a true alliance with Western countries. This, however, is obviously a matter of the rather distant future.

However, what remains and even is theoretically increased is the danger of applying greater military-political pressure on Russia should political relations worsen, and the assumption of power in Russia by forces which the West would consider hostile, or else not consistent with Western interests. The unclear future and an entire array of other arguments dictate the need for having a sufficiently convincing, although not mandatorily equal, reduction in the nuclear potential. Deep cuts beyond certain quality parameters may turn out to be politically disadvantageous.

1.3.6. Despite the current increased activity of contacts with the outside world, Russia faces the threat of a new semi-isolation. Economic relations with the outside world are being curtailed. Difficult to surmount obstacles to extensive foreign investments remain. The crisis in the petroleum extraction industry threatens to worsen the situation even further. The geostrategic separation of Russia from Europe and our disappointing inability to become economically "open" to the outside world, as well as our diminished economic and political influence lower, to a certain extent, the interest of the Western countries in Russia (this is one of the main reasons for the current weakening of relations with Germany). The sharp decline in the role of the nuclear factor will contribute to lowering the interest in Russia. To a certain extent the value of Russia as a geopolitical partner as well is being reduced (worsened by the withdrawal of Russian diplomacy from a number of key countries. Without being our opponents, these countries have not become useful partners).

The already existing noticeable irritation caused by our incompetence and confusion may increase. It is becoming clear that in the next few years possibilities for economic expansion and involvement with Russia will be extremely limited. Russia is threatened less by "economic enslavement" than by lack of interest in investing in its economy, without which its upsurge becomes impossible. Potential partners are showing restraint also because of the fear that Russia would either go through a stage of uncontrolled chaos or else will collapse. The isolation could worsen if the Western security structures (NATO, EEC) are stretched to include countries in Central and Eastern Europe, with the exception of Russia.

Neo-isolation is encouraged by the geo-economic factor (increased cost of exports and imports because of the distance separating Russia from the principal markets, and loss of the virtually free and unhindered access to most ports of the former USSR).

Neo-isolation is not inevitable if Russia continues to pursue the path to reforms and does not convert to rigid authoritarian forms of governance. The threat exists, however, and requires a suitable policy. Should Russia turn to neo-fascism or to a neo-communist restoration or begin to break down, as we already said, a virtually total hostile isolation becomes inevitable.

1.3.7. A zone of relatively strong but unstable countries will develop south of the borders of the former USSR. Their policies and interests will be very similar to those of the European countries during the period of early imperialism (end of the 19th and beginning of the 20th century). They will begin to struggle for greater influence in world affairs and for a certain redivision of the world. Whereas in international relations as a whole there will be a reduction in the role of military force, in that area that same role will be retained. A headlong saturation of the area with conventional armaments will occur. A number of countries in that area have the theoretical ability to develop mass destruction weapons, including nuclear. The challenge originating in that zone may intensify with the increased instability and appearance of a security vacuum in the former Soviet Central Asia, and the spreading within it of Islamic fundamentalism. However, this last threat is being obviously exaggerated. A Sunni rather than Shiite population is in the majority in the Central Asian republics. The local elites are developing mostly on national, regional, political, and noncommunist grounds, i.e., on a laic basis, and much less on the basis of religious grounds and are leaning more to the Turkish rather than the Iranian system. In general, Russia's policy blocks the political fear of Islam felt in the West but not the aim of promoting cooperation with its supporters which, incidentally, could rely on rich historical tradition and mutual interests.

Therefore, the challenges to Russia from the south have not been concretized and are not a direct threat to security. They remain dispersed and scattered. Their military and political containment requires flexible power instruments which could support a diplomacy of possible involvement in police operations aimed at encouraging divisions and peace-making operations, preferably coordinated within the framework of a common policy pursued by the Euro-Atlantic community. As a whole, Russia's possibilities of controlling the situation in this potentially dangerous area are limited. Efficient control requires flexible diplomacy and cooperation with the West. At the same time, cooperation with many countries in Asia is not only advantageous in itself but also could greatly contribute to the preservation and even strengthening of foreign policy opportunities in other directions. This particularly applies to India, Pakistan, Saudi Arabia, Syria, and Israel.

1.3.8. Russia's diminished potential, compared to that of the USSR, and the long-term economic crisis in the country encourage new relations with China. China's GNP is almost double that of Russia. China is and must remain a friendly state. However, it could either enter a period of destabilization or else begin to display a tendency to engage in territorial-economic expansion. The prevention of such a possibility by political means alone, through the organization of friendly relations or reliance on the restraining power of a conventional potential may prove ineffective. The Chinese factor is encouraging Russia to retain its political reliance on nuclear containment and of strategic alliance with the West.

1.3.9. A process of conversion of Japan's economic into political power has started and is rapidly progressing. However, Japan remains relatively little interested in economic cooperation with Russia. A long-term possibility exists of Japan developing a major military potential. Reliance on economic dynamism and the political vacuum in the ATR [Asia-Pacific Region], provide an opportunity for major political and military-political changes in the area.

1.3.10. Russia is urgently facing the problem of loss of political face and trust and dignity as a state, i.e., of political capital. This is the result of a frequently automatic effort to get around the Western partners. Self-exposing ties with the former partners of the USSR (although, as a rule, they were quite unattractive), whether in the intelligence community, the communist parties, and other left-wing movements (even among social democrats) and circles which could be accused of international terrorism, and endless leaks of confidential data about partners, agents, and influence in other countries are causing particularly serious damage. Such self-exposures place Russia not in the position of a privileged partner but in that of odd man out, of the "village idiot," with whom one cannot engage in serious and confidential affairs.

1.3.11. Russia finds itself in a profound economic dependence on the outside world, without any alternate options, in the areas of servicing the debt and critical imports.

1.3.12. As a whole, changes in relations between Russia and the outside world are relatively favorable, above all as a result of eased external pressure and threats, and the establishment of new relations with a number of the most powerful countries, as well as efforts to secure for Russia the status of the main successor of the USSR. New challenges could arise to neutralize such a correct policy. However, we are facing a limited possibility of making use of external aid for the internal restructuring and a reduced opportunity for exerting foreign political and other types of influence.

1.4 CHALLENGES ORIGINATING FROM THE FORMER USSR

1.4.1. Following the accords of Belovezhskaia Pushcha, the former USSR entered not an age of "disintegration of the empire," "decolonization," disintegration or "recreation of statehood" (although all such processes occurred), but an age of building new countries. All states on the territory of the former USSR and even within the Russian Federation have, as a rule, a weak historical legitimacy, particularly in their present borders and/or their present ethnic and socioeconomic population structure. Historically, the process of building new states has almost invariably been paralleled by a lengthy series of wars. The current processes could last as long as several decades. Throughout this time the main task of Russian security strategy will be to avoid wars and to settle conflicts on the territory of the former USSR.

1.4.2. Essentially it is a question of "low-intensity" conflicts which, actually, may show a tendency to escalate. In that sense, the threat of local wars facing Russia has increased.

1.4.3. There is great likelihood that the territory of the former USSR will become a zone in which military power will continue to play an essential role in politics. There is the threat of militarization of intergovernmental relations. There also is an obvious need for political and other reliance on armed forces, adapted to the new conditions and objectives. In order to contain and prevent conflicts and promote peace, Russia may have to rely on clearly superior power.

1.4.4. A belt of unstable and relatively weak states has developed to Russia's west and south. Their policies may show a degradation toward hostility. Theoretically, Ukraine can develop a substantial military potential, which could intensify its foreign political ambitions. Some of these countries could struggle and are struggling for increasing the isolation of Russia and for becoming subjects of primary attention by the outside world.

1.4.5. The erosion of governmental authority, particularly of the executive branch which, as a result of hasty economic reforms, indecisiveness, and differences in the leadership and a weakening of traditional factors for the consolidation of the Russian state—outside threat and internal political coercion, and upsurge of nationalism and national communism, and the overall global process of the weakening of states as subjects of international relation—have created a real danger of Russia's disintegration. Should this occur, the Lebanization or Yugoslavization of the virtually entire former USSR will become practically inevitable.

We are faced with the indecisiveness of the Russian leadership in defining its attitude toward the potential division of the country, the lack of a special policy which would identify the dynamics which threaten the country's territorial integrity.

1.4.6. Another threat comes from the assumption of the prerogatives of the state by political, social, national, and, frequently, also criminal groups in the localities. The state is losing its ability to protect the individual and is surrendering its own power. Mass violations of human rights are beginning to take place on a new level and in new forms. The most obvious although, perhaps, not the most dangerous example of usurpation of power is the political aspects of the upsurge of the Cossack movement and its arming in a number of areas.

1.4.7. The continuing economic decline leads to the impoverishment of the population and the erosion of the former Soviet middle class—the majority of intelligentsia groups. The establishment of a new middle class is falling behind. We are witnessing the fast growth of crime and comprehensive corruption. The state is unable to protect the citizen. The alienation of society to the new system is growing. Democratic values and constitutional limits are being discredited along with the forms of the political process. A social foundation is being laid for radical political movements which, should they come to power, would almost inevitably lead Russia into the path of foreign adventures and militaristic policy.

Similar and potentially even more drastic processes are occurring in the contiguous states, Ukraine in particular. The temptation to shift the growth of popular discontent to the external "enemy" will intensify. In a number of cases, this enemy will be Russia.

The crisis of the transitional period and the need for social and economic reform are becoming the main determining factor of Russia's interests.

1.4.8. A new phenomenon in Russia and the CIS is that of a regionalized foreign policy, in which individual oblasts and regions are starting to develop their own systems of foreign policy interests and economic and other relations. This process is universal. It is essentially healthy but also may prove to be dangerous. It should be corrected and monitored.

1.4.9. The status of the ethnic minorities, which are becoming or could become targets of pressure or discrimination and forced to emigrate, presents a particular challenge. This is a question not only of 25 to 28 million Russians but of at least 70 million people, including Ukrainians, Belarusians, Armenians, Tajiks, etc., who live outside their ethnohistorical areas. If prerequisites for mass migration flows are established in the former USSR the situation will become explosive, and not only in Russia.

1.4.10. The situation in the former USSR is characterized by a "security vacuum," by a weakness or total absence of efficient structures which would control security in the former USSR.

1.4.11. The situation in the armed forces presents a particular challenge to security. Management and military control over them have been weakened in virtually all republics of the CIS. Political control over such forces is even less than in the past. The level of political and social discontent within them is extremely high. The extent to which the latest changes in the Ministry of Defense of the Russian Federation can neutralize such processes remains unclear.

1.4.12. Unforgivable militarization of potentially unstable areas by letting units deployed in such areas arm the local authorities is taking place on CIS territory. Such actions have already brought about the escalation of a number of conflicts. Pursuing such a policy in Central Asia could have catastrophic consequences in terms of regional stability.

1.4.13. The reform in the armed forces will take place against a background of a worsened demographic situation, making it virtually impossible to maintain their numerical strength on the currently planned level without broadening the category of individuals subject to the draft and without corresponding social and political consequences, including those affecting the armed forces themselves.

1.4.14. The crisis in the armed forces and economic difficulties undermine the system of control over nuclear weapons.

1.4.15. The threat that a number of countries (Ukraine above all) may gain control over nuclear weapons has not been eliminated. Such a development of events would not only increase the threat of their use in unsanctioned launching. The leadership of a country which has obtained nuclear weapons will almost inevitably become radicalized.

1.4.16. The situation in the VPK [military-industrial complex] is triggering an entire array of familiar problems. The concept and the systematic policy for its adaptation to the new realities have still not been formulated. A problem which has been discussed little is the virtually total alienation of the elite sectors and population strata linked to the VPK from the new economic and political processes and their very small possibilities of interacting with the outside world.

1.4.17. In virtually any upturn in the internal political situation a further reduction of military expenditures is inevitable. This makes necessary the fastest possible definition of priorities in military construction and, above all, a concentration on the social area within the armed forces and the laying of scientific and technical foundations.

1.4.18. As in the past, the trend toward disintegration within the former USSR remains prevalent. An economic collapse could bring to power even stronger radical-nationalistic forces. At the same time, the level reached in independence and international recognition and the cost and threat of disintegration are beginning to intensify the trend toward integration.

2.1. RECOMMENDATIONS: GENERAL STIPULATIONS

2.1.1. Russia's safety depends to a decisive extent on the success of the reforms and the preservation of the basic democratic gains. The unquestionable support of democratic values and the rights and freedoms of man must retain their priority even despite the fact that in reality this will not be very easy, bearing in mind the nature of the most likely regime to come. In all other cases the suggested scenario would automatically assume its "worst variant."

Absolutely mandatory in this sense is preserving the freedom of the press and of information as well as the strengthening of the "fourth estate."

2.1.2. At the present stage, the most acute overall problem of national security is that of strengthening the governmental power structures and controlling society in the normal and legal rather than the totalitarian understanding of this term, and making it possible for the state really to protect the rights and the lives of the citizens.

2.1.3. The present condition of Russia and the historical traditions of Russian statehood would be most consistent with establishing a type of presidential republic rather than a parliamentary or a "mixed" one (presidential-parliamentary as has been actually proposed in the official draft Constitution submitted for approval by the sixth congress).

2.1.4. However, any major disruption of the established balance of powers is inadmissible. Any undermining of the legislative branch, despite its entirely obvious imperfection, would inevitably bring about the totalitarian degeneracy of the state. We must strengthen the executive and, particularly, the judicial authorities while strictly retaining the essential features of the present balance.

2.1.5. A policy aimed at strengthening the state must be based on social groups which are most interested in strengthening and preserving its integrity and preventing the growth of disintegration processes within the former USSR. This applies to the corps of directors, which is rapidly becoming bourgeoisified, to the new private enterprise bourgeoisie and, finally, the officer corps. We must have a purposeful policy both of the state as well as of these groups in order to surmount and smooth the contradictions existing among them and to formulate a single ideology as well as to upgrade the living standards of the officers.

2.1.6. Development following a relatively peaceful democratic way requires the clear determination of realistic yet understandable and attractive development targets. This may apply to a socially oriented capitalist economy and a law-governed state which can protect human rights and life. This must not be a path to a sterile "bright future," socialist in the past and capitalist now, but a clear program of steps leading to a society of universal prosperity, making use of the experience of foreign countries where such a society already exists, above all by applying the North European model (Germany, Scandinavia), but adapted to the specific features of Russia with its historical characteristics and psychological mood of the people.

2.1.7. A prime task for the immediate future in the area of national security, defense, and foreign policy is not only the formulation of a long-term policy (although, naturally, this too is necessary) but shaping the respective structures into a relatively streamlined system. Currently, due to bureaucratic lack of organization and diversity of opinions, it is impossible even to aspire toward the pursuit of an ideal political line.

2.1.8. One of the possible ways for the development of such a structure is strengthening the Security Council, strictly subordinating it to the president, granting it real rights to formulate a rational policy for national security and coordinating its implementation. However, if the SB [Security Council] were to function in virtually all areas of state policy, thus duplicating the Council of Ministers, it would find itself in the position of a superministry or of the former Politburo and, having acquired a dangerous total permissiveness, would begin to display political ambitions while becoming incapable of performing the functions of information-analytical support of the president in coordinating a policy of national security in the practical sense and would be unable to become an instrument for additional control by the civil political departments over the power structures.

2.1.9. No strategy of national security or any long-term foreign and defense policy could be implemented before resolving the problem of whether Russia will preserve its territorial integrity as a state. The main priority of state policy at the present stage must be to prevent the disintegration of Russia both through sensible prevention compromises in the division of rights between the central and local power authorities, as well as the strict prosecution, within the law, of any official or any political and social organization whose activities threatens Russia's territorial integrity. Such a policy must be public. An end must be put to the still used policy of unsystematic agreements between the center and the local authorities, which, in a number of cases, have brought us close to disintegration.

2.2. POLICY TOWARD THE OUTSIDE WORLD

2.2.1. Despite the obvious need for drastically upgrading the intensity and the level of cadre support for work among the "immediate neighbors," the policy toward the traditional outside world must remain a priority item. Obviously, it is impossible to modernize Russia without opening it to the world of developed countries and without interacting with them in the economic and security areas.

Although Russia will have to make the main efforts and find its own funds for modernization, controlling the situation within the CIS would be difficult without interacting with the outside world. Russia's self-isolation and further plunging into provincialism would also limit possibilities for democratic development.

Russia is not endangered by the status of being the weaker partner within the system of interdependencies (such as a "raw material appendage" or "source of inexpensive manpower"). For a while such a model is inevitable. Such a phase was covered quite quickly by some of the "new industrialized countries" among the developing states. Russia's educational, scientific, and cultural standards and defense potential allow it to fear this stage less than would other countries.

2.2.2. Preventing the outbreak of new challenges from the West and, particularly, from the Southeast, the tasks related to regulating the situation within the CIS and controlling the worsened geostrategic status of Russia and the task of compensating for the growing influence of Japan clearly dictate the need for the formulation of a long-term course of strategic alliance with the West (including Japan and South Korea).

2.2.3. In the long term, the possibilities of the United States and its role as Russia's partner would diminish while those of Western Europe would potentially increase. However, this does not dictate the expediency of converting to a "Eurocentrist" model of politics. The organization of maximally close interaction with the United States will maintain Russia's positions in Europe, positions which have weakened and will continue to weaken over the next decade. Russia's interests are consistent with maintaining a constant balance between America and Europe.

2.2.4. Russia's long-term interest lies in maximum rapprochement with the European Community and, in the final account, joining the single European economic and political space, the center of which will be the EC. However, this does not mean the total identification of Russian interests with those of the Community. Russia is interested in maintaining the possibility for political maneuvering and for a multipolar European policy and limitation of the military-political functions of the European Community. Hence its long-term interest in the preservation of NATO and developing partnership relations with it.

2.2.5. We must drastically enhance our efforts along the most unsuccessful line of Russian politics: toward Germany. Russia is rapidly losing its "German legacy." It is obvious that there can no longer be a question of a "special relationship." Germany, however, remains the economic leader of Europe and the country which is potentially most interested (although less than in the past) in the stable development of Russia, of the former USSR. Russian-German interaction is a key factor in determining Russia's possibility to regulate its relations with the European countries which were part of the USSR.

2.2.6. The formulation of a purposeful strategy to prevent Russia's neo-isolation from the developed countries is vital. This means developing the export sectors and a maximal economic involvement of the developed countries in the West, East, and South, which leads to relations of uneven but existing interdependence and the establishment of a strategic alliance in which Russia would play the role of an important partner in settling the situation in Eastern Europe, Central Asia, and the Far East. Also important is the knowledgeable use of the "negative" factors which are of interest to the outside world, the West in particular, in ensuring the favorable development and modernization of Russia during its transitional period. This applies above all to its powerful and efficient nuclear potential.

Another reserve is the deliberate policy of exposing the Russian countryside to the outside world and introducing the outside world inside the Russian countryside.

2.2.7. It is obviously necessary to make an effort to energize the policy aimed at countries in Central and Eastern Europe, particularly in the areas of economic, cultural, and personal relations.

In principle, Russia is not interested in letting the countries in Central Europe become members of any broader security system which would exclude Russia.

However, we must also realize the fact that these countries will not assume any priority status in Russian politics. They are hurrying to join the West, being now geographically separated from Russia. They have neither the funds nor the technology which would ensure their major participation in Russia's revival. Therefore, any effort at including such countries in the list of Russian political priorities would be unrealistic.

By virtue of its geopolitical position, the most important to Russia in that area are Poland and, possibly, Bulgaria (we could also add Slovakia).

2.2.8. The limited possibilities and unwillingness of the West to participate in Russia's revival, its international-political positions, and the difficulties which will develop in the next few years in entering the Western markets urgently demand a diversification of Russian policy. The Western direction inevitably retains its priority. However, any one-sided alignment with the West would be counterproductive. Russia must consistently pursue a line of developing political and economic relations with partners in Asia, which are important from the political or else advantageous from the economic viewpoint. This includes India, Saudi Arabia, Egypt, the United Arab Emirates, Israel, and Iran. Partnership relations with those countries would strengthen Russia's positions in its relations with the West. They are also necessary in order to control the situation in the Central Asian republics and the Transcaucasus.

2.2.9. Any attempt at preserving the global nature of Russian politics (from the viewpoint of direct involvement, particularly military-political) is doomed to failure and would hasten the further exhaustion of resources and the disintegration of Russia.

2.2.10. A shift in the ratio of forces between China and Russia requires a sharp increase in the attention paid to China by Russian policy. In terms of priority, it should be equal to Europe and America, and become determining in a number of other policy areas.

2.2.11. The Russian state must formulate and actively implement a strategy of aggressive promotion of Russian economic interests and Russian business abroad, where it faces a limited business practice and unconscientious competition. Finally, there simply is a shortage of necessary experience and contacts. It is important to preserve and not allow the wasting but instead make use of potential bridgeheads for future Russian economic expansion, of the property owned by armed forces abroad. Also expedient is maintaining the export of armaments and creating an efficient system for its control, which would not allow, on the one hand, the causing of any harm and, on the other, would harm the interests of Russian exporters. At the same time, we must clearly realize that the arms market is extremely unreliable and hopes for exports do not eliminate the need for the accelerated conversion of defense production facilities which have no future in the domestic market.

2.3. POLICY TOWARD COUNTRIES ON THE TERRITORY OF THE FORMER USSR

2.3.1. In terms of these countries, Russia has three possible courses it could follow:

1. A policy aimed at restoring the former USSR although on a different basis (the alternative of the red-brown part of the population which does not accept the breakdown of the USSR, and some of the bureaucratic structures suffering from the consequences of this breakdown).

2. Total withdrawal and isolation, abandoning the former republics in the USSR to their own devices, and refusal to try to strengthen the CIS (option of some radical democrats and ultranationalists, so-called Russian party).

3. Various options of an enlightened post-imperial course, which would include efforts to preserve and develop intergovernmental structures and a new community, and an active (if possible internationally sanctioned) participation in preventing and ending conflicts, if necessary even with the help of military force, and preventing any mass and gross violations of human rights and freedoms.

2.3.2. The first course would almost inevitably degenerate into a series of major wars and conflicts. Wars and their consequences would quite likely bring about the disintegration of Russia. This course is fraught with a war of all against all, disintegration of the military machine, and loss of control over arsenals of mass destruction weapons. The outside world is not interested in a restoration of Moscow's control over the former USSR. This interest, as well as a reaction to the inevitable mass violence would result in a hostile and virtually total political, economic, and military-political isolation of Russia, and efforts on the part of the outside world to undermine its positions. In the best of cases a return to a relatively normal life would be possible in 30 to 50 years.

2.3.3. On the surface, the neo-isolationist radical-democratic option appears attractive: it implies distancing ourselves from culturally different and, as a rule, poorer and more backward, parts of the former USSR. In its pure aspect, this political option promises a relatively faster (10-20 years) conversion to a new type of society. The reaction to it by the outside world could be quite calm and even favorable. However, it is unrealistic, speculative, and fraught with the danger of enhancing aggressive nationalism in both Russia and the other countries within the former USSR. Problems involving minorities become inevitable. Mass internal migration and the spreading of conflicts throughout Russian territory would bring down any regime. Refusal to protect ethnic minorities is immoral and would undermine even further any confidence in and prestige of Russia.

2.3.4. An enlightened post-imperial integrationist course in its various options seems to be the only realistic although not the easiest way. In a number of its manifestations it would invariably clash with the suspicion or even opposition of a segment of the international community which is not interested in a strong Russian state as a center of a community involving other countries. However, flexibly promoted, this course would meet with the understanding of Russia's basic partners who are interested in guarantees for maintaining stability in the area of the former USSR and fear the intensification of the "geostrategic hole."

2.3.5. Obviously, such a course should proceed from the post-Belovezh reality and reject as unrealistic and counterproductive the objective of achieving a new and fast unification within a union. The main objective (post-imperial) of the policy should be to avoid quite likely wars and conflicts and to control the transformation of the former USSR. As a long-term practical objective, it could aim at the creation of a viable community of the EC type, i.e., the reintegration of a substantial portion of the former USSR on the basis of conditions acceptable to all countries.

Despite this entire labored and conditional nature of the CIS formula, it makes it possible, albeit on the symbolic level, to identify the real commonality of interests of millions of people who inhabit the space of the former Union and, at the same time, leaves the door open to the search for a new and even as yet unclear configuration of structures of profound cooperation among areas and territories which may eventually unite within a single Russian state.

2.3.6. Any sensible policy requires the unconditional acceptance of the principle of inviolability of borders despite their obviously artificial nature. The rejection of such a principle would open the way to literally dozens of conflicts and to national catastrophe.

2.3.7. Particular effort must be focused, despite all difficulties, on developing a close network of permanent intergovernmental authorities which would regulate relations in all areas of life: economic, transport, power industry, finance, education, culture, and defense. Such a network is needed not only in order to prevent or ease conflicts and soften the consequences of the break up. It should serve the establishment of personal relations and the personal interests of the new elites in widening them.

2.3.8. Naturally, on Russia's part the efforts to recreate relations which were broken by force should be very painstaking and twice as delicate in order not to encourage local national extremists which would deliberately provoke its leadership to display and assert its great-power status. This should not be left in the hands of nonprofessionals on any level, regardless of their official position. It is only thus that we could hope to maintain in the future, until the present generation of politicians has been replaced, any possibility for the revival of a natural Russian foreign policy and, consequently, the opportunity to regain Russia's legitimate historical place in the international arena.

2.3.9. The new policy of the CIS toward the former USSR should be based on a tripartite alliance with states which are of key importance to Russia from the viewpoint of its vital interests: Belarus and Kazakhstan, as well as Georgia in the Caucasus. Unless Russia is able to establish, even by making concessions, the closest possible friendly relations with the first two countries, the CIS is doomed. Disintegration and conflicts will increase, possibilities to control them will diminish, and the isolation of Russia (and the other states) would intensify.

2.3.10. A sharp increase in political action and institutional development on the territory of the former USSR should not push aside the other lines of traditional foreign policy. We must clearly realize that such provincializing of Russian policy would bring about the loss of many opportunities to influence not only the entire outside world but also the "immediate foreign vicinity," that the situation in it is not very hopeful even in the medium time range and that it is a question of controlling the crisis without any particular hope that it can be rapidly surmounted. Finally, Russia and its partners will find it obviously quite difficult to institute such control without quite extensive internationalization and without involving foreign countries and international organizations.

2.3.11. The strategy toward CIS should be oriented toward long-range development and toward strengthening and creating in the contiguous states the type of social and economic structures and special interest groups which will favor a sensible policy which would not clash with the interests of their own peoples and those of Russia.

2.3.12. Russia unquestionably is interested in the preservation and blossoming of the Russian (or Russian-speaking) diaspora in all countries belonging to the former USSR, the countries of the former "socialist camp," and all other countries. In that sense, the breakdown of the USSR has paradoxically given Russia political, economic, and social trump cards of substantial potential power.

For that reason, everything possible should be done (above all through diplomatic methods) to guarantee the rights of the Russian-language population wherever it

resides. In that connection it is possible, and perhaps even necessary, to establish a special ministry or state committee in charge of affairs of our compatriots abroad, which would gather all the necessary information in this area and will formulate a general governmental strategic line in this matter.

2.3.13. Another part of Russia's long-term interests is the preservation of the Russian language as a means of communication and achieving high-quality education in all countries within the former USSR. It is necessary to develop a "Russian Language" state program which would not be aimed at violating the use of any other language used in Russia but would be aimed at preserving for the Russian language the priority status it had already earned.

The secondary and higher education system in the Russian language must be preserved intact (and its quality must be improved). Furthermore, we must strengthen this system and ensure the possibility for training in Russian VUZs high level cadres for the republics of the former USSR.

It is important for military cadres of the new states which were part of the former USSR to continue to be trained essentially in Russia.

2.3.14. We need a long-term strategy of support of private and government investments in and export of Russia's capital to Russia's immediate neighbors. Increased investment will provide not only commercial gains but will also enable us to acquire further political influence. It will strengthen the forces interested in establishing an efficient commonwealth.

2.3.15. Controlling the situation on the territory of the former USSR would require the comprehensive spreading and instilling of the norms and rules of the CSCE [Commission on Security and Cooperation in Europe] and the standards of international law, and filling the legal, political, and military-political vacuum which has formed on the territory of the former USSR and in Central and Eastern Europe, with the help of the CSCE and other European organizations. The best option for filling this vacuum is creating within Europe, including the territory of the former USSR, a collective security system. Establishing an effective collective security system on the territory of the former USSR is a desirable although unlikely possibility, although its elements must be developed.

2.3.16. Although it is clearly preferable, so far we have not fully relied on internationalization in controlling conflict situations in the former USSR. In some cases, however, such an instrument may prove to be too slow or ineffective. Russia must make it clear that, in exceptional circumstances, it does not exclude the possibility of unilateral action—political and economic sanctions—and even, in extreme cases, direct use of force in a situation of mass and gross violations of human rights (and not only of the rights of so-called Russian-speaking minorities) and, to an even greater extent, in cases of open violence against the civilian population. The unequivocal readiness to protect human rights and freedoms in accordance with the standards of international law and morality, and in close cooperation with international organizations and other states within the CIS and the global community, in itself will act as a restraining factor. Like other countries, Russia cannot avoid the responsibility for the development of events on the territory of the former USSR. It is necessary to recognize this reality and to formulate a policy which would be maximally consistent with its UN partners and with European organizations. It is necessary to do everything possible in advance so that any use of force is maximally and internationally sanctioned.

2.4. DEFENSE POLICY

2.4.1. We must unequivocally acknowledge that Russia needs armed forces not only in order to contain aggression and prevent the escalation of crises but also to ensure the defense of its constitutional system, and legality and stability, which are threatened in the current period in its history, and to protect it from disintegration.

2.4.2. In the present critical situation, the priority task is to restore full military control over the armed forces and to strengthen the still extremely weak political control over them.

2.4.3. Political and demographic conditions and scientific and technical requirements dictate the need for the fastest possible conversion to voluntary military service.

2.4.4. The state of crisis in which the armed forces have found themselves, along with the rest of the country, requires the formulation of clear priorities in their development. This applies, above all, to preserving, with a maximally possible reduction, of the cadre backbone of the Army and Navy—the officer corps and the fundamental elements of the training system; it means preserving and developing the scientific and technical base and production capacities (while maximally reducing the purchase of serially made armaments); finally, it means a gradual reform of the armed forces consistent with the new circumstances.

2.4.5. In accordance with the new strategic realities in the development of general-purpose forces, it would be expedient to abandon the old concept which calls for their concentrated deployment in several strategic directions and convert to the concept of "defense in all azimuths" and "mobile defense." This requires the existence of numerically small forces kept in permanent state of readiness, capable of quickly and efficiently influencing local conflicts; a mobile reserve or rapid deployment force which could be transported within the quickest possible time to any area along Russia's periphery; strategic reserves to be set up in war. Subunits and units of rapid reaction forces which could be used in operations to maintain the peace both within the CIS, the UN and the CSCE.

2.4.6. In equipping the Army and Navy priority should be given to high-precision aero-mobile long-range means of destruction and types of armaments and military ordnance and means of reconnaissance and control which, in terms of their quality indicators, could substantially reduce the amount of armaments while retaining adequate firepower.

2.4.7. Russia's present economic and political weakness and other political interests call for retaining in the foreseeable future a political reliance on nuclear weapons and for a strategy of nuclear containment of aggression. In the foreseeable future (0-20 years) Russia will not be interested in any radical reduction of the role of the nuclear factor in the system of means for ensuring its security and political interests either as a result of an extremely radical reduction of strategic armaments or the deployment of broad global anti-missile defense forces. However, the gradual reduction of clearly excessive arsenals would be useful and necessary. As a whole, the liquidation of tactical nuclear armaments as well would be consistent with Russia's interests.

2.4.8. Russia is interested in strengthening strategic stability by creating an integrated early warning and control integrated system and preventing unsanctioned launches by creating zonal anti-missile defense systems. However, clearly, efforts which lead potentially to the creation of a comprehensive global anti-missile defense and a fundamental revision of the principles of the anti-missile defense treaty violate its interests.

2.4.9. Russia's long-term interests are consistent with the maximum possible coordination of its military efforts with other countries and the creation of strategic alliances with the countries within the Atlantic zone, Japan, and South Korea. However, Russia is not interested in such an alliance to be aimed at any one of its southern neighbors.

2.4.10. Conversion measures, based on the smooth conversion of military-industrial complex enterprises and shifting their intellectual potential to civilian tracks should be prepared and carried out in an atmosphere of maximum possible openness, taking into consideration the opinion of the personnel within this complex and its organizations, for it is only thus that one would be able to avoid or reduce the strength of social outbursts. At the same time, the lack of any kind of clear policy in that area and lengthening the agony of unnecessary production is inconsistent both with the interests of society and, in the final account, those of the personnel of such enterprises.

• The Foreign and Defense Policy Council (SVOP) is a non-governmental organization which currently numbers 37 members including politicians, entrepreneurs, members of the military, diplomats, and scientists. One of its main tasks is to assist in the formulation of strategic concepts for the development of the country, particularly in the foreign policy and defense areas. This report was drafted by a working group of SVOP members, consisting of L. Vaynberg, A. Grachev, K. Zatulin, S. Karaganov, Ye. Kozhokin, M. Masarskii, N. Mikhailov, V. Rubanov, V. Tretiakov, A. Tsalko, and I. Yurgens. The authors of this report are grateful to A. Arbatov, S. Blagovolin, S. Kolesnikov, A. Konovalov, V. Mozhaiev, V. Nikonov, S. Oznobishchev, S. Rogov, K. Sorokin, S. Stankevich, and G. Yavlinskii, whose materials were used in drafting the theses. Also used were unclassified documents of the Russian Ministry of Defense and the Ministry of Internal Affairs. The authors of these studies and developments bear no responsibility for the text of the theses. The theses were discussed at the 30 July 1992 meeting of the SVOP, after which they were slightly edited and submitted for exclusive publication in NG.

Nezavisimaia gazeta, 19 August 1992, in FBIS-USR, 8 September 1992, 54-64.

NEW APPROACHES TO RUSSIAN MILITARY DOCTRINE, JULY 1992

Col. Gen. I.N. Rodionov

Russia is reviving and developing statehood in a complicated military-political situation: the Warsaw Pact Organization has been eliminated, the Soviet Union has disintegrated, a shaky political situation has taken shape in the CIS, the Union's unified Armed Forces have disintegrated, its defensive system has fallen apart, and world military-strategic balance essentially has been disrupted.

One task of the Russian Federation Ministry of Defense is to develop the fundamentals of a Russian military doctrine, to determine its overall direction and to substantiate the ways, means and mechanisms for protecting the homeland's vitally important interests. After determining the substance and content of the Russian state's military doctrine, it is also possible to resolve other questions connected with Armed Forces force generation and devise methods of employing them to repel possible aggression.

It must be noted that changes occurring in the world require not only Russia, but literally all states to interpret and work out anew the content of their military policy and military doctrine. The United States, the European NATO countries and many Eastern European states already have refined their military-strategic aims. In particular, a new NATO strategy has been developed and the bloc's military system has begun to be restructured with respect to it.

The question of developing a military doctrine for Russia arises especially acutely under the conditions at hand. It is also pertinent in connection with the fact that the country presently is on the verge of making very crucial decisions on defense matters.

Military Doctrine is a system of fundamental views and provisions on questions of the defense of the country officially adopted in a state in a given time period for mandatory fulfillment by all state, including strictly military, entities. It reflects a state's attitudes toward war and defines the nature of possible military missions which may face it, methods of accomplishing them and primary directions of military force generation. Arguments and discussions on particular questions connected with military doctrine may go on during its development and formation, but when provisions have been incorporated in legislative and government documents, they become doctrinal, i.e., mandatory for everyone, and serve as it were as the aims of supreme political and military authority on national defense questions. Of course this does not mean they are eternal and faultless. Some provisions of military doctrine, and possibly the entire doctrine, may be revised with a change in the internal and external situation. Now it is a question of adopting a fundamentally new military doctrine for Russia

Just where are basic provisions of military doctrine reflected? In a separate document or in other official sources? Doctrine fully encompasses a large range of questions and it is simply impossible to set them forth in one separate document (there is no such thing in a single country in the world). But fundamental provisions of a political and military-technical nature can and must be set forth in a separate document similar to how it was done in the Warsaw Pact (1987) or NATO (1991).

Based on this it is advisable to set forth only approaches to forming the most important provisions and general content of Russian military doctrine, and not the doctrine itself, on which we still have to work.

In forming the political fundamentals of military doctrine, the following must be determined: the state's attitude toward war and use of military force; Russia's national interests and factors opposing them; the nature, dimensions and sources of military danger as well as the possibility of a military threat; the probability and methods of preventing war and the personnel and equipment necessary to do so; the military-political goals of war; and probable enemies and allies. The Russian state's peaceable policy, the fact that Russia does not plan to attack anyone and will not use military force first, and that Its Armed Forces will be directed toward protecting the country's national interests and the state's territorial integrity and independence and repelling aggression must be made the basis of the political aspect of military doctrine. In other words, the political fundamentals must reflect the principal idea, that Russia will not impose its ideology on anyone, recognizes the preservation of peace as a priority goal, rejects initiation of war and aggression against other countries, and favors its prevention and resolution of conflicts which arise by peaceful means above all. The state's military might also must contribute to attaining Russia's political aspirations.

The most difficult of these fundamental questions in developing Russia's military doctrine is for the state's political leadership to determine Russia's national (state) interests.

As one of the world's largest states, Russia has global and regional national interests. On a global plane it is interested in progressive development of civilization; strengthening economic, political, cultural, scientific and other relations with all countries; participating in existing international and regional organizations and creating new ones contributing to strengthened peace and stability in international relations; and establishing a world order which would rely not on the domination and diktat of one country or group with respect to other states, but on collective resolution of urgent problems under UN auspices. Instances of attempts to isolate Russia in political, economic, scientific and cultural development, whether it be in Europe, Asia or other parts of the world, and of the establishment of military-political alliances directed against it will be viewed as actions affecting its national interests.

The Russian Federation's spatial dimensions in Europe and Asia predetermine its vital interests on the Euro-Asiatic continent from the Atlantic to the Pacific. As a European state, Russia has interests in Eastern European countries contiguous with the CIS which previously were in the Warsaw Pact. These states' entry into military-political groupings targeted directly or indirectly against Russia will substantially affect its security and seriously worsen the strategic situation. There-fore, friendly relations with Eastern European states and at the very least their neutral attitude would be in Russia's national interests.

For many centuries Russia fought for an outlet to the Baltic and Black seas, since the impossibility of a free outlet to them always ran counter its national interests. Therefore, the Baltic countries' recognition of Russia's right to free access to seaports on commercial terms with the condition that stationing of "third country" military forces on their territory or their entry into military blocs directed against the Russian Federation would be precluded, and also with unconditional assurance of civil rights of the Russian population in these states would be quite fair for Russia.

With respect to the CIS countries, all Commonwealth states are in the sphere of Russia's vitally important interests. Relations with them are of paramount impor-tance for Russia in the political, economic and military spheres. Collective efforts must be aimed at ensuring that our closest neighbors with many centuries of tradi-tions of living together in friendship do not turn into countries of a unique "buffer zone" or *cordon sanitaire* separating Russia from countries of the West, South and East. This would contradict not only Russian Federation national interests, but also the interests of all peoples of the Commonwealth countries. Attempts by cer-tain internal and external forces to take advantage of artificially aroused separatist and nationalist sentiments can create a situation where if any state of Europe, America or Asia tries to use existing differences and contradictions among CIS members for its own purposes and in this way attempts to strengthen its influence in particular Commonwealth states, this will destabilize international relations and in the final account may have a negative effect on its own position. With respect to Russia, that development of events would signify infringement of national interests and an influence on its security. In the Middle and Far East Russia also is interested in preserving peaceful, mutually advantageous good-neighbor relations with all countries and using ocean waters for free navigation and for economic activity. Those are Russia's national (state) interests.

Other questions also arise in connection with an interpretation of the nature of Russia's national interests. For example, do any threats to its interests exist? This question can be answered in the affirmative! The fact is that national interests of different states often do not coincide, which creates certain contradictions among them. Take just Russia's interests in any of the aforementioned areas (the Baltic, Eastern Europe, and the Near, Middle and Far East); to a certain extent they are opposite to interests of other states and above all the United States in these areas. An attempt by some states or coalitions to dominate individual regions and the world as a whole, dictate their will, intervene in the regions' internal affairs, and help stir up internal contradictions cannot help but trouble Russia. In addition, there exist territorial, ethnic, economic and religious contradictions as well as uncertainty and instability of a rapidly changing world, which also affects Russia's national (state) interests.

It is impossible to ignore that major states (the United States and other NATO countries) have enormous military might and they not only are preserving it, but also are reinforcing it, and that a certain quantitative reduction in armed forces quickly made up for by adopting new, more effective kinds of weapons. Everyone is familiar with figures on the size of US and NATO armed forces. NATO countries presently have around 20,000 different offensive air weapons and a developed system of their basing near Russia's borders, so that they have enormous offensive might which is being developed rapidly by the way, maintaining superiority in aerospace and at sea is one of the US strategic principles). Under these conditions it is not at all precluded that these countries may employ military force to resolve contradictions in various spheres of society's life and to achieve their military-political goals. Many military conflicts which have broken out since World War II, including the Persian Gulf war, attest to this.

A military threat to Russia's national interests exists and hardly will disappear in the near term. This is confirmed by conclusions from an analysis of actions by probable enemies and allies, which are very important in forming the state's military doctrine.

That assessment is not at all simple and lately has been distinguished by extremes. Previously it was considered that almost the entire world was the probable enemy, but now we declare that we have no probable enemies nor can there be any, that all former enemies are friends. That approach is profoundly erroneous. Russia in fact does not now have direct enemies which would immediately threaten it with attack. At the same time, military conflicts are occurring on ethnic, territorial and religious soil in a world which still preserves tension. All this demands that we correctly assess the military-political situation and promptly determine the impending threat. It is necessary to consider the possibility of a change in the political course of individual countries, the desire to revise postwar borders and, for some states, the desire to preserve and strengthen large groupings of armed forces. It makes sense to carefully observe military preparations of particular countries, attempts to move troops into contiguous countries, and a disturbance of military-political stability in border areas.

It is impossible to agree with the opinion that no one now threatens us and that military danger is gone for Russia since the difference in ideology with foreign countries, which previously had been the source of military danger, is disappearing. This is absolutely incorrect. It is necessary to recall that World Wars I and II began between groupings of states with the same ideology and socioeconomic system. This also goes for the Persian Gulf war to a certain extent. With respect to allies, it is necessary to have them above all among Commonwealth states. Russia must strive to organize defense in the Commonwealth system together with other sovereign states based on the existing Collective Defense Treaty. Integration of military efforts will conform to the interests both of Russia as well as of Commonwealth states. This will allow the sovereign states to rely on each other and make maximum use of the preserved elements of the former USSR's defensive system in a joint defense.

The military-technical aspect of military doctrine in the most general statement of the question must respond to the following fundamental questions: What is the strategic nature of a possible war for which one must prepare? What are the methods of waging it? And what armed forces must one have for this? Up to the present time principal attention in military doctrine was given to provisions on world nuclear war and conventional war. Insufficient attention clearly has been given to local wars and low-intensity military conflicts essentially have not been examined at all, the more so as people in the former USSR feared even to mention conflicts disturbing stability within the country. Russia's new military doctrine must give enormously more attention to interpreting the conduct of local wars, low-intensity conflicts, and military operations to restore stability within the country. This is occasioned by the fact that such wars and conflicts are most likely in the future, while the possibility of the initiation and conduct of a world war has diminished considerably.

Just what is the nature of wars which Russia may be forced to wage?

First of all, a global nuclear threat will be preserved as long as other states have nuclear weapons and the capability of using them. This is a reality with which it is impossible not to reckon. Statements by state leaders about non-use of these weapons against Russia cannot be sufficient grounds for our nuclear disarmament, especially as the Americans are in no hurry to make the very same statement with respect to Russia. Everything appears just the other way around. For example, the US Defense Directive for 1994–1998 notes that American nuclear weapons will continue to be aimed against Russia's military targets. The Directive states: "American missiles will continue to threaten the most significant targets...of Russia and other possible enemies."

If war with use of nuclear weapons is not prevented, it can acquire a global scale and will have catastrophic consequences for all mankind. Therefore, Russia opposes such a war. All means (political, diplomatic and military) must be directed toward preventing it, but the deciding role here will rest with Russia's capability to inflict damage on the probable enemy in a retaliatory nuclear strike under all conditions.

Secondly, major aggression against Russia with conventional weapons also is possible in the future. The initial period of such a war can differ, and its feature is that an enemy invasion most likely will begin in air and sea space with delivery of strikes by aviation and naval forces, and in the future also from space. It is not precluded that this option of an aggressor's initiation of war will become the most realistic as a result of the existing military-political, military-strategic and military-technical situation (for Russia and the CIS as a whole). This is also confirmed by the fact that developed countries have powerful, effective means of precision air attack and have an advantage in their development. Under certain conditions a war also can begin by an invasion of enemy ground force groupings with simultaneous delivery of strikes from air and sea. A large-scale conventional war also can arise as a result of the development of local wars and military conflicts into a major military clash, as well as because of military assistance being given to one or more countries which have been subjected to aggression. Such a war, using precision weapons and enhanced-yield munitions, can have serious consequences, and if opposing sides set for themselves the achievement of decisive goals, it is fraught with the constant threat of developing into a nuclear war. Because of the reality of these options, Russia must openly declare that it has the right to use the entire arsenal of weapons at its disposal, including nuclear weapons, to repel aggression.

Thirdly, local wars and military conflicts affecting Russia's national interests may arise subsequently. Such wars are possible both near the borders of Russia and other CIS countries as well as in other countries. They can be waged with limited involvement of armed forces and the extension of military operations to relatively small territories. But local wars and military conflicts are fraught with developing into major military clashes both from escalation as well from ruling circles of individual countries using them as a pretext to carry out large-scale aggression.

Fourthly, the country's internal situation can be destabilized by conflicts on ethnic and religious soil, by civil war, and by the intervention of armed forces in these processes. It is curious to note that the concept of employing armed forces for accomplishing internal missions is rejected by opposition forces fighting for power until they obtain it, after which they begin to look differently on the role of the armed forces.

Thus the Russian Armed Forces must be capable of conducting military operations of any nature and on any scale.

The methods of military operations of the Russian Armed Forces at the beginning of a war can vary. Previously the state's military doctrine envisaged only defensive operations in the initial period. Later it was presumed that the enemy would be expelled from captured territory with the help of a counteroffensive and military operations would cease without invading the aggressor's territory in case of reaching his state border. "Hitting the enemy not on foreign, but on friendly territory" was intended. The mission of defeating the enemy was not assigned; it was a question of pushing him back beyond the state border. It was also said that subsequently one must strive to end the war, but how to do this was not explained. It was impossible to be reconciled any longer with such doctrinal provisions on the methods of conducting military operations. They clearly reflected specific political sentiments and did not consider the laws of warfare. These provisions, predetermining defeat in a future war in advance, essentially are very dangerous for a state.

History attests that an indifferent defense, passiveness and loss of strategic initiative never before brought victory to belligerents. It is useful to recall that in the Great Patriotic War we seized the strategic initiative once and for all only in the summer of 1943. According to the doctrine existing in that period, the initiative was given to the enemy in advance. The principal argument in favor of such a strictly defensive concept was considered to be the fact that otherwise a contradiction arises between defensive political and offensive military-technical aspects of doctrine. In fact, the fallaciousness of this approach was as follows: political aspects were transferred to military-technical aspects, and the time before the beginning of war was identified with the time after its beginning.

The new Russian military doctrine must precisely, clearly and unequivocally reflect the proposition that if an enemy has begun aggression and armed conflict, its evaluation must proceed from the laws of warfare. In this case the armed forces must choose and carry out those forms and methods of military operations most effective in a given situation: the offensive, the defense, and the delivery of fire strikes against the enemy no matter where he is located. This includes strikes that must be delivered above all against the aggressor country's territory and against his most important military and economic installations.

It is also time to reject such concepts as "defensive doctrine," "defensive strategy," "defensive armed forces" and so on. Such concepts are not used abroad, particularly in the United States and NATO. One simply says doctrine, strategy and armed forces without the adjective "defensive."

Russian military doctrine must determine the principal directions of its armed forces force generation, which must be based above all on the national interests for whose defense the armed forces are created; on missions which may face the armed forces in order to attain these goals; and on the country's economic and S&T capacities for comprehensive outfitting and support of the armed forces. The priority in armed forces force generation must be, not the residual principle, but specifically national Interests and missions of ensuring one's security. References to norms in effect in so-called civilized countries and to general coefficients of the numerical strength of the population in determining the makeup of the Army and Navy are inappropriate in the given instance.

Each state has a geopolitical and strategic position inherent only to it and has its own features, capabilities and interests in accordance with which armed forces force generation must be carried out. It is fully understandable that one should consider here the economic and S&T capacities for upkeep and outfitting of the Army and Navy, but they must be strictly calculated, coordinated and brought into agreement with missions and national interests for ensuring security of society and the state. Otherwise these missions cannot be performed. And if there is some kind of discrepancy, it is necessary to begin not with an arbitrarily established numerical strength of armed forces and allocation of an arbitrarily established part of the budget, but with clarification of national interests and political goals, conclusion of favorable political alliances, and conduct of other political and economic actions which would permit relieving tension or reducing the need for armed units to a certain extent.

In establishing the Russian Armed Forces it is necessary to set a course not toward their quantitative, but toward their qualitative development. The priority should be given to new, most effective means of warfare (aerospace weapons, precision guided weapons, and modern command and control and reconnaissance equipment). This will permit increasing the armed forces' combat capabilities with their lesser numerical strength. But with regard to structure, evidently it is inadvisable to cardinally change it in the near future. It is necessary to preserve existing branches of armed forces and make maximum use of the command and control system and agencies. A cardinal restructuring in this area will rapidly involve enormous expenditures and reduce combat readiness. Now everything must be based and substantiated on what exists, and only later can it be adjusted and improved.

In the makeup of the Russian Armed Forces it is necessary to have permanent readiness forces of limited numerical strength; mobile, air-transportable reserves capable of movements to any region of the country in short time periods; as well as strategic reserves formed in a period of threat and in the course of war to conduct large-scale military operations. During a strategic deployment the Russian Armed Forces must he capable of establishing three major groupings—western, southern and eastern—which would have the capability of independently accomplishing strategic missions if necessary on their own axes. They must be built on one-man command, which is called upon to be strengthened and developed in every way. And it is advisable to carry out armed forces manpower acquisition on a mixed basis—military obligation and contract. On the whole, a course must be set toward creating a professionally prepared, well trained cadre army.

The Russian Ministry of Defense has drawn up a draft of principles of the state's military doctrine which can be taken as a basis, but requires serious discussion and substantial corrections. A concept such as "deterrence from possible aggression against Russia" needs further interpretation. This is one of the basic principles; Russia must concentrate its political, economic and military efforts to implement it in the future as well. Not only do circumstances which have formed in the world point in favor of this, but so do provisions of US national and military strategy published in 1992, for example. About deterrence they state that US national interests and most important goals include the following: deterring any aggression which may threaten the security of the United States and its allies and, in case deterrence policy fails, repelling armed attack or defeating the enemy and ending the conflict on terms favorable to the United States; deterring nuclear attack remains the very first priority in the matter of US defense even in the new era; the fundamental mission of the American Armed Forces remains unchanged—deterring aggression. These statements are backed up by political, economic and military measures and by open publication in the mass media. There are few who doubt that the US Armed Forces will in fact carry out the deterrence function, and not just by using nuclear weapons, but also using the full might of the Armed Forces and general purpose forces, to whom Russia's territory is accessible from all sides and to the full depth.

Russia also supports the principle of deterrence, but the question of by what forces this can be realized is legitimate. The United States and many other possible enemies are inaccessible to general purpose forces. There remain the Strategic Nuclear Forces and above all the Strategic Missile Forces, but the new doctrine again states that Russia will not be first to use nuclear or any other mass destruction weapons. Statements about "non-first use of nuclear weapons," "retaliatory strikes," and "defensive character" indicate a repetition of mistakes of past years designed for political leaders' self-advertisement and irreparably damaging our defense. And in what state possessing nuclear weapons does the President place millions of lives of his citizens and the existence of the state itself under a first nuclear strike by one such statement? Only in ours?

In the future nuclear weapons are the primary means for deterring possible aggression, which also means preventing war. It is advisable to entirely exclude wordings about use of nuclear weapons from the content of military doctrine. The main thing is for us not to be the aggressor in any case, and as to the rest everyone must know firmly that in case of aggression against Russia it will employ all means it has to protect its interests.

There are very few who wished to see a strong, independent, free RUSSIA in the world either before 1917 or afterwards. But Russia became great over many centuries of struggle with aggressors for survival against the attempts of other states. It is erroneous to hope that with a revision of our ideological concepts everyone will rush to help revive Russia. An economically stable, renewed, prospering Russia rid of wars is needed only by Russians, and the military doctrine being adopted is called upon to give them help in this not in words, but in action.

Voennaia mysl (July 1992), 6-14, in JPRS-UMT, 30 September 1992.

RUSSIAN MILITARY DOCTRINE, JULY 1992

Army General Pavel S. Grachev

We are concluding four days of work of the extraordinarily timely Russian Federation Ministry of Defense scientific conference. The goals which were set basically have been achieved. There was a useful exchange of opinions on various problems of Russia's military security.

The theme of the scientific conference was not chosen by chance. We are faced with the need to form, reorganize and reduce the Russian Armed Forces in short time periods. It was gratifying to sense a desire in the majority of presentations to create those Russian Armed Forces in short time periods which would meet modern demands and he a reliable guarantor ensuring our Motherland's security. The tone for these presentations was set by the bold, meaningful briefing of General Staff Military Academy Chief General L.N. Rodionov. Presentations by generals and officers comrades I.S. Danilenko, N.P. Klokotov, L.I. Volkov, M.M. Kasenkov, F.M. Kuzmin and V. Ya. Abolins were no less meaningful. We are grateful to the comrades from the Russian Academy of Natural Sciences and Russian Academy of Sciences, to representatives of military industry, and above all to academicians V.S. Pirumov, Ye. A. Pozdniakov and A.A. Chaldymov, who took an active part in conference work.

Today we are faced with many issues, one being the development of a military doctrine, and this was given special attention during the conference. It is the basis of the concept of Russian Federation Armed Forces organizational development and of practical measures for upgrading them.

I agree with briefer General Rodionov and with other speakers that doctrine must be developed based on conclusions from an objective analysis of the present world military-political situation and long-range scientific forecasts. Doctrine must become an integral continuation of the concept of Russian security in which state policy goals and tasks are formulated and the Russian Federation's priority interests are defined. In it our state's attitude toward war and toward use of military force as a means of achieving political goals should he expressed; missions facing the Russian Armed Forces should he confirmed; and the nature of military danger and of possible wars in which Russia's involvement is possible, and ways to deter and repel aggression by military means should he defined. In addition, basic provisions of strategic concepts and principles of Armed Forces organizational development and preparation of the Russian Army and Navy and the country as a whole for defense of the homeland must he reflected in military doctrine.

Yes, today there is no one who denies that the degree of military danger has lowered—world war or other large-scale war hardly is possible in the foreseeable future. But the probability of so-called small, local, and even regional conflicts being initiated has grown. Therefore we still are far from an era of general world prosperity. Under present conditions there can he no guarantees against an increased decree of military danger and its development into a directed, immediate military threat under certain conditions. By confirming this we are not supercharging the situation or calling for a hunt for an enemy, but as persons to whom the people have entrusted the defense of their security against outside threats, we take account of the possibility of such a fully realistic development of events. Therefore it would he criminal not to devote the most serious attention to military questions. Preventing war is a statewide political goal. There is no question that under present conditions the priority must he given to political means, but they will he effective only when policy relies on sufficient state economic and military might. Consequently the Armed Forces along with other state institutions also must take an active part in solving this important problem. It is they who are called upon to ensure our state's territorial integrity against an outside threat and the deterrence and repulse of aggression by methods of force.

With respect to certain specific provisions of the military doctrine being developed, one of the most difficult tasks is a determination of forms and methods of conducting combat operations and their practical introduction in the process of Armed Forces training.

The nature of our military doctrine stems from fundamental principles of Russian policy and envisages the rejection of first use of nuclear weapons and of military force for resolving international disputes as well as adherence to the idea of disarmament and so on. Many understand these provisions literally and interpret them in such a way that we allegedly must only defend ourselves always and everywhere. It is difficult to agree with that interpretation. It is impossible to ignore the objective principles and laws of warfare. If an enemy has begun aggression, we have the right to choose and use those kinds, forms and methods of military actions which are most effective in a given situation. This may he both the offensive and the defense. A differentiated approach must he taken to accomplishing missions of repelling aggression in different TYD's [theaters of military operations] and sectors, taking account of the political, economic and strategic situation realistically taking shape. We must not give contiguous states occasion to assess our actions as provocative, but at the same time we do not have the right to lag behind a probable enemy in preparing the Armed Forces and economy for the beginning of military actions. We should not forget the lessons of 1941.

Let us recall the majority of exercises of recent years. As a rule, a situation was created in them in which the enemy conducted a real, planned preparation for aggression over several weeks and even months, and we were forced merely to take certain measures to increase our combat readiness covertly under the guise of exercises. We thereby consciously gave the aggressor the strategic initiative. Can such actions force him to reject aggression? Hardly. This only stimulates the enemy's desires, while he can be deterred exclusively by adequate actions, not hiding our readiness and ability to repel aggression. Herein lies the essence of the principle of deterrence.

Having analyzed the opinions expressed at the conference and without burdening ourselves with ideological aims, it is necessary to determine our position on possible methods of the initiation of aggression against Russia and on the nature and classification of future wars, and to build the Armed Forces and prepare the country to repel aggression based on this.

With respect to basic directions of Armed Forces organizational development, an analysis of the main briefing and of other presentations on this problem shows that we still do not have enough precise studies in this respect.

It is obvious that the Russian Armed Forces will he established and their functioning will be supported in a difficult internal political and economic situation in the country and abroad. While these tasks are being accomplished, it should he taken into account that the state presently does not have the necessary material means for a radical Armed Forces reform. At the same time, a swift, poorly thought-out breakup of existing military structures can lead to loss of command and control. This cannot he allowed, considering Russia's nuclear status and its responsibility for fulfilling the Paris Agreements on a Reduction of Conventional Arms. This is why a phased program for establishment, reform and reduction of the Russian Federation Armed Forces is necessary. Moreover, many now have been convinced that a "landslide" conduct of this process, an insufficiently thought-out elimination of arms and ammunition, as well as defense industry conversion not only do not provide a saving of funds but, to the contrary, demand additional material inputs.

At the present stage our primary task is to establish the Ministry of Defense as a capable entity of military leadership. This will permit beginning the immediate formation of the Russian Armed Forces and resolution of problems above all concerning the situation of Russian servicemen and their families outside Russia, chiefly in "hot spots." By the way, many states which previously were in the USSR express the desire to begin bilateral and multilateral talks to determine the status of forces located on their territories which did not become part of their national armed forces. We should begin resolving this problem without delay.

We presume that in the next few days the structure of the Russian Ministry of Defense and General Staff will he approved with new elements meeting today's demands. This will ensure interworking and coordination of activity of the Ministry of Defense with authoritative structures of the Russian Federation, with structures which are called upon to deal with questions of military policy, questions of interworking with CIS states and foreign countries, and also problems of conversion and servicemen's social protection.

Forming the Armed Forces is no less important a task. For purely military and economic considerations, during their organizational development there must he maximum use of the existing military potential and the created structure and groupings of Armed Forces stationed on the territory of the Russian Federation as well as of forces being withdrawn from the territories of Germany, Poland and the Baltic states, troop units of the Caucasus region, and subsequently formations and units which did not become part of armed forces of other CIS member states.

In accordance with the Russian Federation Presidential Ukase, all forces stationed on the territory of Russia and under its jurisdiction were included in the Russian Armed Forces. At the same time, the Strategic Nuclear Forces were operationally subordinated to the CIS Joint Armed Forces High Command for the transition period.

Forces included in the Russian Armed Forces must be substantially reduced and reorganized, the ultimate goal being to establish modern Armed Forces corresponding to the level of real military danger and new political and economic conditions. With consideration of Russia's geo-strategic position and geopolitical interests, its peacetime Armed Forces should be mobile and well equipped for actions in accordance with the strategic concept of deterrence and guaranteed repulse from any direction.

First of all they are required to ensure prevention of military actions using only conventional weapons, above all local conflicts and wars; prevention. of their escalation; and defense of Russia's national interests and, as part of coalition forces, also the interests of CIS allies. For this it is necessary to establish and upgrade groupings of general purpose forces deployed in regions (in the West, South and East) in such a makeup which would allow them to perform the aforementioned missions.

In our view, Armed Forces organizational development must be carried out with consideration of demands of the mobile defense concept. Implementation of this concept presumes the presence of small but powerful force groupings ready for immediate actions where a real threat arises. In this connection it is advisable to have the following in the Armed Forces: permanent readiness forces capable of effectively influencing local conflicts; rapid deployment forces consisting of airborne troops, naval infantry, light motorized rifle divisions, army aviation and other necessary means of support and reinforcement, with the assignment of military transport aviation for movement to any region in the shortest possible time to reinforce the permanent readiness force groupings stationed there and to perform missions in regional conflicts; and strategic reserves formed in peacetime, deployed in a threat period as well as during war, and earmarked for performing missions in large-scale wars.

It is advisable to leave the branch structure of the Russian Federation Armed Forces unchanged for the period of their formation, although some circles express ideas on the need for its unconditional change. As already stated, however, a radical breakup will require significant material inputs, which we cannot allow ourselves to do today. This involves a significant perestroika of systems for command and control, orders, procurements, cadres training and so on. Therefore in my view a solution to this problem should not be forced. It unquestionably will face us in the future, but it hardly can be recognized as an immediate problem now.

In connection with the fact that under present conditions all the questions examined will be resolved with the involvement of higher state authorities, we should convince members of the Supreme Soviet and government and the mass media of the need for a balanced Armed Forces organizational development, and that they should not compel us to take hasty steps, but support our ideas.

It must be borne in mind that the Strategic Nuclear Forces have been and remain a guarantor for Russia and all CIS countries against the initiation of any war, not just nuclear war. Domestic and international security demands a precise determination of their status and of state guarantees of nuclear safety.

It is important to note that the position of Kazakhstan, Belarus and Ukraine as non-nuclear states already has been determined today. In this connection a real opportunity has appeared to legally confirm Russia's status as the only CIS nuclear power, to ratify the Treaty on Reduction of Strategic Offensive Arms with retention of the 1972 ABM Defense understandings, to elaborate specific options for the order of battle of the Strategic Nuclear Forces, and to develop proposals for radical reductions of strategic offensive arms that are optimal in the military-strategic and economic respects. In so doing it is necessary to observe the military-strategic parity between Russia and the United States.

Military-technical policy problems should hold a special place in Russian Armed Forces organizational development. Under conditions of inflation and reduced financial appropriations for defense, it is possible to maintain the minimum necessary level of Armed Forces technical outfitting only by determining the priorities in development and procurement of arms and military equipment. In my view, priority must be given to development of highly mobile forces, strategic arms, air defense weapons, military-space weapons, long- range precision weapons, army aviation, and reconnaissance, EW, and command and control equipment.

It is also impossible to ignore defense enterprise conversion questions, which represent a very important statewide task. I emphasize this in connection with the fact that an opinion exists that conversion is a matter only for the Ministry of Defense. That approach is incorrect. We all have to seriously think how to preserve the existing S&T potential of the defense industry within reasonable limits. I consider it impermissible to lower the level of RDT&E financing. If we permit this, then we hardly will be able to accomplish the task of making a transition to quality indicators of Army and Navy outfitting with new kinds of arms and military equipment.

Those are some of the general approaches to Russian Armed Forces organizational development. I will reemphasize that their establishment is an extraordinarily difficult, laborious process demanding significant material inputs. In beginning its realization, it is necessary to have detailed, economically substantiated plans with precise argumentation on all aspects of problems connected with the withdrawal, reduction and reform of forces. Questions of destroying and recycling arms and military equipment which have served the prescribed time periods as well as which fall under reduction in accordance with concluded agreements demand serious attention.

Inasmuch as military reform includes a large set of complicated, large-scale problems of a radical reorganization of the Armed Forces with a simultaneous significant reduction in their numerical strength, a certain time—usually decades—is required for this, as attested by historical experience. We do not have that time, but we also do not plan to excessively accelerate the process without considering economic capabilities, social tension in society and transformations occurring in the state. Therefore it is proposed to carry out forces reform in three stages over 6-8 years.

In the first stage (during 1992), establish the Russian Federation Ministry of Defense; develop and approve the numerical strength and structure and determine the sequence and time periods for reform of the Russian Armed Forces and refine their command and control system; create a legal base for their functioning with consideration of rules of international law and agreements which have been reached, and also create a system of social guarantees for servicemen, their families, and persons discharged from military service.

In the second stage (2-3 years) basically complete the withdrawal of Russian forces from the territories of other states into the limits of Russia and establish force groupings; continue the reduction of forces; bring the Armed Forces numerical strength to 2.1 million by 1995; and make the transition to a mixed manpower acquisition system.

In the third stage (34 years) completely withdraw the Northwestern Group of Forces; complete the reduction of Armed Forces in accordance with previously adopted international obligations, and complete their reform and transition to new organizational structures with consideration of the reorganization of branches of the Armed Forces and combat arms. The numerical strength of the Russian Federation Armed Forces can be taken to 1.5 million.

It should be noted that those time periods are tentative. They may be seriously adjusted under the influence of processes of the development of the domestic political and economic situation in Russia as well as of interstate relations.

The European part of our state previously was the deep rear and its operational preparation was given insufficient attention. You also know full well the state of affairs in Siberia and the Far East in this respect. Added to this today is a disruption of previously established systems of communications, command and control and the military infrastructure.

Questions of preparing the country and Armed Forces to repel aggression were examined during the third day of conference work. Supporting the activity of the defense complex under conditions of fundamental transformations of our economic system is the problem of all problems. It is important here to determine our position as quickly as possible regarding the direction and tasks of all economic structures both in peace and wartime and create conditions for their normal, stable functioning under these conditions. No less serious problems face us in working out the Principles of Russian Armed Forces Employment both for the transition period and over the long term. Our military theory largely lags behind today's, not to mention tomorrow's, demands. Where are the weakest places in development of military art?

First of all, we have been saying steadfastly since 1985 that our immediate task is to deter aggression. But how must the Armed Forces act in order to perform those missions? There are no precise answers for now. I realize that this is not only and not so much a matter for military scientists, but we too must not remain aloof from elaborating this question. In our view, first of all it is necessary to arm ourselves with the principle of deterring aggression proposed at the conference. Its essence lies in our creating an opposing grouping of adequate strength in case a threat appears. This will force the enemy to think about the fact that in case of attack his costs can exceed the planned benefits.

Secondly, we have insufficiently thought out and substantiated questions of preparing and conducting combat operations in local and regional wars. Evidently they will have their features, which have to be theoretically interpreted and practical conclusions have to be drawn. This must be done as quickly as possible, and the General Staff Military Academy must become the leader in resolving this question.

Thirdly, our theory of conducting military operations in continental TYD's bears an "infantry-tank" character, if it can be thus expressed. We say much about the increased role of offensive air weapons and others including precision weapons, and even more about the need to revise the existing system of forms and methods of waging warfare and bring it into line with today's demands. But what practical recommendations have we developed for the troops? How has this been reflected in our guidance documents? I believe extremely little has been done here.

Fourthly, I am very much troubled by questions of strategic deployment, and particularly shifting the Armed Forces from a peacetime to a war footing. The European part is the most densely populated part of Russia, but it falls under the effect of the Paris Treaty. Equipment can be stored in Siberia, but how can it be moved from there in case of necessity? How can human resources from the central part of Russia be linked up with reserves of equipment and arms beyond the Ural Range? How can large strategic formations that have been formed be moved from the interior of Russia to the necessary axis if such capabilities do not exist? The questions are extraordinarily complicated and important; they demand careful attention and, unfortunately, enormous expenditures.

Fifthly, I would say many of our studies in the area of military art bear an abstract character. They often are separated from our country's real life and economic capabilities. Of course, scientific investigations must be directed toward the future, but they cannot be allowed to go over into the area of fantasy, and many here specifically fantasized. It turns out as in the familiar saying: "It went smoothly on paper, but they forgot about the ravines, and that is what you walk through."

It may seem to some that I am excessively emphasizing the significance of the practical direction of scientific research, but it must be remembered that we live in a special time. There are very difficult tasks in the military sphere, many of which previously were not accomplished on the scale of Russia. Today the role of military science has grown considerably. This is connected above all with the fact that on the one hand we have a time shortage and consequently science is required to have a special promptness and a preemptive nature; on the other hand, as you realize, miscalculations in solving the problems raised are inadmissible now and avoiding them requires an exceptionally precise assessment of many objective and subjective factors of the political, economic and strategic situation and all trends in the development of military affairs. Based on this assessment, military science must provide a substantiated forecast in the shortest possible time on collective security problems of Russia and CIS member states, develop proposals on military organizational development in Russia, take a new approach to solving problems of military art, and determine ways of further upgrading Russian Army and Navy operational and tactical training. The conduct of our conference gains exceptionally great significance in this respect. Valuable theoretical proposals were expressed during the conference which must be brought to practical realization as quickly as possible. In this connection the Ministry of Defense, with the involvement of specialists of scientific research establishments and military higher educational institutions together with representatives of Russia's legislative and executive entities, must generalize all proposals expressed during the conference, take them into account in the draft military doctrine, and pass the modified draft to the interdepartmental commission by 1 July of this year for examination and submission to the President of Russia.

The Ministry of Defense which is being established, the General Staff, military academies and scientific research organizations are to complete work on substantiating' the Armed Forces development concept, which in accordance with instructions of the Russian Federation President must be submitted to him for approval prior to 1 September, and to the Minister of Defense prior to 15 August.

In solving major organizational development problems, above all we need a thorough theoretical substantiation of the missions, structure, optimum makeup, and tasking and makeup of each branch of the Armed Forces, combat arm, and special troops, and not just for the transition period, but for the long term as well.

Questions connected with the system of strategic leadership and command and control of the Armed Forces demand further elaboration. This problem always has been acute, and at the present time in connection with many factors it becomes especially pertinent and directly connected with Russia's security.

The altered nature of a possible war also dictates the need to seek new approaches to the problem of preparing the country and Armed Forces to repel aggression. Comprehensive studies are needed encompassing all interrelated factors. I ask you to turn attention to mobilization preparation of the Russian national economy in peacetime and arrangement for its transfer to operation under wartime conditions, to methods of transferring the Armed Forces to a wartime footing, and to their manpower acquisition and training.

A serious problem of elaborating the theory of employing the Armed Forces under present conditions now is being advanced to the agenda. We must clarify the adopted system of operations and the employment of branches of the Armed Forces and combat arms by missions to be accomplished and by their spheres of employment. There are many unresolved problems in tactics.

It is important for the General Staff, staffs of branches of the Armed Forces, and military academies to correctly assess and consider the new trends which now have appeared in connection with the development of military affairs. Some already have been identified in the course of local wars; others are latent for now, but must be anticipated. In developing new combined-arms regulations, we must take account of Russia's historical military experience and all that is best and most valuable which has accumulated not only in the former Union's Armed Forces, but also in armies of other states. This task is being given to staffs of branches of the Armed Forces and of combat arms.

The General Staff and leading scientific research institutes should begin developing fundamental documents of regulations for strategic and operational levels in which demands and recommendations must be set forth on preparing and conducting operations and combat operations both for large strategic formations of strategic forces as well as for front, army and corps large strategic formations which are part of the General Purpose Forces. These documents must be widely discussed prior to publication.

Prior to 15 June of this year chiefs of military academies and of scientific research institutes of branches of the Armed Forces are to prepare and submit proposals to the General Staff for establishing commercial structures in the Ministry of Defense for selling recycled and surplus arms and military equipment. Funds recovered from sales must be directed toward strengthening the material base of forces and social needs of the Armed Forces. Measures must be provided for in those structures precluding abuses by officials who are to engage in this activity.

The General Staff is to prepare a draft order establishing a provisional commission to carry out an inspection of the Russian Armed Forces during which staffs of branches of the Armed Forces and central directorates are to pay special attention to studying the state of affairs in the troops, the strength level, status of combat readiness, and level of training.

As you see, we are faced with difficult, capacious tasks demanding the efforts of large scientific collectives.

Preserving the level of the scientific potential will remain one of the principal tasks. It is necessary to take a very circumspect approach to scientific cadres, not destroy the scientific schools which have formed, not lose prominent scientists, and not break the well worked out ties. Some servicemen's positions can be filled by military scientists discharged to the reserve.

Respected colleagues! Life confirms that a change in the nature of military organizational development and in the appearance of the Armed Forces is gaining more and more dynamism. Fulfillment of a complex, many-sided set of measures making up military reform must ensure establishment of Russian Armed Forces of a fundamentally new quality corresponding to the features and trends of the modern world military-political situation and to the content and direction of development of military affairs.

The Armed Forces should retain their genuinely popular character, become modern and civilized, and be an authoritative and effective factor for deterring an aggressor and preserving peace and stability.

Voennaia mysl (July 1992), 108–117, in JPRS-UMT, 30 September 1992, 58-63.

V BIBLIOGRAPHY

RUSSIA AND EURASIA ARMED FORCES, 1992–1993

Kathleen Addison

1. "Russian Nuclear Accident Opens Up Military Complex," *Nature*, Vol. 362, No. 6421 (15 Apr 1993), 579-579.
2. G. Akhmetov and A. A. Khodakov, "Nekotorye voprosy planirovaniia ognevogo porazheniia v armeiskikh operatsiiakh," *Voennaia mysl*, No. 4 (1993).
3. Ulrich Albrecht, *The Soviet Armaments Industry* (Chur, Switzerland, 1993).
4. I. Aleksin, "Preduprezhdenie avariinosti v VMF," *Voennaia mysl*, No. 1 (1993).
5. Svetlana Alexevich. *Zinky Boys. Soviet Voices from a Forgotten War* (London, 1992).
6. Roy Allison, ed., *World Congress for Soviet and East European Studies. Radical Reform in Soviet Defence Policy. Selected Papers from the Fourth World Congress for Soviet and East European Studies, Harrogate, 1990* (New York, 1992).
7. Roy Allison, *Military Forces in the Soviet Successor States. An Analysis of the Military Policies, Force Dispositions and Evolving Threat Perceptions of the Former Soviet States* (London, 1993).
8. A. Andreev, "Posle Mukkdena i Tsusimy," *Voenno-istoricheskii zhurnal*, No. 8 (1992).
9. Iu. A. Andreev, "Ob aeromobilnykh voiskakh NATO," *Voennaia mysl*, Nos. 4-5 (1992).
10. G. Andronikov, "Pervyi rubezh reshaiushchikh pobed (K 50-letiiu razgroma nemetsko-fashistskikh voisk pod Moskvoi)," *Voenno-istoricheskii zhurnal*, No. 1 (1992).
11. Artamonov, "Petr I i reguliarnaia armiia," *Voenno-istoricheskii zhurnal*, No. 9 (1992).
12. N. Artsibasov and Iu. N. Zhdanov, "Pravovaia osnova voennoi doktriny gosudarstva," *Voennaia mysl*, No. 12 (1992).
13. S. Aushev, "Sokhranim svoiu sovest'," *Voenno-istoricheskii zhurnal*, No. 1 (1992).
14. Banerji, "Military as a Factor in Russian Politics," *Economic and Political Weekly*, Vol. 28, No. 46, 13 Nov 1993, 2543-2546.
15. B. Baraev and A. A. Gerasimov, "Problemy sovershenstvovaniia sistem bazirovaniia i obespecheniia aviatsii," *Voennaia mysl*, No. 11 (1993).
16. V. Barylski, "The Soviet Military Before and After the August Coup. Departization and Decentralization," *Armed Forces & Society*, Vol. 19, No. 1 (Fall, 1992), 27-45.
17. Bass and L. Dienes, "Defense Industry Legacies and Conversion in the Post-Soviet Realm," *Post-Soviet Geography*, Vol. 34, No. 5 (May 1993), 302-317.
18. Robert F. Baumann, *Russian-Soviet Unconventional Wars in the Caucasus, Central Asia, and Afghanistan* (Fort Leavenworth, Kan., 1993).
19. Evgenii S. Berezniak, *Operatsiia "Golos." Rasskaz razvedchika* (M., 1992).
20. Coit D. Blacker, *Hostage to Revolution. Gorbachev and Soviet Security Policy, 1985-1991* (New York, 1993).
21. Christoph Bluth, *Soviet Strategic Arms Policy before SALT* (Cambridge, 1992).
22. A. Bogdanov, "O sistemnom podkhode k issledovaniiu razvitiia artillerii," *Voennaia mysl*, No. 10 (1993).
23. P. Bogdanov, *Voennye poseleniia v Rossii* (M., 1992).

24. I. Bologov, "O mobilizatsionnoi gotovnosti i podgotovke voisk, stabov v usloviiakh stroitelstva Vooruzhennykh Sil Rossiiskoi Federatsii," *Voennaia mysl*, No. 8 (1993).

25. Astrid von Borcke, *Sinn und Unsinn der Geheimdienste. Die Lehren aus den Erfahrungen des KGB und der neue russische Nachrichtendienst* (Cologne, 1992).

26. Borodavko and A. Manachinskii, "Malozametnye samolety F-117A. Opyt boevogo primeneniia," *Voennyi vestnik*, No. 12 (December 1992), 69-72.

27. Ulrich Brandenburg, *The "Friends" are Leaving. Soviet and Post-Soviet Troops in Germany After Unification* (Cologne, 1992).

28. Edward F. Bruner, *Soviet Armed Forces in Transition* (Washington, 1992).

29. Taras Bulba-Borovets, *Armiia bez derzhavy* (Lviv, 1993).

30. Leszek Buszynski, *Gorbachev and Southeast Asia* (London, 1992).

31. Glenn R. Chafetz, *Gorbachev, Reform, and the Brezhnev Doctrine. Soviet Policy Toward Eastern Europe, 1985-1990* (Westport, Conn., 1993).

32. Michael Checinski, *Military-Economic Implications of Conversion of the post-Soviet Arms Industry* (Jerusalem, n.d.).

33. Marjorie Mayrock Center for Soviet and East European Research, Hebrew University of Jerusalem, 1992.

34. N. Chichkan and S.L. Velesov, "Nekotorye voprosy primeneniia sil spetsialnykh operatsii," *Voennaia mysl*, No. 2 (1992).

35. Stephen J. Cimbala, *US Nuclear Strategy in the New World Order. Backward Glances, Forward Looks* (New York, 1993).

36. Kenneth M. Currie, *Soviet Military Politics. Contemporary Issues* (New York, 1992).

37. Alexander Dallin, ed., *Civil-Military Relations in the Soviet Union* (New York, 1992).

38. Danilenko, V.A. Dvurechenskikh, S.A Proskurin, B. M. Kanevskii, and L. P. Malyshev, "Voennaia bezopasnost i problemy oboronnoi politiki gosudarstva," *Voennaia mysl*, No. 1 (1992).

39. A. Danilevich and Iu. P. Tikhomirov, "Natsionalnye voennye doktriny stran SNG. Nekotorye podkhody i otdelnye polozheniia," *Voennaia mysl*, No. 2 (1993).

40. G. Dashkov, N.B. Kaplunov, and Yu. A. Nikolaev, "Problema utilizatsii voenno-tekhnicheskikh sredstv," *Voennaia mysl*, No. 8 (1993).

41. P. Dawydow, and D.W. Trenin, "The Future of Russia's Armed Forces. The Dissolution of an Empire and the Problem of a Military Reform," *Europa Archiv*, Vol. 47, No. 13 (10 July 1992), 353-364.

42. S. Deinekin, "Osnovnye napravleniia stroitelstva i podgotovki Voenno-Vozdushnykh Sil v sovremennykh usloviiakh," *Voennaia mysl*, No. 7 (1993).

43. C. Desch, "Why the Soviet Military Supported Gorbachev but Why the Russian Military Might Only Support Yeltsin for a Price," *Journal of Strategic Studies*, Vol. 16, No. 4 (Dec 1993), 455-489.

44. Yu. L. Diakov and T.S. Bushueva, *Fashistskii mech kovalsia v SSSR. Krasnaia Armiia i Reikhsver. Tainoe sotrudnichestvo, 1922-1933. Neizvestnye dokumenty* (M., 1992).

45. Ole Diehl, *Postsowjetische Risiken. Neue Herausforderungen an die deutsche Sicherheitspolitik* (Bonn, 1992).

46. Durov, *Ordena Rossii* (M., 1993).

47. V. Eremin, "Mokshanskii polk na sopkakh Manchzhurii," *Voenno-istoricheskii zhurnal*, No. 10 (1992).

48. Erickson, "Fallen from Grace. The New Russian Military," *World Policy Journal*, Vol. 10, No. 2 (Summer, 1993), 19-24.

49. S. Fedorov, "Vooruzhenye Sily i rynok," *Voennaia mysl*, No. 10 (1992).

50. Neil Felshman, *Gorbachev, Yeltsin, and the Last Days of the Soviet Empire* (New York, 1992).

51. I. Firsov, *Petra tvorene. K 300-letiiu russkogo flota* (M., 1992).

52. Fitzgerald, "Chief of Russia's General Staff Academy Speaks Out on Moscow's New Military Doctrine," *Orbis*, Vol. 37, No. 2 (Spring, 1993), 281-288.

53. Willard C. Frank, Jr., and Philip S. Gillette, *Soviet Military Doctrine from Lenin to Gorbachev, 1915-1991* (Westport, Conn., 1992).

54. Andreas Furst, Volker Heise and Steven E. Miller, eds., *Europe and Naval Arms Control in the Gorbachev Era* (Oxford, 1992).

55. V. Fuzhenko, E.V. Malyshev, and N.S. Olesik, "O roli gorodov v dostizhenii strategicheskikh tselei sovremennykh voin i voennykh konfliktov," *Voennaia mysl*, No. 11 (1993).

56. Yu. A. Galushko, *Shkola rossiiskogo ofitserstva. Istoricheskii spravochnik* (M., 1993).

57. Garcia, "Vooruzhennye sily v usloviiakh perekhoda ot totalitarnogo gosudarstva k demokraticheskomu," *Voennaia mysl*, Nos. 8-9 (1992).

58. A. Gareev, "O nekotorykh voprosakh Rossiiskoi voennoi doktriny," *Voennaia mysl*, No. 11 (1992).

59. A. Gareev, "Problemy podgotovki Vooruzhennykh Sil v svete sovremennoi voennoi doktriny Rossii," *Voennaia mysl*, No. 11 (1993).

60. Frank Gaudlitz, *Die Russen gehen. Der Abzug einer Armee* (Berlin, 1993).

61. Harry Gelman, *Russo-Japanese Relations and the Future of the US-Japanese Alliance* (Santa Monica, Cal., 1993).

62. Georgievich, "Kompiutery i neirokompiutery v artillerii," *Voennyi vestnik*, No. 9 (September 1993).

63. Giskho, "GKO postanovliaet," *Voenno-istoricheskii zhurnal*, Nos. 2, 3, 4-5 (1992).

64. Bradley R. Gitz, *Armed Forces and Political Power in Eastern Europe. The Soviet/Communist Control System* (New York, 1992).

65. Glantz, David M., "The Ghosts of Demiansk. In Memory of the Soldiers of the Soviet 1st Airborne Corps," *Journal of Military History*, Vol. 56, No. 4 (October 1992), 617-650.

66. David M. Glantz, *The Military Strategy of the Soviet Union. A History* (London, 1992).

67. Gorlov, "Peregovory V.M. Molotova v Berline v noiabre 1940 goda," *Voenno-istoricheskii zhurnal*, Nos. 6-7 (1992).

68. Grachev, "Aktualnye problemy stroitelstva i podgotovki Vooruzhennykh Sil Rossii na sovremennom etape," *Voennyi vestnik*, No. 8 (August 1993).

69. Idem, *Voennaia mysl*, No. 6 (1993).

70. I. Gribkov, "Doktrina Brezhneva i polskii krizis nachala 80-kh godov," *Voenno-istoricheskii zhurnal*, No. 9 (1992).

71. I. Gribkov, "Karibskii krizis," *Voenno-istoricheskii zhurnal*, Nos. 10, 11, 12 (1992).

72. N. Gromov, "Natsionalnye interesy Rossii na more i Voenno-Morskoi Flot," *Voennaia mysl*, No. 5 (1993).

73. V. Gurkin and A. I. Kruglov, "Oborona Kavkaza 1942 god," *Voenno-istoricheskii zhurnal*, No. 10 (1992).

74. Kazuyuki Hamada, "The Soviet Defense Industry's Conversion Program. US and Japanese Responses" (Ph.D. diss., University of California, San Diego, 1992).

75. Hamburg, "After the Abortive Soviet Coup and What is to Be Done. The Post-Soviet Military," *Journal of Political and Military Sociology*, Vol. 20, No. 2 (Winter, 1992), 305-322.

76. *Harmonizing the Evolution of US and Russian Defense Policies,* Center for Strategic and International Studies and Council on Foreign and Defense Policy. Fred C. Ikle, et al. (Washington, 1993).

77. Andreas Heinemann-Gruder, *Das russische Militar zwischen Staatszerfall und Nationbildung* (Cologne, 1993).

78. Gut, ed., *In Erwartung des Umbruchs. Beobachtung und Analyse der Entwicklungen in der ehemaligen Sowjetunion. In memoriam Prof. Ivo Tschirky, 1930-1992* (Zurich, 1993).

79. Steedman Hinckley, *Department of Defense Assistance to the Former Soviet Republics. Potential Applications of Existing Army Capabilities* (Santa Monica, Cal., 1993).

80. Hlopiev, "The Military Aspect of National Security in the Estimates of Russians," *Sotsiologicheskie issledovaniia*, 12 (1993), 88-94.

81. Arthur T. Hopkins, *Unchained Reactions. Chernobyl, Glasnost, and Nuclear Deterrence* (Washington, 1993).

82. Iarmak, "Vopros pervostepennoi vazhnosti," *Voennyi vestnik*, No. 2 (February 1992), 4-8.

83. F. Iashin and V. I. Kuznetsov, "Armeiskie kontrnastupatelnye operatsii," *Voennaia mysl*, No. 1 (1992).

84. Ignatenko, *Politicheskaia rol' vooruzhennykh formirovanii na Kavkaze. Analiticheskaia otsenka* (M., 1993).

85. S. Iukhnovets and O.N. Novikov, "Rol i mesto primeneniia aerozolei vo frontovykh operatsiiakh," *Voennaia mysl*, No. 10 (1993).

86. P. Ivanov, "Chernobyl. Glazami ochevidtsa," *Voenno-istoricheskii zhurnal*, Nos. 4-5, 6-7 (1992).

87. L. Ivanov, "O putiakh perestroiki sistemy upravleniia kosmicheskoi deiatelnostiu," *Voennaia mysl*, No. 2 (1992).

88. L. Ivanov, "Voenno-kosmicheskie sily. Perspektivy i problemy stroitelstva," *Voennaia mysl*, No. 9 (1993).

89. Geoffrey Jukes, *Russia's Military and the Northern Territories Issue* (Canberra, Australia, 1993).

90. Kashitsin and V. Kharitonov, "Aviatsiia v ognevom porazhenii protivnika," *Voennyi vestnik*, No. 12 (December 1992), 30-35.

91. A. Kersnovskii, *Istoriia russkoi armii v chetyrekh tomakh* (M., 1992-1994).

92. A. Kersnovskii, *Istoriia russkoi armii* (M., 1992-1994).

93. A. Kharitonov, "O podgotovke boevogo primeneniia aviatsii v obshchevoiskovom boiu (operatsii)," *Voennaia mysl*, No. 6 (1993).

94. V. Kirilenko and D.V. Trenin, "Formula besopasnosti. Ot pariteta k strategicheskoi stabilnosti," *Voennaia mysl*, No. 8-9 (1992).

95. V. Kirilenko and Iu.A. Kuznetsov, "Nekotorye ekonomicheskie voprosy voennoi reformy," *Voennaia mysl*, No. 4-5 (1992).

96. F. Klimenko, "O roli i meste voennoi doktriny v sisteme bezopasnosti Sodruzhestva nezavisimykh gosudarstv," *Voennaia mysl*, No. 2 (1992).

97. T. Klimov, "Nekotorye aspekty tylovogo obespecheniia voisk na udalennykh TVD," *Voennaia mysl*, No. 2 (1992).

98. A. Kokoshin, "Protivorechiia formirovaniia i puti razvitiia voenno-tekhnicheskoi politiki Rossii," *Voennaia mysl*, No. 2 (1993).

99. Iu. M. Kostin, "Stroitelstvo mnogonatsionalnykh formirovanii NATO," *Voennaia mysl*, No. 11 (1992).

100. G. Kozyrev, "Stanovoi khrebet Voenno-Morskogo Flota," *Voennaia mysl*, No. 6-7 (1992).

101. Joachim Krause and Charles K. Mallory, *Chemical Weapons in Soviet Military Doctrine. Military and Historical Experience, 1915-1991* (Boulder, Colo., 1992).

102. F. Krivosheeva, ed., *Grif sekretnosti sniat. Poteri Vooruzhennykh Sil SSSR v voinakh, boevykh deistviiakh i voennykh konfliktakh* (M., 1993).

103. I. Krotov and A.A. Tsyganov, *Voennye Rossii* (M., 1992).

104. I. Kushnirsky, "Lessons from Estimating Military Production of the Former Soviet Union," *Europe-Asia Studies*, Vol. 45, No. 3 (1993), 483-503.

105. M. Kuzivanov, "O rabote vserossiiskoi nauchnoi konferentsii 'Kakoi flot nuzhen Rossii?,'" *Voennaia mysl*, No. 6 (1993).

106. N. Kuznetskov, "Tekhnicheskie vozmozhnosti kosmicheskikh sredstv SShA," *Voennaia mysl*, No. 8-9 (1992).

107. M. Kyrov, "Zabudet li Otechestvo pogibshikh desantnikov?" *Voenno-istoricheskii zhurnal*, Nos. 6-7, 9 (1992).

108. Laskiewicz, *Russia and World War III. A National Political Study of Russia* (London, 1993).

109. Lebed, "14-ia rossiiskaia obshchevoiskovaia. Garant mira i stabilnosti," *Voennyi vestnik*, No. 1 (January 1993).

110. G. Lebedko and V. V. Barvinenko, "Voprosy organizatsii vsaimodeistviia voisk i sil PVO na primorskom napravlenii," *Voennaia mysl*, No. 6 (1993).

111. Lebedev, "Kak 'lomali' marshala G. K. Zhukova," *Voenno-istoricheskii zhurnal*, No. 12 (1992).

112. Derek Leebaert and Timothy Dickinson, *Soviet Strategy and New Military Thinking* (Cambridge, 1992).

113. Sharon Leiter and Claire Mitchell Levy, *Russian Military R&D. Are the Regions Taking Charge?* (Santa Monica, Cal., 1993).

114. Nathan Constantin Leites, ed., *Soviet Style in War* (Santa Monica, Cal., 1992).

115. Leonov, "Voennoe stroitelstvo v Rossii v XIX veke," *Voennyi vestnik*, No. 5-6 (May-June 1992), 102.

116. W. R. Lepingwell, "Soviet Civil-Military Relations and the August Coup," *World Politics*, Vol. 44, No. 4 (July 1992), 539-572.

117. Nan Li, "Bureaucratic Behavior, Praetorian Behavior, and Civil-Military Relations. Deng Xiaoping's China (1978-1989) and Gorbachev's Soviet Union (1985-1991)" (Ph.D. diss., University of California, San Diego, 1993).

118. Ligachev, *Inside Gorbachev's Kremlin. The Memoirs of Yegor Ligachev* (New York, 1993).

119. M. Lisovoi, "O zakonakh razvitiia vooruzhennoi borby i nekotorykh tendentsiiakh v oblasti oborony," *Voennaia mysl*, No. 5 (1993).

120. Jonathan Samuel Lockwood and Kathleen O'Brien Lockwood, *The Russian View of U.S. Strategy. Its Past, Its Future* (New Brunswick, 1993).

121. Malcolm Mackintosh, *The New Russian Revolution. The Military Dimension* (London, 1992).

122. Maiatskii, "Voennaia khimiia. Realnost i den zavtrashii," *Voennyi vestnik*, No. 11 (November 1993).

123. Makarov, "Demokratizatsiia armii i obshchestvennye struktury," *Voennyi vestnik*, No. 1 (January 1992), 35-40.

124. Thierry Malleret, *Conversion of the Defense Industry in the Former Soviet Union* (New York, 1992).

125. Maltsev, "Voennye posoleniia v Rossii XIX veka," *Voenno-istoricheskii zhurnal*, No. 12 (1992).

126. Marchenko, "Boegotovnost obespechat professionaly," *Voennyi vestnik*, No. 2 (February 1993).

127. McKeehan, and R.E. Campbell, "The International Conflicts in the Soviet Army," *Sotsiologicheskie issledovaniia*, 1 (1992), 94-104.

128. M. Meyer, "How the Threat (and the Coup) Collapsed. The Politicization of the Soviet Military," *International Security*, Vol. 16, No. 3 (Winter, 1992), 5-38.

129. I. Mironov, "Gumanizatsiia voinskoi deiatelnosti i dukhovnoe vosrozhdenie rossiiskoi armii," *Voennaia mysl*, No. 8 (1993).

130. M. Miroshnikov, "Minister of Defense Industry Zverev, Sergei Alekseevich and Soviet Optics (on the 80th Anniversary of his Birth)," *Soviet Journal of Optical Technology*, Vol. 59, No. 12 (December 1992), 755-765.

131. Moskvin, "Ukreplennye raiony. Uroki i vyvody," *Voennyi vestnik*, No. 7 (July 1992), 21-27.

132. S. Muzychenko, "Strategiia konversii," *Voennaia mysl*, No. 4-5 (1992).

133. Hiromasa Nakayama, *The Military Context for the Disintegration of the USSR* (Yokohama, 1992).

134. Nakhieon, "Korea to Help Russia Commercialize Defense," *Electronics*, Vol. 65, No. 14 (26 October, 1992), 5.

135. Namsaraev, "Oruzhie porazheniia ili sredstvo samoubiistva?" *Voennyi vestnik*, No. 12 (December 1992), 36-40.

136. Naumova, and V.S. Sicheva, "Public Opinion about Social Problems of the Russian Army," *Sotsiologicheskie issledovaniia*, 12 (1993), 73-83.

137. Thomas Nichols, *The Sacred Cause. Civil-Military Conflict over Soviet National Security, 1917-1992* (Ithaca, 1993).

138. Nikolaev, *Dengi beloi gvardii* (SPb, 1993).

139. S. Novikov, "Armiia i Russkaia Pravoslavnaia Tserkov," *Voennaia mysl*, No. 4-5 (1992).

140. *O polozhenii v vooruzhennykh silakh i oboronnoi politike. Po materialam VII Sezda narodnykh deputatov Rossiiskoi Federatsii* (M., 1992).

141. Petra Opitz, *Chancen regionaler Rustungskonversion in Russland. Die Regionen St. Petersburg und Novosibirsk* (Cologne, 1993).

142. N. Osipova, "Posle Krymskoi voiny," *Voenno-istoricheskii zhurnal*, No. 2 (1992).

143. N. Osipova, "Russko-turetskaia voina 1877-1878 gg," *Voennyi vestnik*, No. 7 (July 1992), 82-91.

144. I. Ostankov, "Osnovnye printsipy organizatsionnogo stroitelstva inzhenernykh voisk," *Voennaia mysl*, No. 7 (1993).

145. Ovechkin, "Professionalnaia armiia SShA. K voprosu o distsipline," *Voennyi vestnik*, No. 3-4 (March-April, 1992), 24-29.

146. Pechen, "Traditsii v russkoi armii," *Voennyi vestnik*, No. 6 (June 1993).

147. Claiborne Pell, *US Relations with the Former Soviet Union. At the Crossroads of History. A Report to the Committee on Foreign Relations, United States Senate* (Washington, 1992).

148. Ia. Petrenko, "Chto pokazyvaet analiz voennoi doktriny," *Voennaia mysl*, No. 1 (1992).

149. Petrov (general-polkovnik), "U khimicheskikh voisk est budushee," *Voennyi vestnik*, No. 1 (January 1993), 12-17.

150. Petrov, "Voiska radiatsionnoi, khimicheskoi i biologicheskoi zashchity. Reshaemye zadachi i perspektivy razvitiia," *Voennyi vestnik*, No. 11 (November 1993).

151. P. Petrov, *Pereorientatsiia voennosluzhashchikh na grazhdanskie professii. Kak naiti rabotu uvolennym iz vooruzhennykh sil. Sovety psikhologa* (M., 1993).

152. D. Plotnikov, "Kavkazskaia kazachia brigada na Balkanakh," *Voenno-istoricheskii zhurnal*, No. 12 (1992).

153. A. Potto, *Kavkazskaia voina* (Stavropol, 1993-1994).

154. A. Pozdniakov, "Rossiia i natsionalno-gosudarstvennaia ideia," *Voennaia mysl*, No. 4-5 (1992).

155. Iu. Proniakin, "Rossiiskaia armiia vo vtoroi polovine XVIII veke," *Voennyi vestnik*, No. 2 (February 1992), 76-80.

156. A. Prudnikov, "Osnovnye napravleniia stroitelstva i podgotovki Voisk PVO na sovremennom etape," *Voennaia mysl*, No. 10 (1993).

157. G. Putilin, "Voenno-tekhnicheskie aspekty voennoi doktriny SshA," *Voennaia mysl*, No. 4 (1993).

158. Andrei Raevsky, *Development of Russian National Security Policies. Military Reform* (New York, 1993).

159. Riazanov and A. Kokushkin, "Professionalnyi podkhod k professionalnoi armii," *Voennyi vestnik*, No. 5-6 (May-June 1992), 25-26.

160. Riazanov, "Ekonomicheskie aspekty voennogo iskusstva," *Voennyi vestnik*, No. 8 (August 1992), 25-28.

161. M. Rodachin, "Armiia i politicheskaia vlast," *Voennaia mysl*, No. 5 (1993).

162. N. Rodionov, "160 let Rossiiskoi akademii Generalnogo shtaba," *Voennaia mysl*, No. 11 (1992).

163. Sergei Rogov, ed., *Russian Defense Policy. Challenges and Developments* (Alexandria, Va., 1993).

164. E. Rudnev, "Voennaia doktrina i vooruzhenie," *Voennaia mysl*, No. 2 (1992).

165. Russia (Federation), *Zakon Rossiiskoi Federatsii "O pensionnom obespechenii lits, prokhodivshikh voennuiu sluzhbu, sluzhbu v organakh vnutrennikh del, i ikh semei." Tekst zakona i kommentarii* (M.,1993).

166. *Russian Defense Business Directory.* Prepared by US-Russia Business Development Committee, Defense Conversion Subcommittee (Washington, 1993).

167. V. Rutskoi, "Voennaia politika Rossii. Soderzhanie i napravlennost," *Voennaia mysl*, No. 1 (1993).

168. Thomas Sachse, *Russische Rüstungsexportpolitik 1992. Umfang, Organisationsstrukturen, Perspektiven* (Cologne, 1993).

169. Jacques Sapir, *Les bases futures de la puissance militaire Russe* (Paris, 1993).

170. Hans-Henning Schroder, *Die Militärreformdebatte in der Sowjetunion, 1989-1991* (Cologne, 1993).

171. Hans-Henning Schroder, *Eine Armee in der Krise. Die russischen Streitkräfte 1992-93. Risikofaktor oder Garant politischer Stabilität?* [Bundesinstitut für Ostwissenschaftliche und Internationale Studien] (Cologne, 1993).

172. Hans-Henning Schroder, *Kameradenschinderei und Nationalitätenkonflikte. Ein Rückblick auf die inneren Probleme der sowjetischen Streitkräfte in den Jahren, 1987-1991* (Cologne, 1992).

173. Hans-Henning Schroder and Eberhard Schneider, *Moskau, Minsk, Kiew. Sicherheitspolitische Perzeptionen im Werden. Eindrucke von einer Fact-Finding-Mission* (Cologne, 1992).

174. Ulrich-Joachim Schulz-Torge, *Who was Who in the Soviet Union. A Biographical Dictionary of more than 4,600 Leading Officials from the Central Apparatus and the Republics to 1991* (Munich, 1992).

175. Mirali Seiidov, *Rusja-azarbaijanja izahly harbi terminlar lughati* (Russko-azerbaidzhanskii tolkovyi slovar voennykh terminov) (Baku, Azerbaijan dovlat nashriiiaty, 1993).

176. Amnon Sella, *The Value of Human Life in Soviet Warfare* (New York, 1992).

177. M. Semenov, "Sukhoputnye voiska. Zadachi i problemy razvitiia," *Voennaia mysl*, No. 6 (1993).

178. Sergeev, "Sluzhit Rossii," *Voennyi vestnik*, No. 6 (June 1993).

179. D. Sergeev, "Raketnye voiska strategicheskogo naznacheniia. Problemy stroitelstva i reformirovaniia," *Voennaia mysl*, No. 6 (1993).

180. I. Shapovalov, "Posle Pskova i Narvy," *Voenno-istoricheskii zhurnal*, No. 9 (1992).

181. A. Shcherbina, "Istoriia Kubanskogo kazachego voiska," *Voenno-istoricheskii zhurnal*, Nos. 8, 9, 10 (1992).

182. G. Shevelev, A. Ol. Lugovskii, and V.V. Nikulin, "Tendentsii razvitiia teorii voennomorskogo flota," *Voennaia mysl*, No. 5 (1993).

183. N. Sheveleva, *Nagrudnye znaki russkoi armii. Iz sobraniia Voenno-istoricheskogo muzeia artillerii, inzhenernykh voisk i voisk sviazi. Katalog* (SPb, 1993).

184. Shpak, "Trudnoi dorogoi peremen," *Voennyi vestnik*, No. 9 (September 1993).

185. A.E. Sikorskii and V.A. Mikhalev, "Puti resheniia problemy razmeshcheniia krupnykh voennykh obektov," *Voennaia mysl*, No. 10 (1992).

186. G. Simonenko, "Marshal Pilsudskii i Oktiabrskaia revoliutsiia," *Voenno-istoricheskii zhurnal*, No. 3 (1992).

187. Iu. G. Sizov and A.L. Skokov, "Znachenie vysokotochnogo oruzhiia v sovremennoi voine," *Voennaia mysl*, No. 12 (1992).

188. Mark Smith, *Pax Russica. Russia's Monroe Doctrine* (London, 1993).

189. Richard Felix Staar, *The New Russian Armed Forces. Preparing for War or Peace?* (Stanford, Cal., 1992).

190. V. Stefashin, "Osnovy sovremennoi voennoi doktriny Yaponii," *Voennaia mysl*, No. 11 (1993).

191. V. Stefashin, "Sovremennaia voennaia doktrina Kitaia," *Voennaia mysl*, No. 1 (1993).

192. V. Stepashin, "Demokratizatsiia obshchestva i problemy gumanisatsii voinskoi deiatelnosti, *Voennaia mysl*, No. 8 (1993).

193. Viktor Suvorov, *Akvarium* (M., 1993).

194. Viktor Suvorov, *Osvoboditel* (SPb, 1993).

195. Suzdaltsev, "Ne budem upriamy i samouverenny," *Voennyi vestnik*, No. 4 (April 1993).

196. Sverdlov, *Evrei-generaly Vooruzhennykh Sil SSSR. Kratkie biografii* (M., 1993).

197. Svezhintsev and E. Shakhmatov, "Sistema RITM. Pervye shagi," *Voennyi vestnik*, No. 5-6 (May-June 1992), 21-24.

198. Raymond J. Swider, *Soviet Military Reform in the Twentieth Century. Three Case Studies* (New York, 1992).

199. Thakur, "The Impact of the Soviet Collapse on Military Relations with India," *Europe-Asia Studies*, Vol. 45, No. 5 (1993), 831-850.

200. *The Defense Industries of the Newly Independent States of Eurasia* (Washington, 1993).

201. Heinrich Tiller, *Machtkrise und Militär. Die russischen Streitkräfte während des Machtkampfes zwischen Präsident und Parlament im Herbst 1993* (Cologne, 1993).

202. P. Timokhin, "Voennaia strategiia SshA. Novyi etap," *Voennaia mysl*, No. 8-9 (1992).

203. "Tipovoi uchebnyi plan na 1993 god," *Voennyi vestnik*, No. 1 (January 1993).

204. A. Tsaturian, "Ekonomicheskaia reforma v Rossii," *Voennyi vestnik*, No. 2 (February 1993).

205. David T. Twining, ed., *Beyond Glasnost. Soviet Reform and Security Issues* (Westport, Conn., 1992).

206. Frank Umbach, *Der sowjetische Generalstab und der KSE-Vertrag* (Cologne, 1992).

207. Frank Umbach, *Die Rolle des sowjetischen Generalstabes im politischen Entscheidungsprozess unter Gorbatschow* (Cologne, 1992).

208. United States Congress, House Committee on Science, Space, and Technology, Video-teleconference, *Exploring the US/Russian Relationship in the Post Cold War Era. Hearing Before the Committee on Science, Space, and Technology, US House of Representatives,* One Hundred Second... (Washington, 1992).

209. United States Congress, Senate Committee on Armed Services, *Assisting the Build-Down of the Former Soviet Military Establishment. Hearings before the Committee on Armed Services, United States Senate,* One Hundred Second Congress, Second Session, February 5 and 6, 1992 (Washington, 1992).

210. United States Congress, Senate Committee on Armed Services, *Current Developments in the Former Soviet Union. Hearings before the Committee on Armed Services, United States Senate,* One Hundred Third Congress, First Session, February 3, 17, 24; March 3, 1993 (Washington, 1993).

211. United States Congress, Senate Committee on Foreign Relations, *The START Treaty. Hearings Before the Committee on Foreign Relations, United States Senate,* One Hundred Second Congress, Second Session (Washington, 1992).

212. United States Congress, Senate Committee on Foreign Relations, *The START Treaty in a Changed World. Hearings before the Committee on Foreign Relations, United States Senate,* One Hundred Second Congress, First Session, September 19 and 25; October 23; and November 7, 1991 (Washington, 1992).

213. United States Congress, Senate Committee on Foreign Relations, *US Plans and Programs Regarding Dismantling of Nuclear Weapons in the Former Soviet Union. Hearing Before the Committee on Foreign Relations, United States Senate,* One Hundred Second Congress, Second Session (Washington, 1992).

214. Ustinov, "Solntse Austerlitsa zakatilos v Rossii," *Voenno-istoricheskii zhurnal*, Nos. 10, 11 (1992).

215. L. Vakhitov, A.N. Kuznetsov, V.P. Chigak, "Novye prioritety programmy SOI," *Voennaia mysl*, No. 2 (1992).

216. Brenda Jones Vallance, "Neotraditionalism and the Military. The Challenge of Reform in Communist Systems" (Ph.D. diss., University of California Los Angeles, 1992).

334 BIBLIOGRAPHY

217. Vasilev, "Russko-iaponskaia voina 1904-1905 gg," *Voennyi vestnik*, No. 10 (October 1992), 77-80.
218. Vedernikov, "Yadernaia voina s tochki zreniia spetsialista," *Voennyi vestnik*, No. 11 (November 1993).
219. Vinitskovskii, "Tserkov, Obshchestvo, Armiia," *Voennyi vestnik*, No. 10 (October 1992), 81-83.
220. Vladimirov, "Krymskaia voina (1853-1856)," *Voennyi vestnik*, No. 5-6 (May-June 1992), 98-101.
221. Vlahos, M.J. Deane, and M.J. Berkowitz, "Aerospace Defense Requirements in Post-Soviet Russia," *Comparative Strategy*, Vol. 11, No. 4 (October-December 1992), 431-445.
222. Voloshin, "Istoriia uchit ostorozhnosti," *Voennyi vestnik*, No. 5-6 (May-June 1992), 14-18.
223. N. Vorobev, "Kakie mobilnye sily nam nuzhny?" *Voennaia mysl*, No. 11 (1993).
224. Zoia Voskresenskaia, *Teper ia mogu skazat pravdu. Iz vospominanii razvedchitsy* (M., 1993).
225. Edward L. Warner, *The Decline of the Soviet Military. Downsizing, Fragmentation, and Possible Disintegration* (Santa Monica, Cal., 1992).
226. Stephen White, *Gorbachev and After*, 3rd ed. (New York, 1992).
227. Charles Wolf, Jr., and Steven W. Popper, eds., *Defense and the Soviet Economy. Military Muscle and Economic Weakness* (Santa Monica, Cal., 1992).
228. Charles Wolf, Jr., ed., *The Role of the Military Sector in the Economies of Russia and Ukraine. Proceedings of the RAND-Hoover Symposium, November 1992* (Santa Monica, Cal., 1993).
229. Yang, "The Transformation of the Soviet Military and the August Coup," *Armed Forces and Society*, Vol. 19, No. 1 (Fall, 1992), 47-70.
230. David Youtz and Paul Midford, *A Northeast Asian Security Regime. Prospects After the Cold War* (New York, 1992).
231. Yu, "Sino-Russian Military Relations. Implications for Asian-Pacific Security," *Asian Survey*, Vol. 33, No. 3 (March 1993), 302-316.
232. Kim Yu-Nam, *Soviet Russia, North Korea, and South Korea in the 1990s. Nuclear Issues and Arms Control in and Around the Korean Peninsula* (Seoul, Korea, 1992).
233. Zadvornov, "Osnovnye etapy stanovleniia i razvitiia rossiiskoi gosudarstvennosti," *Voennyi vestnik*, No. 1 (January 1993).
234. V. Zagorskii and Vladimir Egorov, *Die militarisch-politische Zusammenarbeit der GUS-Staaten* (Cologne, 1993).
235. Steve Zaloga, *Target America. The Soviet Union and the Strategic Arms Race, 1945-1964* (Novato, Cal., 1993).
236. Zimmerman and Berbaum, M.L., "Soviet Military Manpower Policy in the Brezhnev Era. Regime Goals, Social Origins and Working the System," *Europe-Asia Studies*, Vol. 45, No. 2 (1993), 281-302.
237. Kimberly Marten Zisk, *Engaging the Enemy. Organization Theory and Soviet Military Innovation, 1955-1991* (Princeton, N.J., 1993).
238. K. Zmeev, "Ekonomicheskii podkhod k voprosu o sushchnost voennoi reformy," *Voennaia mysl*, No. 10 (1992).
239. Zmeev and A. Nikolaev, "Opyt i traditsii podgotovki voennykh kadrov v Rossii," *Voennyi vestnik*, No. 10 (October 1992), 6-10.
240. Zmeev, "Voiskam nuzhny professionaly," *Voennyi vestnik*, No. 9 (September 1993).

FROM ACADEMIC INTERNATIONAL PRESS*

THE RUSSIAN SERIES

*Request catalogs. Sample pages, tables of contents, more on line at www.ai-press.com